Experimental Psychology

Ram Nath Sharma
Rachana Sharma

ATLANTIC®

PUBLISHERS & DISTRIBUTORS

Published by

ATLANTIC®

PUBLISHERS & DISTRIBUTORS

B-2, Vishal Enclave, Opp. Rajouri Garden,
New Delhi-110027
Phones : 25413460, 25429987, 25466842

Sales Office
7/22, Ansari Road, Darya Ganj,
New Delhi-110002
Phones : 23273880, 23275880, 23280451
Fax : 91-11-23285873
web : www.atlanticbooks.com
e-mail : info@atlanticbooks.com

Printed in India
at Nice Printing Press, Delhi

PREFACE

Experimental psychology is the most important branch of psychology. The credit for establishing psychology on a scientific basis goes to experimental method. This method is now being used more and more in psychological studies. Therefore, it is in the fitness of things that experimental psychology constitutes compulsory part of courses of psychology for the under-graduate and post-graduate students in Indian universities and also everywhere in the world.

Experimental Psychology is a textbook focusing on the experimental methods in the fast growing area of psychology. It includes experiments in physiological psychology, nervous system, mental processes and aspects of human behaviour. Without going into minute details, the book, covering the latest trends in experimental psychology, aims at presenting the broad outline of the subject with an eye on the examination question papers of different Indian universities. It is based upon authentic sources. The language used is lucid, simple and unburdened by technical jargon. The presentation of subject matter has been made from the pragmatic viewpoint, following a tried and tested pedagogical style, enabling the reader to understand and grasp the subject.

Suggestions, if any, from the readers for further improvement of this book in the next edition will be highly appreciated.

RAM NATH SHARMA
RACHANA SHARMA

CONTENTS

1

INTRODUCTORY

What is Experimental Psychology?

Experimental psychology is the branch of psychology in which behaviour is studied through experimental method. Psychology is the science of behaviour. Behaviour includes inner experiences and overt activities. The behaviour is studied in relation to the environment, part of which is controlled and part uncontrolled. Experimental psychology studies behaviour in controlled environment. Some aspects of behaviour and environment cannot be controlled. Those, therefore, fall outside the scope of experimental psychology. Thus, the scope of experimental psychology is extended to include all those aspects of behaviour which are subject to control. Experiment is controlled observation. Experimental psychology uses controlled observation.

Nature of Experimental Psychology

As is clear from the above discussion, experimental psychology is a science. Its nature is scientific. Experimental psychology is veridical. It discovers the cause-and-effect relationship between the various phenomena. On the basis of this discovery it predicts the future course in the various spheres of life. Experimental psychology as a science, uses scientific methods. It very widely utilises the experimental method which is as much scientific as any other method in the strict sense of the term. It is factual because it depends on the facts. The experimenter observes behaviour with an objective attitude, notes it, classifies and compares it and finally finds out general principles based on common factors. He does not pass a judgment on behaviour, but only discovers its general principles. These principles of experimental psychology are universal if the circumstances do not change. They can be verified by any one at any time and at any place. On the basis of these principles the psychologist can predict the future course of human beings and groups. Thus, experimental psychology is a positive science. This will be further clear from the following discussion :

(1) *Use of Scientific Method* : Almost all the methods of psychology are, more or less, scientific in their nature. Of these the experimental method is the most exact. It is no less scientific than any other method, used in other sciences. Experimental psychology widely uses this method in all its branches. In the experimental method the dependent and

independent variables are distinguished, the dependent variables controlled and the effect of the independent variables observed. Thus, in the experiment, the psychologist observes a certain phenomenon in strictly controlled situations. He also uses various types of instruments, *e.g.*, chronoscope, a highly sensitive clock, used to determine the interval time down to the thousandth part of a second in reaction experiments. The psychological laboratories are continuously developing and new and more exact instruments are being constantly put to use. With these instruments the psychologist observes the phenomenon, notes it, compares and classifies it and discovers various principles through generalization. These general principles in experimental psychology are as much veridical as a science demands.

(2) *Factuality* : Psychology studies the facts of behaviour. The psychologist is detached and objective in his observations and experiments. The proper field of psychology is not values but facts.

(3) *Universality* : The laws of experimental psychology have been found to be correct at every time and place, under the same conditions. The general principles of experimental psychology are universal, whatever differences there may be in the psychology of different individuals, *e.g.*, the psychological fact that human beings and animals are emotionally disturbed by any impediment in the satisfaction of their impulses, is applicable everywhere.

(4) *Veridical* : Thus, by verification and re-verification principles have been found to be true everywhere. They may be verified by any one. To illustrate, it is a psychological fact that wherever there is some conflict, there are some frustrations behind it. This fact has been verified by the clinical psychologists. By discovering these frustrations, one may trace the causes of the particular conflict.

(5) *Discovers the Cause-effect Relationship* : Experimental psychology not only observes behaviour, but also finds out cause-effect relationship in it, *e.g.*, it has discovered why and in what circumstances a D.L. is constant. These findings have been put to use and found correct. Thus experimental psychology discovers the 'how' of behaviour together with its 'what'.

(6) *Predicts Behaviour* : By discovering the cause-effect relationship, experimental psychology also predicts behaviour and these predictions are generally correct. Thus, in the modern progressive countries, appointments to different Government posts are made by relying on the predictions made on the basis of psychological tests. On the basis of these psychological tests, it is predicted that such and such person will be a good soldier and so and so a good administrator; and generally this proves true in actual experience.

Scope of Experimental Psychology

Experimental psychology studies external behaviour as well as the internal processes of the different stages of human development as also of animals. Only those phenomena fall outside its field which cannot be studied in controlled situations. But the scope of experimental psychology is gradually widening with the invention of new tools and instruments for experiments. The most important areas covered by experimental psychology include psycho-physics, animal psychology, learning psychology, psychology of individual differences, child psychology, educational psychology, clinical psychology and industrial psychology etc.

Experimental Method

Psychology is the positive science of behaviour. Science is a method. It is distinguished from philosophy on the basis of methodological difference. Science is the study of any object by scientific method. Hence if psychology is to be called a science, it should use scientific methods, *e.g.*, introspection, case history and observation etc. But experimental method is the most important method in the study of psychology. It is this method which has the credit of bringing psychology to the level of an exact science. Hence modern psychology lays greatest emphasis upon experimental method.

What is Experimental Method?

According to Garret, experiment is a question asked systematically. Thus in experiment, the experimenter has a problem before him. He experiments to find out the answer to this problem. The clarity of the answer depends upon the clarity of the question. The question is based on a hypothesis. This hypothesis is proved or disproved by the experiment, *e.g.*, suppose that while studying or teaching some one thinks that motivation has its role in study: this is merely a hypothesis. To examine it, it is placed in the form of a question — does motivation effect study? To get an answer to this question, it requires psychological experiments. Suppose by the experiments one arrives at the result that motivation is useful in the study : this proves the hypothesis. Now another question might be raised as to how far motivation helps in study? This question will lead to further experiments in this direction. In this way various types of enquiries can be made through the method of experiment *e.g.*, experiment regarding the effect of motivation on study. Similarly, the effect of smoking on study, of family environment on the child, the effect of intelligence and practice in learning etc., may be put in the form of the questions and experiments can be performed to get answers to them. In the experimental method, the observation is held in certain predetermined conditions. Thus, experiment is a controlled observation. It is the observation of the behaviour or activity in fixed circumstances. The characteristic of this observation is that it can be repeated in different places and times without difference in results.

Steps in Experiment

There are the following steps in a typical experiment :

(1) *Raising a problem* : The first step in an experiment is the raising of the problem *e.g.*, it is said that smoking is harmful to the students. On the other hand some say that it helps in concentration. Those who are neither for nor against smoking may say it is not smoking but the personality of the student which is relevant to his results in examinations. This discussion creates a problem about the effect of smoking on physical or mental capacity. This problem may lead to further experiments.

(2) *Formulation of a hypothesis* : The second step in experimental method is the formulation of a hypothesis. In the example of smoking, the problem of its effect on physical and mental capacity can be put in the form of a hypothesis. This hypothesis will be like this "smoking is harmful for physical and mental efficiency". Now this hypothesis will be tested by experiments.

(3) *To distinguish independent variable and dependent variable* : The third step in experimental method is the distinction between independent variables and dependent variables. In the example of smoking, the physical and mental capacity will be the dependent variables, since they will be fixed in experiment. Smoking will be an independent variable since the aim of the experiment is to find out the effect of its presence and absence.

(4) *Controlling the environment or situation* : The fourth and the most important step in the experimental method is controlling the environment or situation. There are several difficulties in the above mentioned experiment on smoking. It is just possible that the subject may try to prove that smoking has no effect on physical or mental capacities. But to neutralise these possibilities the experimental situation is controlled. In the experiment on smoking, the eyes of the subject were closed by bandage. Two exactly similar holders were used. One of these holders had an electric wire through which the subject might inhale the warm air, while the other holder had a common cigarette. In all the sessions of the experiment all types of sounds, related to smoking were made *e.g.*, the rubbing of the match etc. At the end of the experiment there were sticks and ashes lying round about, so that the subject might think that he really smoked. The subject cannot touch cigarette at any time. The experimenter himself puts and takes away the holders from his mouth. In the sessions when cigarette was not given to the subject, the experimenter himself smoked. To stop the signs received by the smoking sequence of giving and taking away the holders, the sessions of smoking and not smoking were kept irregular. These special arrangements in the case of experiment on smoking are necessary in all types of experiments. The arrangements of control differ according to the nature of experiments. In the case of man some special types of controls are necessary so that the subject may not know the principles of the experiment, since it is feared that this might make difference in his mental attitude. But in the case of experiments

on animals this difficulty is not there. So there are different types of controls in the experiments on animals, *e.g.*, Pavlov, in his experiment on conditioned reflex in the dog made special arrangement for the flow of saliva and to gather it outside dog's mouth.

(5) *Analysis of the result*: The fifth important step in the experimental method is the analysis of the results. Generally, the subjects of the experiment are divided into two groups — one controlled and another experimental. In the experiment on smoking every subject was also his controlled subject. All smoked half times and in the remaining half they inhaled warm air. The experimental group is often called independent variable, since the experimenter can stop it or modify it. In the experiment on smoking, cigarette is an independent variable and the results of its presence have been compared with the results of its absence. For the analysis of the results of the experiment, statistical technique is used.

(6) *Verification of the hypothesis by the result of the experiment*: The final step in experiment is the verification of the hypothesis by the result of the experiment. The result of the experiment exhibits whether the hypothesis was right or wrong. In the experiment on smoking, it was found by the comparison of the sessions of smoking and non-smoking that there was very little difference in the results. Smoking increased heart beat and the trembling of the hand. This effect was observed more in non-smokers than the smoker subject. No influence was observed on mental capacities known by mental tests. After 18 days of smoking it was concluded that it had very insignificant effect. This result disproved the hypothesis.

Limits of Experimental Method

Like other methods, experimental method has also its own limitations. The following are the most important limitations of experimental method :

(1) *Artificial situation of Laboratory*: Artificial situation of laboratory is characteristic of experimental method as well as its limitation. In the experimental method the experimenter leaves some variables. But it is very difficult to ascertain all the variables working in a particular situation, *e.g.*, in the attainment of scholarship, the hours of work, the hours of extra-curricular activities, anxiety for future, interest in the social work, motivation for social work, hours of study etc., were controlled and the time given for student's activities was increased and decreased. The result by the increase and decrease of the hours of study shows its effect on scholarship. But it is possible that the variables controlled in this experiment may not include all those which effect the attainment of scholarship. As a matter of fact it is very difficult to ascertain all the factors affecting the attainment of scholarship in a man and the result is that the effect of some of the factors might be alluded to some other.

(2) *Difficulty in the control of the attitude of the subject* : Another limitation in the experimental method is the difficulty in the control of the attitude of the subject. In experiments on men it is often very necessary to control their attitudes, since if the subject is opposed to the experiment or careless towards it, he might give wrong answers or keep silent. But it is not always easy to control the attitudes of the subjects specially when they are children or students. This makes the result of the experiment unreliable.

(3) *Difficulty of securing the co-operation of the subject* : Another difficulty in experimental method is the difficulty of securing the co-operation of the subject. Experimental method is impossible without the co-operation of the subject, but the co-operation is not always easily forthcoming. It is possible that the subject may show himself fatigued or not fatigued according to his attitude or give false replies. This difficulty makes experimental method unreliable.

(4) *Limited Field* : The last but not the least important limitation of the experimental method is the limitation of its field. In several matters it cannot be applied at all, *e.g.*, if one has to know the effect of bad environment on child's development, it is not possible to place some children in bad environment and to wait for the results. Again, in the case of the mental states, like love etc., it is neither possible to control them nor to create them in the laboratory. These and many other phenomena may be studied only through observation or introspection etc.

In spite of the above limitations of the experimental method, it is undoubtedly the most important and valuable method in psychology. It is by this method that the psychologist arrives at the most exact conclusions about behaviour. But experimental method is limited to only those aspects of human behaviour, where one may hope to arrive at exact conclusions. On the other hand, some aspects of human behaviour are so changeable and complex that one should be satisfied with their observation and arrive at some workable conclusions. The field of experimental method, however, is gradually being widened with the advent of new inventions regarding tools and instruments. If observation and introspection methods have widened the field of psychology and made it more useful in daily life, it is experimental method which has secured a respectable place for psychology among the sciences. In the world outside the limits of laboratory, man will always learn by experience and observation but it is on the experimental method alone that the future of psychology as a science depends.

Control in Experimental Method

In an experiment, the subject is studied in controlled situations. The experimenter divides different factors in the experiment into dependent and independent variables and controls the former to watch the influence of the latter. Without such a control, the result of the experiment can never be dependable, *e.g.,* in the experiment to determine the effect of smoking on study, the constancy of the age of the subjects, their intelligence, work at schools etc., are necessary because all these factors influence the study. If these do not remain the same or constant, the difference by the influence of either of them may be mis-interpreted as the difference due to smoking or non-smoking. In ordinary life the importance of such a controlled observation is not so much emphasized. Hence, most of the conclusions are far from being accurate. They are at the most, merely workable inferences. By seeing some smokers in good health, it is often concluded that smoking has no bad effect on health. Similarly, when a patient is cured, no effort is made to ascertain whether he has been cured by the medicine or owing to some other causes. For example, normally a man is relieved of his cold after the third day, but some people do not give the credit of this relief to Nature but to the medicine. Psychological processes are influenced in great measure by certain factors *e.g.,* the age, intelligence, motive, intention, education and the physical and mental states such as hunger, fatigue etc. All these may influence the result of the experiments. Hence, no definite conclusions may be drawn without controlling all these factors.

Thus, every experiment has certain conditioning factors. Among them, the general condition of the subject is very important. In the psychological experiment the attitude must be controlled. For example, if an experiment is being conducted with regard to learning, it is necessary that the subject should not be averse to learning since that will lead to the failure of the experiment. In such experiment, the subjects are told that they should attend to such and such stimuli and leave such and such. Sometimes the subject is kept in illusion. He is told that a certain thing is being examined, while actually it is something else which is under examination, *e.g.,* in order to determine the influence of a certain medicine sometimes the water and sometimes the medicine is injected. In experiments on animals, the attitude of the subject need not be controlled. But in experiments on human beings, specially adults, it is necessary to control the attitudes of the subjects.

Side by side with the internal attitude, the external stimuli should also be controlled. Stimuli include all those internal and external factors which have some effect on the subject to be studied, *e.g.,* light, sound, touch, temperature, smell etc., are external stimuli and nervous excitements are the internal stimuli. Both these types of stimuli affect the subject. Hence they are controlled. The external stimuli are controlled with the help of various types of room and apparatus. The internal stimuli are controlled by administering certain medicines or particular type of food or by keeping the subject hungry etc.

In certain experiments, the heredity should also be controlled, *e.g.,* if the psychologist has to determine the effect of training and maturity on the development of the child, he should take two types of subjects *i.e.* trained and untrained. Along with this both these subjects should also be the same. Similarity of heredity is found only in identical twins. Hence in such experiments the psychologist should take identical twins. Now, one of these should be trained and the other untrained. The comparison of the development of both these will exhibit the influence of training on development. Thus, in the experiments on human beings, many factors are to be controlled. In the experiments on animals, sometimes some external or internal organ has to be removed through operation, *e.g.*, in order to determine the influences of a certain endocrine gland, the behaviour of the animal is noted, the endocrine gland is removed and the behaviour is again noted. Now a comparison of the behaviour with and without the particular endocrine gland will give the influence of that gland on behaviour.

Dependent and Independent Variables

As has already been pointed out, the different factors in an experiment are divided into independent and dependent variables. Independent variables are stimuli or particular states of the subject which can be changed as desired. Often the independent variable is one because the experimenter has to see the effect of every factor separately. But if the effect is due to two factors, which are not separated from each other, it will be difficult to determine how much influence is exercised by each of them. In the statistical method, there may be more than one independent variable because statistical analysis separates the influence of each factor.

Dependent variable, as is clear from its name, depends on the independent variable. The experimenter keeps all the factors of his experiment constant and changes some one factor. This change results in a certain effect in the subject. These factors are the dependent variables. These include the external behaviour of the subject *e.g.*, speaking, hearing, laughing, weeping etc. as well as internal processes. The internal processes are determined with the help of certain instruments.

The analysis of various factors of control in an experiment, as given above, clearly shows that the method of experiment very much depends on the control of the various factors in the particular experiment.

QUESTIONS FOR EXERCISE

1. Explain the nature and scope of experimental psychology.
2. Explain the characteristics of a psychological experiment. What is the meaning of experimental control.
3. Describe the set up of a typical psychological experiment indicating the function of controls in it.
4. Describe the different steps in performing a psychological experiment. Illustrate your answer.

5. Clearly distinguish between independent and dependent variables and explain what is experimental control of variables.
6. Explain the significance of independent and dependent variables and the parameters in experimental method.
7. How is the necessary control of variables effected in an experiment? Illustrate by means of an example.
8. Discuss the nature and classification of variables in experimental psychology.

2

PIONEERS OF EXPERIMENTAL PSYCHOLOGY

Experimental psychology was born in Germany. Wilhelm Wundt established the first psychological laboratory at Leipzig and encouraged psychological experiments. He himself performed many experiments which deserve special mention.

WILHELM WUNDT

Early Life and Education

Wilhelm Wundt was born in a place called Neckaran in the year 1832. His early education was received under the guidance of a priest. Later on he studied medicine at the Tubingen University. After this he went to Heidelberg University where he studied physiology. In 1856, he went to Berlin to further study physiology. Here he made a detailed and experimental study in physiology under the guidance of Muller. At that time Muller was famous as the greatest physiologist. Wundt learnt a lot from Muller.

In 1857, Wundt agreed to deliver lectures at the Heidelburg University and continued on this post for 7 years. During this period he wrote a book on physiology. In 1864, he became associate professor. Helmholtz did not encourage Wundt in conducting experiments in physiology as Wundt's mathematical knowledge was not sufficient for such experiments. In 1874, Wundt accepted the post of professor of philosophy at the Leipzig University. Here he performed physiological experiments and established the world's first physiological laboratory. Now his fame spread far and wide and students from different countries started coming to him. Two Americans, Cattel and Hall, were among his first students.

Wundt wrote many psychological articles and books. In 1863 he published, one of his articles the subject of which was sense perception. In this he threw light on the scientific facts related to sensations. The most famous of his books entitled *Outlines of Physiological Psychology* was published in 1874. This book had three parts and contained nearly 2400 pages. Wundt did considerable labour on this book and it became so popular that by 1911, six editions of it had come out.

In addition, Wundt also wrote some textbooks for the teaching of psychology. These books were most useful for the students of psychology. In fact, Wundt remained busy throughout his life in continuous study and writing. He wrote another book on Folk psychology which was published in ten volumes. A special feature of this book was that he started writing this when he was 70 years old. Wundt had an interest in experimental psychology, and this is clearly indicated in all his works.

Contributions to Psychology

To clarify the nature of psychology, Wundt organized its various subjects into a systematic form and at the same time made these subjects clear. In other words he made psychology systematic and in this way made it easy for the students to study psychology.

Wundt analysed and explained such mental processes as sensation, perception and concepts. The basis of this study was experimental. He explained the part that was played by the nervous system and sense organs in the development of sensation. He accepted sensation and feeling to be a necessary element of the mind and described intensity, quality and duration in defining sensation. He performed different psycho-physical experiments concerned with intensity in sensation and defined them on this basis. While defining it, he threw light on the simple form of sensation. He made direct perception the basis of extent and duration.

Study of Feelings

According to Wundt there are three dimensions of feeling. First dimension of feeling was pleasant or unpleasant. In other words on one end of the dimension of feeling, pleasant feeling is found and on other unpleasant feeling. In this way both ends are completely different from each other. On the one end of the second dimension is prest and on the other opposite to it exists excitement. Similarly, in the third dimension rest and tension are found. Wundt discovered by experiments that during pleasant feeling there is also a feeling of peace and rest. On the contrary, unpleasant feeling also has excitement and tension in it. Similarly, aiming at the arousal of feeling, three out of the six kinds of mental conditions should necessarily exist. This theory of Wundt is famous as the theory of tri-dimensional feeling.

Study of Ideas

According to Wundt a concept is related to direct perception. He said about the nature of perception that it was the combined form of feeling and memories. Ideas and concepts emerge from direct perception. Wundt has classified ideas and concepts on the basis of their qualities. According to this classification there are three kinds of ideas :

1. Intensive Ideas
2. Space Ideas
3. Time Ideas

Wundt said about the intensive idea that its development occurs when the ideas are associated on the basis of consonance and resistance. Intensive ideas are related to those sounds and thoughts in which similarity and dissonance are found. Intensity in ideas is due to the unity in their form. Opposite ideas cannot combine to become intense. Wundt has written about space ideas that these are ideas which are connected with space. Similarly, time ideas are those ideas which are related to time. As the individual goes on gaining experience on the basis of physiological activities, time and space ideas go on increasing at the same rate. The amount of time consumed by a work is known by the time idea and similarly distance from one place to another is perceived by space idea.

According to Wundt the evaluation of feeling and emotion is related to the nervous system. In other words some physiological change takes place in the creation of feeling and emotion. When feeling occurs in a person then some peculiar reactions occur in his body. Feeling is the cause which impels man to action and movement in some direction.

Study of Apperception

Wundt said about apperception that it was related to the upper portion of the brain. The action of apperception occurs by the combination of nerves. Association has an important role in the development of apperception. The awareness of association goes to the brain through the medium of the nerves, where perception evolves. The sensations of the individual acquire meaning on the basis of association. In the action of remembering there is the contribution of both apperception and association. Ideas and concepts develop on the basis of association and the action of remembering takes place on this basis. When any special fact or concept needs to be remembered, then both association and apperception are helpful in its selection. It will be appropriate to say that if there is no co-operation of association and apperception in the action of remembering then many thoughts will come in a single memory and it will be hard to decide as to which idea is needed.

It is clear that Wundt studied mental processes on a physiological basis. However, he made it clear that the actions of mind and body do not depend upon each other to such an extent that there cannot be any consideration of them separately. Wundt accepted that mind and body are distinct but emphasised that they are intimately associated to each other. In other words, mind and body are parallel to each other. But Wundt has not clarified why they have this close relation between them.

In psychology too Wundt has laid stress on experimental psychology. For his experiments he chose only those subjects on which not much information was available. In addition to visual and auditory sensations, Wundt is credited with the experimental study of other sense organs.

He experimented to determine the time for physical reactions. He also found out the time taken for the related reaction when the appropriate stimulus occurs. In this way psycho-physics was strengthened by the experiments of Wundt. He also studied association and apperception.

Wundt's greatest contribution to psychology lies in the method of the study of psychology. In fact, Wundt started experimental psychology. Even before Wundt psychologists had written from time to time on the scientific study of psychology but it was Wundt who applied this in practice. He found out many facts by experiments in the laboratory. It must also be remembered that Wundt established the world's first psychological laboratory.

HERMAN VON HELMHOLTZ

After Wundt the name of Helmholtz is most notable in the development of experimental psychology. As is obvious from his name, Helmholtz was a German, born in 1821 at Potsdam, a place near Berlin. His father was a teacher of linguistics and philosophy and Helmholtz's early education took place under his guidance. But he was never a brilliant student. May be the cause for this was that from childhood his health was not satisfactory. Thus, he could not lead a more active life though he had great interest in games.

Helmholtz was interested in science, especially in physics. Hence he started studying physics and very soon acquired considerable knowledge in it. In those days it was not sufficient for livelihood to study science. Hence Helmholtz also had to study medicine. At the age of 21 he published an article on medicine in which he said that the cells of gangalia were attached one by one to different veins. Before this there had not been any study on this subject. Hence this subject was welcomed in the medical field. From here, Helmholtz's career started.

Helmholtz was enlisted in the army. He was appointed as a surgeon. During his stay there he performed many psychological experiments and made intense study of energy. He also wrote an essay on the conservation of energy. In this essay he described the importance of energy and that how necessary was its conservation. Psychologists had not yet paid any attention to this subject.

Helmholtz was interested in experimental psychology. His most important work in psychology was the *Principles of Physiological Optics* published in three volumes in 1856, 1860 and 1866 respectively. These three volumes were on physiological optics but physics has been used as the basis in the first part, physiological dynamics in the second and psychology in the third.

Young-Helmholtz Principle of Colour Vision

Helmholtz conducted an experimental examination of Thomas Young's principle of colour vision and found it to be defective. He amended this principle, which came to be known as the Young-Helmholtz principle of colour vision. Before we understand this principle we must know about Young's principle. In brief, Young's principle was that in fundamental form there are three colour sensations. They are Red, Green and Violet respectively. In their different mixtures were seven colours, as Yellow is formed by mixing Red and Green, Orange from Violet while Red and Blue are formed by Green and Violet. The seventh colour is white light which is formed by the mixture of the three primary colour sensations. Helmholtz amended this principle. According to him the three main colours were Red, Green and Blue. While defining these three colours, he conceived of three cones of retina which are known as R. Con., G. Con. and B. Con. The nerves of these are related to the Red, Green and Blue colours. When these cones are stimulated separately, then the sensations of red, green and blue colours respectively occur. When the cones of red and green colours are equally stimulated by the light waves then yellow colour is seen. When the three cones are equally excited by the light waves then individuals have colourless sensation.

In criticism of this theory of Helmholtz it may be said that there is no clear definition of colour-blindness in it. It has been seen by experiments that those persons who are blind to red and green colours may see yellow colour. It is not possible to explain this phenomenon by the principle of Helmholtz. Still the importance of Young-Helmholtz principle cannot be questioned. Enough light has been thrown by it on physiological colour optics and the interest of other scientists has been directed towards this subject.

(2) Auditory Sensation

Helmholtz studied auditory sensation and maintained that there are thousands of nerves in the inner membrane of the ears. Their number is between 18 and 24 thousand. The nerves of the membrane of the ear may be compared with any stringed musical instrument. By the agitation of one specific wire of an instrument a special kind of sound is produced. The same work is done by the nerves of the ear membrane. These also resonate sound into the ear.

This fact has also been criticized. It has been proved that the nerves of the ear membrane do not have the capacity to resonate sound.

(3) Unconscious Inference

While defining unconscious Helmholtz has said that for an unconscious inference is most necessary. Every person indulges in unconscious inference, and this action is natural. It is often seen that when a person sees a colour then he forms an unconscious inference about the opposite colour. In addition to it development of unconscious inference depends on experience. By and by when experience increases in a person, his capacity for unconscious inference also improves. The action of unconscious inference is similar to conscious inference. But while unconsciously inferring, a person does not know that he is doing so.

(4) Perception

Helmholtz has also defined perception. According to him perception is related to the stimulus and the specific sense organ. It is also related to the pre-conceptions of man and his unconscious inference. While defining the characteristics and qualities of things Helmholtz has written that they help in gaining perception. No person can change the qualities or characteristics of an article. These are unchangeable.

In addition to this, Helmholtz also studied temperature and said that it may be measured. Helmholtz accepted the relationship between psychology and human physiology and defined mental processes on this basis. In fact, he contributed greatly to the development of experimental psychology and did much labour in this direction.

J. MCKEEN CATTEL

In American psychology the name of J. McKeen Cattel is very important. Cattel was born in Estan in 1860. He had his early education at the Lofaet College of which his father was the president. Later, Cattel went to Europe for higher education. For three years (1883-1886) he remained a student of Leipzig University where he came in contact of the famous German psychologist Wundt. From Wundt he learnt the experimental method of psychology.

From Germany, Cattel went to England and took admission in Cambridge University. Here he had the honour of becoming a student of Galton. Later on he was appointed as a lecturer at Cambridge University. He established a psychological laboratory here. He returned to America 2 years later and was appointed as a lecturer in psychology at Columbus University. Here too he established a laboratory.

Till the first world war he worked on this post but during war he resigned from this job. Cattel was a believer in peace and hence opposed war. When he expressed his opposition against war then differences occurred between him and the university officials and due to this he resigned. From this it is clear that Cattel was a determined and fearless person. He strictly adhered to his principles.

A noteworthy thing about Cattel was that he remained a pupil of three pioneering psychologists of Europe, Britain and America — In Europe under Wundt, in Britain under Galton and in America under Stanley Hall. While working with Wundt he obtained his Doctorate. He studied experimental psychology and designed suitable apparatus for experiments. From Galton he learnt the use of statistics in psychology and here too he designed some apparatus.

Contribution to Psychology

Cattel's field was experimental psychology. Hence, in psychology he always stressed the experimental aspect. He did experiments concerning reaction and worked in the field of measurement of direct knowledge. He used an apparatus called tachitoscope for this purpose. He found out the fact on studying the direct knowledge of children that in the beginning it is unified but later on it may be analysed in categories. It was learnt from his experiments that separate letters should not be used while teaching language to children but they should be taught complete words.

Cattel designed many necessary mental tests to measure individual differences. In fact, he wanted to measure mental abilities. He also wanted to know what mental ability lay at the root of the work done by man.

Hence, Cattel experimented on individual differences. He also experimented on reaction time, association, direct knowledge and psycho-physics etc. He also used statistics in the experiments on reaction time. Thus, conclusions relating to reaction time may be definitely found by this method. In 1887, he published a description of experiments concerning association and two years later published an essay on free association. Important suggestions on language teaching also resulted from Cattel's experiments related to reading. As has been written earlier, Cattel studied direct knowledge of children and suggested about their language teaching that they should be taught not by letters but by complete words.

In 1890, he published an essay on individual differences. In this he emphasized the need of mental experiments to measure individual differences. It is noteworthy in this respect that it was Cattel who used, for the first time, the word mental test in psychology. In this essay Cattel described many mental experiments which are used every year to determine the mental level of college students. Cattel included the power of muscles, intensity of speed, pain absorbing power, vision and visual intensity, weight discrimination, reaction time, memory etc., in his mental experiments. Since determination of mental level depends on measurement, hence only those mental experiments should be chosen which may be easily measured.

In addition to mental experiments, Cattel developed many new fields in psychology. He had the ability to organise. He published his writings from time to time in a magazine called *Psychological Review*. Cattel is also credited with arranging for the publication of *Psychological Monograph* and *Psychological Index*.

Cattel edited many reference books among which the notable were – *Scientists of America* and *Leaders in Education*. He also published a Directory of American scientists and scholars. In addition, he published a monthly magazine concerning science.

In 1896, Cattel was elected President of the American Association for the Advancement of Science. Later on in 1926, he was elected Chairman of the Ninth International Psychological Congress. In 1931, he organised the American Psychological Corporation. The main aim of this organisation was to organise various psychological experiments and even today this organisation is doing useful and important work.

In the end, it may be said that Cattel made important contributions to experimental psychology. He studied individual differences on an experimental basis and accepted the importance of mental tests in this subject. He established psychological laboratories. He studied perceptions of children on the basis of experiments and presented important facts.

Cattel was an able Editor. He contributed to the development of psychology by editing many books and magazines. He had a great personality. His behaviour with his friends and pupils was very cordial and he was fearless and resolute in his principles. He fearlessly and openly criticized those whom he wanted to.

In the history of modern psychology he is known as a pioneer. He did work of considerable importance for the development of psychology. He died in 1944.

QUESTIONS FOR EXERCISE

1. Discuss the chief contribution of Wundt to the growth of experimental Psychology.
2. Write a note on the contribution of Herman Von Helmholtz in Experimental Psychology.
3. Write a note on the contribution of Cattel to Experimental Psychology.

3
PSYCHO-PHYSICAL METHOD

Among the methods used in experimental psychology, psycho-physical methods are the most quantitative methods. They are specially used in psycho-physics. The chief of these methods are given below :

(1) Method of Limits

This method has been specially used in studying sensory threshold. In this method different environments are controlled first of all. After that the person, experimented upon is made to sit in an easy position and a wooden screen is placed between the experimenter and the subject. Absolute threshold and differential threshold are found out through this method. Their methods are given below :

1. *Measurement of absolute threshold* : Suppose we want to know absolute threshold relating to cutaneous sensation. Now the person, subject is made to sit in a suitable position as described above and then the experimenter will instruct him like this — "Your skin will be touched at such a place with such a kind of thing. If you feel the touch, say 'Yes' and 'No' if you do not feel it." After issuing these instructions, the experimenter will touch the specified part of the body with a specific thing which he may surely feel. Now he gradually goes on decreasing the force of stimulus to a degree where the stimulus is no more felt. After this stage is reached, the experiments are stopped. In this way, after experimenting from increased to decreased stimulus, the experiment is restarted with decreased stimulus which is again gradually increased unless it is clearly felt. Thus, we get at two kinds of sensations — from increased to decreased and gradually from decreased to increased. In both the kinds of these stimuli, we reach such a transition point where a change of stimuli is clearly felt. This shows the average threshold of both the transition points. In this way, absolute threshold is the average of the descending and ascending series. Both the kinds of series, descending and ascending, are taken so that the result of the experiment may be reliable and factual. The average of the threshold of both the kinds of chains shows the absolute threshold.

2. *Differential threshold* : Two kinds of stimuli are needed to find out differential threshold which is also known as D.L. — standard and

variable stimuli. In this also, descending and ascending chains are gone through. In this the subject notes the difference between the two stimuli after comparing — variable and standard. Weber widely employed this method in his experiments.

(2) Method of Right and Wrong Cases

The modern name of this method is Method of constant stimuli. In this, the number of mistakes due to habituation or expectation, is very small and therefore it has a greater scientific quality. Absolute threshold and differential threshold are known through this method. Their methods are given below :

1. *Method of finding out absolute threshold* : For this, some fixed stimuli are repeatedly presented before the subject randomly and he gives judgment about them. For example, suppose you find, with the help of aesthesiometer, the minimum distance between the two points which provides sensation of both the points to the subject. Now you will instruct him like this, "A sensation will be given to your skin at such and such place, you will say 'one' when you feel one point and 'two' when you feel two points." Now, by giving some practical trials, the highest and the lowest limits of sensation are found out. When it is found out, the distance of the highest limit is reduced a little and the stimuli is aimlessly presented before the subject. Every time the skin of the subject is touched at two points with aesthesiometer. In reaction when the subject says 'two', it is regarded to be correct, but when he says 'one', it is incorrect. Now, the correct and incorrect reactions are enlisted and absolute threshold is found out with their help. Sensation of this absolute threshold is felt in 50 per cent attempts of the subject of experiment.

2. *Method of finding out differential threshold* : Like the method of limits, standard variable stimuli are presented before the subject of experiment to find out differential threshold in the method of constant stimuli as well, and every time he is asked whether the variable stimulus is bigger than, smaller than or equal to the standard stimulus. Stimuli are repeated in an irregular form. The subject is instructed : "Two lines at a time will be presented before you, you will look at them and tell which of them is bigger and which is smaller." Now in 75 per cent attempts, the threshold declared as big will be regarded big and the threshold declared as small, in the same number of attempts, will be regarded small. The differential threshold will be found out by dividing the total of the highest and the lowest threshold by two.

(3) Method of Mean or Average Error

Whereas in the method of limits as well as in the method of constant stimuli, the experimenter brings about a change in controlled stimulus, this change, in the method of mean error, depends on the subject. The subject, after his observation of the standard stimulus, gradually increases and decreases the variable stimulus. In this process,

he sometimes over-estimates and sometimes underestimates the
. standard stimulus. Due to this, the variable stimulus, instead of being
equal to the standard stimulus, sometimes becomes bigger and at
other times smaller than the standard stimulus. The subject, after
making different attempts, finds out the mean error by taking out the
average of the errors of evaluation. For example, suppose there is a
standard line measuring 40 millimeter and the subject has to draw a
line equal to it; its error, in different trials will be noted in the method
given below :

Trial No.	Right side	Left side	Trial No.	Right side	Left side
1	41	42	6	43	37
2	42	38	7	37	39
3	44	36	8	39	41
4	38	44	9	42	43
5	36	41	10	41	42
	201	201		192	192

Average on the right side $= \dfrac{402}{10} = 40.2$ millimeter.

Average on the left side $= \dfrac{384}{10} = 38.4$ millimeter.

Average of the total evaluation $\dfrac{40.2 + 38.4}{2} = 39.3$ millimeter.

∴ Mean Error $= 40 - 39.3 = 0.7$ millimeter.

It is clear from the above result that a line of 40 millimeter in
length will, on 50% or more occasions, appear to the subject to be
different from the line of 40+.7 millimeter. This has been found out
through the method of mean error used in taking out threshold. Before
beginning the above experiment, the subject will be instructed in this
way, "Draw another simple line equal to the given simple line through
your own presumption and do not use any scale in doing so." The
subject will draw this line at one time to the right and at another time
to the left of the standard line. When the number of trials in drawing
lines to the right is equal to the number of trials in drawing lines to
the left, space errors are avoided. In the same way, the subject is given
stimulus at one time much greater than the standard stimulus and
much less at another time in order to reduce the errors of habituation.

Errors of Psycho-Physical Methods

Although Psycho-physical methods are considered to be very
important in experimental psychology, yet they are not found to be all
correct. The errors occur due to the difference between the actual
measurement of the stimulus and its evaluation by the subject. As a
matter of fact, this very difference is the error. The main errors of the
psycho-physical methods are given below :

(1) *Accidental errors* : Accidental errors, as is clear from their name, are those errors which occur due to chance or to some unknown reasons. The experimenter, the subject or any person inside the laboratory may cause such errors. For example, the experimenter's observation may be erroneous due to the experimenter's mental and physical condition being unfavourable for the experiment. Such errors are possible in all experiments. An attempt is, therefore, made to reduce them as far as possible or at least their effects are traced so that they may be borne in mind at the time of evaluating the results of an experiment.

(2) *Constant errors* : Constant errors, as is clear from their name, are those errors which occur constantly. These errors are such as cannot be avoided even if their causes are known. For example, out of the two equal stimuli, the subject takes one to be bigger or smaller than the other. The main forms of constant errors are given below :

(a) *Time errors* : When two stimuli, instead of being presented at one and the same time, are presented one after the other, it is natural for the subject to err in evaluating them. In the same way, time error occurs due to the difference of time in presenting two stimuli. For example, if a second line is presented a few seconds after the presentation of the first simple line, there is every possibility of an error on the part of the subject in evaluating it.

(b) *Space errors* : When two stimuli are presented one on the right or the left side of the other, there is a possibility of an error in evaluating them. The error is called space error due to a change of space. To avoid this error, the changing stimulus is sometimes presented on the right side of the standard stimulus and sometimes on the left side, although it does not remove the error completely.

(c) *Variable error* : Variable errors keep changing with the subject in particular and depend on the condition of the subject. For example, errors gradually decrease with the increase of habituation in evaluation. On the other hand, when the subject is tired of doing the same kind of work continuously for some time, it may also cause an error in evaluation. The effect of habituation and tiresomeness may be stopped to some extent by decreasing or increasing the working method, but it cannot be stopped completely because the alternating errors depend on the particular subject to a great extent. One subject becomes habituated in a short time and the other may take a long time. One may get tired very soon and the other may take some more time to get tired. A similar working method, therefore, cannot be decided in all cases.

In spite of the above errors, the psycho-physical methods are scientific. As a matter of fact, it is through the knowledge of these errors that the experimental result may be scientifically decided. It is needless to say that the credit of placing experimental psychology in the position of pure science goes to the psychological methods.

QUESTIONS FOR EXERCISE

1. What do you mean by Psycho-physical Methods? Discuss their importance in experimental psychology.
2. Describe 'Method of Limits' or 'Method of right and wrong cases' and give examples.
3. Write short note on — 'Psycho-physical Methods'.
4. Discuss with example, the method of average error in psycho-physical measurement.
5. Discuss the method of Average Error.
6. Describe the procedure of the method of average error. Indicate the characteristic features of this method.

4

SAMPLE INVESTIGATION

In the quantified research, the sampling technique is made maximum use of and in no field of research can its importance and value be belittled. In researches in the educational, economic, commercial and scientific domains, the sampling technique is used and considered most apt for research. Sampling technique also has very high value in day-to-day activities. In making our daily purchases of food-stuff, vegetables, fruits etc., it is not considered necessary to examine each and every piece of the commodity; only a handful of goods are examined and the idea about the whole is formed and this usually proves a justified procedure. In the words of Snedecor : "A cart load of coal is accepted or rejected on the evidence gained from testing only a few pounds. The physicians make inference about a patient's blood through examination of a single drop. Samples are devices for learning about large masses by observing a few individuals." In education, sampling is a widely used technique. The census technique is rarely used, its most striking example being population count.

In the technique of sample investigation certain units from the whole domain of survey are selected as being representative. Now these are studied in detail and the conclusions arrived from these are extended to the entire field. Unlike census investigation, not all units are studied in sample investigation, but only some of these are selected for study on a certain definite basis. An example would make this clear. If one has to study the monthly expenditure of the students of a university one may not study all the students. One may collect figures of about 5% of them only. Supposing there 10,000 students : then one may collect expenditure figures of only 500 and extend his conclusions to all of them. If full caution is taken in the selection of representative students and data is collected faithfully, the applicability of these conclusions to the entire set will be of very high reliability.

Characteristics of Sampling Technique

The sampling technique has following characteristics and these bring into relief its value and significance :

(1) *Economical* : The sampling technique is much less expensive, much less time-consuming than the census technique.

(2) *Reliability* : If the choice of sample units is made with due care and the matter under survey is not heterogeneous, the conclusion of the sample survey can have almost the same reliability as those of census survey.

(3) *Detailed Study* : Since the number of sample units is fairly small these may be studied intensively and elaborately. They may be examined from multiple viewpoints.

(4) *Scientific Base* : This is a scientific technique, because the conclusions derived from the study of certain units may be verified from other units. By taking random samples one may determine the amount of deviation from the norm.

(5) *More Suitable* : Most of the surveys are made by the technique of sample survey, because wherever the matter is of a homogeneous nature, the examination of few units suffices. This is the case in the majority of situations.

Defects of Sampling Technique

(1) *Less Accuracy* : In comparison to census technique the conclusions derived from sample are more liable to error. Therefore, sampling technique is less accurate than the census technique.

(2) *Changeability of Units* : If the units in the field of survey are liable to change or if these are not harmonious the sampling technique will be very hazardous. It is not scientific to extend the conclusions derived from one set of sample to other sets which are unlike or are changeable.

(3) *Misleading Conclusions* : If due care is not taken in the selection of samples of if they are arbitrarily selected, the conclusions derived from them will become misleading if extended to all units. For example, in assessing the monthly expenditure of university students if we select for sample study only rich students, it will be highly erroneous to extend the results to all students.

(4) *Need for Specialized Knowledge* : The sample technique may be successful only if a competent and able scientist makes the selection. If this is done by average scientist, the selection is liable to be wrong.

(5) *When Sampling is not possible* : Under certain circumstances it is very difficult to use the sampling technique. If the time is very short and it is not possible to make selection of the sample, the technique cannot be used. Besides if we need 100% accuracy the sampling technique may not be used. It may also not be used if the material is of heterogeneous nature.

When and Where Sampling Technique is Appropriate

The foregoing discussion of *pros and cons* of sampling technique shows very clearly that certain defects and limitations notwithstanding, it is very widely used. Following are the criteria to determine the appropriateness of sampling technique :

(1) *Vast Data* : When the number of units is very large, sampling technique must be used as it economizes money, time and effort.

(2) *When Absolute Accuracy is not Required* : The sampling technique is very suitable in those situations where cent percent accuracy is not required; otherwise census technique is unavoidable, because 100% accuracy is available only by its means.

(3) *Infinite Data* : If the data are unlimited, one must use sampling technique.

(4) *Where Census is Impossible* : If one wants to know the amount of mineral wealth in a country, one cannot dig all mines to discover and count. Here sampling technique may be used.

(5) *Homogeneity* : If all the units of a domain are alike, sampling technique is very apt to use.

Essentials of an Ideal Sample

An ideal sample has following qualities :

(1) *Representative* : An ideal sample must be such that it represents adequately the whole data. We should select those units which have the same set of characteristics as are found in the whole data. It should not lack in a quality found in the whole data.

(2) *Independent* : The second feature of a sample is independence, that is, interchangeability of units. Every unit should be free to be included in the sample.

(3) *Adequate* : The number of units included in a sample should be sufficient to enable derivation of conclusions applicable to the whole data. A sample having 10% of the whole data is adequate but if it has only 1 or 2% it is not adequate.

(4) *Homogenous* : The units included in sample must bear likeness with other units; otherwise the sample will be unscientific.

Methods of Sampling

From a given data the choice of sample is made by various methods. Which method will suit in a given problem will depend upon its nature, scope and the investigator. Therefore, the choice of method in the selection of a sample must be made with utmost care. The main methods of selecting a sample are the following :

(1) Deliberate sampling or purposive sampling
(2) Random sampling
(3) Stratific sampling
(4) Quota sampling
(5) Multi-stage sampling
(6) Extensive sampling
(7) Convenient sampling.

(1) *Deliberate or Purposive Sampling*: In this method the investigator has complete freedom in choosing his sample according to his wishes and desires. The investigator chooses certain items from the whole data and studies them. To choose or leave an item for the purpose of study depends entirely upon the wishes of an investigator and he chooses those items or units which in his judgment are representative of the whole data.

This is a very simple technique of choosing the samples and is useful in cases where the whole data is homogeneous and the investigator has full knowledge of the various aspects of the problem. Though deliberate or purposive, this method does not imply arbitrary choice. In fact, it means that only those units will be selected which represent the whole.

Criticism of Deliberate Sampling Technique

In criticizing the deliberate sampling technique it is pointed out that in this the selection is completely under the control of the investigator and his prejudices and predilections are liable to interfere with his sense of objectivity. If this happens, and there is no theoretical check against this possibility in this technique the selection of the sample will be unfair. For example, if a scientist is investigating the monthly expenditure of students living in a hostel and he has a preconception that students spend maximum amount on cinemas and other source of entertainment, he may select only those students for study whose rooms are stacked with film magazines. This may be true only of 20% students but upon this basis of his sample he may conclude that 75% students spend more than 50% of their total expenditure on cinema and cinema literature. Another investigator who may have the preconception that students are much excited by sexual literature and other sources of sexual entertainment may come out with an unrealistic estimate about the amount spent by students on call girls, prostitutes and blue films.

For these reasons this technique is considered highly unsatisfactory and most statisticians have not a single word of praise for it. According to Parten, "Statisticians as a class, have nothing to say in favour of purposive selection."

If very great care is taken and the investigator is an expert scientist, this technique may still be useful, otherwise, as a rule, it is inappropriate and unsuited to objective study. Its main drawback is lack in it of any inherent check.

(2) *Random Sampling*: Of all the methods of selecting the samples, Random Sampling technique is made maximum use of; and it is considered the best method of sample selection. In this technique every item or unit of the domain has an equal opportunity for selection and this selection is in no way influenced by personal bias and

predilection of the investigator. No item is selected on account of likes or dislikes of the investigator and the selection is left entirely to chance. This provides every item fair and equal chance for selection; so it is not investigator's whim but Nature which determines the selection.

Random sampling is made in the following ways :

(i) *Lottery Method* : This is the simplest way of making the selection. The number of items in a data are written on sheets of paper or cards and they are thrown into a box. Now a neutral observer or the investigator blind-folding himself selects the number of items required in the sample. Here there is no partiality in favour of any item. The play of chance is allowed to determine the items selected in the sample.

For this method it is necessary that sheets of paper should be of equal dimensions and none should be bigger or smaller than the other.

(ii) *By rotating the drum* : This procedure is a slight modification of the lottery method. In it the pieces of wood, tin, or cardboard of equal length and breadth, with number 0, 1 or 2 printed on them, are used. Now a list of items in the domain are prepared and divided in 0, 1 or 5 categories. The pieces are rotated in the drum and then requisite numbers are drawn by an impartial person. Now, if the pieces drawn are 20 zeroes, 10 ones and 15 twos, we shall take 20 units from the zero list, 10 from list 1 and 15 from the list 2.

(iii) *Selecting from Sequential List* : In this procedure units are broken up in Numerical, Alphabetical or Geographical Sequence. Now one may decide to choose 1, 5, 10, 15 and so on, that division is alphabetical we decide to choose every item starting a, e, m, o, etc.

(iv) *Tippet's Numbers* : On the basis of population statistics, Tippet has constructed a random list of four digits each of 10,400 institutions. These numbers are result of combining 41,600 population statistics reports.

The first forty numbers in Tippet's list are :

2952	6641	3922	9792	7969	5911	3170
5634	4167	9524	1545	1396	7203	5356
1300	2693	2370	7483	3408	2762	3563
1089	6913	7691	0560	5246	1112	6107
6008	8126	4433	8776	2754	9143	1405
9025	7002	6111	8816	6446		

Upon the basis of Tippet's numbers it is very easy to select samples. If a domain has 8000 items and we wish to select first 30, then we shall first arrange serially items 1 to 8000, and then select from the above schedule first thirty such items which do not exceed the number 8000. Tippet's numbers are widely used in making random selections.

Precautions in the Choice of Samples

In random selection one should take care of the fact that the item chosen is representative and sufficient. Following points should be borne in mind in making the selection of samples :

1. The investigator should be well acquainted with the entire range of items or population out of which selection is to be made. What are the chief features of the field, what is its scope and what is the number of items in it, all this should be known to the investigator; otherwise he would not be able to make a fair selection.

2. The different items of a field should be alike and homogeneous. If there is too much of heterogeneity, the sample cannot be representative.

3. The various items of the field should be independent of each other. If they are interlinked, random selection will not be possible. It is not possible in random selection to select other units having resemblance and dependent upon the selected units.

Every unit should be easily accessible to the investigator and there should not be any item which is obscure to the investigator.

3. *Stratified Sampling* : This method of selecting sample is a mixture of the deliberate and random sampling techniques. In this, first of all the data in a field is split into various classes on the basis of their characteristics and immediately thereafter certain items are selected from these classes by the random sampling technique. That is why this is known as mixed technique of sampling. This technique is suitable in those cases in which the data has sub-data having special characteristics. The stratification is made on the basis of the special attributes and from these strata items are selected random. For example, if we wish to collect information regarding income-expenditure of the male population of a town, firstly we shall split the whole population in various strata on the basis of special professions pursued. We shall get the classes of service people, businessmen, shopkeepers, workers etc. From these we shall select random some units for study of income-expenditure.

Process of Stratifying : The stratification of a data should be done with great care, because upon successful stratification depends the success of this technique. Following points should be borne in mind :

(i) One should possess extensive information of all the items included in a domain and should also know which items make a coherent whole on the basis of similar traits and which others are different from them and why?

(ii) The size of each stratum should be large enough to enable use of random sampling technique.

(iii) In stratifying it must be kept in mind that various strata should have similar relation to the domain and should themselves be homogeneous.

(iv) The various strata should differ from each other and be homogeneous by themselves. If two strata are alike, there is no need for stratified test.

(v) The proportion of random sample from each stratum should be the same as the proportion of stratum from the field. Suppose a field had four strata : accordingly the proportion of each stratum to domain is ¼. Now, if the number of total items of the sample is 64, one shall select 16 items from each stratum and thus the proportion of selected items from each stratum will be of the total items.

If the above mentioned precautions are taken one may get very good results from this method as it combines the virtues of deliberate sampling and random sampling methods.

(4) *Quota Sampling* : This method of study is not much used. In it the entire data is split up into as many blocks as there are investigators and each investigator is asked to select certain items from his block and study. The success of this method depends upon the integrity and professional competence of investigators. If some investigators are competent and others not so competent, serious discrepancies will appear in the study. Therefore, as remarked above, it is a method which is sparingly used.

(5) *Multi-stage Sampling* : This, again, is not a favoured procedure of sampling. In this items are selected in different stages at random. For example, if we wish to know per acre yield of various crops in U.P., we shall begin by studying a single crop in one study. Here we shall begin by making at random selection of 5 districts in the first instance, then of these 5 districts, 10 villages per district will be chosen in the same manner. Now, in the final stage we shall select again by random selection 5 fields out of every village. Thus, we shall examine per acre yield in 250 farms all over U.P. This number may be increased or decreased depending upon the opinion of experts. Following table makes this procedure clear :

Domain of Whole Data
(U. P.)
↓
(Districts)   →   First Stage
↓
Villages   →   Second Stage
↓
Farms   →   Third Stage

(6) *Extreme Sampling* : This method is virtually same as census except that irrelevant or inaccessible items are left out. Every other item is examined. For instance, if we are to study sexual behaviour of Indians, we may leave foreigners living in India from our study. This method has all the merits and demerits of census survey and is very rarely used.

(7) *Convenient Sampling* : This is hit or miss procedure of study. The investigator selects certain items from the field as per his convenience. No planned effort is made to collect information. This is a method by which a tourist studies generally the country of his visit. He comes across certain people and things, has transactions with them, and then tries to generalize about the entire populace in his travelogue. This is essentially unscientific procedure and has no value as a research technique. But as is characterized by "hit or miss" method, at times clear hits are scored. That is why we discover profound truths expressed about a country by perceptive travellers.

The selection of a sampling procedure from the above mentioned techniques depends upon the nature, scope, number of units etc. in a field. Also another factor determining our choice is the amount of accuracy and refinement desired. The choice of a method therefore, is bound up with the nature of circumstances. However, mostly random and stratified sampling techniques are used, rest are rarely preferred.

QUESTION FOR EXERCISE

1. What is the meaning of representative sample? What is the method of achieving representative samples?

5

PSYCHOLOGICAL TESTING

Importance of Psychological Tests

Psychological tests have been proved to possess great utility in many spheres. Briefly, the utility and importance of mental tests can be observed in the following spheres :

1. *Guidance :* As has been indicated earlier, psychological tests are indispensable in all forms of guidance.

2. *Appointments* : Psychological tests are now-a-days resorted to for the appointment of appropriate individuals to posts in offices, factories and government services. It has the doubly beneficial effect of securing proper and desirable jobs for individuals according to their interests inclinations, intelligence and abilities, as well as ensuring that the highest level of efficiency is achieved by the right man being in the right job. In this way, both the employee as well as the employer are benefited.

3. *Selection of training* : An individual can benefit from training for some particular job only if he is initially in possession of the requisite intelligence, abilities and qualities, besides the necessary interest in the work involved. It is evident, that the individual should be tested in respect of these qualities before any training is imparted to him. Hence, in all advanced nations of the world, all kinds of training institutes make use of psychological tests for selecting the required candidates. In India, for example, the recruitment to the Police Training Colleges, the Govt. Teachers' Training Colleges and other technical institutions is done only on the basis of psychological tests. In public schools, the students who receive scholarships are selected on the basis of psychological tests in order to ensure that the scholarships are not wasted, as well they might be if they are provided to the wrong individuals. Psychological tests are further used for selection of candidates for the National Defence Academy in the country. Such use of psychological tests for the selection of personnel in training schools is constantly on the increase.

4. *Classification according to level of intelligence* : Now-a-days, all educationists agree that the success of education depends upon the

student being provided education of a kind that accords with his level of intelligence. Hence, individual students are classified and stratified according to their level of intelligence, and different curricular and extra-curricular programmes devised for the three categories of students, the brilliant, the average and the retarded. The classification is based on intelligence tests. It is not only in the field of education but also in various vocations, armed forces and industries that intelligence tests are used to classify individuals so that they can be given the proper kind of work that is within their capacity to perform with reasonable success.

5. *Prediction* : The term indicates the forecasting of success in the case of an individual. While guiding the individual, a psychologist can normally make fairly accurate predictions as to the degree of success that one is likely to achieve. This prediction is based upon psychological tests, the greater the capacity of a psychological test to assist in prediction, the greater is its validity and its reliability.

6. *Diagnosis* : Before giving any guidance, the directing psychologist makes a diagnosis of the problem present before him. He gives suggestions for alleviating a certain condition only after he has decided upon a diagnosis, since it is only upon diagnosing some problem that he reaches the root causes. And psychological tests are essential for diagnosis; without them a proper diagnosis cannot be achieved.

7. *Research* : Psychological tests are of use even in the field of psychological research. Intelligence tests, interest inventories, personality tests, tests of mental abilities and personal qualities help in research in these specific directions.

What are Psychological Tests?

Importance of psychological tests is fairly evident from the preceding exposition of the subject. Before proceeding to a study of the various kinds of tests, it is essential to know the kinds of psychological tests that are in use, and the principal elements active in them. Defining psychological tests, Mursell writes : "A psychological test, then, is a pattern of stimuli selected and organised to elicit responses which will reveal certain psychological characteristics in the person who takes them."[1] In this way, psychological tests are an organisation of some stimuli. These stimuli are selected with some special objectives in view. The object is to discover some psychological characteristics of the person being tested. Stimuli present in psychological tests are called test items and they can be of all kinds — pictures, figures, wooden blocks, word groups, sentences and figures, etc. and the way in which these stimuli uncover psychological characteristics will be evident from a description of each of them.

---

1. Mursell, J.L. : *Psychological Testing,* New York : Longmans Green (1953), p. 1.

Classification of Psychological Tests

Psychological tests are of various kinds. They have been classified from various different viewpoints. Classifications are as follows :

1. *Classification according to method of testing* : Tests have been divided into two classes, in this case classification is based on the method involved :

(a) *Individual tests* : These tests are administered to one individual at one time, as indicated by the term denoting them. They include only performance tests. In addition to these, they also include tests that require linguistic ability. Some examples of these are Stanford Binet intelligence test, Weshler Belleviue intelligence tests, Kohez's block design test, Rorschach's ink blot test and T.A.T. test, etc. These tests are particularly appropriate for testing of individuals, but they are not financially suitable as they are expensive, in addition to requiring more expert training than in many other cases. Secondly, they are less objective than group tests.

(b) *Group tests* : In this category the tests included are performed upon a large number of people simultaneously. Some examples are the group intelligence tests of the Psychological Bureau of Uttar Pradesh, interests lists, vocational lists etc. They are more objective and less expensive, requiring very little, if any, specialised training that may prove expensive. But in these tests no real rapport between the subject and the examiner is established. Hence, they are less useful for solving problems of individuals, than are the individuals tests. Nevertheless, they have proved really useful in the case of educational and vocational guidance requirements.

2. *Classification according to the medium of instruction* : In these tests, classification is based upon the, medium of teaching of the subjects. The psychological tests, from this viewpoint, are divided into the following two classes :

(a) *Verbal tests* : This classification comprehends tests in which questions are orally asked, linguistic and concerned abilities being essentially required. One of the best examples of verbal tests is Dr. Sohan Lal's intelligence test utilised at Allahabad. These tests are not intended for, and cannot be used in the case of illiterates, only slightly educated persons and small children, since such people lack linguistic ability.

(b) *Non-verbal tests* : This classification includes tests that do not require the use of language, but substitute figures, pictures, blocks and other implements for it. Examples of it are Pidgon's non-verbal tests and Raven's progressive matrices. Their particular felicity lies in the fact that they can be applied to the testing of illiterates, very slightly educated individuals and very young children. This category includes all non-verbal tests.

3. *Classification according to the objectives of testing* : Division of tests on the basis of their individual objective or aim leads them to be put into the following categories—

(a) *Intelligence tests* : These help to test the intelligence in the form of both verbal and non-verbal tests. They can be administered both to the individual and to a large group.

(b) *Testing of mental abilities* : In this are included the various tests of mental abilities such as tests of spatial ability, artistic ability, mechanical ability etc.

(c) *Interest tests* : These tests help to discover the interest of the individual, some examples of which are Strong's Vocational Interest Blank and Cudor's Vocational Inventory. Both of them are described in detail at a later stage. Besides these, the vocational interest list devised by the Bureau of Psychology, Uttar Pradesh, is also an effective test.

(d) *Aptitude test* : These tests or lists are devised by combining the different tests of mental abilities.

(e) *Personality tests* : These help to find out the individual's personality traits or characteristics. The main methods of personality testing are Rorschach's Ink Blot test and T.A.T.

Characteristics of Good Tests

Good tests of a psychological nature bear the following features :

1. *Reliability* : The higher the degree of reliability that results of a test have the greater is considered the reliability of the test itself. And the reliability of its conclusion means that if the same test is performed upon the same individual more than once, results obtained in each individual list should be the same or commensurate with the first one, if it is modified by changed circumstances.

2. *Validity* : The validity of a test lies in the fact that it succeeds in testing the particular quality which it is designed to test. For example, intelligence tests can be valid only if they, in fact, test correctly the intelligence level of the individual subject.

3. *Objectivity* : A test can achieve a high level of objectivity only if the answer to each of its various questions is distinct and precise, and if there is no difference of opinion, regarding it, among the various examiners. Its efficacy lies in the fact that the conclusion or result is, in no way, influenced by the examiner's individual thoughts or opinions, so that the conclusions or results are obtained no matter what the number of examiners who examine the same subject.

4. *Comprehensiveness* : Another feature of a good test is its comprehensive nature. This feature involves inclusion of all features or qualities allied to the one in question. It will provide information on qualities concerned with the one quality actually being tested. In this manner, in a comprehensive test, questions cover the quality in

question as well as allied qualities so that no aspect of the measured or tested ability escapes attention.

5. *Discriminating power* : This term applies to the ability which helps to distinguish between persons with greater or less ability so that they score more or less points or marks.

6. *Utility* : This feature concerns the extent to which a particular test can be used with facility. And for this it is essential that the questions asked should be simple, the method easy, the time involved less and the expenses negligible.

Of the above mentioned characteristics, the most important are validity and reliability. Hence, both these qualities will be described in detail here.

VALIDITY

What is Validity?

It is apparent from the description of intelligence tests that all tests do not have a common degree of validity, it being completely dependent upon the extent to which any judgment based upon the test's result is objective. For example, validity in the case of intelligence tests can be attributed only to those tests that actually succeed in testing the individual's level of intelligence. A test can be accepted as valid only to that degree to which it can correctly gauge the intelligence of the subject. In this way, validity of a test is that quality on the basis of which the correctness or incorrectness of judgments based upon it is evaluated. For example, the validity of interest tests is less than the case of intelligence tests. Here there is a slight difficulty. Suppose, for the moment, that the intelligence of some students was measured by one particular method. Now the validity of the test will depend upon whether the students tested do, in fact, possess the intelligence that they are indicated as possessing. The problem that arises here is how can one ascertain whether the students do or do not possess the intelligence indicated by the above test. Evidently, there must be some independent criterion for deciding upon the validity of the particular test in question or tests in general. In this case, of the intelligence level of students, the examination results can be the basis for measuring the validity of the test. Generally speaking, it can be said that if there is a correlation between marks obtained at an examination and the result of the test, then the test is valid.

Kinds of Validity

But as is evident from the foregoing description, validity is a relative term, as no test can have complete validity. Hence, whenever a particular test is termed valid, or whenever the lack of validity of a test is in question, it is necessary to indicate the sense in which it is considered valid or invalid. Apparently, validity is of many kinds. Psychologists have roughly accepted the following kinds of validity :

1. *Face validity*: Face validity is concerned with the form of the test. Such a validity is attributed only to the test which provides an item or subject that appears valid.

2. *Content validity* : Another kind of validity is content validity in which the validity of the test is based on the validity of its contents. In order to obtain this kind of validity in a particular test, it is essential that the items of a test should achieve the objective for which they are originally designed. For example, content validity in the case of an intelligence test will be attributed only in the event of its succeeding in discovering all factors concerned with intelligence.

3. *Factorial validity* : This is inclusive of the validity of the factors in the test and in order to judge whether a test has factorial validity, it is examined by the method of factor analysis, and a correlation between this result and the evident factor resultant of tests is established.

4. *Predictive validity* : This is the most popular form of validity. In this, results are obtained on the basis of a particular criterion, and correlation between the scores and the criterion is established. In this, the choice of a criterion requires much care and attention. The coefficient obtained by this correlation between scores and criterion is called the validity coefficient. The validity coefficient varies between 0.5 and 0.8. A lower coefficient makes the test inapplicable and lacking in utility, while a higher coefficient is not normally obtained.

5. *Concurrent validity* : It resembles the predictive validity since in it, too, a correlation between the test and some definite standard is established. But, despite these common features, there are also some definite variations.

From the above analysis of the various kinds of validity it is evident that validity exists in a particular context, or in other words, every test is valid for a particular objective and for a particular age group in individuals. It can just as well be invalid for a particular age group in individuals and in a particular context. Hence, to attribute validity to a test without qualification is completely unjustified and inaccurate. For the sentiment to have any value or meaning, it is essential to state the context and conditions in which it is applicable.

RELIABILITY

What is Reliability?

In addition to validity, it is essential that in every test there be a definite element of reliability. It is only then that the conclusions of the test can be considered reliable and worthy of trust. Reliability of a test consists in any quality in the test that may inspire confidence and trust. And this quality can be attributed to only that test which provides the same score every time it is performed on the same individual. Now, if some intelligence test yields one score for an individual at one time, and another if it is applied to the same individual at a different time, it is only too evident that such a test cannot be considered reliable and his reliability of the test does not reside in any one part of it, but in its wholeness or completeness. Its reliability will considerably be weakened and decreased if even one part of it is injured in some respect. Hence, it is essential that the internal parts of a test possess internal consistency and uniformity. It is only on the basis of such a reliable test that guidance can be given.

Means of Measuring Reliability

Reliability can be measured in the following four ways :

1. *Test retest method* : One method of gauging reliability is to perform the same test of the same group of individuals on two different occasions, and to test the scores or results obtained. One group of individuals can be subjected to the Binet intelligence test. Then later on the same group of individuals can again be subjected to the Binet intelligence test. If the results obtained in each case do not tally, then the tests cannot be considered reliable.

2. *Parallel form method* : Another method of judging the reliability of a particular method is to prepare a method similar to the one being judged and examined. Now the same group can be examined through the basic and then through the modified or parallel methods. Finally, the results of the two can be compared to judge the reliability of the test. Gulliksen has suggested that more than one parallel method be devised for greater accuracy.

3. *Split half method* : Another method of judging the reliability of a test is to divide the components of the test into even and odd times whose results can be individually obtained. Now the results can be compared to show the reliability of the test.

4. *Inter item consistency* : In this method of measuring the reliability of a psychological test only one method is applied at one time. The mutual relation between the scores obtained for each specific item in the test is observed. At the same time the relation between the marks obtained for one specific question and the marks obtained for the whole test is also ascertained. As this method of measuring reliability involves considerable statistical skill in correlation, psychologists Cudor and Richardson, have devised some formulae for application in this method.

As has been indicated previously, the implication and meaning of reliability also change the method of judging reliability. Hence, it is not sufficient to remark that a particular test is reliable. It is equally essential that the sense in which reliability is judged also be mentioned, or in other words mention must be made of the method by which its reliability has been established.

Of the above mentioned methods of judging reliability of psychological tests, the third is the most prevalent and useful, since it is the most easy. In this method, the necessity of collecting the same group of individuals more than once is obviated. Reliability is known from the coefficient of reliability, and this coefficient is known as the reliability coefficient.

In this manner, both reliability and validity are important qualities of tests. Validity is related to the scale or structure of the test while reliability is an attribute of its ability of testing.

The aim and object of education is the comprehensive, overall development of the child. This development and progress is gradual. Hence, it is essential to examine the child at regular intervals to find out the extent to which he has progressed. In the school, students study a number of subjects. To test one in respect of these subjects from time to time is essential as it makes clear the success with which he is studying and understanding them. It is the examination that makes it possible for one to know the child's achievements in terms of ability in learning these subjects. Hence, in almost all schools some mode of examining the children, in respect of their attainments in learning and retaining all that is taught to them, is present.

INTELLIGENCE TESTS

Historical Outline

As the new individual dissimilarities came to light, psychologists tried to measure the various individual differences, and to this end, different tests were evolved. Among these tests, those devised to measure intelligence achieved a lot of fame. Near the close of the 19th century, Galton developed some tests to measure the function of the different organs. By these, Galton measured sensory discrimination, sensory perception and sensory acuity. Though these measures are not directly related to intelligence they may be accepted as the forerunners of intelligence tests.

In 1880, Ebbinghaus prepared several tests to measure the differences in the intelligence of various individuals. In 1890, a famous American psychologist Cattel evolved some mental tests. On the basis of these, Cattel measured individual differences between some students of Columbia University in respect of the speed of reactions, sensory acuity, memory and some other simple mental activities.

But in fact, the first concrete step in the direction of intelligence tests was taken by a famous French psychologist Alfred Binet. Alfred Binet was conducting some research in the mental activities of school-going children. In the course of his research he observed that in order to give any useful education to the feeble-minded children it is essential to put them in special classes. In order to investigate this subject a committee headed by Binet was formed in 1904. The first difficulty, concerning the study of feeble-minded children, was need of a scale with which to measure the intelligence of children.

With Simon's assistance Binet developed and published a scale in 1905, known as the Binet-Simon Scale. In this scale, some 30 tasks, from the simplest to the most complex, were prescribed in a serial order. On the basis of experiments with the average and feeble-minded children carried out with the help of this scale Binet and Simon determined norms for various age levels. According to the Binet-Simon intelligence tests, if a five-year old child is capable of performing tasks which an average child of three can perform, his mental age will be rated as three years and if that child fails to perform more than the first five among the thirty tasks he will be classed as idiot.

Binet and Simon made revisions in this scale from time to time. The first revised scale was published in 1908. From the success of this revision, psychologists of other countries developed intelligence tests suitable to the environments of their own countries. Among them, Burt's London Revision and Terman's Stanford Revision are well-known. The modern revised edition of the 2nd revision was published in 1937 under the name of Terman Merrill Scale.

In the Terman Merrill Scale which was a revision of the Stanford Binet Scale, some more subjects, related to intelligence tests were included. It now became useful for the age range of 2 to 18 years. In this scale, there were provisions for two types of tests, yearly and half-yearly, for children belonging to the age group of two to four years. Many other subjects were included for the adult people. For every age group there were six to eight subjects. In this scale there are tests which enable the examiner to examine the intelligence of an individual in a very short time.

In Indian conditions, Binet's test was adopted for the first time by Dr. C. Herbert Rice. But its revised form is almost completely different from the Binet tests. These tests were compiled in Urdu and Punjabi. There are two types of scale in it, one having 10 tasks, the other 35 tasks, and it was the smaller scale of tests which proved dependable. In 1927, Dr. J. Munry of Christian College started verbal group tests in Urdu, English and Hindi. In 1933, Mr. Lajja Shankar developed group tests for children from 10 to 18, which adopted a revised and studied form of Terman group tests. Besides these, the group tests started by Dr. Jalota of Lahore, in Hindi, Urdu and English — proved very valuable. In Bihar, under the direction of Dr. S.M. Mohsin, a test battery was constructed to measure mental abilities and intelligence of participants in many group tests. In the non-verbal group tests, Menzel has created tests founded upon the ability of Indian children in drawing. Besides, Mr. I.R. Kumaria organised group tests for college students. The other important contributions in this direction have come from Dr. Lalit Kumar Shah, C.T. Philip, H.C. Banerjee, D.H. Roy, T.P. Bhowmick and H.P. Maiti. The above description makes it quite clear that not much work has been done in the direction of non-verbal tests. There is hope of development in this direction in the future.

Types of Intelligence Tests

Intelligence tests are classified as follows according to the activities prescribed in them :

1. Verbal Tests,
2. Non-Verbal Tests.

As the name itself suggests, verbal tests make use of language while the non-verbal tests include such activities which do not necessitate the use of language. Both these types are suitable for individual as well as group tests. Consequently, verbal and non-verbal tests are further sub-divided into two classes — individual and group. Thus, finally there are four types of intelligence tests :

1. Verbal Individual Intelligence Tests,
2. Non-Verbal Individual Intelligence Tests,
3. Verbal Group Intelligence Tests,
4. Non-Verbal Group Intelligence Tests.

Verbal Individual Intelligence Tests

The very name verbal individual intelligence tests suggests that there are intelligence tests given to individuals or in other words they are meant to test the intelligence of individuals. Language finds adequate use in them. Binet-Simon tests and the various revisions are all included in this classification.

The State Manovigyanshala of Uttar Pradesh has made a Hindi version of the Terman Merrill Scale. This revision includes a variety of material, from solid object to difficult questions. The activities in the beginning are simple like constructing a bridge or a tower of blocks or fitting in irregular wooden blocks in their proper place supplied for them. At the same time, at the end of the tests there are difficult questions which need considerable thinking. This test is divided into several age groups. The higher groups use language and its use gradually declines with the age group. For example, the two years' group includes the following activities :

1. To form panel with three holes,
2. Recognising of objects by name,
3. Recognising the organs of the body,
4. Making a tower of blocks,
5. Naming an object from its pictures,
6. Word building.

Non-verbal Individual Intelligence Tests

It is quite apparent from the above example that in verbal test the child's knowledge of language is more in demand, and therefore, the use of these tests is limited to students and literate persons. But these verbal tests cannot be used in the case of illiterate individuals as these tests involve an extensive use of language which fails as a medium to measure the individual differences between the illiterates. Consequently, illiterate individuals are tested with the help of non-verbal individual intelligence tests. The name itself indicates the nature of these tests. These tests involve the least possible use of the linguistic ability and are similarly almost unaffected by knowledge derived from books. An example of these non-verbal tests is the Performance Intelligence Tests.

It would be in keeping with the context of our discussion to understand in detail the performance intelligence test as an example of the non-verbal individual intelligence tests. The word 'performance' is usually applied to tests which require a minimum use of understanding and language. Thus, these tests make use of items requiring performances and not language and these tests can be applied to children, illiterates, feeble-minded individuals as well as foreigners.

Merrill-Palmer Block Building Tests

One of the most important of performance tests for children is Merrill-Palmer Block Building Test. Besides Seguin Form Board it includes block building test as well. In the Fig. 1 given below a four-year old boy is making a structure by means of blocks as demonstrated by the tester.

Pintner-Paterson Performance Scale

An example of the performance intelligence tests is the Pintner-Paterson Performance Scale. It was evolved by Pintner and Paterson in 1917. In this scale there are 15 types of tests, of which 4 are form boards, 6 picture completion, memory span and the rest picture puzzles and imitations etc.

Porteus Maze Test

Another example of the performance intelligence tests is the Porteus Maze Test. In it, paper and pencil mazes are used. For his tests, Porteus created mazes for children from 3 to 14 years. It gets difficult, corresponding to the increase in age. The subject is allowed two chances and if he fails in the attempts then the conclusion is that his intelligence is not of that age level. Children of 12 to 14 years are given four opportunities. These tests designed by Porteus not only measure intelligence, but they also reflect

Fig. 1

the temperament of the individual. It is distinguished from other tests in as much as that it includes some aspects ignored by such tests as the Stanford-Binet tests.

Form Board Test

A comparatively simple example of the performance intelligence test is the form board tests. Among them the tests of Seguin and Goddard deserve special mention. In the form board test, there are numerous blocks and a board in which there are holes corresponding to this block. The subject as shown in Fig. No. 2 has to fit the blocks in these corresponding holes in the board, the time taken and mistakes committed being noted from which the score test is calculated.

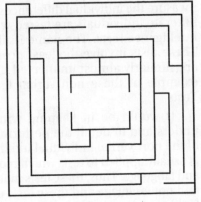

Fig. 2

Wechsler Bellevue Test

Another example of the performance intelligence tests is the Wechsler Bellevue test, evolved in 1939, meant for people from 10 to 60 years of age. In a modern clinic, these tests are included in Binet class, as one of the most important. In this way it is the most apt test for measuring the intelligence of adults. In this test there are five verbal tests and five performance tests. This test affords not only an index to mental abilities but also a profile of abilities.

Fig. 3

Bhatia's Battery of Performance Tests

The description of performance intelligence tests is incomplete without reference to Bhatia's Battery of Performance Tests. It is the battery created by the former Director of Uttar Pradesh Manovigyanshala Dr. Chandra Mohan Bhatia. It has the following 5 sub-tests :

1. *Kohez block design test* : 10 items of tests out of the Kohez block design test have been included in the battery. There is one card on

every subject upon which is depicted a colour design. The subject or the examinee sees this design and makes a similar one out of the blocks as shown in the Fig. 4. These designs become correspondingly more and more complex, having been simple at the start.

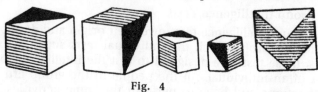

Fig. 4

2. *Alexander Pass along test*: The Bhatia battery also includes Alexander pass along test, in which, too, there are some designs. As shown in Fig. 5 the subject shifts coloured pieces in an open box and places them in similar design.

3. *Pattern drawing test*: This test has been developed by Dr. Bhatia himself. In this, there are eight cards on each of which there is a particular form. The subject draws a particular figure or pattern after seeing this form.

4. *Immediate memory test* : Some digits are recited, which are immediately repeated by the subject, this activity throwing some light on the immediate memory of the subject.

Fig. 5

5. *Picture construction test* : In this sub-test there are five subjects in which pictures relating to the rural life are fragmented into 2, 4, 6, 8 and 12 pieces respectively. At one time pieces of a picture are placed before the subject who puts them in order and constructs the picture.

Difficulties in the Individual Intelligence Tests

Some difficulties are faced in both the verbal and non-verbal types of individual intelligence tests. They are roughly as follows :

1. *The difficulty of time* : The individual intelligence test takes an hour usually and only one person can be tested at one time. Obviously, at this rate it would be essential to have a very big number of trained examiners and in spite of that it would be difficult to test all the people.

2. *Need for experienced examiners* : The second obstacle in the individual intelligence tests is the need for experienced examiners because the correct result cannot be arrived at if the examiners are inexperienced. At the same time, the availability of such a large number of trained personnel is almost impossible.

Notwithstanding these difficulties, in some circumstances the individual intelligence tests become unavoidable. This is because the level of accuracy reached by the individual intelligence tests, in the assessment of a person's intelligence, is beyond the reach of the group intelligence tests.

Verbal Group Intelligence Tests

The group intelligence tests owe their origin and development to the difficulties from which the individual tests suffer. As the name suggests, these tests are designed to test the intelligence of a group and not of an individual. All the people in the group are given the same directions and have to perform the same activities. Even the score of the result of group intelligence tests is calculated by machines thus dispensing with the necessity of skilled examiners, resulting in an economy of time.

Army alpha and beta tests : An excellent example of group intelligence tests is afforded by the Army alpha and beta tests, which were evolved during the World War I in order to test the American soldiers. For example, it revealed separately the feeble-minded, men capable of becoming skilled specialists, men capable of becoming officers, men needing some training, etc.

Naval and army general classification tests : Due to the success which attended these tests, some group tests for classification of naval or army soldiers were evolved during the World War II. Of these two particular forms deserve mention. These two are : (1) Naval general classification tests and (2) Army general classification tests.

With the type of calculations made by Cruze, some one billion people were tested by the military general classification tests during the years 1941 to 1946. In these tests there are three subjects, *viz.*, those relating to vocabulary problems, relating to mathematics, and relating to problems of counting blocks.

From the above example, it is quite clear that these verbal group intelligence tests examine the reasoning ability, ability of comparing and contrasting sense of directions, ability in numerals and language, of the individuals who constitute the group. It is essential that the examiner should be fully acquainted with the test and he should also understand the corresponding directions. Thus, often the examiner examines himself to start with. At the same time, it is necessary for the examiner to have some knowledge of the mechanical aspects of the conditions of examination such as the proper seating arrangement of the examinees, the distribution of test blanks and the preparation of material related to tests, like pencils etc.

Difficulties in the Verbal Group Intelligence Tests

Even after taking all the precautions, some difficulties are discernible in the verbal group intelligence tests which can be eliminated only by reverting to the individual intelligence tests. It is due to these difficulties that the individual intelligence tests are considered more realistic than the group intelligence tests. The difficulties of the verbal group tests are fundamentally as follows :

1. *Difficulties relating to co-operation in tests* : In these tests it is difficult to judge whether the examinee is extending his full co-operation or not.

2. *Difficulties related to the balance of the subject* : In these tests it is difficult to determine whether the physical and emotional balance of the examinee is even or disturbed.

3. *Difficulty related to the ease of the subject* : In the verbal group intelligence test it is difficult to ascertain if the examinee is feeling at ease and free or restrained.

4. *Possibility of cheating by the subject* : Another difficulty in these tests is that no one can testify whether the person has written the answer himself or copied it from his neighbour.

In spite of difficulties which arise in the verbal group intelligence tests, they have their own advantages due to which they are used comprehensively. As has been said before, the advantages are the same as the difficulties of the individual intelligence tests.

Non-verbal Group Intelligence Tests

As has been mentioned before, the verbal intelligence tests are meant only for the literates because of the requirement of linguistic ability. It is for this reason that the non-verbal group intelligence tests have been developed, the examinee making a minimum use of language but performing, instead, many activities. One example of the non-verbal

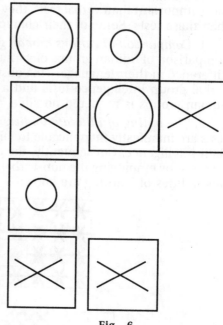

Fig. 6

intelligence test is Cattel's Culture Free test and the N.I.I.P. test. An example of the subjects given in these tests is as follows :

In the Fig. 6, there are 3 squares with some figures drawn in the three squares. On the left, various figures are shown in five squares. In the given diagram, the fourth square has to be filled with one such figure from the five squares that its relation to the third square must be the same as the relation which the figure in the first square bears to the figure in the second square.

In these non-verbal group intelligence tests the examiners have to explain to the examinees even the simplest directions which are also demonstrated as far as possible. All this is done to make the least possible use of language. There are some performance tests in these group intelligence tests, in which the examinee draws some lines according to his abilities, fills in some empty spaces, draws some simple figures, or performs some simple activities. Some psychologists do not give credence to these non-verbal tests in their role of measuring intelligence of the subjects, while on the other hand some psychologists consider them to be better than verbal tests. For example, in Alexander's opinion, "A complete performance battery will be a better measure than a complete verbal battery."

Characteristics of the Non-verbal Group Intelligence Tests

The truth is that even if non-verbal group intelligence tests are not more important than verbal tests, they are certainly not less important than these tests. Some of their characteristics are as follows :

1. *Comparison of various human groups* : The first obstacle in the comparison of human groups of various languages and cultures is the difference in their language. This obstacle can be overcome by non-verbal group intelligence tests and a comparison between different human groups is rendered possible.

2. *The testing of illiterate soldiers* : The verbal group intelligence tests are manifestly inapplicable to illiterate soldiers for the testing of their intelligence. Consequently, the abilities of illiterate soldiers are assessed by employing the non-verbal group intelligence tests and the possibilities of learning are known.

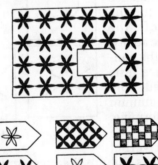

Fig. 7 : Matrix similar to Raven's Progressive Matrices.

3. *Intelligence testing in children* : The linguistic ability is very low in the case of children and consequently the verbal group intelligence tests cannot be given to them.

Reliability

The reliability of a test depends not on any one item in the test but on the test as a whole. The reliability of the test diminishes if any one item of the test is defective. This is why there must be a uniformity and internal consistency between the various items of the test. It is only on the basis of such a reliable test that correct directions can be given.

Reliability is investigated in three ways. These ways are as follows :

1. The test is applied to the same group under two different conditions and the results thus compiled are compared. Suppose, for example, the group is tested for its intelligence using the Binet test. Now, after sometime, the same group is tested employing the Binet test. If the I.Q. resulting from both the tests is the same, the Binet tests will be accepted as reliable. If there are some differences between the I.Q. received from the two tests, they will be considered unreliable.

2. In a test in which there are many items, the results of the even and the odd items are compared to examine its reliability.

3. Another method of examining reliability is to prepare a test parallel to the one whose reliability is under examination. Now a group should be tested by both the original and the transformed forms of the test. This is followed by a comparison of the two results and the reliability of the test is, in this way, examined. Gulliksen has advised the preparation of more than one parallel list.

Among the three methods of examination of reliability, the second is the most popular because it is also the easiest. This method does not necessitate the collection of the group time and again. Reliability is known from the coefficient of correlation which is known as the reliability coefficient.

Thus, both validity and reliability are essential qualities of tests. While validity is related to the scale or structure of the test, reliability is related to the capacity of the test.

MEASUREMENT OF PERSONALITY

Psychologists employ a number of methods to measure personality, *e.g.*, situation test, psycho-analytic test and projective method etc. Besides these, the case history method, interview and questionnaire and rating methods have their own importance. Briefly, the methods of measuring personality are :

1. Case History Method
2. Interview Method
3. Questionnaire Method
4. Performance Method
5. Rating Method
6. Situation Test

7. Psycho-Analytic Test

8. Projection Techniques.

Among the above mentioned methods the projection techniques are the most popular. A brief description of the other methods, before we make a detailed description of this specific one, would be quite in keeping with the context.

1. *Case history method* : In the case history method, as the name obviously indicates, the facts concerning the life of the subject are collected. This case history supplies all the facts related to man's environment and heredity. This method can be employed to study both normal and abnormal personality but it needs experienced testers.

2. *Interview method* : The interview method is the most common of all the methods for the study of personality. It is the method widely used in the selection of people for government, semi-government and private services. In this, the subject and the tester sit facing each other and the former answers questions asked by the latter. Besides the answers which the subject offers, his personality is indicated by his expression. This method, like the case history method, needs very experienced testers who ask questions which may probe the correct thing and enable the subject to express himself without any apprehension. Thus, the interview method depends as much on the tester as it does on the subject.

3. *Questionnaire method* : Questionnaires have been used extensively in the investigation of personality. The name suggests that it is a list of selected questions the answers to which throw light upon different traits of personality. 'Yes' and 'No' are written in front of these questions. The subject either strikes out the wrong answer or indicates the correct one. Questionnaires are used to gain knowledge of traits like self-confidence, sociability, introversion or extroversion, tendency to dominate or be dominated etc.

There are some difficulties in the questionnaire method. It has the following limitations :

(a) Often the subjects conceal the facts and give wrong answers.

(b) Sometimes the framing of the questions is such that the tester takes them to mean one thing and the subject another.

(c) Usually the subjects write the answer without an adequate amount of thinking thus leaving possibility of mistakes.

In spite of these difficulties, the questionnaire method has proved to be of tremendous value. Allport and Minnesota etc. have formed questionnaires which help in the study of some subtle traits of personality. It affords a lot of assistance to comparative study because of the various answers of the subjects to the same questions. The conclusions based on these questionnaires are comparative as well as numerical. They also facilitate wide study because a number of people can be studied simultaneously.

4. *Performance method* : The performance method was developed by May and Hartshorne. In this method, the subject is given a variety of specific jobs to be performed and the particular trait of his personality is examined. For example, in order to test the honesty of children some weights with little difference between them, were presented to them. The exact weight of each was written under it and the children were told to place them in the correct order. The honest children experienced great difficulty while the dishonest read the weights under them and placed them in order promptly. A very simple method of judging the honesty of the students in the class could be something like this. Some piece should be dictated and the copies collected and examined. The mistakes of each should be secretly noted without any markings on the copy, following which the copies should be returned with the direction that the mistakes are to be noted and marks allocated. The dictation should be written on the black board. The honest will mark their mistakes while the dishonest will quietly correct them. The honesty of the students can be judged by comparing these with the mistakes previously noted.

5. *Rating method* : Another method of measuring personality is the rating method, in which the procedure is of two types. One, the subject is asked to answer questions related to traits of personality. The answers which the subject offers or selects exhibit his personality. Another way of applying the rating method is to place the subject in real situations and then study his behaviour and reactions. For example, in order to judge personality traits a person is given a variety of jobs to perform.

As it is, the rating method is very simple. But it needs more skilful testers. Roughly speaking, it presents the following difficulties :

(a) Much skill and capability are essential in the tester.

(b) The possibility of prejudice is very great.

(c) It is very difficult to enumerate or evaluate the subtle traits. Mistakes are often made in this.

In spite of the above mentioned difficulties, both social and industrial psychologists make much use of this method. As has been pointed out previously too, it can be made useful to a large extent if the tester is very skilful.

6. *Situation test* : As usual, the name suggests the nature of the method. In it, the subject is placed in some specific situations and the traits of his personality are ascertained. Actually, it resembles the performance method, the difference lying in the fact that in this case the person is placed in a situation while in the performance method he is given some work to do.

7. *Psycho-analytic method* : In the psycho-analytic method of measurement of personality two types of tests are more popular—Free Association and Dream Analysis. Both these tests show the traits of the

personality, in its unconscious aspect. In dream analysis, the subject describes his dream and without using reasoning, associates freely the dream objects and activities. Because of the absence of reasoning the truth of the unconscious mind is expressed by this association, by which the psycho-analyst discovers many characteristics of personality. The psycho-analytic method is mostly used in discovering the personality traits and mental ailments of abnormal people. Its main condition lies in the need for a skilled and experienced psycho-analyst. Often, the psycho-analyst has to analyse his own mind in order to remove the possibility of any prejudice.

8. *Projective techniques* : The most popular of all the methods for the investigation of personality is the projective method. Its name suggests the fact that it is founded upon the element of projection. The Taj Mahal, to take an example, is a marble building which many people go to see. Different people find in it different things, in keeping with the peculiarities of their personalities. An emotional person sees it in the form of a formal symbol of emotions while, to the person who gives importance to political and economic questions, it may be a symbol of exploitation. This is an example of a material object but it does make clear the fact that a human being does not see an object as it is but also projects the traits of his own personality upon it. Many peculiarities of the personality are investigated by an analysis of this projection and a comparison of it with the projections affected by others.

Two tests in the projective techniques are more widely used :

1. Rorschach ink-blot test.

2. Murrey's Thematic Apperception Test, known in brief as T.A.T.

They are extensively used in the investigation of personality. These will, therefore, be described briefly here.

1. *Rorschach ink-blot test* : This test was developed by the Swiss scientist Hermann Rorschach. He used 10 original ink-blot cards which are still in use today. There is no picture made in these blots. Five of these are black, two black and red and the other three multicoloured. To investigate personality, they are exhibited before the subject one after the other and he is asked to describe everything he sees in the blot. These are shown for a definite interval of time. Then they are shown to the subject for a second time and he is asked to point out the location, of whatever he had seen, on the blot. In order to establish the meaning of the subject's reaction to the blots, the psychologist analyses the location, determining factors and the object. The analysis of the location serves to indicate whether the subject reacted to some particular spot on the blot or towards the blot as a whole. As a general rule, it is believed that the person who reacts more completely is more principled. The analysis of the determining factors is an attempt to find out whether the reaction of the subject is towards the shape of the

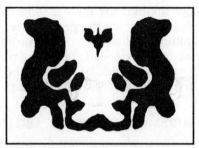

Fig. 8

blot or to the colour or motion in the blot. As to the object, the analysis shows whether the subject sees in it, the figure of a man or an animal or anything else.

Besides the above analysis, facts like the time taken by the subject to react to the whole blot, the number of activities which he did and whether he did them normally or not, are also noted and observed. All these things tend to help in the analysis and investigation of the unconscious peculiarities of the subject.

The difficulty in the ink-blot test is that the description of the subject's reaction becomes quite subjective, which conceals to some extent the correct personality traits of the subject. But efforts are being made to make this test more objective.

2. *Murrey's thematic apperception test* : The founder of this test, Murrey investigated the personality traits with the help of some pictures. These pictures are still considered to be standard. Observing these pictures, the subject, by projection, identifies himself with the characters in the picture. The pictures are presented one by one to the subject who has to compose a story on each of them within some fixed time period, say five minutes. Unknowingly, the subject expresses many of the peculiarities of his personality in these stories by projection. He does not get time to think. Therefore, the story expresses his natural desires, emotions, sentiments etc. On the basis of these stories, the psychologist analyses the personality of the subject and uncovers its traits.

Fig. 9. An Indianised picture from T.A.T.

As in the Rorschach ink-blot test, there is some difficulty in Murrey's thematic apperception test, since the personality investigation done by it is not numerical but qualitative with possibility of mistakes. But there is no doubt that an experienced and skilful psychologist can use this method to uncover many hidden traits of the personality of the subject. This test helps in the discovery of many abnormalities of personality as well.

MEASUREMENT OF SPECIAL ABILITIES

Such problems as the profession an individual may adopt, or the course of study a student may profitably pursue are ones that need guidance and for this guidance it is essential that in addition to measuring the individual's level of intelligence, his special abilities are investigated. Hence, efforts have been made to devise tests to discover special mental abilities, and they are being extensively used.

Before going on to a description of the special mental testing of abilities, it is necessary to know the age in which these tests can be suitably administered. This question arises for the simple reason that in childhood, these special abilities are not distinctly present and psychologists are not unanimous in their opinions regarding the age in which these abilities become distinct and separate. According to some, man's special mental abilities can be separately distinguished at the age of 11, while in the opinion of Cyril Burt, it is at 13 that these abilities become distinct. Generally, it is the former opinion that is accepted. Accordingly, all educational guidance is rendered at the age of 11 or thereabout.

Number of Special Mental Abilities

Having determined the age in which the special mental abilities become distinct, it is now essential that their number also be determined. In fact, it is very difficult to determine the exact number of special abilities, and there is no unanimity of opinion on this question. In 1938, Thurston and his associates fixed the number of special fundamental abilities at seven, calling them Primary Mental Abilities — verbal abilities or V, numerical ability or N, reasoning or R, memory or M, word fluency or W, and spatial ability or S, and perceptual speed or P. The Chicago primary mental abilities test has been based on these mental abilities. Another test battery formed on the same principle is used in the American Psychological Corporation. It contains the following seven tests :

(1) Verbal reasoning,
(2) Numerical ability,
(3) Abstract reasoning,
(4) Space relation,
(5) Mechanical reasoning,

(6) Clerical speed and accuracy,

(7) Language uses.

Now, we can go on to a slightly detailed account of some special abilities tests.

1. *Thurston's S.R.A. Tests of primary mental abilities* : To repeat, Thurston has discovered the presence of seven fundamental abilities through his study. This conception of primary mental abilities wrought a great change in the field of guidance and counselling. Following this discovery, in the field of guidance even more importance began to be attached to these abilities, than to intelligence, since mental abilities of different individuals with similar levels of intelligence were found to differ in the extreme. On the other hand, people with the same mental abilities were found to have different levels of intelligence. In fact, the choice of a course of study to be taken up by a student or the choice of a profession by a person requires a test of special abilities more than it requires intelligence tests since success in these fields depends more upon innate as well as acquired ability than upon intelligence. Hence, in England and America, many tests of mental abilities were evolved, and they were combined to form test batteries. Then, these test batteries were used extensively in the field of education and professions.

Thurston constructed three batteries of tests for special abilities for various children in the following, three age divisions and used different test items in each of them :

1. *For children between 5 and 7* : In the test battery for this division, he included tests of verbal reasoning, spatial ability, speed of perceptual knowledge and of motor ability.

2. *For children between 7 and 11* : Test battery for this classification includes tests of verbal ability, numerical ability, speed or logic and perceptual knowledge.

3. *For children between 11 and 17* : Test battery for this division includes tests of verbal ability, numerical ability, word fluency, spatial ability and power of abstract reasoning.

Tests for Individual Abilities

Test batteries devised by Thurston reveal the main mental abilities of children of different ages, but in addition to this, there are individual tests for separate mental abilities. It would be in keeping with the context to describe them also.

1. *Spatial ability tests* : This reveals the person's spatial or form ability. One example of this is the N.I.I.P. form relation test devised by the National Institute of Industrial Psychology, London. It has been described earlier. The Psychological Bureau of Uttar Pradesh has been making use of it for quite some time; besides the Bureau has also formulated its own test for measuring spatial ability. Another example

of such a test is the Minnesota Paper Form Board which includes 64 test items in which one has to combine various incomplete geometrical forms to complete the figures. In the Minnesota Spatial Relation Test, there are four tests of the form board. Both these tests have proved to be of immense value.

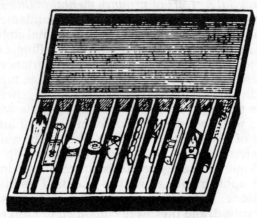

Fig. 10. Box of Minnesota Test.

2. *Mechanical ability tests* : Through these tests, the person's ability of handling mechanical devices is measured. For this, some laboratories use paper and pencil while others use mechanical tools and objects. One example of this is the Minnesota Mechanical Assembly test. In this, there are three boxes that contain the various parts of some common mechanical device. In the test, these parts have to be put together to form the complete objects. Other tests of mechanical ability that are famous are the Bennett Test of Mechanical Comprehension, and MacQuarrie Test for Mechanical ability.

3. *Motor dexterity tests* : In these tests, the motor ability of the hands and fingers is measured. Examples of such tests are Bennett Hand Tool Dexterity Test, Purdue Peg Board Steadiness Tester and O'Conor Tweezer Dexterity Test. Only the first two will be described here.

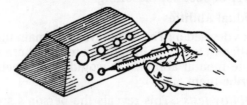

Fig. 11. Steadiness tester

(a) *Steadiness tester* : This device examines the steadiness of the hand and the fingers. In this, there is a box on one side of which there are numerous holes arranged systematically so that they proceed from the widest to the smallest. The subject takes an instrument called the stylus into his hand and inserts it completely and draws it out of these holes successively. If in doing so, the stylus touches any of the walls of the hole, a bell rings. The test consists in the ability to prevent the stylus touching the wall while inserting it into the hole and drawing it out. The hole in which the bell rings is tried thrice by the subject. This test helps to discover the individual's dexterity with his hand and fingers, and the extent to which he can handle minute instruments.

(b) *O'Conor's Tweezer Dexterity test :* In this test, there are 100 small holes on a board, in rows of ten each. There are 100 pins placed by the side. The subject has to use a tweezer to place each of these pins in this board, one in each hole. He scores according to the short time that he takes to complete this task.

4. *Clerical tests :* These tests measure the individual's ability concerning writing and composition. It is composed of tests in arithmetic, word groups, distinct reading and good writing, tests in direct knowledge, etc. One example of the clerical tests is the Minnesota Clerical test which has two parts. In one part there are pairs of numbers, the correct pair having to be marked in which both numbers are given. In the other part one has to point out pairs of names that are similar.

5. *Artistic or Aesthetic Ability test :* In these, the individual's ability concerning art is tested. One example of this is the McAdory Art Test. Sea Shore Measure of Musical Talent measures the individual's ability in respect of music. Meier Art Judgment Test is another test of artistic and aesthetic ability. In this test, there are 100 pairs of pictures. In every pair there is one original and the other copy, and the student has to select the original and its copy in respect of every pair. Success in this depends upon his aesthetic ability and acuity since the original has more beauty than the copy.

QUESTION FOR EXERCISE

1. Evaluate the significance of psychological testing in measuring fitness for work.

6

INDIVIDUAL DIFFERENCES

Meaning of Individual Differences

According to Skinner, "Today we think of individual differences as including any measurable aspect of the total personality." From this definition of individual differences it is evident that it comprehends every aspect of the human personality, albeit all aspects that are in some manner measurable. Aspects of this nature can be many such as variability, conformity, difference in the rate of learning and development, mutual relationship between the various characteristics of the personality, etc. In this manner, various individuals exhibit differences of physical and mental development, nature, rate of learning, ability, specific abilities, interest and personality, etc.

TYPES OF INDIVIDUAL DIFFERENCES

(1) **Average Intelligence.** The following brief description may serve to make individual differences a simple concept that can easily be grasped. Individuals are seen differing in considerable measure in respect of their general intelligence. It is not possible to send children with an intelligence quotient of below 50 to schools. Children with a higher intelligence quotient go to school. Children with intelligence quotients between 50 and 70 can learn only the simplest tasks. Even the small schools trouble children whose intelligence quotient varies between 70 and 80. Children between 75 and 90 I.Q. are considered morons, and they have considerable difficulty in progressing, along with the other children, in their learning. Generally, 40 to 60 per cent of the children in school have I.Qs. varying between 95 and 105, being the children with average intelligence who form the basis for the formulation of the syllabus and curriculum as well as the method of teaching. Children who are either above or below this level of intelligence require special educational methods and conditions. Children with intelligence quotients varying between 115 and 120 are considered brilliant or intelligent. The following facts have come to light concerning individual differences of intelligence in children :

(a) However good and beneficial the environment and the method of education, the moron invariably reaches his highest level of learning before the average or the intelligent child.

(b) In favourable circumstances the average child generally gives a good account of himself in his academic pursuits.

(c) If the circumstances are favourable, the intelligent child shows great alacrity in the process of learning.

(d) Adverse circumstances have the worst effect on all children, and their learning activities are hindered.

(2) **Special Abilities.** During the junior and senior high school as well as the college stage, the individual's differences in respect of special abilities, in addition to the general intelligence, are also important since special professions and specialised fields of vocation all need certain specific abilities. Abilities of this kind are concerned with mental personality or motor ability.

(3) **Differences of Background.** In school, the differences that the children exhibit are the outcome of their different families and their communities. Attitudes towards education and authority differ in each family, culture and class. Some of these attitudes are favourable while others are unfavourable to education. In either condition the differences of attitudes result in differences among children. Besides these attitudes, the child's emotional, social, aesthetic and moral development is influenced by his family and the neighbourhood. Hence, differences of background are also manifest in individual differences.

(4) **Alacrity in Learning.** Difference in the quickness or alacrity in learning is visible not only in children of different ages but also among children in the same age group. This difference is dependent upon their maturity and educational background. Differences in the alacrity of learning result in benefits accruing from formal education.

(5) **Mental Age.** Children of differing ages as well as children of the same age show differences in their respective mental ages. Generally speaking, all students studying in the same class differ according to their mental ages. It has been observed that in the age of 6, differences in mental age range up to 5 years. Mental age and education are intimately related. The child's level of education is determined according to his mental age.

(6) **Motor Ability.** The individual's movements of the hand and feet and other physical abilities are seen to be very individual as they do not resemble another's to any great extent. Till the individual attains adulthood, his manual dexterity, rate of muscular movement and resistance to fatigue develops continually. In this manner, the same individual in different ages and different individuals in the same age group manifest considerable differences in manual dexterity.

(7) **Sex Differences.** Makneimer and Terman discovered the following differences between men and women, on the basis of some studies —

(a) Women have greater skill in memory while men have greater motor ability.

(b) Female handwriting is superior while men excel in mathematical logic.

(c) Women shows greater skill in making sensory distinctions of taste, touch, smell etc. while men show greater reaction and consciousness of size-weight illusion.

(d) Possessing greater linguistic ability women are superior to men in language, similitudes, word building, compositions and use of long sentences, etc. On the other hand, men are superior in physics and chemistry.

(e) Women are better than men in mirror drawing. Faults of speech etc., in men were found to be three times of such faults in women.

(f) Women are more susceptible to suggestion while there are three times as many colour blind men as there are women.

(g) Young girls take interest in stories of love, fairy tales, stories of the school and home and day-dreaming, and show various levels in their play. On the other hand, boys take interest in stories of bravery, science, war and scouting, stories of games and sports, scouts stories and games of occupation and skill.

(8) Racial Differences. Many scientific studies have indicated the presence of various kinds of differences between individuals of different races, although differences of environment are a normal factor in causing these differences. Karl Brigham has composed a test on the basis of differences in the levels of intelligence among people who have migrated to United States from other countries.

On the basis of these average differences between the races, the mental age of a particular individual of a definite race cannot be calculated since this difference is based on environment.

(9) Nationality. Many studies have led to the conclusion that individuals of different nations differ in respect of nature, physical and mental differences, interest and personality, etc. Such a difference is only natural since their cultural and geographic environment is distinctive.

(10) Economic Situation. Economic differences are seen causing differences in the children's interests, tendencies and character, etc.

(11) Differences Relating to Learning. In respect of learning, children manifest such differences as past experience and learning, ability in the use of various kinds of apparatus, rate of learning, interest in learning, etc.

(12) Difference in Respect of Development. Difference in development is in evidence not only in individuals of different age groups but also between individuals of the same age.

(13) Difference of Interests. As has been pointed out, the difference in sex leads to a difference in interests. Similarly, factors such as family background, level of development, differences of nationality and race, etc., cause difference of interests.

(14) **Personality**. Differences in respect of personality have led psychologists to much study, and on the basis of this study individuals have been classified into many groups. Jung, for example has divided individuals into three groups — (a) Introvert, (b) Extrovert, and (c) Ambivert. This is the psychological classification of people. Stephenson has divided human beings into two categories — preservator and non-preservator. In this division, people of the first group are very sensitive and susceptible to experience while people of the second group are not influenced by it to quite that extent. Cattel has put people into the surgent and the surgeless or non-surgent classes. The former is similar to Jung's extrovert while the surgeless resembles his introvert individuals. Terman has put people into 9 classes according to their level of intelligence — (a) Genius, (b) Near Genius, (c) Very superior intelligence, (d) Superior, (e) Average, (f) Backward, (g) Feeble-minded, (h) Dull and (i) Idiot.

Thorndike has divided people into four categories on the basis of thinking — (a) Abstract thinkers, (b) Ideational thinkers (c) Objective thinkers, (d) Thinkers in whom sensory experience is predominant. These names indicate the peculiarities of thinking in these individuals.

From the viewpoint of nature, personality has been divided into three classes — (a) thought dominant, (b) emotion dominant and (c) action dominant.

Concerning these classifications of the human personality, it should be remembered that although one specific person may exhibit the main broad characteristics of one class of personality, he cannot be said to belong to only that class of personality as the differences between various personalities are so subtle and minute that it is not scientifically feasible to divide them into classes.

QUESTION FOR EXERCISE

1. What do you understand by individual differences? Discuss in detail.

7

PSYCHO-PHYSICS AND WEBER-FECHNER FUNCTION

E.H. WEBER

Experimental method has the credit of bringing psychology to the scientific level. It is experimental psychology which is the solid foundation for psychological principles. In the development of experimental psychology E.H. Weber of Germany can be accepted as the founder. Weber was interested mainly in the physical structure of sense organs. He did detailed experiments on the sensations of eyes, nose, ears and skin. Many scientists of Germany and other countries have experimented widely in these fields but Weber for the first time found out new facts by the experimental method and from them arrived at psychological conclusions. Till his death in 1820, Weber remained professor of physiology at Leipzig University in Germany. His experiments and publications gave great encouragement to research work in the fields of medicine, zoology and physiology. Till now physiology is a part of medicine.

From the view of the history of psychology, the most important contribution of Weber is the principle which later on became famous as the Weber-Fechner Law. Before discussing this law it will be appropriate to survey Weber's experiments on different sensations.

To know the effect of temperature on the skin Weber performed a simple experiment. He examined, by successively putting his hand in cold and hot water that the sensations of temperature depend not on the temperature of objects but on the temperature of the skin. The temperature of skin increases by putting the hand in hot water and consequently we feel hot. We feel cold by putting the hand in cold water due to the decrease in temperature of the skin and not due to the coldness of water. This principle also supports the simple experience that the skin of a person feels less warmth or cold when he becomes used to winter or summer. By bathing in cold water in winter we feel less cold. Here we have to keep in mind that the more intense this experience of the temperature of the skin, the greater will be the experience of heat or cold.

For example by coming to a warm place from a cold one, we feel more heat. On the other hand if temperature is changed very slowly then probably cold or warmth will not be felt because skin gradually acclimatizes with the temperature and becomes used to it.

Experiments Concerning Smell

Weber tried to find out about sensations related to smell and whether gas or liquid has more effect on it. To see this he dropped a 10% solution of eudicologne on the outer membrane inside the nose and by sinking the head established contact between membrane and solution. By the contact of liquid and membrane he experienced no smell. From this he concluded that the liquid is not a powerful stimulus for the sensations of smell.

Weber also experimented on sensations related to hearing. He experimented by bringing two alarm clocks near his ears and then by bringing both the clocks near one of his ears. He found that when the clocks are brought near the ears then the sensations are not equal while when both are brought near one ear then both seem to sound at the same time.

Experiments Concerning Vision

Weber also experimented on sensations related to vision. He wanted to see the difference between two lines that should exist so that it is seen. While experimenting on this he saw that a 101 mm. long line seems to be longer than a line 100 mm. long with great difficulty and a line 51 mm. long seems longer than a line 50.5 mm. long with great difficulty. Weber saw by his other experiments that when two lines are very close to each other then both seem to be the same. When the difference between them increases then they seem to be different lines. Weber found out the minimum difference between the two lines that should exist so that they may be seen to be different from each other.

Experiments on Doubleness

In relation to cutaneous sensations Weber did research work on the perception of doubleness. He kept a compass on the skin at various distances so that there may be difference between the two points of the compass touching the skin. The precaution was taken that eyes were not used. Now it had to be found without the use of eyes that what difference between the two paints should exist so that they may be seen to be two. It was seen in these experiments that in the early stages clear difference between the two points was not perceived by the subject but gradually when the difference between the two points was increased then a time came when they could be perceived as two different points of the sensation. From this, Weber reached the conclusion that to establish the sensation of doubleness of the points a definite threshold had to be crossed. It must be kept in mind that even before Weber the idea of limen was in use in the measurement of sensations but Weber for the first time used this idea in an organised form. By performing another experiment on tactile sensations, Weber saw that the difference between the two points required for perception of doubleness are not similar at various points of the body. For example, very little difference is needed for the sensation of doubleness on the fingers and the tip of the tongue. The difference gradually increases on the lips, palms, wrists and shoulders. Weber found out difference in various persons in the experiments related to the skin. For the sensation of doubleness different differences in the points of the compass were required for different individuals. Of the difference with which the sensation of doubleness occurs in one individual, there is no sensation of doubleness with that difference in other persons. Decrease or increase of difference among points is needed due to individual difference. To define this fact of individual difference, Weber presented the theory of sensation cycle. According to this different persons have different sensations. In these sensation cycles doubleness does not appear due to excitement. But this theory of Weber could not be proved by experiments because it was seen that these cycles get smaller by practice. In other words, a change occurs in the necessary difference for a sensation of doubleness.

Experiments Concerning Muscles

The most important of Weber's experiments is concerned with the sensations of the muscle. On its basis the famous doctrine of Weber was developed. It is a common experience that when very little difference exists it becomes difficult to separate two sensations. For example, if you are asked to lift two boxes one at a time which have very little difference then you cannot tell which is heavier and which is lighter. If a small thing is kept inside a box and if one is asked to tell the difference by picking up the box then it is not necessary that the difference will be perceived. Here the question arises that what difference in the weights of the boxes should be kept so that the difference is known or when the minimum weight in one of the box is increased in comparison to the other so that the weight is felt to be increased. Similar questions related to other sensations may also be raised. Weber, the pupil of Wundt, also had interest in this kind of experiments. We experimented to know what must be the difference among weights so that they may be felt by manually lifting them or what minimum weight should be increased so that difference between two weights is known.

Weber saw in his experiments that 29 ounce in comparison to 30 ounce and 30 ounce in comparison to 31 ounce is felt to be slightly heavier by close observation. This difference of 1 ounce may be recognised and Weber saw by experimenting that a difference of ½ ounce is known with great difficulty but less than this difference cannot be felt.

By his experiments on temperature, smell, hearing, vision, sensations of the skin and muscles, Weber reached the conclusion that to make out the difference between two sensations, relative difference and absolute difference is needed. This difference, as has been shown earlier by the description of various experiments, is different in different persons and even for the same one person. Weber saw that the perception of the difference in sensations does not depend directly on their difference as much as it depends on their relations. To verify this conclusion he did some experiments related to the eye. He produced pairs of lines in front of the subject and asked him to say which line seemed to be longer. These experiments further strengthen the theory of relativity. Weber saw in his experiments that in comparison to sensations of the muscle difference in visual sensation can be recognized in spite of factorial difference.

On the basis of experiments, Weber conceived of the minimum recognisable difference which exists in the case of different sensations. This difference came to be known as J.N.D. or Just Noticeable Difference. In the language of experiment it is known as Difference Limen (DL). Here, an objection was raised that how many times a difference should be recognised to be called DL. It was decided in this respect that it should happen 75 times out of 100. Weber also saw that DL was always a fraction of the stationary thing out of those compared and is always stationary. For example, the weight of 30 ounce is stationary and by comparing it with a weight of 31 ounce, 1 ounce DL is found. This DL is 1/30 of the stationary substance. Now even if 30 is made 60 then too DL will remain 1/30 of the stationary substance or the substance recognised should be $\frac{1}{30} \times 60 = 2$ ounce more than the other. By experimenting on suitcases, Weber saw that to be recognized suitcases weighing 31 pounds in comparison to 30, 62 pounds in comparison to 60 and 93 pounds in comparison to 90 pounds should be used. In this, it was seen that for the difference to be recognizable it should be 1, 2 and 3 lbs for weights of 30, 60 and 90 lbs.

From this, it is clear that in every condition DL is the same fraction of the standard.

From this conclusion, Weber formed the law that 'The increase in any given stimulus which is correctly perceived in 75 per cent of the trials is a constant fraction of the size of the stimulus.' In the examples of suitcases the constant fraction of the standard in every case remained 1/30. In this way in 75 per cent experiments in suitcases of 30, 60 and 90 pounds the correctly recognised increase was 1, 2 and 3 respectively.

In various fields, Weber tried to find support for his own theory in the experiments of other scientists. For example, Weber mentioned Delezenne's experiments related to hearing in support of his own ideas, though his view was wrong.

Many scientists criticized Weber's theory and it was refused later on, but his importance in the history of psychology cannot be determined by the correctness or wrongness of his theory. Weber appeared in Germany at a time when German scientists had been busy in various kinds of experiments since the last century. French findings were being welcomed in the beginning of 19th Century in the German Universities. At this time associationism predominated in England. Though Hamilton experimented with the problems of attention, they had no effect on the majority of the scientists. A generation before the age of Weber Bouguer in France had experimented with the sensitivity of eyes towards light. But no special results came out of it. When this was the state of experimental science in other countries, at that time Weber established experimental psychology on a firm footing in Germany. The thing to be noted in Weber's experiments is that he tried to express in quantitative words the law of the sensations of different sense organs. He saw his problems from the experimental point of view. He tried to find out a universal law on the basis of various laws. This experimental viewpoint is the peculiarity of Weber. By this experiments many physiologists were inspired to start work in their laboratories on psychological problems. It was the problem presented by him on which scientists Helmtholtz, Fechner and Lotze performed useful experiments. Weber not only presented problems but himself experienced to solve them and the most important thing is that he led the path to organised study.

In the history of psychology, Weber's importance lies in this that he tried to gauge the reactions of man towards the outer world. From his time to the present the sphere of measurement in the field of psychology has gone on increasing. As the sphere goes on increasing psychology becomes more scientific. Nowadays in psychometry from small sensations and feelings to complicated social tendencies all are measured. It need not be said that Weber establised this system of measurement by his experiments. Gardener Murphy has written correctly about Weber and his theory, "Important as this law was to become as a hypothesis of voluminous research, Weber's greatest significance lies rather in his conception of an experimental approach to psychological question, and in the stimulation of research through which ultimately a vast variety of problems other than this have been incisively studied."

FECHNER

Often Fechner's name is taken along with Weber. But it will wrong to think that in the history of psychology there is no independent importance of Fechner. One main branch of psychology is psycho-physics. In psycho-physics the relations between physical stimuli and mental actions are realistically studied. In 1879, when the famous German psychologist Wundt established the first psychological laboratory at Leipzig the foundation of psycho-physics was laid but the credit should go to Fechner for encouraging Wundt and other contemporaries to experiment with various psycho-physical problems. In the words of Gardener Murphy, "Indeed, Fechner's long and careful research did much to give Wundt and his contemporaries the plan of experimental psychology." Before the establishment of Wundt's laboratory, Fechner published in 1860, his famous book *Elemente der Psychophysics*. Before this book was published, Fechner had written a scientific article on mental measurement in 1858. In this article, Fechner had given the definition of psycho-physics and detained its sphere. According to Fechner, psycho-physics was a science studying the relations of interdependence between the mind and the body, as well as the functional relations, sensations, perception, feelings, actions, attention etc. come in its sphere. According to Fechner sensations can be most successfully measured. In this way according to him sensation is formed by various sensation units and standardization of these units can be done. The standardization would be done on the basis of their relationship with the stimulus. Fechner differentiated between inner psychophysics and outer psychophysics in which a comparison between physiological responses and internal feelings is made. On the other side in internal psychophysics the relationship of subjective feeling with physical feelings can be measured, for example the relation between the sensations and mental changes can be studied.

Fechner experimented for years with Weber's law and found that when a uniform increase is effected in the stimulus, then there is a similar increase in the sensations resulting from them. This increase does not occur in a simple ratio but is in comparison to the increase in the excitement. Hence, relation between excitement and sensation is shown by a curve. It is seen that this curve always bends down in the graph of stimuli and sensation.

On the basis of the above finding, Fechner discovered a law that the sensations are in a ratio of the Log of the stimulus responsible for them. If sensation is shown by S, stimulus by R and constant as C then Fechner's law can be expressed by this that $S = C \log R$. This equation is known as Weber-Fechner's law. In it, both sensation and stimulus are changeable, only C is constant. This law is the amended form of Weber's law. Hence, it is famous in the name of both Weber and Fechner.

But there is a great difference in the hypotheses of Weber and Fechner though they reached agreement over a law. Weber was only interested in the just recognisable difference while on the other side Fechner's aim was to mathematically define the relation between physical and spiritual world. Still Fechner developed Weber's method of just recognisable difference by experiments for many years, Fechner experimented on the sensations of eye and temperature. He created experiments similar to Weber's in which two stimuli are presented and one of these is increased or decreased to reach a barely recognisable difference among the two. Here a difference between the viewpoints of Weber and Fechner is noteworthy. Fechner has stressed in this experimenting on proceeding from both ends and found out the average of the just recognisable differences found out by the increase and decrease. Fechner, in addition to his experiments on the sensations of temperature and vision also experimented on sensations of lifting weights and skin sensations.

In the weight lifting experiments, Fechner compared the weights over 67000 times. In this case he experimented with the method of right and wrong cases. The method had been originally started by Vierordt. In the method of right and wrong cases the stimulus remains constant and decisions are changed. In this way by taking any particular difference which can be generally equally recognisable but whose being recognised is not absolute and correct, incorrect and doubtful decisions are taken. Then necessary difference is found out to give percentage to correct cases in the basis of the theory of probability. In this way the aim of this method is to find that stimulus by which correct decisions in a definite ratio are provided.

Fechner found out the method of average error for experimenting on the measurement of sensations related to skin and vision. He developed this method with the cooperation of Volkmann. This method had been in use in palmistry. This method is based on the belief that the errors of observation and decision are also dependent on variability and quantity of stimulus as much as upon the internal and external circumstances. In this method a stimulus is left constant and with its help a variable stimulus is adjusted according to intrinsic similarity. The stimulus adjusted by the observer is the error stimulas. The mean value of the difference of given stimuli will be determined by the subject's error of observation in the controlled conditions. For example, in the experiment of lifting weights, the subjects take up a particular weight and try to form another weight similar to it. When he fixes a second weight similar to the first then he weighs it to find his own fault. In this way he tries to give the weights to various quantities and every time finds out his mistake by weighing the guessed weight. Now, by finding out the average of the results of the experiments the average error can be found.

To understand Fechner's experiments it is necessary to know their philosophical background. The aim of Fechner's experiment is to find out the extent to which science might be helpful in the study of man in relation with nature. Fechner wanted to experiment upon actual methods being used successfully in the natural sciences in the outside world. His problem was to find some way so that the soul be visible and seen in observable conditions.

Fechner was influenced by the philosophies of Fichte and Schelling. The philosophy of nature in search of a spiritual meaning in the events in their natural order influenced Fechner. On the other side, he was a student of medicine and he had deeply studied physics and chemistry. He was also interested in mechanics and contemporary inventions regarding electricity. The fact is that Fechner was an authoritative scholar of physical sciences in his time.

Being influenced by both philosophy and science a strange combination of the two was seen in Fechner. As is evident in his problems, he wanted to find a way to solve his problems without being tied down to any ideology. In finding a path he adopted many things from the philosophy of nature but then opposed other things. He wrote many sarcastic articles on mechanistic science. He saw that the spiritual legacy was so complicated that it could not be understood by scientific ideas. He opposed the description of biological sciences by the ideas of mathematics and physics. His view was that it was an effort to boycott life and mind. He found this effort to be opposed to the nature of biology and psychology. For him every particle of nature was meaningful and due to this it was not appropriate to study it by the methods of physics and chemistry because it opposed all the life element of the world.

On the other side, Fechner felt the necessity for a sure and correct method in zoology and psychology. He saw that observed facts in these sciences could not be defined by existing methods. Hence, whereas on one side he was writing satirical articles under a pseudonym, he was also doing research in the field of physics. In fact, by writing satirical articles his aim was not to oppose science but to understand it. He wanted to find an aspect of science, and to find a method by which actual knowledge of things both in the human soul and external world could be gained. He put great labour in his effort. He even lost his health. He was studying after-images by taking the high stimulus of the solar rays. This caused great pain in his eyes and for many years he was unable to see clearly. He could not read and think properly. He would have definitely lost his health but he slowly regained it with the help of his wife.

As has been told earlier the main problem for Fechner was to find out the mutual relations between mental and physical actions. As a result of thinking and experiment he learnt one day that quantitative relations exist in the facts of our physical life. In other words, with the increase of stimulus there is no equal increase in sensations. Instead, if a stimulus is taken in geometrical progression, then sensations occur in arithmetical progression. For example, if a bell is ringing then the effect on us by ringing a second bell along with it is not the same if we add the sound of the first bell to ten bells. It means that the effect of one bell combining with ten bells, is much less than the effect due to its combining with another bell. Another example is that if 4-6 candles are burning then by adding another candle to them, no great difference in the light is seen. On the other hand, if a single candle is burning, a sufficient difference in light occurs by burning another candle. It is clear that the effect of stimulus cannot be similar under all circumstances. Its effect depends on the existing stimulus. Or the effect of stimulus is relative to the already existing stimulus. If the already existing stimulus is so great that no great difference is seen in it by the addition of new stimulus then there will be no difference in the effect too.

In his many experiments, Fechner saw that with some increase in a definite ratio in our sensations in the different sensory sensations a difference in the sensation is seen. In this way, like Weber, Fechner arrived at the theory of just recognisable difference which has been described earlier.

In this way by the theory of just recognisable difference, Fechner reached the quantitative relation between the mental and the physical worlds. A mathematical relation has to be established between these two worlds by the Weber-Fechner law. Fechner has described this finding in his book *Zend avcsta*. In this book he has elaborated his philosophy of nature. As is evident from its name, there is a mark of Persian philosophy and its dualism on Fechner's philosophy of nature. According to Persian philosophy there is the dualism of good and bad in human beings. Fechner saw the world not in the form of a contradiction between the mental and physical but in the form of their combination. The world is natural, but still a mental definition of it can be made.

In this way, the problem which Fechner took up seems to be solved by both experiment and reasoning. But he was not satisfied with his conclusion and hence he continually experimented. In these experiments he laid the foundation of experimental aesthetics. He tried to find out by many things of daily life like books, windows, cards etc., the relations that existed in their shapes and which can be termed as beautiful. Along with articles of daily life he also studied samples of art. His effort was towards establishing some facts about experimental method in the field of aesthetics. He was against evaluation of beauty by some definite principles. He wanted to give an experimental basis to aesthetics.

Fechner tried throughout his life to combine the scientific and mystic ideas. Nowadays most of the scientists believe this combination to be difficult if not impossible though still in every sphere of science scientists can be seen agreeing with Fechner's views. Fechner saw the whole world in the form of a living organic being. He saw life and soul in every particle of nature. There is consciousness in every object of the world and it reacts towards other objects. In this way, Fechner's view of nature is totally monistic. Hence, Fechner should not be understood as a parallelist in psycho-physical relations. He does not differentiate between man's internal experience and the reality of the outer world. We experience objects as they are or if a causal study of the outer world could be made then a similar study of the internal world can also be made. In this way, Fechner stressed the use of the methods of physics and mathematics in zoological and psychological experiments. Every science studies life in different ways. Everywhere there is life, consciousness, soul etc. Everywhere its different relations can be measured. Everywhere it can be learnt by mathematical methods. Everywhere it can be causally or quantitatively defined. There may not be complete truth in these views of Fechner and even if all do not agree with his view, there is no doubt that he encouraged experimental study in the field of biology, psychology and aesthetics. In the history of psychology he should be acknowledged as the actual creator of psycho-physics.

JOHANNES MULLER

Johannes Muller was born in 1801 and was a contemporary of Fechner. He was interested in physiology. In 1833, he was appointed Professor of Physiology in Berlin University. Muller is known as a great experimentalist of the 19th century because he performed many important experiments related to the sensations and propounded many new facts. He made a profound study of physiology in his period of teaching and threw light on the various actions of the body. He published a book 'Elements of Physiology' on the science of physical actions which soon became popular. This book was published in 1833 in the German language and in English in 1833. In this book many subjects had been defined which were of great importance from the psychological view-point.

Muller was generally interested in the actions related to sensation and he centred his study on optical sensation. Mostly, his experiments were related to the action of the external organs of the eyes and space perception. These facts were influenced by Kant's principle of space perception. Kant had accepted the knowledge of space to be subjective and had said that it was a natural characteristic of the soul. Berkeley had said about visual space perception that whatever we see is a sign or symbol which prepares us for necessary action. Herbert considered space to be a combination of some special experiences. But Muller threw light on the question that in what way a thing is affected by inspection and how are they again remembered. He said that every person has the ability to know space but he cannot know definitely its distance, shape and position. Man knows by his experiences whether a certain thing is within his reach or not.

Muller also threw light on reflex action. He said on the basis of his experiments that the brain and the spinal cord is concerned with all physical actions and reflex action is based on them.

Muller has propounded a very important principle related to sensation which is known as the doctrine of 'specific energy'. According to this doctrine there is a special kind of energy in the nerves of the body. When a nerve is connected with a stimulus, then a unique reaction occurs. For example, visual nerves only perform the function of seeing and auditory nerves that of hearing. Similarly, there is sensation of cold by dropping cold water on the skin. Sensation related to temperature also occurs in the same way.

Hence, Muller made it clear that the nature of sensation depended on that nerve which comes in contact with the stimulus. In this way he said that the idea was wrong that the nature of sensation depends upon the stimulus related to it. In fact, the basis of sensation is the nerve and the energy in it.

Muller also defined mental actions. He said that a person's images related to experience are formed on the basis of the nervous system and then these exist and are transferred to the memory. Equality and co-existence help in association. In fact, these are the different forms of association. The individual has the ability to limit association according to his need and in this way brings in memory the objects and images directly concerning him. If he does not do so, then association related to many things will occur at the same time and mental work will become confused. In this way, Muller defined the limited and general aspects of association.

Muller has written about feeling that in favourable circumstances feelings are created by similarity of difference of ideas. In this way the feeling of happiness occurs in man when he is successful in his efforts while a feeling of sorrow is due to failure.

Muller has also accepted body to be the basis of emotion. In a condition of emotion there is sensation inside the body. In other words, the sensations which occur in the body on the basis of nerves are known as emotions.

Muller has also thrown light on will power. Will power is related to attention. Will power can work towards that object on which our attention is centred. Here, it is necessary to know the difference between voluntary and involuntary actions of a person. A person can only control those actions which occur according to his will. The actions which do not occur according to his will cannot be controlled by the individual.

It is clear in the above brief description that Muller had said while throwing light on the mutual relation between Physiology and Psychology, that the basis of psychology was physical. He gave great importance to the nervous system and whatever he wrote in this respect is the basis of the study of modern neurology. He stressed greatly the physiological aspect. The reason for this is that his main subject was physiology. He is among the famous German psychologists of the 19th Century.

QUESTIONS FOR EXERCISE

1. Explain Weber-Fechner Law.
2. What is Weber-Fechner Law? Does it hold good for all ranges of stimuli?
3. Distinguish between absolute and differential threshold. Explain and illustrate Weber's law in this connection.
4. Describe in detail the procedure followed in the method of constant stimuli or obtaining differential limen.
5. Write short note on the following — Fechner as a psycho-physicist.
6. "Fechner in distinction from Weber was an event making man." Comment.
7. Assess the contribution of Muller in the development of modern psychology.

8

PHYSIOLOGICAL PSYCHOLOGY AND NERVOUS SYSTEM

Physiological psychology is a relatively younger science. This science grew out of physiology about a century ago. The development of this science was the result of curiosity of some physiologists. These physiologists wanted to make a detailed study of the functioning of human brain. It was known from general observation that functions and activity of the human brain have relationship with the behaviour. Activity of the one affects the other. If any area of the brain has some defect or it does not function normally, there is a definite and certain change in human behaviour. Physiological psychology was developed to have a combined study of the functions of brain and behaviour. This science not only studies the functions of brain but also the functions of other parts of body in behaviour. Thus, it is evident that physiological psychology is concerned with both physiology and psychology. Subject-matter of psychology and physiology were different and limited before the development of this new science of physiological psychology. For example, aspects of human behaviour like perception and learning were studied by a psychological approach in pure psychology. Structure of the body, changes in it and its diseases were the main problems of study in physiology. But after the development of physiological psychology, structure and internal changes in the body related to perceiving and other psychological activities are also studied and combined results are obtained. It is also important to know the influence of different bodily activities and changes of behaviour in it. Besides this, facts established in this science can be taken for the selection of essential hypotheses for the new experiments in psychology and physiology.

It is clear from the above discussion that physiological psychology is related to two sciences of physiology and psychology. But it is essential to point out here that this is not a separate science. In fact, physiological psychology is a form of link joining the two separate sciences. Its task is to interrelate physiology and psychology. This fact has been stated by Harthway in these words. "Physiological psychology is not a separate science but is, as the name implies, a link between two basically similar sciences, physiology and psychology." After its historical development Physiological Psychology today is accepted chiefly as a science concerned only with Neurology and Psychology. Thus, physiological psychology is situated in the border land of these two sciences. This fact has been stated by James Drevel in these words, "Physiological Psychology, historically equivalent to Experimental Psychology, is now used mostly for the borderland between Psychology and Neurology."

PSYCHOLOGY AND PHYSIOLOGY

Psychology is the positive science of behaviour. Physiology studies body structure and body activities. Physiology is the science of bodily functions. It studies respiration, blood circulation glandular and muscular activities. All these activities have some influence on behaviour. "Healthy mind in healthy body", is a popular saying. Therefore, a close relationship between psychology and physiology is natural. Some correlation can be seen between mental states and physiological states. Neurosis is closely related with psychosis and the one may give rise to the other. It has been proved from experiments in psychology that physiological functions have a great influence on mental activities. On the basis of this close relationship between mental life and physiological states some thinkers have accepted psychology as a branch of physiology. According to them, mind is only a function of the brain. According to this theory consciousness is the product of the various activities of the body. But this theory has been disproved by both logic and facts. The study of physiological activities does help in understanding the mental life but it does not mean that both are identical. Therefore, psychology is not a branch of physiology.

The fields of psychology and physiology are different. The field of Physiology is bodily functions whereas the field of psychology is mental activities or behaviour. The points of view of psychology and physiology are also different.

The unit of the study of psychology is human organism. Physiological psychology studies the behaviour of human organism. Physical activities like movement of hands and feet, laughing widening of the pupils of the eyes, acceleration of the rate of heart beat etc. are parts of behaviour. Nervous system also comes in it. Physiology also studies the Nervous System, but physiological psychology studies the nervous system and other physiological processes from the point of view of behaviour, i.e., it tries to know which behaviour is expressed from different physiological activities. Thus, physiological psychology studies the mental activities hidden behind the physiological activities. Description of human body will be the description of physiology, whereas the description of physiological activities involved in human behaviour, experiences, efforts, desires and needs will be the description of physiological psychology.

DEFINITION OF PHYSIOLOGICAL PSYCHOLOGY

From the above discussion about the nature of Physiological Psychology, its definition also becomes clear. Some modern definitions are given below :

1. Definition by Freeman. The famous Physiological Psychologist G.L. Freeman has defined physiological psychology in the following words : "Physiological psychology is the study of the relationship between integrated behaviour and the bodily processes of intact organism."[1] The definition by Freeman makes clear the subject matter of physiological psychology. It is clear from this definition that physiological psychology studies all those physiological processes which are related to behaviour and the interrelationship of these processes and human behaviour. In other words, physiological psychology studies the relationship by which bodily processes and behaviour are interrelated.

2. Definition by Wenger and Jones. Wenger and Jones have given a definition which is similar to the one given by Freeman. Their definition is as follows : "Physiological psychology is the study of relationship between bodily processes and behaviour."[2] It is also clear from this definition that the relationship of bodily processes and behaviour is studied in physiological psychology.

3. Definition by Morgan and Stellar. Morgan and Stellar have given a broad definition of physiological psychology. In this definition these authors have explained the meaning and fields of study of psychology and physiology separately.[3] After this it has been explained as to how these two sciences are studied together in an integrated way in physiological psychology. In the words of Morgan and Stellar, "Physiology is the science of bodily functions; it has to do with the processes going on in the organs and tissues of the body. Psychology, on the other hand, is the science of behaviour; in psychology we try to see human beings and members of animal kingdom adjust to the world they live in. Our task in physiological psychology is simply to put these subjects together and see how the physiological processes of the body are related to behavioural adjustments."

The meaning and field of the study of physiological psychology becomes clear by the above described definitions. It is also important to know the problems of physiological psychology for a detailed study in this connection.

---

1. G.L. Freeman : *Physiological Psychology*, D Van Nostrand and Company. New York, p. 31.
2. Wenger and Jones : *Physiological Psychology*, Henry Holt and Co., New York, p. 5.
3. Morgan and Stellar : *Physiological Psychology*, McGraw Hill Book Co., New York, p. 1.

PROBLEMS OF PHYSIOLOGICAL PSYCHOLOGY

Some main problems are selected for the study of each subject. The broader a subject is, the more are its problems of study. Besides this, the problems of study of a complex subject are also complex. Physiological psychology is a complex subject. Its problems are also complex. Problems of this science have increased in modern times. It is not easy to describe all the problems of physiological psychology in detail. Some main problems will be described here in brief. The field of the study of physiological psychology will also become clear by this description.

The main problems of physiological psychology have been classified into the following five groups :

1. Problems of the Activity of Nerve and Receptor cells.
2. Problems of Cortical Function and Behaviour.
3. Problems of the Patterns of Nervous Action.
4. Problems of Physiological Factors in Abnormal Behaviour.
5. Problems of Biochemical Influences.

A brief introduction to these problems is given below :

1. Problems of the Activity of Nerve and Receptor Cells. All the problems of the activity of receptor cells and nerve cells are studied in this group. Excitation of these cells and sensation etc. are observed. Following are the sub-problems in this group :

(a) *The Nature of Excitation* : There are various receptor cells in the organism. These cells are excited differently by different stimuli. Outer stimulation received by the receptor cells gives rise to sensation. Knowing the nature of this excitation is a problem of physiological psychology.

(b) *The Nature of Impulse Conduction* : This problem is similar to the first problem. Various cells in the organism are connected with each other. After the stimulation is received by receptors, it is conducted from one nerve cell to the other and so on. Here it is essential to know as to how impulses are conducted in nerve cells.

(c) *The Nature of Inhibition* : Can a stimulation received by one nerve cell be inhibited by another nerve cell? If it is so, then it is important to know how this type of inhibition of impulse takes place? What is its nature?

(d) *The Nature of Receptor Adaptation* : Adaptation takes place in receptor cells. One problem of physiological psychology is to know the mechanism of receptor adaptation. Another question is about the place of this adaptation : Whether it takes place in the peripheral nervous system or in the central nervous system.

2. Problems of Cortical Function and Behaviour. Main problems in this group are the following :

(a) *Sensation and Perception* : This is considered a general problem.

Many aspects of this problem are known now. But some problems regarding the difference in excitation of receptor cells and attributes of sensation are yet to be explained.

(b) *Problem of Learning and Memory* : Learning and Memory are related with the brain. But it is essential to know as to which parts of the brain are related to learning? Whether all parts of the brain are equally active in the learning process?

(c) *States of Consciousness* : Consciousness, hypnosis and unconsciousness are different states of consciousness. One problem in physiological psychology is to explain the neural basis of these states of consciousness.

(d) *Experience of Pleasure and Pain* : How are pleasure and pain experienced in the brain? Which stimuli are responsible for these experiences? What are the different centres in the brain for these experiences? This is a very complex problem in physiological psychology.

(e) *Problem of Imagination and Thinking* : Imagination and thinking are special capacities of human beings. Man is different from other animals because of these capacities. One problem in physiological psychology is to find out as to where do these capacities lie?

3. Problem of the Patterns of Nervous Activity. Following problems come in this group :

(a) *Self-limiting Function of Nervous System* : Self-limiting function also takes place along with conduction in the nerve cells. These two activities differ from each other. Self-limiting function is concerned with individual differences in rates of reaction of nerve cells and synapses. It is essential to know this self-limiting psychology.

(b) *Rhythmic Functions* : Many activities going on in the body are of rhythmic nature. Heart beating and respiration are the two examples. But there are many others like tremors of the finger, potentials from the brain etc. The study of the nature and influence of various rhythmic activities is a fascinating problem in physiological psychology.

(c) *Compensatory Phenomena* : Compensation is a natural characteristic of the organism. Feeling of need for rest after fatigue, need for water, sweating and needs for other substances in the state of their deficiency in the body are the main examples of compensatory behaviour. These are important for maintaining homeostasis at both physiological and psychological level. Understanding of various compensatory functions is an important problem in physiological psychology.

4. Problems of Physiological Factors in Abnormal Behaviour. Sometimes the behaviour of a person becomes abnormal. Before the acquisition of sufficient scientific knowledge there were many superstitions about the causes of abnormal behaviour. But as result of the developments in Physiology, Medicine and Psychology, these superstitions are now no longer accepted. Now it has been established that both organic and mental factors operate in the causation of abnormal behaviour. Following problems related to abnormal behaviour are studied in physiological psychology :

(a) *Hysteria* : Hysteria is an abnormal behaviour. Causes of this disease are both physical and mental. These causes are studied is physiological psychology.

(b) *Psychoneuroses, Fatigue and Anxiety* : Intense anxiety, fatigue and other psychoneuroses result because of psychological as well as physical factors. Their causes and methods of treatment are studied in physiological psychology.

(c) *Physiological Stress* : Physiological stress is a problem which is studied only in physiological psychology.

(d) *The Psychoses* : Psychoses are of different types. Nature and causes of psychoses are also understood in physiological psychology.

5. Problems of Biochemical Influences. Many problems of physiological psychology are concerned with the body of organisms. In this position, it is also essential to know the influence of various chemicals on the body. Following are some of the problems of this group which are studied in physiological psychology :

(a) *Biochemical Influences on the Activity of Muscles* : The muscles of the human body are influenced by various biochemicals. This influence may be in the form of exciting or inhibiting the muscle activity. Some biochemicals excite the muscles and some have an opposite influence on their activity. An understanding of this influence is a problem of physiological psychology.

(b) *Influence of Biochemicals on Behaviour* : There are many chemicals inside the human body. A notable change occurs in the behaviour of the organism by a change in the equilibrium of these chemicals. Why does this change occur? How does the change occur? Answers to these questions can be given only by the study of physiological psychology.

(c) *Influence of Biochemicals on Nerve Cells* : Biochemicals have a very important influence on the activity of nerve cells. Now it has been established that nerve activity has both electrical and chemical aspects. Chemical events underlie the electrical events in the nerve impulse. Some chemicals facilitate and accelerate the nerve activity while others retard it. The study of the properties of biochemicals and physiological reactions is a problem of physiological psychology.

A person can only control those actions which occur according to his will. The actions which do not occur according to his will cannot be controlled by the individual.

It is clear in the above brief description that Muller had said while throwing light on the mutual relations between physiology and psychology, that the basis of psychology was physical. He gave great importance to the nervous system and whatever he wrote in this respect is the basis of the study of modern neurology. He stressed greatly the physiological aspect. The reason for this is that his main subject was physiology. He is among the famous German Psychologists of the 19th Century.

The nervous system is generally considered responsible for the behaviour of organisms. It is the nervous system which regulates and organises the behaviour of the organisms. But it is not true that only the nervous system regulates the total behaviour. Beside the nervous system, there are some bio-cells, tissues and other organs inside the body which affect the behaviour of organisms in various ways. Their role is important. But all these bio-cells, tissues and organs do not influence the behaviour directly. These cells and organs influence bodily and mental processes through a common medium. This medium is called Internal Environment. The internal environment has a special function in human body. The behaviour of the organism is also influenced by the processes going on in the cells and organs of the body. Its composition changes from time to time because of these influences.

This internal environment supplies necessary materials to the cells, tissues and organs of the body for their normal functioning. It also relieves the body of its waste products from time to time. In this way the internal environment helps the various cells of the body in their work by supplying necessary energy to them whereby their activities in the body go on normally. Thus, though the internal environment does not control and regulate the behaviour directly, it definitely contributes in important ways for the normal functioning of whole body.

It is clear from the above discussion that the study of Internal Environment is essential for a complete understanding of the behaviour of the organism. Therefore, special emphasis is laid on the study of internal environment of the organism in physiological psychology.

On analysing the functions of the internal environment of the organisms it is found that these are of five types. The description of these functions is given below :

1. Metabolism of Cells. Various complex chemical reactions take place in metabolic functions of cells. The aim of these chemical reactions is to supply necessary energy for the bio-cells and to excrete waste products from the body.

2. Intermediary Metabolism. These are also special types of chemical reactions. Food eaten by the organism is in the form of complex materials. This food is broken down to simpler compounds by these chemical reactions. Food in the form of these simpler compounds is used by the cells of the body as a source of energy through other chemical reactions.

3. Metabolism of Genes, Vitamins and Enzymes. Genes propagate hereditary features of each individual. Enzymes and vitamins influence the behaviour of organisms. The behaviour of the organism is changed by the deficiency or increase of vitamins and enzymes in the body. Equilibrium and adjustment of the organism behaviour depends upon their normal activity.

4. Homeostasis. Homeostasis is a special condition of the internal environment of the organism. All the organs of the body do their functions normally in this state. This is a state of normal equilibrium in the body.

5. Psychoactive Drugs. These are chemical substances which have special influence on the internal environment of the organisms. When introduced into the body, these drugs become a part of the internal environment and through it act primarily on the nervous system. In recent years, psycho-active drugs have come into increasing use for the specific purpose of modifying psychological conditions.

METABOLISM OF CELLS

Cell is the basic unit of the organism. All living organisms are made up of a special complex organisation of these cells. The internal environment of the organism supplies various substances like food and oxygen to these cells. These cells live because these substances form the internal environment and physiological processes go on normally. Besides this, these various cells of the body eliminate useless and waste products from the body through the medium of the internal environment. In this way, these processes of give and take go on in the cells of the body. These processes are called metabolism of cells. Morgan and Stellar have defined metabolic processes of cells in these words. "The metabolism of cells are the biochemical processes that are vital to the existence and life processes of the cells of the body." The usefulness of metabolism of cells becomes clear by this statement of Morgan and Stellar. Francis Leukel has also described metabolism of cells. According to him, "Metabolism of cells refers to the chemical reactions that go inside the cells and where the activities of the cells are involved in transforming food and oxygen into cellular structure and eliminating waste from the cells." The process of metabolism becomes clear by the statements of these authors. The complex process of metabolism has two aspects. In the first phase food is received and conserved whereas in the second phase food is conserved and waste products eliminated. The process of building up and conservation is called Anabolism. On the other hand, the second process of destruction is called catabolism. Many types of chemical reactions go on in these metabolic processes. These chemical reactions supply and transform the energy of the cells. The growth of the body is possible because of this energy only. Following are the major types of chemical reactions in metabolism of the cells :

(1) **Oxidation-Reduction.** Oxidation is a very important chemical reaction of compounds in the internal environment. Oxidation is a chemical reaction in which removal of electrons or hydrogen ions from the molecule of a compound takes place. It is also defined as the addition of oxygen to a compound or element. Reduction is the converse process of oxidation. In it oxygen is removed from a compound or electrons or hydrogen ions are added to the compound.

(2) **Hydrolysis.** This is a chemical reaction in which water is added or removed from a compound in the body. This reaction helps in the normal working of many processes in the cells of the body.

(3) **Decarboxylation.** In some special circumstances some products are formed which have a molecule containing carboxyl group (— COOH). This carboxyl group is low in energy and it is beneficial for the body to eliminate this group and raise the average energy potential in the cells. This process of removing carboxyl group from the body is called decarboxylation.

(4) **Phosphorylation.** Phosphorous is especially useful for the bio-cells of the organism. Phosphorus is responsible for energy transformation in the cells of the body. This energy is released in the body in the form of heat when organic phosphates are broken down. Such a process of breakdown of phosphates and thereby releasing energy is called Dephosphorylation. In the process of phosphorylation, phosphorous is added to a compound.

(5) **Deamination.** Protein is a major element of the food of each organism. Break-down of these proteins in the body gives rise to amino-acids. These amino-acids are useful in many chemical reactions in the body. Amino group or NH_2 group is an essential feature of amino acids. In the process of deamination the amino group is broken down from the amino-acids and set free. This causes transformation of energy in the cells.

INTERMEDIARY METABOLISM

Man and other animals get different kinds of food substances from the outside world. It contains mainly proteins, carbohydrates, fats, minerals, amino-acids, fatty acids and vitamins. After these substances are eaten, they are broken down to simpler compounds in the Alimentary canal. Then these materials reach liver via the intestines. Various chemical reactions take place in the liver. These substances are further broken down by chemical reactions here to produce energy for the cells of the body. In this way complex food substances are transformed into energy for the cells. The processes regulating this transformation are called Intermediary metabolism. Morgan and Stellar have defined the process of intermediary metabolism in these words, "Intermediary metabolism are the biochemical events in which food materials are broken down into simpler compounds, then recombined in various ways to make the materials from which the various cells of the body get the energy for their activities."

Francis Leukel has also given his ideas about intermediary metabolism like Morgan and Stellar. According to him "Intermediary metabolism refers to the chemical reactions that go on outside the cells where the fats, proteins, carbohydrates used by the body as food are broken into the simple compounds which specialized cells can use, and when cellular waste is transformed for removal from the blood stream."

Thus, the processes of intermediary metabolism are very complex. A brief introduction of some main features is given below :

(1) **Oxidation.** A sufficient amount of oxygen is required in the internal environment for carrying out the process of intermediary metabolism. To fulfil this need the body gets oxygen from the outside environment. The process of consumption of oxygen is called oxidation. Here it is essential to note that if the body has to do hard work or more work, more oxygen is required for the intermediary metabolism.

(2) **Carbohydrate Metabolism.** The process of carbohydrate metabolism and metabolism of fats and proteins also comes in intermediary metabolism. In this type of metabolism fats and proteins are broken down into glucose. Glucose obtained by the metabolism of these products is used in the body in three ways. This glucose stores energy in phosphate bonds in the bio-cells. This glucose is used as a source of energy for the muscles of the body. It is deposited either in muscles or in liver in the form of glycogen. This glucose is also helpful in the transformation of energy in the activities of bio-cells.

(3) **Basal Metabolic Rate.** Intermediary metabolism is also concerned with breathing in of the oxygen and breathing out of carbon-dioxide by the body. For getting energy oxygen is inspired in the body and the same amount of carbon-dioxide is expired out. The state of body metabolism is known by measuring the rate of breathing in of oxygen and breathing out of carbon-dioxide. This rate generally increases when the body is doing strenuous work. On the other hand, this rate decreases in the state of rest and in some physical abnormalities. This rate is called basal metabolic rate or BMR. The BMR is seen in order to know about the different aspects of physical health.

(4) **Respiratory Quotient.** For the consumption of food by the cells in the body, oxygen is breathed in and carbon-dioxide is breathed out. The ratio of oxygen breathed in the body and carbon-dioxide breathed out is called respiratory quotient. This quotient can be expressed by the following formula :

$$\text{Respiratory Quotient} = \frac{\text{Carbon-dioxide breathed out of body}}{\text{Oxygen used by the body}}$$

$$= \frac{CO_2}{O_2}$$

(5) **Energy Transformation.** Transformation of energy is a very important event in the body. This transformation takes place in intermediary metabolism. Bio-cells of the body receive energy because of various chemical reactions in intermediary metabolism. Energy is transformed in these reactions. This energy builds necessary fats and proteins for the body by means of other chemical reactions. This entire process is called Energy Transformation.

(6) **Circulatory System.** Circulatory system has a special importance in the body. It gives sufficient co-operation in intermediary metabolism. The major function of the circulatory system is to maintain physical and chemical adaptation of various fluids present in the body. This system influences 96% of the fluids in the body.

(7) **Action of Hormones.** Hormones have a very important role in maintaining equilibrium in the body of man and other animals. These hormones influence and control many physiological processes and mental behaviour of the person. It can be said in this connection that the unique behaviour and the unique personality of a person is the result of unique functioning of hormones in his body. These hormones have a unique contribution in regulating the metabolic processes in the body. Now question arises : "What are Hormones?" Hormones are chemical substances produced in the body itself. These hormones are secreted from a number of glands in the body, called ductless or endocrine glands. Endocrine glands secrete hormones directly into the blood. There are a number of endocrine glands in human body and they secrete different hormones. Hormones of different glands have different influences on human behaviour and personality.

METABOLISM OF GENES, VITAMINS AND ENZYMES

The metabolism of genes, enzymes and vitamins have important functions along with other processes of the internal environment. Their contribution is important in producing normal behaviour and a balanced personality. A brief introduction to their function and importance is given below :

(A) GENES

Chromosomes are found in the body of human and other organisms. These chromosomes contain genes. Genes are made up of an acid called Deoxyribo Nucleic Acid (DNA). Genes have a great importance in the life of organisms. Hereditary characteristics of the organisms are transmitted from one generation to the next through the medium of genes. Racial characteristics like eye colour, colour of body skin, physical constitution etc. are determined through the genes. These genes also determine some aspects of the metabolic processes in the cells. The influence of genes on metabolic reactions is carried generally by enzymes which have a very close link with genes.

(B) VITAMINS

What are Vitamins?

Before the discovery of modern scientific knowledge it was believed that only carbohydrates, proteins, fats and some minerals are essential food elements for the proper growth and other life processes of the body. But now it has been established by modern scientific researches that besides these food elements the body needs some other chemical substances for various purposes. It is essential to take these chemical substances regularly for the growth and proper functioning of the body. These chemical substances are known as vitamins. Vitamins are also called accessory dietary factors. Now the question arises. What are these vitamins? Vitamins are complex chemical compounds. These are not produced in the body but are to be taken in the diet from the external environment. The role of vitamins is to regulate the metabolic processes of the body in a normal way. Vitamins also help in maintaining the equilibrium of physiological processes in the body.

Properties of Vitamins

In fact, vitamins are complex chemical substances having many different properties. They have a unique contribution in the body. Vitamins do not take part directly in the metabolic processes of the body, but they have important contribution in smooth functioning of metabolic processes. There are different kinds of vitamins on the basis of difference in chemical structure and function in the body. Each vitamin has a specific function. The body gets some specific disease in its absence. Therefore, vitamins are helpful in the prevention and treatment of various diseases. Vitamins are not produced in the body but they are taken in the form of diet from the external environment. Most vitamins are received from vegetables, fruits, milk and other food substances. Vitamins are needed in only small amounts in the body.

Classification of Vitamins

It has been said earlier that there are many vitamins. It is essential to classify them for the sake of convenience in studying their functions. There is no fully appropriate system as yet for the classification of vitamins. In fact, their classification is not simple because of their complex chemical structure. In this state, vitamins have been classified on a crude basis. All vitamins have been classified into two groups on this basis :

(1) Fat Soluble Vitamins.

(2) Water Soluble Vitamins.

1. **Fat Soluble Vitamins.** Vitamins which are soluble in fats come under this group. Important vitamins in this group are vitamin A, vitamin D, vitamin E and vitamin K.

2. Water Soluble Vitamins. Those vitamins which easily dissolve in water come in this group. Vitamin B complex, vitamin C and vitamin P are the major vitamins in this group.

In short, it can be said about vitamins that these are complex chemical structures which the organism receives from his diet. The body needs only small traces of them, but these vitamins control certain vital chemical reactions in the body. These vitamins are closely related to enzymes in different metabolic reactions in the body.

(C) ENZYMES

Enzymes are essential for the normal functioning of the bodily processes and equilibrium in behaviour. The enzymes give essential speed to the chemical reactions in body metabolism. In fact, these enzymes work as catalysts. Because of the nature of their catalysts, chemical reactions in the body go on easily and quickly in their presence. It is essential to make it clear here that enzymes are not used in the chemical reactions. These influence only speed of those reactions. They help various processes of synthesis and disintegration in the body. The enzymes also act in an important way on the body temperature.

Enzymes are of various types. The action of each enzyme is different according to its nature. One enzyme acts on some specific substances and in specific conditions. For example, enzyme acting on fats is useful only in reactions of fat metabolism. This enzyme has no action on proteins. Besides this, an enzyme working in acidic medium cannot act in an alkaline medium.

The structure of an enzyme molecule is very complex. This complex molecule contains sufficient quantity of protein apo-enzyme and a minute quantity of non-protein coenzymes. Generally, two molecules of enzyme work together in their catalytic action. Here it is essential to make clear that where the body essentially needs enzymes, another type of chemical substances are also simultaneously present in the body. These chemicals are called anti-enzymes or enzymes inhibitors. The main function of these enzyme inhibitors is to control the action of enzymes. Intermediary metabolism of the body go on smoothly because of their control. Thus, it is clear that enzymes act in regulation and catalysis of various chemical reactions in the body.

HOMEOSTASIS

It is generally seen that changes go on in the internal and external environment of the body of organism. But inspite of these changes a state of equilibrium exists in the body. What is the reason for this? In fact, it is a characteristic of the body of the organism. This condition results because of an appropriate adjustment between the bio-cells and their environment. All the bio-cells of the body are not responsible for this adjustment. There are some specific systems in the body which make possible the state of equilibrium. Thus, the bodily characteristic of maintaining equilibrium in the internal environment in the face of changing conditions is called homeostasis.

Many examples of homeostasis in the life of an organism can be given. The normal temperature of human body is 98.4°F. Because of the homeostatic property of the body, its temperature does not fluctuate much from 98.4°F in the cold atmosphere of Mount Everest and in very hot atmosphere. Besides body temperature, blood pressure, heartbeat rate, balance of water and salts in the body and the amount of many other substances remain almost stable in all conditions. This equilibrium of various conditions in the body is called homeostasis.

Francis Leukel has presented this homeostatic property of the body in his own way. He writes : "Homeostasis is that state of balance between changes in which the external environment and internal changes caused by metabolism are reacted to by the tissues, organs and system of the body to keep the internal environment within narrow limits of pressure, oxygen content, acid-base balance, blood sugar level, chemical composition and temperature."

Now the question arises that how is this state of homeostasis maintained in the body? There are many factors which work to maintain this state. Hormones present in the body have a special influence on the homeostatic process. Beside this, the activity of lungs, circulatory system, function of kidneys, metabolic processes, and also the activity of nervous system contribute in important ways in maintaining homeostasis in the body. Homeostasis process in the body is mainly regulated by three processes. A general introduction of these processes is given below :

(1) **Blood Sugar Level.** Sugar is always present in some fixed amount in the blood of the organism. This level of blood sugar is essential for the homeostasis in the organism. The essential amount of sugar is needed for the activity of the nervous system. This behaviour of the human organism becomes abnormal if the level of sugar falls or becomes higher in the blood. The person goes in a coma if the amount of blood sugar falls below a particular level. This state is called hypoglycemia. If the proper treatment of this state is not done for some time, the person may die. On the other hand, if the level of sugar in the blood rises higher, there is also disturbance in the body functions. This defect is called diabetes.

A continuous process goes on in the body to maintain the normal level of sugar in the blood. This activity is done by liver in the body. To maintain this normal level, the liver deposits carbohydrates in itself in the form of glycogen. If the level of blood sugar is less, this glycogen is converted to glucose by the liver and it is released into the blood. On the other hand, if the level of sugar in the blood rises higher, the liver draws out extra glucose from the blood and deposits it in the form of glycogen. In this way the level of sugar in the blood remains normal because of this double action of the liver. Behind this whole process is the influence of endocrine glands. Also important is the amount of carbohydrates which the body takes. Another characteristic of liver is also important. The liver converts fats and proteins into carbohydrates by means of various chemical reactions. These converted carbohydrates also work in the production of sugar in the body. This chemical process is called gluconeogenesis. The liver functions in another way to reduce the level of sugar in the blood. It increases the secretion of hormones from thyroid, anterior, pituitary and adrenal certex. The increase in these hormones helps in maintaining the normal level of sugar in the blood. Two other things also influence the level of blood sugar. First, intestines absorb some amount of sugar from the blood. Secondly, tissues of the body absorb some amount of carbohydrates. These processes help in maintaining a constant level of sugar in the blood.

(2) **Hydrogen-ion Concentration.** Generally, acids and bases are produced when metabolic processes go on in the internal environment of the body. Dissociation of these acids and bases in water gives rise to Hydrogen ions (H^+) and Hydroxyl ions (OH^-) respectively. The relative amount of the two types of ions produces acidity or alkalinity in the internal environment. Homeostasis in the body depends on the balance between these two. On the other hand, homeostasis is disturbed if ratio between the amounts of acid (H^+) and base (OH^-) is disturbed.

(3) **Oxygen Supplied.** The body continuously needs oxygen for the metabolic processes and other activities. This oxygen is received by lungs from the external environment. Inside the body, this oxygen is absorbed in the blood. There are some red corpuscles in the blood. Oxygen received by the lungs is absorbed in the hemoglobin of red corpuscles. In normal circumstances, the process of intake of oxygen and its absorption in the blood goes on normally. In unusual circumstances when there is less intake of oxygen, its level in the blood falls. The deficiency of oxygen in the blood is called anoxemia. Deficiency of oxygen is compensated by the acidity of the blood. Generally, the rate of breathing increases whenever acidity in the blood is increased. More amount of oxygen reaches in the body as a result of increase in the rate of breathing. Simultaneously, the rate of blood circulation in the body also increases because of increase in the acidity of blood. More oxygen reaches the various cells and tissues of the body as a result of these two effects of acidity. Thus, the body itself takes more amount of oxygen which results in smooth functioning of all processes in the body.

THE RESPONSE MECHANISM

Response mechanism is that system which helps the organism to adjust itself to the environment and control its activities. Thus, it is due to response mechanism that one finds selection, adjustment, combination etc., in human behaviour. The response mechanism in animals is divided into the following parts :

1. Receptors. Cells of the eyes, nose, ears, tongue and skin etc., are receptors. They receive the sensation. Human behaviour begins through the receptors. It is only after the receptors have received the sensation that the response in the organism begins.

2. Effectors. Effectors include muscles and glands. They make the actual response possible.

3. Nervous System. Nervous system controls the response. It joins the receptors and motor-organs.

Human organism is affected by the environment. The sun, heat, cold etc., affect our body. The body responds to external stimuli. This response changes the external environment. When something pinches, the pinched one feels a sensation. The sensation is received by the nervous system through which the receptors and motor organs are connected and the muscles of the hand re-act immediately so that the pinching object is removed. Thus, the receptors receive stimuli from the environment and the motor organs change the environment by response. The human organism has innumerable receptor-cells. In the eye alone there are lakhs of cells. Similarly, the receptor organs *e.g.,* muscles etc., have innumerable muscles-fibres. The nerves connect the receptors and the muscles and thus make response possible. These nerves carry the message from the receptors to the muscle. This communication has a speed of 75 yds., a second. This response takes a very small portion of a second. In times of emergency it becomes even more rapid.

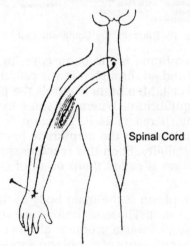

Spinal Cord

Fig. 12. Functioning of Response Mechanism

The functioning of response mechanism is shown in the Fig. 12. In this figure, the stimulus is being received by the receptor on the hand. The nerves are connecting the receptor with the muscles. The nerves go from the hand to the spinal cord and from there take the message to the muscles. This completes the circle of the response mechanism.

CELL AND ITS FUNCTIONS

Robert Hook found for the first time in 1665 that all organisms are made up of cells. This is called cell doctrine since 1838. As these cells are the building blocks of all the organisms, a Physiological Psychologist intensively studies cell. There are three parts in any cell — (1) Membrane, (2) Cytoplasm and (3) Nucleus.

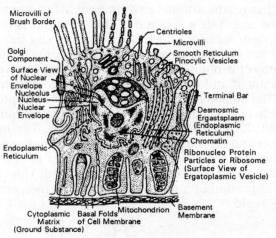

Fig. 13. Diagram of a Composite Cell

1. Membrane. Membrane is the outer covering of a cell. Some substances can come and go through it in the cell. But it maintains a separate identity of a cell. Membrane controls the pressure on a cell and maintains the equilibrium. Whenever some external substance affects the membrane, it reacts as its function is to maintain the equilibrium. Dis-equilibrium in the membrane because of the outer influence is called irritability. Soon this reaction spreads to the total membrane. This reaction is called the process of conduction in the cell.

2. Cytoplasm. Cytoplasm is the main body of the cell. Processes of secretion take place in it. These secretions are very useful for the cell. Secondly, excretion of waste products also occurs through it. A contractibility is another property of cytoplasm. Process of metabolism also takes place through it.

3. Nucleus. Nucleus of the cell has two main functions. First, it looks after the functions of the cytoplasm. Its second function is the reproduction of cells. In reproduction, cells are increased by the process known as cell division.

The above division of functions of different parts of cell is not hard and fast. In fact, these parts are so intimately related with one another that hard and fast distinction cannot be made in their functions.

PRIMITIVE RESPONSE MECHANISM

In Fig. 14 shown below are shown those parts of the Primitive Response Mechanism in which Physiological Psychologists take special interest. These are called Primitive because they appeared in the beginning of the evolution of organisms. These parts are — Receptors, Adjusters and Effectors. Receptor cells are shown in Fig. 14. Muscle cells are Effectors. Ganglion cells shown in the figure are Adjuster cells. The characteristics of these three types of cells are different. In evolutionary history first of all developed the muscle effector cell. Its example is sponge. After this developed receptor cell and adjuster cell or neuron developed last of all. In different organisms these three types of cells show their specialized properties. They are very similar in nature in mammals and higher organisms like man. Physiological Psychologist is interested in the study of these cells.

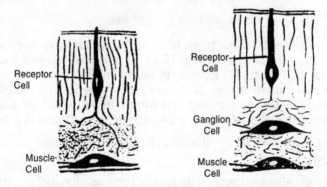

Fig. 14. Diagram of Primitive Response Mechanism

NEURONS

Our nervous system is mainly made up of adjuster cells of neurons (nerve cell). Their main function is in the adjustment of activities between receptors and effectors. For this purpose, they have specialised properties of irritability and conductivity.

Structure of a neuron is shown in Fig. 15. Each neuron has three parts : (1) Dendrites, (2) Cell body and (3) Axon. Dendrites and axon have separate features. Dendrites are found in positions where they can be excited by other cells or by the environmental stimuli. Dendrite is the "receiving" end of the neuron and it carries nerve impulse to the cell body. Axon receives the impulse from the cell body and it is connected to effectors or to other neurons to which it 'delivers' the nervous impulses. A nerve cell generally has several dendrites, but on the other hand, it has only one axon. Both dendrites and axons are generally called fibres.

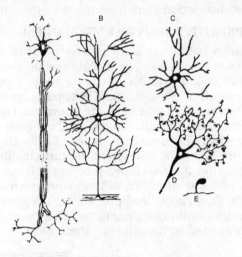

Fig. 15. Different types of Neurons.

There are five different types of neurons which have been shown in Fig. 15. Neuron shown in Fig. 15 (A) is a motor neuron found in spinal cord. In Fig. 15 (B) neuron is found in the motor area of the brain. Neuron shown in Fig. 15 (C) is connecting neuron called golgi type. In Fig. 15 (D) is a bushy cell found in networks of neurons. Neuron shown in Fig. 15 (E) is a bipolar neuron of sensory nerves.

RECEPTORS

What are Receptors?

Receptor cells are those cells which receive physical stimulation from the environment and start the process of adjustment of the organism to his environment. Receptors have developed gradually. In this evolution, they have specialized, their structure and position in the body have changed. Their structures change for responding to different types of physical energies. In the early period of evolution they became more sensitive than other cells. Later on, some receptors became more sensitive to one type of stimulus energy and other receptors specialized to receive other kinds of stimulus energy.

Kinds of Receptors

As a result of this differentiation, there are four main types of receptors in man : (1) Thermal receptors, (2) Mechanical receptors, (3) Chemical receptors and (4) Photic receptors. Photic receptors receive light energy more readily. Similarly, chemical receptors easily receive chemical stimulation, mechanical receptors are sensitive to mechanical energy and thermal receptors to hot and cold stimuli. But it does not mean that any of these receptors cannot react to other types of stimulus energy. In fact, each type of receptors is influenced by different kinds of stimulus energy but it has much more sensitivity to one particular stimulus energy than other receptors. For example, thermal receptors are also influenced by chemical energy but these are more sensitive to thermal energy than other receptors. Similarly, mechanical energy is more effective for mechanical receptors but thermal stimuli also influence them. The energy to which a receptor is more sensitive is called 'Adequate stimulus' for that receptor. Other types of stimuli can influence it only when they are presented in a very high quantity. These are called 'Inadequate stimuli' for it because they are inadequate and insufficient to activate this receptor. Thus, light energy is the adequate stimulus for receptors in the eyes. Adequate stimulus for ear is mechanical energy and it is called a mechanical receptor. Skin feels pressure. Therefore, it is the receptor for pressure. Skin also contains receptors which react to heat and cold. Thermal receptors are complex and their power of discrimination is very fine. Smell receptors are the most developed of all chemical receptors. They are nerve cells reactive to different chemicals. Receptors for touch are relatively simple, whereas auditory receptors are very complex.

Position of Receptors

Different receptors are situated on different positions in the body so that they are able to receive different kinds of stimulation. From the point of view of their position in the body, receptors have been classified as follows :

(1) **Exteroceptors.** These receptors are situated on the surface of the body in such a way that they are easily affected by the physical energies of the external environment. Hence, these are called exteroceptors. Receptors in the eye are the example of this type.

(2) **Proprioceptors.** These receptors are present almost everywhere inside the body. The word 'proprio' means self. Therefore, self-receptors or proprioceptors give information to the organism about sensations

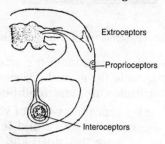

Fig. 16. Position of Receptors

of his own body. The example of this type of receptors are the sensory cells in the muscles. They are affected by the changes in the muscle.

(3) **Interoceptors.** These receptors are found in the inner surface of stomach and intestines. They receive visceral sensations.

The three types of receptors have been shown in Fig. 16.

All receptors are connected with dendrites of afferent neurons. These will be discussed in connection with nervous system. Nervous system relates to receptors and effectors. These three together make response mechanism. Effectors will be discussed before studying nervous system.

EFFECTORS

Effectors are those cells or group of cells by which an organism responds or does activities. Effectors are of two main types :

(1) Muscles and (2) Glands.

1. Muscles. There are three types of muscles. These are : (1) Striped Muscle, (2) Smooth Muscle and (3) Cardiac Muscle. The distinction between these muscles is based on the difference in their functions or the type of fibres in them. The structure of the fibres of different muscles is shown in the Fig. 17.

Fig. 17. Structure of Different Muscle Fibers

In Fig. 17, (A and B) are shown the structure of striped muscle fibres, (C) cardiac muscle fibres and (D) smooth muscle fibres. Now the three types of muscles are described here in brief.

(a) *Smooth Muscle* : From the point of view of evolution, smooth muscle cells are the most primitive and least differentiated of the muscle cells. These cells are unstriped and spindle-shaped. Smooth muscle cells contain a special substance upon which its contractual properties depend. Smooth muscle cells are found in the walls of intestines and stomach. They receive excitation from autonomic nervous system and, therefore, they are autonomous in function.

(b) *Striped Muscle* : From the point of view of evolution striped muscle cells evolved after the smooth muscle cells. These muscle cells are longer than the smooth muscle cells. The activity of these muscles is controlled by the central nervous system and they contract and expand according to the will of the person. Therefore, they are also called voluntary muscles. Striped muscles are present in hands, arms, legs etc. Their fibres are made up of two types of substances, one of which is darker than the other. This gives striped appearance to these muscles. Striped muscles are enclosed in a special elastic membrane called sarcolemma.

(c) *Cardiac Muscle* : As is clear from the name, cardiac muscle is present in the heart. It is a special kind of striped muscle. Its chief distinction is that its fibres are not arranged parallel or enclosed in a membrane as are the striped muscle cells, but branch and unite with each other in a network. Like smooth muscle, activity of the cardiac muscle is also controlled by the autonomic nervous system.

Striped muscles are voluntary and the other two muscles are involuntary. All muscles, whether they are striped or smooth or cardiac, are specialized in one function — contraction. The excitation transmitted through the adjusters of the nervous system starts essential physical and chemical activities in the muscle. These changes lead to the release of muscle's energy in the form of contraction. Contraction is the final step which determines the behaviour of the stimulated organism.

(2) **Glands.** Glands are a special type of cells whose main function is to produce different types of secretions in the body. They are called effectors because like muscles they are connected with the cells of the nervous system and they respond in the form of secretion to excitation from it. They look very much like simple cells of the skin. Their secretory function is not prominent in their structure. But they differ in their chemical function and in the way in which they deliver their secretions into the body.

The Nervous System

Nerve is the most important part of response mechanism. It joins the receptors and the effectors. The nervous system is divided into two parts : (1) Central nervous system and (2) Autonomic nervous system. In the human organism there is a whole network of nervous system. The central nervous system too has two parts : (a) Spinal Cord and (b) Brain, which has three parts — (i) Cerebrum, (ii) Medulla oblongata and (iii) Cerebellum. The autonomic nervous system has two parts — (a) Sympathetic and (b) Parasympathetic. The following chart shows this structure :

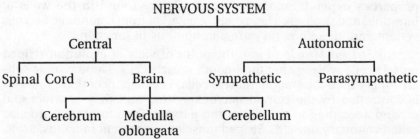

A nerve network spreads throughout the body, similar to the telephone cable network spread over the city. These nerves reach every receptor and muscle just like cables which reach every business centre, office, hospital, college, etc. All the nerves of the body are connected to the spinal cord and this central body resembles a telephone exchange where all the wires from the different telephones meet. Information is sent from any telephone in the system to the telephone exchange and the desired telephone connection is got. Thus, the exchange of information between two centres is always through the medium of the telephone exchange. A similar state of affairs exists in the nervous system. Sensory nerves bring information to the centre from the receptors and the motor nerves carry direction to the muscles. But there is a big difference between the telephone system and bodily nervous system. The telephone exchange is merely a medium which has no say in anything which goes on. On the other hand, the nervous centre is not merely a medium because it decides upon the response to the stimuli

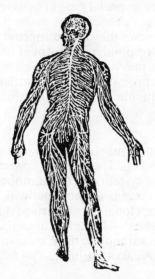

Fig. 18. A general view of Central Nervous System

and part of the body to obey it. So, in reality it is the centre which controls the whole response mechanism.

The nerves of the central nervous system reach every sense organ and muscle. These nerves are connected with the central ganglia of the spinal cord. All the nerves meet at this centre. The nerves carrying the message from the receptors to the centre are known as sensory nerves. The nerves carrying the message from the centre to the muscles are known as motor nerves. The response mechanism works by systematic working of the sensory and the motor nerves. Besides these two types of nerves there are nerves connecting them.

Thus, various responses of the human body function through nerve centres. These nerve centres are very complex. When seen with the help of a microscope, many subtle fibres are seen in other nerves. These fibres are very thin but reach from the receptor to the nerve centre and from the nerve centre to the muscle. Thus, some of these are even some yards in length. The complexity of the nerve centre can be imagined from the fact that the optic nerve alone has about 4,00,000 fibres. A nerve is made up of a bundle of fibres. Fibres are connected outside the nerve centre, but again meet in the nerve centre. It is not necessary that one fibre should carry one message. Sometimes an outgoing fibre takes several messages. When the nerves are broken and the muscles are unconnected with the centres, these become useless.

The nervous system is made up of nerves. The nerve system and the nerve cells are connected through the blood vessels. These nerves also include their branches. These branches are of two types — axons and dendrites. Axon is one and alone while dendrites are many. Axons are several feet long. The dendrites extend like the small branches of a tree. The axon is covered by an insulating substance. The axons of the sensory nerves are sensory while axons of the motor nerves are motor. A motor axon extends from the brain or spinal cord to the muscle or gland. The sensory axon extends from the nerve cells of the brain. Thus, these axons connect the receptors and the nerve centres.

The connection between the two cells is known as synapse. In this synapse an axon of a nerve finishes in fine branches and these fine branches get connected with the dendrites of some other nerves. Thus, a synapse is formed when the axons of a nerve get connected with the dendrites of some other nerves, and a sensation is carried from one to another. The axon carries the sensation and the dendrites receive it. Thus, the message is communicated from the axon of the nerve to the dendrite of another nerve. This message is in form of nerve impulse which is like an electro-chemical current found in the nerve. The force of the reaction of any muscle depends on the total number of these electro-chemical currents per second, as it increases and decreases simultaneously.

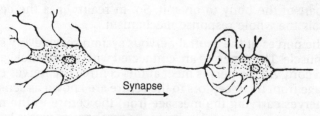

Fig. 19. Synapse

EFFECTORS : ENDOCRINE GLANDS

Effectors are of two types : (1) Muscles and (2) Glands. Muscle effectors have already been discussed. Now we shall discuss about glands and their functions in behaviour.

Glands have a unique place and function in the body of the organism. They influence every aspect of the body. Besides influencing the body, human behaviour and personality are also influenced by their activity. Life is active only because of the normal activity of glands. Now the question arises, "What are these glands?" In fact, bodily glands are structures formed by the special composition of cell molecules. Their function is also specific. The gland, produce and secrete various chemical substances. Secretions of one class of glands are called hormones. Each gland of this group secretes a specific hormone. The hormones of various glands have very important influence on human behaviour and his personality.

Classification of Glands

It is clear from the above discussion that the main function of glands is the discharge of secretion. There are some glands which do not pour their secretions into the blood but pour them out on the body surface through some tubes. Because of this characteristic, these glands are called Duct glands or Exocrine glands. The second type of glands have different characteristics. These second type of glands pour their chemical secretions directly into the blood stream without the help of any duct (tube). Their secretions reach various organs of the body through blood and influence their activity. Because of this characteristic, these are called Ductless or Endocrine glands. There are, thus, two types of bodily glands :

(1) Duct or Exocrine glands

(2) Ductless or Endocrine glands.

Endocrine Glands

Endocrine glands pour their secretions directly into the blood stream without the help of any tube (duct). These glands have unique importance in animal and human body. These glands are located at different parts of the body. Chemical substances secreted by endocrine glands are known as hormones. These hormones influence various parts of the body and behaviour. Hypo or hyper secretion from these glands have bad and good influences on body functions. Some of the hormones of these glands also take part in the metabolic processes in the body. Emotional behaviour of human beings is also influenced by their action. A description of the general characteristics of endocrine glands will be given first before discussing their functions in detail.

General Characteristics

Each endocrine gland has its own unique characteristics and functions. But there are some characteristics which are common in all the endocrine glands. Some of these common characteristics are given below :

(1) All endocrine glands pour their secretion directly into the blood without the help of any tube. These secretions reach the whole body through the blood vessels.

(2) Secretions of endocrine glands are called hormones. Hormones of each endocrine gland have their unique properties and functions.

(3) Whereas, different glands have specific functions in the body, they also affect the activity of each other. In fact, different glands work as a system.

(4) Normal secretion of endocrine glands is beneficial for the body and behaviour. But, on the other hand, their abnormal activity results into various symptoms in the body. Abnormal activity may be of two types. First, if secretion from the gland is more than normal, it is called hyper-function. Secondly, if the secretion is less than normal, activity of the gland is low then it is known as Hypo-function.

(5) Secretions of endocrine glands influence human body functions and behaviour. Their hypo or hyper functioning have different influences. These influences are on all cells, tissues and organs of the body.

Major Endocrine Glands

There are various endocrine glands in the human body. Their location in the body and functions are different. Following are the major endocrine glands in the human body :

(1) Thyroid gland.
(2) Parathyroid glands.
(3) Adrenal glands.
(4) Pancreatic gland.
(5) Pituitary gland.
(6) Pineal gland.
(7) Thymus gland.
(8) Gonads.

Location of these glands in human body has been shown in Fig. 20. It is now believed that thymus and pineal glands have no importance in human behaviour. A detailed discussion of the functions of other endocrine glands is given below :

1. Thyroid Gland

The thyroid gland is located in the tissue of the neck around the wind pipe. Hormone secreted from this gland is called Thyroxine. Thyroxine contains a large amount of iodine.

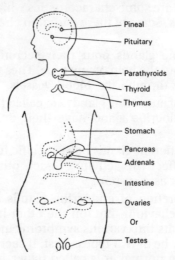

Fig. 20. Location of Endocrine Glands in human body.

Activity of the thyroid gland influences various bodily activities. Its hormone thyroxine controls the rate of various metabolic processes. Various processes of oxidation going on in the body are regulated by this hormone. Thyroid gland gives enough co-operation in the activities of various tissues of the body and in the stimulation of the process of general growth in the body. Activities of various muscles of the body are influenced by the action of its hormone. Regulation of body temperature, control of blood pressure and rate of heart beating are influenced by the action of the hormone thyroxine.

Influence of Hypo and Hoper Secretion

In some cases secretion of hormones from thyroxine gland is low. In this state of hypo secretion, metabolic processes in the body are slowed down and energy production in the body is reduced. This state occurs in human beings when there is acute deficiency of Iodine in their diet. Different diseases occur in children and adults as a result of hypo-function of the thyroid gland. Deficiency of thyroxine in children gives rise to an abnormality called cretinism. In cretinism body growth is arrested and there is weakness in it. Body is lethargic and disformity comes in many of its organs. Brain does not function normally and mental processes are slowed. Normal growth of sex organs is arrested. Resistance to various diseases is reduced in the body. In adults, low secretion of this hormone gives rise to a disease called Myxedema. In this disease skin of the body becomes fat and dry. Hair become brittle and begin to fall. Face becomes ugly and tongue becomes fat because of which the voice becomes hoarse. The person is usually very sluggish and sleeply. He lacks drive and is unemotional. His thinking power is reduced. For the treatment of this disease, medicines containing iodine are given.

Hyper secretion of this gland also gives rise to abnormal conditions. Metabolic processes in the body are speeded up because of increased thyroxine in the blood. Rate of heart beating and respiration are increased. The person becomes more active and seems to have more energy. The person suffering from this disease becomes irritable and restless. This disease is called Exophthalmic goitre. There is slight temperature in the body and the skin remains wet. These symptoms can be eliminated by giving a thyroid-inhibiting drug.

2. Parathyroid Glands

Parathyroid glands are situated in the neck near the wind pipe. They are four in number and two glands are attached to each thyroid. Secretion from the parathyroids is called Parathormone.

A major function of this gland is to regulate the level of calcium and phosphorous in the body. The growth of the body, bones and their strength depends upon this gland. Growth of teeth and their proper function is also influenced by the secretion of this gland. It is essential for the normal activity of muscles.

Function of Parathyroid

As discussed above, the normal amount of the hormone from parathyroid is essential for the growth and strength of bones and teeth. Hypo-secretion of this gland in the human body gives rise to a disease called tetany. There is generally high temperature in the body. Muscles become weak and muscle twitches occur. Sometimes respiratory muscles fail, breathing and heart beating stop and the person dies. This abnormality is because of the loss of calcium from the blood as a result of the absence of parathormone. For treating this abnormal condition, the person should be given calcium salts. Use of vitamin D is also helpful.

Hyper-secretion of parathormone results in excess of calcium in the blood. But excess of calcium is associated with a lowered supply of phosphorous in the blood and the result is the disturbance in the balance of calcium and phosphorous in the blood. Excess of calcium slows down the muscular activity. In this condition, sensitivity of the body becomes low and there is nervous weakness. In this state of abnormality the person is sluggish and his appearance becomes ugly. Generally, surgery is used for treating very serious condition of abnormality because of the hyper-secretion of parathyroids.

Influence on Behaviour and Personality

Hormone of this gland has an important influence on human behaviour and personality. Its normal secretion leads to normal emotional behaviour. Its adequate quantity is essential for body balance and normal neuromuscular processes. In the state of hyper-secretion, the person becomes lethargic and sluggish and his sensitivity is decreased.

3. Adrenal Glands

Adrenal glands are situated on the top surface of kidneys in the body. These are two in number and one gland is situated on each side in the body. Though these glands are near the kidneys but their function is not related with them in any way. Each adrenal has two parts. Both parts secrete different hormones and their activity has different influences on the body and behaviour. The two parts of the adrenal glands are :

(A) Adrenal Cortex.

(B) Adrenal Medulla.

Now the location, function and influence of both the secreting parts of adrenals will be discussed separately.

(A) **Adrenal Cortex.** A number of hormones are secreted from adrenal cortex. These are called cortical steroids or corticoids. These hormones influence the metabolism of carbohydrates, water, sodium and other salts. The balance between sodium and potassium in the body is maintained by the function of steroids. Sodium-potassium balance is essential in the body for normal physiological functions. In the absence of this balance, resting potential in the membrane is changed and neural processes are affected. Carbohydrate metabolism is increased by the function of these hormones. This is essential for many processes in the body. Blood sugar is deposited as glycogen in the liver and the basal metabolic rate is increased.

Effect of Hypo and Hyper-secretion

In the case of hypo-function of adrenal cortex when the secretion of cortical steroids is low, many metabolic processes in the body, especially those concerned with carbohydrates and sodium are slowed up. Excessive water and sodium are excreted through urine. The level of water and sodium is reduced in the body. On the other hand, concentration of potassium in the body is increased. This results into a disturbance of sodium-potassium balance in the body. The disturbance of this balance slows neural and muscular activities. Blood pressure is also affected. Level of glucose in the blood is reduced. Body weight begins to decrease gradually. Temperature of the body falls below normal. These are the symptoms of a serious disease called Addison's disease. The person may die due to this disease.

Hyper-secretion of cortical steroids interfere with the normal sexual development of the person. In females, excessive hair growth on the face and other masculine signs appear. Their general softness begins to disappear. Similarly, over-secretion in young boys gives rise to sexual characteristics of adult males.

Influence on Personality and Behaviour

Physiological effects of the hormones of adrenal cortex are clear from the above discussion. It is natural that personality and behaviour of the person is affected by these physiological changes. Hypo-secretion of this gland results in the low metabolism of carbohydrates and salts and the person becomes weak, lethargic and easily fatigued. The person generally suffers from feelings of inferiority if this condition continues. On the other hand, hyper-secretion of this gland results into disturbance in the sexual development of the person and it creates changes in the personality and behaviour of the person.

(B) **Adrenal Medulla.** Adrenal medulla is the inner part of the adrenal gland. It is made up of neural tissues and has strong effects on the visceral functions controlled by the autonomic nervous system.

In normal state adrenal medulla has no particular function. It has a special contribution in emergency situations. In emergency situations, adrenal medulla is stimulated by the activity of sympathetic nervous system and secretes hormones. Its two major hormones are (1) Adrenaline or Epinephrine and (2) Nor adrenaline or Nor epinephrine. Adrenaline has widespread physiological effects and thereby enables the organism to meet the emergency. It increases the heart rate and blood pressure. Pupils of the eyes are dilated and erection of the hairs on the body occurs.

In the state of emergency the body needs more energy. The hormone adrenaline helps in this by raising the blood sugar level by stimulating the liver to convert glycogen into glucose and release it into the blood. Neuromuscular activity is also increased by this change. Effect of this hormone increases the intake of oxygen in the body as a result of which the rate of metabolism is increased. In emotions like anger and fear, the secretion of adrenaline is especially increased.

Influence on Behaviour and Personality

As has been discussed above, the activity of this gland has a direct relationship with a person's emotions and emergency situations. So, it is natural that its hormones affect his personality and behaviour. Normal activity of this gland helps in maintaining the emotional balance of the person. In the state of fear, anger and external emergency the hormone adrenaline is secreted from this gland. Activity of the liver, breathing and circulation of blood are increased. All these result in extra energy and drive in the body. Thus, this gland has a special contribution in producing energy in the body in emergency situations. Qn the other hand, in some states the secretion of adrenalin from this gland is low.

In the state of decrease of hormone the person becomes weak and apathetic. He loses appetite and normal sexual urge. The overall picture is that of a depressed personality.

4. Pituitary Gland

Pituitary gland has unique importance in body functions. This gland controls the functions of many other endocrine glands. Therefore, it is called the Master gland.

Pituitary is located on the ventral side of the brain. It is connected to the posterior part of the hypothalamus. It has three main secreting parts :

    (A) Anterior Pituitary gland.

    (B) Posterior Pituitary gland.

    (C) Intermediate Pituitary gland.

(A) **Anterior Pituitary Gland.** Anterior Pituitary is more important from the point of view of behaviour. It is this part of the pituitary which regulates the activity of other glands. A number of hormones are secreted from Anterior Pituitary. These hormones are very complex and they have many influences on human behaviour. Functions of its major hormones are given below :

(1) *Thyrotrophic Hormones* : This hormone is concerned with the activity of thyroid gland. Activity of this hormone stimulates the thyroid to secrete thyroxine. In its absence, the thyroid gland does not function. Thus, when the pituitary does not secrete thyrotrophic hormone, all the processes controlled by the thyroid secretion are disturbed.

(2) *Gonadotrophic Hormones* : These hormones are mainly concerned with the activity of gonads (Sex glands). Sex glands also secrete some hormones. A person acquires sexual maturation as a result of joint action of hormones of the gonads and thyrotrophic hormones. Thyrotrophic hormones affect testes in males and ovaries in females. One of these hormones is called Follicle-Stimulating Hormone (FSH). Under the influence of FSH, ovaries in the females produce ova cells and testes in males produce sperm cells. A second gonadotrophic hormone is called Luteinizing Hormone (LH). LH also stimulates the activity of two gonads but it is specially important in the activity of female ovaries.

(3) *Adrenocorticotrophic Hormone* : This hormone is concerned with the activity of adrenal cortex. It regulates the secretion of cortical steroids and thus controls the sodium-potassium balance in the body. Nervous system is stimulated by its activity. Some secondary sex characteristics also develop as a result of its influence.

(4) *Somatotrophic Hormone* : This hormone of the anterior pituitary gland has an independent and direct influence on the body. Its normal secretion results into a normal and proportionate body growth. If the secretion of this hormone is low, the body growth is arrested and proportionate growth of the bone is affected. Children suffering from the hypo-secretion of this hormone remain dwarf. On the other hand, if the secretion of this hormone is more than normal, the height of the affected person is increased. In this state the person may achieve a height from 8 to 10 feet. This disturbance is called gigantism.

(5) *Pancreatrophic Hormone* : The only function of this hormone of anterior pituitary is to regulate the secretion of insulin from pancreas.

Influence of Anterior Pituitary

Anterior Pituitary gland affects human behaviour and personality in many ways. In fact, besides affecting the human behaviour directly, it affects it indirectly through the medium of other glands. As has been discussed above, abnormal activity of this gland affects the growth and height of the body. It is natural that the behaviour and personality of a person are affected because of his abnormal height. Besides it, this gland makes the person lethargic, angry or irritable through the medium of other glands.

(B) Posterior Pituitary Gland. Secretion of posterior pituitary gland is called pituitrin. It has three hormones whose functions are different. First hormone is called Oxytocin. It stimulates the contraction of smooth muscles of intestines and uterus. The second is called Anti-diuretic hormone. It helps the excretion of various substances from the body. This hormone regulates the level of water in the body. The third hormone is called Vasopressin which affects the autonomic nervous system and controls the blood pressure.

(C) Intermediate Pituitary Gland. The activity of this part of the Pituitary gland is concerned with the excretion of urine from the body. Its hormone controls the activity of urine excretion.

5. Pancreas Gland

Pancreas is located near the small intestine. It acts both as a duct gland and a ductless gland. Its outer portion is a duct gland. Its central portion is composed of group of cells, called Beta cells which have only endocrine functions. Their hormone is called Insulin. The hormone insulin has a unique role in body functions. Carbohydrates present in the body are burnt and sugar so converted is utilized by the cells of the body through the influence of insulin. If the level of sugar in the blood becomes high because of various reasons, then insulin converts this extra sugar into glycogen which gets deposited in the liver and muscles. Various body organs like brain are able to get a constant supply of sugar because of the influence of glycogen. Thus, the activity of the Beta cells of Pancreas regulates the sugar level in the human body.

Hypo and Hyper-Function of Pancreas

Abnormal activity of this gland has disastrous effects on body functions. Hypo-secretion of its hormone insulin increases the blood sugar level. In this state the amount of sugar in the urine of the person becomes high. This disease is known as Diabetes. The person gradually becomes weak in this disease. He may die if the disease becomes serious. For the treatment of this disease it is essential to lower the blood sugar level. For this purpose insulin injections are given to the person and the intake of carbohydrates in the diet is reduced.

In the state of Hyper-function, the amount of insulin secretion becomes high which results in the lowering of blood sugar level. The body does not remain normal. There are tremors and convulsions in the body. The person becomes restless from time to time. Glucose is given for the treatment of this disease.

6. Sex Glands or Gonads

Sex glands are also called gonads. These are known by different names in males and females. Female gonads are called ovaries and in males these are called Testes. Sperms are produced in the testes and ova in the ovaries. Besides these cells various hormones are secreted directly into the blood from these sex glands. These hormones are responsible for the sex characteristics typical of men and women. Main hormones from the male sex glands are Annrosterone and Testosterone. These hormones have three major functions in the body of males. First function is the normal development of male sex organs. Second function is the inhibition of mammary glands and other female characteristics in males. Third function is the development of other sex characteristics in males. In the case of female gonads, main hormones are Esterone and Progestin. Sex organs of females develop under the influence of Esterone. Menstrual cycle of females is also regulated by it. Growth of mammary glands and other sex characteristics are under its influence. Hormore Progestin has many functions in connection with the development of fertilized ovum in the female uterus.

Influence on Behaviour and Personality

Hormones of sex glands have special importance in human life. Sex characteristics of males and females develop under their influence. In the course of time a girl becomes a woman and a boy becomes a man because of the influence of sex glands. Attraction for the opposite sex develops in both males and females. Thus, the behaviour and personality of boys and girls changes suddenly. Abnormal activity of these glands not only interferes with the normal sex functions but also sometimes results in the development of bodily characteristics of opposite sex. The voice of a woman becomes hoarse, increase of hair growth takes place on her body and softness of body organs goes away. Similarly, the female body characteristics like growth of mammary glands may appear in males because of the disturbance in the activity of sex gland. Thus, the secretions of gonads have important influences on the behaviour and personality of human beings.

Nerve Physiology

In physiological Psychology, active researches are being done in the field of nerve physiology for the last many years. Hundreds of research papers have been published on this subject. But, still there are many problems which remain unsolved.

Nerve cell is the unit of nerve physiology. In this connection, structure of a cell has been explained by giving a diagram of a composite cell under the heading Response Mechanism. Types of cells — Receptors, Effectors and Conductors — have also been mentioned at appropriate place. A neuron has three parts — cell body, one or more dendrites and axon. There is an outer covering or membrane over it : Membrane is the key for understanding the functions of different parts of a cell.

POTENTIALS IN NEURONS

Each cell has an extra cellular fluid around it which is in direct touch with the cell membrane. This fluid is similar to the Intra-cellular fluid. Cell membrane acts as a semi-permeable membrane which allows certain types of ions to pass through it and not others. As a result different types of ions concentrate the two fluids on the two sides of the membrane. This gives rise to the potential difference across the

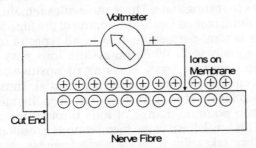

Fig. 21. Measurement of a resting potential

two sides of the membrane. Stimulation and conduction in the cell is ultimately because of the concentration of different types of ions on the sides of the membrane. A polarised membrane has been shown in Fig. 21. Negative ions are inside the nerve cell whereas positive ions are outside it. This gives rise to Resting Potential in the membrane. It can be measured with the help of a Voltmeter. Voltmeter is connected to the membrane by two electrodes — one electrode at the cut end of the nerve fibre and the other on the outside of the fibre. This procedure of measurement of resting potential is shown in Fig. 21.

The value of resting potential is from about 50 to 90 milivolts. Resting state of the cell is called the state of polarization. This state can be changed by any internal or external influence. This change is called depolarization. It decreases the irritability threshold of the nerve cell. When a stimulus is applied to the nerve fibre, depolarization results because of the disturbance in the equilibrium of ions on the two sides of the cell membrane. Ions from the outside enter in the membrane and disturbance gradually builds up and spreads to the neighbouring region. Resulting electrical change in the membrane is known as Action Potential. This is called nerve impulse. In the words of Freeman, "The nerve impulse is a term used to refer to a state of excitation or energy change in the neuron which is conditioned by some stimulating agent from without." Action potential creates complex changes in the distribution of ions. When the disturbance ends, polarization is re-established. In this state membrane permeability is mainly for potassium ions but in the state of disturbance or activity the permeability is mainly for sodium ions.

MEMBRANE THEORY OF CONDUCTION

First of all, in 1890, Ostwald gave membrane theory of conduction of impulse. Bernstein gave it a scientific form in 1908 on the basis of many experiments. Lillie did many new researches on this subject in 1920. Presently, this theory is considered as the most scientific of all theories given to explain the excitation and conduction of nerve impulse.

According to this theory, neuron is surrounded by the layer of various molecules in resting state. These molecules remain connected with a fatty compound named Lipid. Membrane of the fibre surrounded by the molecules is semi-permeable, that is, all types of ions cannot pass through it equally well. While potassium ions pass through it easily, sodium ions cannot pass. Entering of positive ions in the membrane results in a change in the electric potential. Thus, in resting state there are two layers of ions in the nerve fibre. Its membrane is broken at a certain point, exchange of ions through the membrane becomes easier. This breakdown of the membrane as a result of exchange of ions in the fibre takes the form of nerve impulse. According to Hathsway, "The rate of the conduction of the impulse is the rate at which the breakdown travels along the fibre." This theory is proved by measuring the rate of conduction of impulse.

MEASUREMENT OF CONDUCTION

Conduction of impulse can be measured with the help of an instrument called Galvanometer. Galvanometer records the changes of electric potential in the fibre in impulse conduction. Each impulse passing through the nerve fibre is of the same electric potential irrespective of the nature and intensity of the stimulus. When the fibre does not react, it is in the resting state. But when it reacts, it reacts fully. This partial reaction of the fibre is not possible. This law of reaction in the fibre is called All or None Law. Immediately after reacting, a nerve fibre does not react even when the stimulus is very strong. This duration is called Absolute Refractory Period. The time of this period is one thousandth of a second. Following it comes a period when the nerve fibre is excited by a relatively intense stimulus than before. This is called Relative Refractory Period. Number of impulses per second is more in the first condition than in the second. This is because of the Frequency Law.

Experiments in connection with nerve conduction have been done on the following two problems :

(1) Velocity of the nerve impulse.

(2) Electrical changes in conduction.

(1) Velocity of the Nerve Impulse. First of all in 1852, Helmholtz attempted to measure the velocity of nerve impulse. His aim was to find out the speed of conduction of impulse. Muller found in his experiments that the measurement of the speed of nerve impulse is difficult because its conduction is due to speed of electricity.

(2) Electrical Changes in Conduction. It has been explained earlier that action potential in the cell membrane is produced according to all or none law. Changes in membrane potential are maximum at the place of stimulation and these potential changes decrease as we go away from it. Thus, it is essential for exciting the nerve fibre that the intensity of stimuli should be up to its minimum threshold and time duration. Subthreshold stimulation cannot produce action potential in the nerve fibres. When the stimulation is over, the membrane returns to its original state of polarization. There arc different phases of excitability of a nerve fibre after the application of a stimulus. First of all there are local processes which denote subliminal excitation. Second is the phase of spike potential when the nerve impulse starts. Third state is called negative after potential whose value is less than the spike potential. It is a period of super normal excitability when the nerve fibre can be excited by a stimulus weaker than the normal strength. The last phase is that of positive after potential when the excitability of the neuron is subnormal *i.e.,* it needs a larger stimulus than the normal to it.

SENSORY AND MOTOR NERVOUS PATHWAYS

Pathways in the nervous system have been classified into two groups :

1. Sensory Pathways

2. Motor Pathways

Their description is given below :

1. Sensory Pathways

Sensory pathways are also called incoming, afferent or ascending pathways. Sensory pathways, as is clear by their name, bring sensations received by the receptors in different parts of the body, to various parts of the central nervous system. Sensory pathways go from the spinal cord to the brain. Following are their two main types :

(a) **Spino Thalamic Tracts.** As is clear by their name, these pathways go from spinal cord to the Thalamus. Fibres of the lateral group in these are of short and medium size. They transmit sensations of pain and heat. Starting from the lateral group they synapse in the proper sensory nuclei. And then crossing to the other side through the gray matter of the spinal cord they form posterior spine thalamic tracts. Some secondary fibres, without crossing to the other side, ascend through the same side. These are called uncrossed tracts. These also carry the sensations of pain and heat. Fibres in the middle group synapse in the cervical and basal nuclei of the gray matter of the spinal cord and crossing from the anterior commissure to the second part of the gray matter of the spinal cord, form ventral spino thalamic tract.

(b) **Spino Cerebellar Tracts.** It has also two parts — dorsal and ventral. Dorsal spino-cerebellar tract enters the cerebellum from restiform body or inferior cerebellar peduncle and in the end they terminate in the motor centre of the cortex. Mainly, these tracts do not cross the gray matter of the spinal cord. Thus, these tracts are uncrossed. On the other hand, ventral spino cerebellar tract is mainly a crossed tract. These tracts end by going to the dentate nuclei of cerebellum in brachium conjuctivium or superior cerebellar peduncle. In an over all way spino-cerebellar tract received sensations from muscles and cord of the fibres joining muscles with bones.

2. Motor Pathways

Following are the three types of systems in the brain concerned with balance, posture and movement :

(1) The pyramidal system.

(2) The extra pyramidal system.

(3) A system centring about the cerebellum.

Now pathways concerned with these three systems will be discussed respectively.

(1) **The Pyramidal System.** Included in this system are those motor neurons which originate from the cerebral cortex and go down to the brain stem and spinal cord. This is called the pyramidal system because pyramidal tracts going down cross in such a way that they form a pyramid-shaped structure as shown in Fig. 22. Some of the cells of this system in the cortex also happen to be pyramidal in shape, but it is just a coincidence. As it is a crossed system, activity in one side of the cortex produces movements on the opposite side of the body. The largest area of the pyramidal system is the motor area of the cortex, also called pre-central gyrus. Beside pre-central gyrus, pyramidal tracts also originate in the premotor area and in the post central gyrus.

These tracts go down to the ventral side of the medulla and make a pyramid shaped structure. These tracts go down in two main divisions — lateral cortico spinal tract and ventral cortico spinal tract. Lateral cortico spinal tracts cross in the medulla and go to the posterior side of the lateral bundle. Ventral tract cross in the cord and go to the medium bundle of spinal cord. All these fibres end in the multiple motor neurons. Nerve cells of the pyramidal system are long and covered by mylin sheath. These cells are found in layer 5 of the cerebral cortex. These tracts facilitate nerve cells in the spinal cord controlling specific activities.

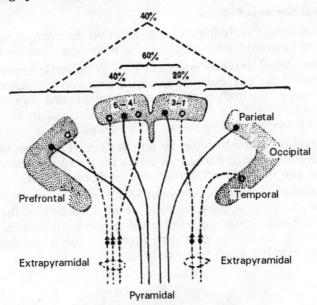

Fig. 22. Pyramidal and Extra-Pyramidal Motor Pathways in the Brain

(2) The Extra Pyramidal System. The pyramidal motor system is simple, whereas the extra pyramidal system on the other hand is quite complex. This system consists of all those descending pathways that originate in the cortex but are not contained in the pyramidal system. Many structures of the brain contribute to this system. It gets contributions from each of the four lobes of the cortex. The cortical areas of origin for the extra pyramidal tract overlap those of the pyramidal system. The pyramidal tract mainly starts from areas around the central sulcus, whereas the extra pyramidal tract mainly originates from areas somewhat forward of the motor area. Extra pyramidal tract also gets contribution from subcortical centres. Two important subcortical centres in this connection are Basal ganglia and Reticular formation. Rubrotegmento spinal tract originates from the Reticular nuclei. Two tracts are included in this group :

(a) *Medial reticulo spinal tract* : It starts from a centre near the medulla and ends in the spinal cord.

(b) *Lateral reticulo spinal tract* : It originates from a rectangular structure near the trigeminal nerve.

(3) System Centring About Cerebellum. The principal structure of the third system involved in the motor functions of the body is the cerebellum. It receives inputs from many senses and has reciprocal connections with the structures of both pyramidal and extra pyramidal system. An important tract of this system is the spino-cerebellar tract which starts from the spinal cord and ends in the cerebellum.

Peripheral Nervous System

Physiological Psychologists have classified the nervous system for the sake of convenience in study in the following three divisions :

(1) Peripheral Nervous System or PNS. Peripheral nervous system is that part of the nervous system which connects various receptors and effectors in the body to the brain and spinal cord. Its ganglia and nerve fibres lie outside the brain and spinal cord. In the present chapter this system will be discussed in detail.

(2) Cerebro Spinal Nervous System or Central Nervous System or CNS. As is clear from its name, this part of the nervous system consists of ganglia and nerve fibres of the brain and spinal cord.

(3) Autonomic Nervous System or ANS. This division of the nervous system consists of those ganglia which control the activity of the internal organs of the body. It functions independently from the central nervous system and in an autonomics way, therefore, the name Autonomic nervous system has been given to it.

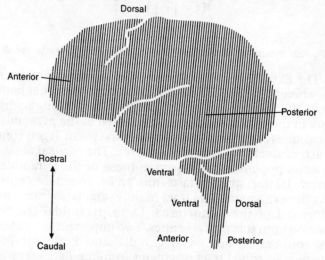

Fig. 23. Peripheral Nervous System

PERIPHERAL NERVOUS SYSTEM

Peripheral Nervous System includes all the ganglia (groups of cell bodies) and nerve fibres which lie outside the brain and spinal cord. Two types of nerves and ganglia are found in this system — (i) Cranial and (2) Spinal. The two parts are discussed below :

(A) **Cranial Nerves.** A cranial nerve is a nerve which arises from the brain itself. Defining these nerves Freeman writes : "Cranial nerves are those which put the CNS in communication with the peripheral parts and especialized receptor organs." Cranial ganglia are found in the recesses of the skull. There are 12 sets of cranial nerves. Some are sensory, some are motor and others have both sensory and motor functions. Thus, cranial nerves connect various receptors and effectors with the middle portion of brain. These are described below :

1. Olfactory Nerve. This nerve originates from the small receptors and carries information to the ventral part of the brain. Its main function is concerned with the sensation of smell.

2. Optic Nerve. This nerve originates from the optic nuclei of the thalamus. It carries visual impulses from the retina to the mid-brain. It serves the ganglion cells of the retina.

3. Oculomotor Nerve. This nerve is made up of motor fibres. It originates from the mid-brain and goes up to the eyeball and produces eye movement.

4. Trochlear Nerve. Fibres of this nerve also originate from the mid-brain and serve the eye muscles. These also function to produce eye movement like the oculomotor nerve.

5. Trigeminal Nerve. The trigeminal nerve has both sensory and motor functions, its sensory fibres originate from the medulla and carry the sensations from face, tongue and mouth to the brain. Motor fibres of this nerve originate from the mid-brain and pons and produce masticatory movements in the mouth.

6. Abducens Nerve. This nerve originates from the ventral part of the Medulla and serves the muscles of the eye. Like the III and IV nerve it is also concerned with the movements.

7. Facial Nerve. Fibres of this nerve originate from the medulla and reach the roof of buccal cavity and the outer surface of the lower jaw. It is also a mixed nerve *i.e.*, it has both sensory and motor functions. Its sensory fibres carry sensations from the roof of the buccal cavity and tongue. Its motor function is concerned with the control of facial movements and salivary glands.

8. Acoustic Nerve. It is purely sensory nerve. It originates from the medulla and reaches up to the semi-circular canals and cochlea in the inner ear. Its fibres have sensory functions in connection with hearing and sense of balance.

9. Glosso Pharyngeal Nerve. It has both sensory and motor functions. It originates from the medulla. Its sensory fibres carry impulses from the tongue and throat. In its motor functions it sends fibres to the throat and salivary glands and helps in swallowing.

10. Vagus Nerve. It is the most complex of all the cranial nerves. It has both sensory and motor functions. Its fibres originate from the medulla. It carries sensory impulses from the heart, blood vessels and viscera. In its motor functions it serves the smooth muscles of the viscera and striped muscles of the larynx.

11. Spinal Accessory Nerve. It is a motor nerve. It originates from medulla and sends efferent fibres to neck muscles and viscera.

12. Hypoglossal Nerve. This nerve also originates from medulla. It sends efferent fibres to the buccal cavity and muscles of the tongue.

Thus, it is clear from the above description that there are 12 cranial nerves and the majority of these nerves enter in the medulla. Whereas, some nerves are sensory and some are motor, there are other nerves which are mixed and have both sensory and motor functions.

(B) Spinal Nerves. Spinal nerves are more regularly arranged and more uniform in their action in comparison to the spinal nerves. There are 31 pairs of these nerves in man. They enter and leave the cord in the spaces between the spinal bones. Spinal nerves have been classified into the following five groups according to the part of the cord with which they are connected.

KINDS OF SPINAL NERVES

1. Cervical Region. It is situated in the neck. There are eight spinal nerves in this region.

2. Thoracic Region. This region is situated in the chest. There are 12 spinal nerves in this region.

3. Lumber Region. This region is situated in the middle of the body. There are five spinal nerves in this region of the cord.

4 Sacral Region. It is situated at the end of spinal column. Five spinal nerves enter in the region.

5. Coccygeal Region. This is the extreme end of the spinal column in the Rectum. Only one spinal nerve enters in this region.

Functions of Spinal Nerves

Motor portions of spinal nerves control all the striped muscles of the arms, legs, and body except the head and neck. Sensory portion has three main functions. It receives the sensory impulses from the tactual, thermal and pain receptors of the skin. Secondly, it receives the impulses from the receptors in the blood vessels. Thirdly, it receives the impulses from the pressure and pain receptors in the muscles, tendons and joints.

QUESTIONS FOR EXERCISE

1. Discuss the status of Physiological Psychology *vis-a-vis* Psychology and Physiology.
2. Show the relationship and difference between Psychology and Physiology.
3. Give a suitable definition of Physiological Psychology.
4. Give a brief survey of the important problems of Physiological Psychology.
5. What is Internal Environment? Explain its functions.
6. Write short note on — Metabolism of cells.
7. Explain in brief the processes of Intermediary Metabolism.
8. Give a brief introduction to the function and importance of the metabolism of Genes, Vitamins and Enzymes.
9. Discuss the process of Homeostasis in the body. What is Homeostasis?
10. Describe the stimulus response mechanism. How does it help in explaining human behaviour?
11. Write short note on — Cell and its functions.
12. Write short note on Primitive Response Mechanism.
13. What are Receptors? Discuss their kinds and locations.
14. What are Effectors? Discuss their kinds and locations in the human body.
15. What are the characteristics of Endocrine glands? Give a brief introduction to their important kinds.
16. Explain the various types of Nervous Pathways.
17. What is Peripheral Nervous System? Explain its different parts.

9

SENSATIONS AND SENSE ORGANS

Sensation is the first response of the organism to the stimuli. Its nature is clear from the following points :

(1) Comparatively Passive State. Sensations are not voluntary in the sense that we cannot produce them at will. They do not depend on our choice. They are, on the other hand, forced upon us by the environment. The sense organs passively receive sensations. Thus, sensation is a comparatively passive state of consciousness. This is amply clear by its comparison with perception.

(2) Partly Subjective and Partly Objective. Sensations form a part of individual's personal experience. Thus, they are subjective to that extent. On the other hand, they are also objective as they are answered by an external stimulus. Thus, sensation is partly subjective and partly objective.

(3) Distinction of Quality. Sensations differ in quality. For example, a sensation of sound differs from a sensation of colour in quality. Different sensations differ in quality.

(4) Distinction of Quantity. Sensations differ in quantity regarding intensity, duration and extensity. An example of the difference in quantity due to intensity is the difference between the loud sound of thunder and the soft sound of whisper. Duration depends on the persistence of the stimuli. As the persistence differs, so does the duration and with it the quantity of the sensation. Extensity *i.e.*, voluminousness depends upon the sensitive surface attended. As the affected surface increases so does the extensity, thereby making a difference in the quantity of different sensations.

(5) Relativity. Hoffding points out to relativity among sensations. A sensation is relative in three senses. Firstly, it is relative to other sensations in so far as its arousal depends on its contrast with other sensations. Secondly, as Weber's experiments have amply demonstrated, the quality of the sensation is also relative to other sensations. For example, if one handles ice first and then water, water will appear more hot than it does normally. Thirdly, the increase and decrease in sensation due to corresponding increase and decrease in stimuli is also relative to foregoing sensations. Thus, Hoffding has rightly said,

"From the moment of its first coming into being, the existence and properties of a sensation are determined by its relation to other sensations."

(6) Distinction in Traits. Different sensations have different traits. For example, the organic, spatial and motor sensations have different characteristics distinguishing them from each other.

(7) Special Sensations are Distinguishable. Special sensations are localized in the external world. They can be easily distinguished from each other.

ATTRIBUTES OF SENSATIONS

Sensations have different attributes. The main attributes have been classified into :

1. Quality
2. Intensity
3. Duration
4. Extensity
5. Local-sign

(1) Quality. Sensations differ in quality. Each sensation has its own quality. Sensations received through different sense organs differ in quality. Again, sensations received through the same sense organ also differ in quality. Different types of colour and taste exemplify this fact.

(2) Intensity. Different sensations have got different degree of strength or intensity. The intensity of a sensation depends upon : (a) the objective strength of the stimulus, (b) the mental state of the individual.

(3) Duration. The duration of a sensation depends on the continuity of the stimulus or of its effect. As this varies with different sensations their duration also varies.

(4) Extensity. Extensity meaning voluminousness or spread-outness of sensation is a spatial characteristic. As this increases, the sensation appears to be bigger, for example, the touch of a palm is more extensive than the touch of fingers.

(5) Local sign. Different sensations are distinguished according to the spot stimulated. This is local sign. It is because of different local signs that one can distinguish among the sensations, having the same quality and same intensity, duration and extensity. Thus, one can distinguish between two pin pricks simply because they are felt as two.

TYPES OF SENSATION

Sensation is the first response of the organism to the stimulus and is a step in the direction of preception. In practice, sensation is not separated from perception. This distinction is necessary in order to facilitate study. Ward expressed it thus : "Pure sensation is a psychological myth." Sensation is felt through the sense organs. We receive sensations through the eye, nose, tongue, skin and ear popularly known as the five sense organs. Apparently, there are many types of sensations but they can be divided generally in the following three categories :

(1) Organic sensations. (2) Special sensations. (3) Kinesthetic sensations. Special sensations correspond to the five sense organs *e.g.,* visual sensation, auditory, olfactory and tactual sensations and sensations of taste.

1. Organic Sensations. The sensations which arise from the conditions of the internal organs are known as organic sensations. They do not need any external stimulation. Hunger creates organic sensation caused by the contraction of the walls of the stomach. Similarly, thirst creates organic sensation which results from the drying up of a membrane located at the back of the neck. Obviously, these sensations indicate the internal conditions of the body and do not convey any knowledge of the outside world.

The organic sensations are of three types, this distinction being based on their location. They are :

(1) Sensations Whose Location can be Determined. Some organic sensations can be easily located. The experience of cutting, burning, blistering etc., is in the tissue. Its location is fixed.

(2) Sensations Whose Location is Undetermined. The position of some sensations cannot be determined. The position of comfort and restlessness are spread over the entire body and no particular part of the body can be assigned to them.

(3) Sensations Whose Location is Vague. Apart from the organic sensations, mentioned above, there are some more sensations about whose location we have a vague notion. We have a hazy idea of the general location of some sensations, like hunger, thirst, pain, though we do not know the exact location minutely.

Organic sensations are of considerable importance due to the role which they play in the affective and motivational aspects of life. Hunger and thirst make us restive and compel us to search for food and water.

2. Special Sensations. It has already been mentioned before that the special sensations are those which are caused by the specific sense organs eyes, nose, ears, tongue and skin. These special sensations can be clearly distinguished from one another. They originate from external stimuli like the waves of either, to mention only one.

Differences between Organic and Special Sensations

There are the following differences between organic and special sensations :

1. The source of special sensations is external stimuli while the source of organic sensations is internal.

2. There are specific organs for special sensations while there is no such provision for the organic sensations.

3. The special sensations give knowledge of the outside world, which the organic sensations do not.

4. The special sensations can be recollected with ease, but the organic sensations cannot be retained easily.

5. The special sensations can be distinguished clearly from each other. This is not the case with organic sensations.

6. It is possible to locate the special sensations while, in most cases, the location of organic sensations is not possible.

7. Special sensations are comparatively more intense in quality and quantity than the organic and motor sensations. The five special sensations are the following :

(1) Visual Sensations. Visual sensations, which are stimulated by light waves are experienced through the medium of the eyes. They are of two types — (i) Sensations of Brightness, (ii) Sensations of colour, of which the following four are primary — red, yellow, green and blue colour. Blind people do not feel these sensations.

(2) Auditory Sensations. These are received through the ears. They are the reactions of the ear to the vibrations in the air. Usually, the local symbol is absent in auditory sensations in which the power of discrimination is high. These sensations are important from the emotional viewpoint.

(3) Taste Sensations. It is the tongue which acquires these sensations. There are many papillae in the tongue. Mostly, there are taste pores in these papillae. There are bag-like structures called taste buds below taste pores, and they contain 10 or 12 taste cells. These taste cells are also the taste receptors. The sensation of taste passes through the taste pores and reaches the taste bud, whence the sensation is transferred to the brain. The result is the experience of taste. The central portion of the tongue cannot receive sensations of different tastes. The tip of the tongue acquires the sweet taste, the rear the bitter taste, the edges the sour taste, while the saline taste is spread uniformly all over the tongue.

(4) Olfactory Sensations. Receptor cells for the olfactory sensations are located in the nose at its apex. As only a part of the breath reaches them, it is necessary to draw a deeper breath in order to smell the odour. The odour carrying air, which is drawn in activates these cells by touching them. The sensation is carried to the brain and odour is perceived.

(5) Tactual Sensations. The skin contains the receivers of somaesthetic sensation. There are two types of sensations, include in somaesthetic sensations — cutaneous and kinaesthetic. Cutaneous sensations include the sensation of pressure, warmth, cold and pain. There are different areas for these sensations, interspersed with insensitive areas. The other type of sensations, kinaesthetic sensations, are felt in muscles, bones and various nervous joints and their covering membrane. These are related to the receivers. There are four types of cutaneous sensations *viz.*, pressure, warmth, cold and pain. They are different from each other and they have different areas of the body assigned to them.

3. Kinaesthetic Sensations. As is obvious from their name, these are the sensations related to motion. Tension, contraction, pulling etc., are examples of motor sensations. They are caused by the muscles, tendons and joints. The nerves embedded in these give the sensations of motivation when the muscles contract or the joints move. The brain receives information of these sensations through the sensory nerves whose fore parts are in the muscles, tendons and joints. The motor sensations put pressure upon the skin. These are as follows :

(1) Sensations of Position. Such a sensation is generated when the arms are motionless in a fully extended position.

(2) Sensation of Free Movement. If the arms are moved in all the directions, then the arising sensations are those of free movement.

(3) Sensations of Impeded Movement. These can be experienced by lifting some heavy weight.

Motor sensations are a means of the knowledge of the primary qualities of objects *e.g.*, their position, distance, direction, weight, etc. These sensations take place automatically and generally pass by unnoticed. They become conspicuous by their absence, if such a contingency is created by some defect in the body.

VISUAL RECEPTOR

The physical sensations of light from the environment are collected by the visual receiver cells located in the eyes. The eyes are connected to the diencephalon which is, in turn, related through the occipital lobes to the cerebral cortex.

Structure of the Eye

Observed from the outside, there appears to be an eye ball in each eye. There is an external covering whose fibres are rather tough and white. It is called the sclerotic coat. It protects the internal parts of the eye and preserves its shape. The foremost part of this coat is transparent and is called the Cornea. Below these there is another coat, called the Choroid coat. It is more of a network of blood capillaries than anything else. In the gap between the external covering and the lens, there is a coloured muscle called the iris. This assimilates the light falling upon the lens. The lens is the transparent cornea.

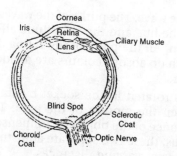

Fig. 24. Eye

The ciliary muscle accommodates the second lens, which is behind the retina. The eye focuses objects at various distances with the help of the ciliary muscles. The retina is a thin membrane stretched over the central part of the eye. It contains the sensory cells which are connected to the brain by means of the nerves. The space between the cornea and the lens and the retina is filled with a fluid which helps to keep the eye healthy. There are seven layers in the retina which contain various types of cells. They are linked to the optic nerve. The sensation of vision is caused by the light falling on the retina. On the retina, there is a spot called the fovea which is identical with the Iris. The vision is clearest when the light falls on the spot. This place where the optic nerves meet the eye is known as the blind spot.

Though the object is visible here, its shape is distorted. The given diagram illustrates the various parts described above.

Visual Receptor Cells

Having understood the structure of the eye, it will be easy to understand the visual receptor cells. This understanding will bring with it a knowledge of the process of seeing. The retina has two types of sense cells : cones and rods.

(1) **Cones.** These, located in the yellow and blue areas exclusively, number something like 70,00,000, in the entire retina. They are concentrated near the fovea. As the distance from the fovea increases, they grow less and become out-numbered by the rods. These cones are indispensable for colour vision and a person becomes colour blind if either they, or their sensory nerve's sensitivity decreases with the intensity of light.

(2) **Rods.** These sense cells assist in vision when the light is dim because their sensitivity increases with the decrease in the intensity of light. Being colourless, they work when the cones do not and that is when object is colourless. The change over to rod vision due to the fall in light intensity is called Purkinge Phenomenon.

How Do We See?

In seeing, light reaches the eye with the help of electromagnetic waves. The sensation of light depends upon the wavelength, purity and amplitude of the wave. The purity of the waves affects the saturation, the length affects the hue and the amplitude affects the brightness of the visual sensation. All the parts of the retina do not absorb colours and the areas which do absorb colours are divided into different parts for different colours.

The eye ball is rotated in the socket by six muscles. There is an adjustment between the motion of the eyes. The retina adjusts the light while the distance of the object is compensated for by the motion of the eye ball. Thus, these two separate adjustments make it possible for us to see objects at varying distances.

VISUAL SENSATION

Visual sensation is received through the eyes. When a certain object is presented before the eyes, light undulations rise from it and fall on the eyes. There are some chemical and physical actions along with the light undulations under which we get the visual sensation of that particular object.

Aspects of Visual Sensation

Three aspects which can be seen in the whole process are given below :

(1) Physical Aspect. According to physical science, every object reflects a special kind of light in a special quantity. The physical aspect of the sensation is formed by these light undulations on the visual stimuli.

(2) Physiological Aspect. As has been said before, when an object presents itself before the eyes it brings about a chemical change in the eyes which is carried to a special part of the brain for information. For an example of visual sensation, these very physical actions, working from the eyes to the brain, form its physiological aspect. The physical aspect can be seen in all the other sensations.

(3) Psychological aspect. Sensation includes not only the physical changes, but it also produces some mental processes. This process is the psychological aspect of sensation. In visual sensation, for example, many psychological actions are seen under the mixture and contrast of colours.

Stimulus of Visual Sensation

As has been said before, visual sensation is stimulated by the light undulations produced by an object. There are two kinds of sources for the production of this light and they are given below :

(1) Incandescent Source. The light produced by switching on the electric light in a dark room is called the light from an incandescent source.

(2) Inminescent Source. If there is phosphorus somewhere in a dark room, the light which is reflected from its gleam is called to have an inminescent source of production.

To define the speed of light undulations, physics has presented the undulatory theory. According to it, the light from an object, before it reaches the eyes, becomes refracted while passing through either which produces a kind of vibration in it. On account of this vibration, light is not received in a straight-line. It is received in the form of undulation or wave. There is seen a difference of length, and purity in different light undulations. The difference is given below :

(1) Difference of Length. The length of light undulations is measured with the help of a photometer in a millimicrone unit. There are 1,00,000 millimicrones in one millimeter.

(2) Difference of Amplitude. There is a difference of amplitude in the light undulations along with a difference of length, although uniformity of length does not mean uniformity of amplitude. Different amplitudes are seen in different undulations.

(3) Purity. Whereas some undulations are pure or similar there are other undulations of different length and amplitude and which, on getting mixed together, are called impure undulations.

The difference of light undulations, as explained above, can also be shown in the form of difference in quality, intensity and complexity. Quality is connected with length, intensity with amplitude and complexity with purity.

Characteristics of Visual Sensations

Some of the objects, which we ordinarily see, are coloured and some are colourless. For example, reddish is white but in water it appears colourless. In psychology, black and white and all the other colour shades falling between these two main colours, are counted among the colourless visual sensations. In psychology, while studying visual sensations, the cause of difference among them is also discovered.

Characteristics of Colours

From physical standpoint, differentiations in colours can be made on the basis of their special features, such as their kind, brightness and purity. A description of these special features is given below :

(1) Kinds of Colours. According to physics, the colour sensation of an object depends on the light reflected from it; and since the reflected light undulation is of different length under different stimuli, difference in colours is seen through them. How a particular length of light undulation will convey a particular colour sensation is shown in the list given below :

	Kinds of Colour	Length of light undulation	
1.	Violet	About 390 to 430	millimicrones
2.	Blue	About 430 to 525	do
3.	Green	About 525 to 590	do
4.	Yellow	About 590 to 650	do
5.	Red	About 650 to 760	do

Light undulations under 390 millimicrones in length convey a visual sensation. They are called ultra-violet rays. They produce a kind of chemical action in the eyes. On the other hand, a light undulation of more than 760 millimicrones in length imparts only a sensation of heat instead of a light sensation. This undulation is called infra red rays. In this way, the light undulations having a length of 390 to 760 millimicrones, can be seen with the eyes to possess one colour or the other. The sun light contains the light undulations of all lengths, and therefore, when they are analysed, they appear to contain all the colours.

Colours are divided into two classes, primary and secondary, according to difference in their kinds; but all the psychologists do not have the same opinion about the colours to be included in one class or the other. Hering has regarded red, green, yellow, blue, white and black as main colours. But most of the psychologists do not consider white and black as colours. On the other hand Helmholtz has regarded the three colours, red, green and blue as the only main colours and yellow colour has been regarded by him to be a mixture of red and green colours. Hering and Helmholtz have both regarded red, green and blue colours as the main colours. On the same understanding, Ladd-Franklin regards the four colours, blue, red, green and yellow as the main colours. Modern psychologists mostly agree with the opinion of Ladd-Franklin. In this way, most of the psychologists regard the four colours, red, yellow, green and blue as the main colours and the rest of the colours are obtained by mixing them. The pyramid formed with the help of these four main colours is called the colour pyramid.

On reaching the white point, all the colours lose much of their brilliance, and on reaching higher up, the colour sensation comes to an end. In the same way, the brilliance goes on decreasing in coming down to the black point and the colour sensation is ended by going down beyond this point. In this way, it is clear that along with an increase or decrease in the brilliance of a colour, its sensation undergoes a change. The light undulation on blue colour is the shortest and it is the longest on red colour.

(2) **Brightness of Colours.** It is a matter of common experience that brightness differs in different colours. For example, blue colour is brighter than violet, red colour is brighter than blue and yellow colours are brighter than blue one. In the same way, some yellow colours are

brighter than some other yellow colours. This brightness of colours is in proportion to their amplitude. It means that a colour will appear more bright with a higher amplitude and less bright with a lower amplitude. For a colour, to appear white, brown or colourless like black depends on the amplitude of the light sensations. The amplitude of the light sensation, in getting lower and lower, reaches a point beyond which the stimulus loses its colour and appears black. By increasing the amplitude of the light undulation of any colour, while maintaining the similarity of its length, a stage is at last reached when the particular colour is lost and begins to appear brown or black.

(3) **Saturation of Colours.** Some colours are deep while others are light. The deeper the colour, the purer it is regarded to be. On the other hand, the lighter the colour, the more impure it would be. Impure or opposite light undulations give rise to impure colour stimuli; while saturated or similar light undulations impart sensation of pure colour. In other words, if an object produces light undulations of different length and amplitude, its colour will appear to be deep and well saturated.

Colour Mixing

It is known from many experiments in physics that colour sensations are conveyed even by a mixture of light undulations of different lengths. For example, it is not necessary that for a sensation of yellow colour, the undulations from an object must be 600 millimicrones. Whatever may be the length of these undulations, if the average length of all of them is 600 millimicrones, it will impart a sensation of yellow colour. It has been seen from colour mixing that, when two different colours are mixed,

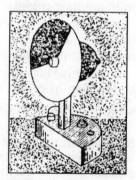

Fig. 25. Colour Mixing Apparatus

they impart a sensation of a third colour. Colour mixing apparatus helps to find out this fact in a laboratory. A picture of the same apparatus is given here. As is seen in the picture, plates of more than two colours are joined and adjusted to this apparatus. When the apparatus works, its axis rotates and along with it, the plates of different colours also rotate. When the speed at which the axis is rotating is slow, the colours appear separately; but when this speed is increased, there is seen a flicker in the colours. If this speed is increased still more, a third colour is seen in place of the flicker. This third colour is the result of a mixture of colours of the different plates. While the axis is rotating, two colours of the two plates stimulate the eye-lens at different places and this is the cause of the sensation of a third colour. This stimulus, working simultaneously, conveys a colour sensation similar to the average of lengths of both the light undulations.

Laws of Colour Mixing

By making experiments with the help of mixing apparatus, psychologists have found out the various laws which tell us how to obtain a new colour by mixing certain colours. Here it is necessary to bear in mind that some colours are complementary and some are non-complementary. A pair of red and green or of yellow and blue is an example of complementary colours. In each pair, each colour is complementary to the other. On the other hand, in both these pairs, any one colour is non-complementary to any one colour of the other pair. In this way, red is non-complementary to blue and green is non-complementary to yellow or red is non-complementary to yellow colour. The three established laws about colour mixing are given below :

(1) A sensation of brown colour is obtained by mixing complementary colours in a particular proportion, the brightness of which lies in the average brightness of both the colours.

(2) If two non-complementary colours are mixed in a particular proportion, a middle colour of both of them is seen. The brightness of this mixed colour is the average brightness of both — the non-complementary colours.

(3) A sensation of brown colour is obtained by mixing all the complementary colours i.e. by mixing red, green, blue and yellow in a particular proportion.

All the three laws, given above, about colour mixing can be verified with the help of colour mixing apparatus.

Flicker and Fusion of Colours

It has already been said that if the plates attached to the colour mixing apparatus are made to revolve in a low speed, the sensation from different colours is separate. The sensation of colours is called the flicker of colours. If the rotating speed of the colour mixing apparatus is increased, the flicker gradually ends; and the separate colours get mixed together after losing their separate existence resulting in the production of a new colour having a brightness similar to the average brightness of all the colours thus mixed. As has been said before a fusion of complementary colours gives a sensation of brown colour, whereas a fusion of a non-complementary colours gives a sensation of a colour in the middle of them. But, when the plates of both the kinds of colours, complementary and non-complementary, rotate at a low speed, there is a sensation of flicker. By decreasing and increasing the speed of the colour circle, the point, which indicates the limit of colour mixing, is found out. If the speed, at which the colour circle is moving is lower than this point, a flicker is seen; but when the speed is higher, the colours get mixed.

Visual Contrast

If you keep looking at a colour for a long time, and later begin to look at some colourless object, the colourless object will appear to have the colour shade of the coloured object. This psychological process is called visual contrast. The main kinds of visual contrast are given below :

(1) **Simultaneous Contrast.** In simultaneous contrast, as is clear from its name, the sensation of contrast is simultaneous to the stimulus *i.e.,* the stimulus and the contrast appear at one and the same time. There are two forms of this kind of visual contrast.

(a) *Simultaneous Chromatic Contrast.* If any two complementary colours are placed close to each other, their brightness increases all the more due to the visual contrast. For example, if a woman is putting on a red blouse with a green sari, the red colour of the blouse and the green colour of the sari will appear deeper red and deeper green respectively. This process is known as simultaneous chromatic contrast. The reason is that each colour in its circumference spreads a complementary colour and if this complementary colour is itself present, the brightness of the original colour is all the more increased. Only the complementary colours, on coming close together, affect each other, is not the fact. Even the non-complementary colours, when they come close together, affect each other, and a colour, formed through the mixture of both these colours, is seen on their sides.

(b) *Simultaneous Achromatic Contrast.* If an object of black or brown colour is placed on an opposite background, the brightness of its colour increases because the brightness of the background is added to the brightness of the object. For example, if two equally brown circles are placed separately, one on the white and the other on the black background, the circle placed on the black background will appear brighter than the circle which is placed on the white background.

The psychological fact at the root of visual contrast in colour sensation is that, if several stimuli join together to effect the eyes, a sensation of simultaneous achromatic contrast is produced through the interaction of these stimuli.

(2) **Successive Contrast.** Successive contrast, as is clear from its name, appears one after the other instead of appearing simultaneously. The sensation of visual contrast in this is not constant but rises at time intervals. In explaining successive contrast, some scholars point at the unconscious state and the mental images. In this connection, nothing has been said finally. Successive contrast is also called negative after image, because the negative after image in this is received a little after the colour sensation. The two kinds of successive contrasts are described below :

(a) *Successive Chromatic Contrast.* It is a matter of common experience that if an object is placed before us for sometime and then removed, its sensation stays for a few moments after it is removed. This sensation which stays even in the absence of the stimulus is known as after sensation. It has been seen from experiments that when a coloured object is seen for sometime and, after it is removed, the eyes are cast upon some colourless object, the colour, which we now see, is complementary to the colour of the first object. In this way, if the first object is red, green or yellow, the colour seen after its removal will be blue. This mental process is called successive chromatic contrast.

(b) *Successive Achromatic Contrast.* Another kind of successive contrast is achromatic contrast. For example, if the eyes are cast on the ground after looking at a white object, an image of a brown colour will be seen. Similarly, if eyes are cast on a brown background after looking at some black object an image of highly bright white colour will be seen.

Retinal Colour Zones

It has been found out through various investigations about different colour sensations in psychology that every colour has its own field in the eye lens, although these fields may not be separated from one another completely. These various colour spheres have individual specialities and differently impressed by the form, purity and brightness of the stimulus. The instruments, known as Campimeter and Perimeter, are used in studying the colour spheres. It has been found out through experiments that all the colours of all the parts of the eye-lens cannot be seen. Sensations of particular colours are received from particular parts. For example, brown and white colour sensations are received from the outer part of the eye-lens, blue and yellow from the middle part and all the colour sensations are received from the central parts the eye-lens. Outer and middle parts do not convey any other lour sensations except these definite colours. It does not mean that, if a particular colour is presented to any such part of the eye-lens which is not stimulated by that particular colour, there shall be no stimulation of any kind. Many important facts have been discovered in this connection by Baird in his studies. It has been found out that red colour appears yellow in the middle of eye-lens and brown in the outer part. If this colour is taken from the outer part to the centre, it gradually appears yellowish, yellow, orange-yellow, yellowish orange, orange-red and red in the end. It is clear that a colour in the outer part of the eye lens appears brown and its saturation goes on increasing when it is gradually taken towards the centre where it ultimately appears in its true colour.

Positive After Image

Negative-after-image has already been referred to while describing successive contrast. Its opposite image is the positive after image. Both the kinds of images are produced after the eye-lens is stimulated. If an object is attentively seen for some time and the eyes are closed, some particular image is still left with the closed eyes. This image can be positive as well as negative to the object seen. There is a negation of colour in the negative image; whereas in the opposite image, the colour and shape of it remain the same as that of the original object. But this opposite image is momentary and is not possible for all. After a few moments, it changes into a negative image.

Visual Constancy

Ordinarily it is quite logical that if an object is gradually taken away from the eye, its size should gradually go on decreasing; and its size should, similarly, go on increasing when it is taken nearer and nearer the eyes. But it has not been experienced always. It has been found out through experiments that, since there is no direct relation between the actual feeling of the object and its image on the eye-lens, its size remains stationary upto a fixed limit. This fact is true, not only about the size but about the colour, brightness and the form as well. It is called visual constancy. A description of its different forms will be worth referring here.

(1) **Size Constancy.** As has been said before, a constancy in the size of an object is seen only upto a fixed limit. An object appears small when it is taken away from this mixed limit and appears big when it is taken close to it. Here a change takes place in the image of the eye-lens but there is no change in the visual action.

(2) **Colour or Brightness Constancy.** Ordinarily, if an object is placed in the sun and in shade, there should appear a difference in its brightness in these two conditions. But it has also been seen that no change takes place in the colour and brightness of an object when it is removed from the sun to a shade. This fact is known as colour or brightness constancy. For example, if you see a crow in the sun and see it again when it has flown to a shade, its brightness will remain the same in both the conditions so far as the visual action goes, although there is a change in its brightness so far as its eye-lens image is concerned.

(3) **Shape Constancy.** Shape constancy means the constancy of the shape of an object like an egg, circle or a square etc. For example, we can see the tables of different shapes. It has been seen through experiments that if a circular object is taken away from the eye-lens gradually, its shape changes into the shape of an egg, but the object appears to be circular even though a change takes place in its eye-lens image. This process is called shape constancy or shape stability. Thouless, through his various experiments, has proved the stability of size and shape and has also thrown light on psychological causes at the root of this process. According to his opinion, even when the image of an object on the eye-lens is small, the object does not appear small when it is seen and it is because of the presence of the deformed image of that object. While describing the stability of colour or brightness, psychologists have maintained that the proportion of reflected light and unreflected light is stable in both, light and darkness. This proportion is called Albedo. Because of this albedo, only swan-white is seen in

both, light and darkness. In defining the stability of shape, the psychologists have taken the help of the correct test theory of the third dimension although it has not been able to clear the whole thing.

THEORIES OF COLOUR VISION

Different psychologists have presented different theories in explaining colours and none of the theories has been able to define colour sensation satisfactorily. The main theories in this connection are given below :

Young-Helmholtz Theory

This theory was presented by Thomas Young in 1801 and Helmholtz supported it in 1860. Since then, this theory is known after the names of both the scientists. In the Young-Helmholtz theory, red, green and blue are the three main colours. According to this theory, these three colours are seen, one after the other, in the retina through three kinds of cones as red, blue and green cones. Although these three kinds of cones are stimulated by a light wave of any length, but different light waves of specific lengths have specific effect on different cones. In this way, the effect of light waves of 600 millimicrones on red cones, of 500 millimicrones on green cones and of 400 millimicrones on blue cones is the greatest. A sensation also is received according to that cone which is stimulated by a wave of the specific length in the highest degree. For example, when a light wave of 400 millimicrones is produced, it affects the blue cone in the highest degree and consequently a sensation of blue colour is received. In the same way for another colour sensation also, the position, in which a specific cone connected with the specific colour is affected in highest degree, is necessary. Young-Helmholtz have explained the colourless and other colour sensations on the basis of these three cones. For example, sensation of white or brown colour is received in the position when some specific light wave stimulates the three cones in a similar degree. In the same way, a sensation of black colour is received from the light wave which does not stimulate any cone. Sensations of different colours are received when the cones of these three colours are stimulated in different proportions. A colour sensation is received in the same proportion in which the different cones are stimulated by a light wave. The colour cone, which is least affected, has no hand in the colour sensation. According to Young-Helmholtz, there is no cone in the eye-lens for yellow colour. The sensation of yellow colour is received when the cones of red and green colour are stimulated in a similar degree and in a less degree outside the blue cone.

Young-Helmholtz have explained colour mixture, after sensation, colour contrast and colour blindness in their theory of colour vision. For a complete understanding of this theory, it is worth-while to throw a little light on its explanation about these various processes.

(1) **Colour Mixture.** Young-Helmholtz have explained colour mixture on the basis of brain actions and, therefore, it is also called Central Theory. According to this theory, the nervous impulses, originated from different cones, are of one and the same kind. They differ only when they reach the brain. Colour mixture is, therefore, not the result of any action in the eye-lens. It takes place in the brain. To prove their theory, Young-Helmholtz have presented evidences from binocular colour mixture when red and green colours are presented before an instrument known as stereoscope, at one and the same time, a sensation of yellow colour is received. Similarly, when two complementary colours present themselves before this instrument, the sensation of brown colour is received. The colour mixture is done through the central nervous system. The explanation of yellow and white colour sensations, advanced by this theory, does not appear satisfactory through experience or any process of argument. For example, according to the explanation of other colours, when yellow and red cones are stimulated, there should be a sensation of greenish red or reddish green, but it is not seen like that in actual experience. Thus, when all the three cones are stimulated, there should be a colour sensation of the shades of all the three colours *i.e.*, red, green and blue and not of white colour. But this is not seen in experience. In this theory, it has been taken for granted that a wave of any length stimulates every cone, more or less. If this theory is taken to be correct, there should arise sensations of all the colours in all the parts of the eye-lens, but as has been written before, there arise sensations of only blue and yellow colours from the middle sphere of the eye-lens. In this way, according to the Young-Helmholtz theory, the explanation of the colour sphere of the eye-lens is not appropriate.

(2) **After Sensation.** In the Young-Helmholtz theory, both the kinds of sensation, positive and negative, have been taken into consideration. According to this theory, when a certain stimulus affects some specific cone of the eye-lens too much, its colour sensation stays for some time even after the removal of that stimulus. This sensation is called positive after sensation. There is one defect in this definition of positive after sensation. It has been forgotten here that positive after sensation is the result of a momentary appearance of the stimulus. It has been given in the definition of the theory of negative after sensation that when some cone is kept stimulated for sometime by any kind of wave, its strength is reduced in comparison to other cones resulting into colour sensation similar to those of the other cones. For example, if red cone is not stimulated for a long period of time by some light wave, it will get tired; whereas green and blue cones will become more active, and this will result in a sensation of bluish green. In brief, in this theory, the definition of negative after sensation is made on the basis of tiresomeness, but, in practice, it is seen that a few moments after the stimulus presents itself, negative after sensation is seen. It is

difficult to believe that the cones of the eye-lens get tired in so short a time.

(3) **Colour Contrast.** Young-Helmholtz have regarded the doubts created with some personal reasons to be the cause of contemporary opposition. For example, blue and yellow colours, when they are presented separately, appear to be brighter in comparison to what is seen ordinarily due to past experience. In this process, the past experience of the person works unconsciously. One defect in this definition of colour contrast is that it has neglected the fact that a past feeling does not help in increasing the sharpness of some present feeling but only creates an obstacle.

(4) **Colour Blindness.** According to Young-Helmholtz, the defect of complete colour blindness is seen in a person when all these cones in his eyes are either absent or have become weak. If a cone of some specific colour is weak or absent, a colour blindness for that specific colour is seen in him. The defect in this definition of colour blindness is that it does not tell us as to why a person, who is blind for some specific colour, becomes colour blind for its complementary colour. According to this theory, the blindness for blue colour should be taken to be the result of a weakness of the blue colour cone. Then how does it create colour blindness for the yellow colour? It is thus clear that this definition of colour blindness is not satisfactory.

It is clear from the above explanation of the Young-Helmholtz theory about the definitions of various visual processes that this theory is satisfactory.

Hering's Theory

Keeping in mind the defects of the Young-Helmholtz theory, Hering presented a new theory about the visual sensation which is known after his name. According to Hering, there are six main colours. They are red, green, yellow, blue, white and black. These six colours can be put in pairs of two each. These pairs will be red and green, yellow and blue and white and black. One colour is complementary to the other in every pair among them. According to Hering, there are three kinds of chemical fluids in our eye-lenses, every one of which is connected with the two kinds of colour sensations. In this way, three fluids are found in the eye-lens connected with the colour sensations of red and green, yellow and blue and black and white. Due to these three fluids, the colour sensations of the three pair connected with them are received. In every chemical fluid, sensation of one colour is received as a result of anabolic process and sensation of the other colour is received as a result of catabolic process. For example, among the three pairs mentioned above, the sensations of red, yellow and white colours are gradually received due to the catabolic process and the sensations of green, blue and black colours are due to the anabolic process. Although all the kinds of light waves stimulate all the fluids, yet this stimulation takes place in different quantities through the light waves of different lengths in different fluids. For example, the light wave, which impresses the blue and yellow fluids, does not impress the white and black fluid to the same extent. Hering has regarded red and yellow as the hot colours and all the rest as cold colours. He considers the sensation of black colour as the natural light of the eye-lens. According to him, there is a feeling of black colour in the absence of stimulus. In Hering's theory, there are three kinds of nervous impulses on the basis of three kinds of chemical fluids. But other physiologists see no difference in the nervous impulses produced in the eye-lens.

Like Young-Helmholtz, Hering also has explained colour mixing and colour sphere, after sensations, colour contrast and colour blindness.

(1) **Explanation of Colour Mixture.** As has already been said, Hering acknowledges two kinds of actions in every chemical fluid anabolic and catabolic. Whenever both these actions take place together, there is a sensation of brown colour. This is an example of the mixture of complementary colours. In the same way, Hering has explained a mixture of non-complementary colours separately. According to Hering's opinion, when two non-complementary colours are placed together, they produce specific action in the related fluids, as a result of which a sensation of the middle of both the colour is received. For example, if the green and blue colours are mixed, anabolic action begins in both the fluids, red-green and yellow-blue and sensation of a colour in the middle of those colours is received.

(2) **Explanation of After-sensations.** Like Young-Helmholtz, Hering has also explained both the kinds of after-sensations-positive as well as negative. According to him, when we see an object, the synthetic action in it becomes weak so that, when we attend to some brown or white background after removing our attention from that object, a positive after sensation is the result. Hering's explanation of the positive after sensation is not regarded appropriate. While explaining the negative after-sensation, Hering has said that the tendency to maintain the equilibrium of the eye-lens is the cause of it. For example, as has been said before, a feeling of colour from the red and green fluids is due to the catabolic action. Now, if the eyes are removed from the red colour and are cast on a brown base, catabolic action, according to the tendency of maintaining equilibrium, is stopped and the anabolic action begins, as a result of which, a sensation of green colour from a brown base is obtained. Most of the psychologists accept Hering's explanation about the negative after sensations.

(3) **Colour Contrast.** Hering has explained colour contrast on physical grounds. According to his theory, whenever a contrast in action begins in part near the eye-lens, we get a sensation of contemporary colour contrast in its consequence. For example, catabolic action works in a sensation of red colour : whereas anabolic action works in a sensation

of green colour which is close to red colour. On account of the presence of these actions, contrasting among them, a sensation of colour contrast is produced. This explanation of colour contrast does not appear satisfactory according to the contrast explained with reference to the Young-Helmholtz theory given above.

(4) **Colour Zones.** According to Hering, sensations of all kinds of colours and brightness are produced in the eye-lens because it contains all the three kinds of fluids. White-black and yellow-blue fluids are found in the middle sphere and sensation of blue-yellow colours is felt. In the outer sphere of the eye-lens there is a sensation of white, black or brown colours alone because it contains the fluids of these colours only. In Hering's theory the question as to how contrasting actions are produced on the stimulations of only one fluid has not been explained properly. In the same way, even if it is accepted that in a position of stimulation, the receiving cell is weak, it cannot be accepted that it has an anabolic action.

(5) **Colour Blindness.** As has been said before, Hering has regarded the absence of visual fluids, connected with specific colours, as the cause of colour blindness. This supposition does not explain the fact why some people are blind for white-black. The theory which has been applied to explain the blindness of the colours does not explain the blindness for white-black colours.

Nonetheless, Hering's theory about-visual phenomena ordinarily appears more satisfactory than the theory of Young-Helmholtz and it is a further step towards a proper direction.

Ladd Franklin Theory

After Hering, Ladd Franklin theory about visual actions was presented in which a synthesis of both the above theories was attempted. Ladd Franklin has explained the colour sensations from evolutionary viewpoint. According to him, receptors of the eye-lens received only white and black in the beginning. Then they evolved gradually and reached a stage where even the blue and yellow colours could also be received in the eye-lens. Gradually after this second stage of evolution, red and green receptors were seen in the third stage. In this way, three kinds of receptive cells are gradually formed in our eye-lens through evolution. Ladd Franklin took the help of evolutionary theory in explaining different colour zones of the eye-lens. According to his opinion, the outer zones of the eye-lens developed in the first stage of evolution, middle zone in the second and the central zone in the third stage of evolution. There is no colour sensation in the first zone, in the second there is a sensation of blue and yellow colours and in the third zone there is a sensation of all the colours. Even in the explanation of colour sensations, Ladd Franklin has maintained the evolutionary viewpoint. According to his opinion, there are four main colours — red and green, yellow and blue, and there are four kinds of chemical fluids similar to these four colours. When an object of specific colour is presented before the eye-lens a reaction in the chemical fluid connected with that colour takes place and consequently the specific colour is formed. Then gradually all the different colours get mixed and take the shape of a new colour. For example, there is a sensation of yellow colour in the presence of red and green fluids. Yellow and blue both together make the brown colour. In the absence of light stimulus there is a sensation of black colour. In this way, Ladd Franklin, instead of regarding colour mixture and colour contrast as central, regards them as related to the eye-lens. According to this opinion, when a person is in the first stage of colour sensation, he cannot tell the difference in colours. This explanation of colour sensation is not correct. Ladd Franklin's explanation about after-sensations and organisation is originally similar to Hering's explanation. In explaining colour blindness, Ladd Franklin has said that the colour receptor fluid, which is not developed completely, produces colour blindness connected to it. If not even a single chemical element is developed in any person, that person is completely colour blind. A great defect in Franklin's explanation of colour blindness is that it is not proved through evidences.

In all the three theories given above about visual actions, only the first *i.e.*, Young-Helmholtz theory is, on the whole, more acceptable, because, in comparison to other theories, very little help from simple concepts has been taken in it. Amendments are constantly being made in this and it will take a little more time to become fully satisfactory.

PURKINJE PHENOMENA

A person named Purkinje was the first to discover that by going from light to darkness and from darkness to light there is a change not only in the cones and rod vision in the eyes but even the sensation of the brightness of colours undergoes a change and becomes just the opposite. In this way, green colour appears the brightest in pitch-dark and yellow colour appears the least bright. On the contrary, yellow colour appears the brightest in a dazzling light and the green appears the least bright. Since Purkinje was the first person to discover this change in the sensation of colour brightness and in cones and rod vision, it is called Purkinje phenomena.

AUDITORY SENSATIONS

The ear is a mechanical receptor of sensations which are of a mechanical nature. The ear with which we hear has three parts :

(1) **External Ear.** This includes all that we can see from the outside, even the opening. The thin membrane in the eardrum separates the external ear from the middle ear.

(2) **Middle Ear.** There are three small bones in the Ear ossicles, which are called the Hammer, Anvil and Stirrup, respectively, so termed because of their shape and function. The hammer and anvil work like

a hammer and anvil respectively, while the part known as the stirrup is shaped like a stirrup. The middle ear is linked with the throat through the Eustachian tube.

(3) **Inner Ear.** The inner ear located in the Ear cavity has three parts : Vestibule, Cochlea and Semicircular canals. The vacant space surrounding these parts is filled with fluid called perilymph. At one end of the vestibule there is an elliptical opening covered by a membrane connected with the stirrup of the middle ear. The tube of the cochlea is connected with the vestibule. This cochlea tube is filled with another kind of fluid, closely related to the act of hearing. In the cochlea, there is an organ called the organ of corti, which is placed on the internal membrane. There are hair cells in the organ of corti, which are connected to the auditory nerve fibres. The semicircular canals are meant more for the balance of the body than for hearing.

How Do We Hear?

The act of hearing involves all the parts of the ear which have been elaborately described above. The first step is the vibration of the tympanic membrane of the external ear. The hammer is put in motion as a result of this disturbance, and the motion is transmitted through the anvil to the stirrup. The agitation passes through the elliptical opening and puts pressure on the fluid in the internal ear. By the time it reaches this point the pressure of the sound wave is magnified 30 times. The pressure on the liquid actuates some local action and disturbs the hair cells in the cochlea.

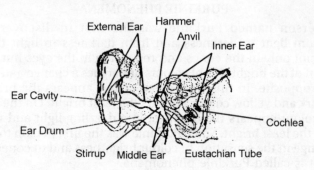

Fig. 26

After the necessary analysis, the sensation reaches the parietal lobes by passing through the auditory nerves. The external ear contains a wax-like substance whose function is to protect the tympanic membrane from high frequency sound waves.

THEORIES OF AUDITION

In explaining the actions connected with audition, different psychologists have presented different theories. Materially, there are three kinds of these theories — place theory, frequency theory and volley theory. All three kinds of theories will be explained here.

(1) **Place Theories.** Helmholtz was the first to present the place theories about audition. He has explained the actions of audition on the basis of the construction and work of basilar membrane. Basilar membrane is a membrane which, by separating tympanic canal from the cochlea canal, forms a boundary between them. Just as the wires in a piano have different lengths and a specific tune is heard from each of them, in the same way the length of fibres goes on increasing in the basilar membrane in advancing from the base towards the apex so much so that the length of apex fibres is threefold of the base fibres. On account of this structural difference, all the fibres of the basilar membrane are not equally impressed by all kinds of repetitive sound waves : specific fibres are impressed by respective waves and consequently produce a specific kind of pitch. Because of a similarity in the structure of piano and the basilar membrane, some scholars also call the place theory of auditory sensation as piano theory. According to this theory, the sharpness of a sound depends on the portion of the basilar membrane stimulated by it. The larger is the portion of the basilar membrane stimulated by a sound, the quicker will be the sound sensation from it. In the same way, the more a sound stimulates some specific portion of the basilar membrane, the more will be its pitch.

The place theory about the auditory sensations has been proved to be true through various experiments. It is known through certain investigations that the deafness of high pitch is due to some defect in the ground sphere of the basilar membrane, and the deafness of low pitch is due to some defect in the apex of the basilar membrane. It is thus clear that different pitches are connected to different portions of the basilar membrane. It has been seen, in the same way, that by stimulating the ear of some animal by high repetitive sound waves, the ground sphere of its basilar membrane is hurt.

Even then, it cannot be concluded from the above experiments that there is a complete and definite relation between the repetition of sound waves and the place of the basilar membrane. As a matter of fact, some motion or the other is seen in all the fibres of the basilar membrane on presentation of some one wave or the other. In other words, although all the fibres do not respond to sound waves in one and the same manner, yet a repetitive sound wave, instead of stimulating some specific part of the basilar membrane, spreads all around. It is clear that a pitch of a specific repetitive sound depends on those specific fibres which are stimulated by it in the highest degree even though its influence, instead of being limited by them alone, spreads to all the other fibres. Forbes and Gregg in 1915, ascertained through their experiments that the decision about the pitch of some sound wave depends on those fibres which are impressed by it and send the greatest number of nervous impulses to the brain. In this way, along with an increase in the sharpness of the stimulus, the repetition of reaction also goes on increasing. It has been found out from some other experimental studies that the place theory about the auditory sensations is true to a great extent. When the other ear is stimulated by some sound wave, there is an electric reaction. This reaction was diagrammatized with the help of electrode. This diagram showed that this electric reaction was produced by increased repetitive sound waves in the base sphere and by decreased repetitive waves in the apex. It is, thus, proved that there is surely some connection between the repetitive sound wave and the different places in the basilar membrane.

(2) **Frequency Theory.** Rutherford was the first to present in 1886 the frequency theory about the auditory sensations but in 1918, Wrightson explained it in detail and presented it in a scientific way. According to frequency theory, sharpness of the sound and the pitch were explained in a method different from that in the place theory. Against the place theory, the advocates of the frequency theory are of the opinion that there is no specific relation between the sharpness of the sound and different place in the basilar membrane, because every sound wave impresses the whole basilar membrane and not any specific part of it. When the basilar membrane is vibrated by a sound wave, an action in the fibres of the basilar membrane is produced. This action creates nervous impulse and pitch depends on its frequency. The more the frequency of a sound, the more is its pitch; and in the same way, the less the nervous impulse created by a sound, the less is its pitch. There is a close relation between the frequency of nervous impulse and the number of circles of a sound wave. The greater is the number of circles of a sound wave, the greater will be the nervous impulse produced on the basilar membrane. The less is the number of circles of a sound wave, the less will be nervous impulse produced on the basilar membrane. The greater is the number of fibres of the basilar membrane impressed by a sound wave, the greater will be the sensation of the sharpness of that sound wave. In the same way, if a sound wave stimulates a small number of fibres, the sharpness of a sensation in that sound wave will be very little. According to frequency theory, the outer part of the ear works like telephone exchange or radio broadcasting centre. The outer part of the ear sends to the brain, through auditory nerve, a nervous impulse of the same frequency as the number of circles of a wave which impresses it. Thus, according to this theory, auditory sensation depends on the brain action and not on the place of the basilar membrane.

According to frequency theory, every fibre in the basilar membrane is impressed by every circle of the sound wave and sends the nervous impulse to the brain. Now, if this ordinary fact, that we can hear through our ear the sound waves of 20,000 circles in one second, is borne in mind the number of nervous impulses going from the ear to the brain should also be 20,000 per second. If it is so, the refractory period must be .05 per second; whereas it has been proved through experiments that this period should be at least 1 M per second which means that any single fibre of the basilar membrane can send to the brain 1000 nervous impulses at the most in one second. It is, thus, clear that frequency theory is not proved through facts.

(3) **Volley Theory**. Waver and Bray presented the volley theory after amending the frequency theory. It has been accepted in this theory that the fibres of the basilar membrane do not react in proportion to the number of the sound circles, specially when the frequency of sound circles is too much increased. The fibres of the basilar membrane, on being stimulated by an increased sound circle, are impressed by a third or fourth wave and not by every wave. On the other hand, if the frequency of sound circles is decreased, sound impulses in them are surely produced. When the sound circles come to a definite number, all the fibres of the basilar membrane are active together at one and the same time, but the sound circles, increased beyond the limit, act on being divided in groups.

For example, all the fibres, after they are impressed by sound circles of 800 per second, are active together at the same time. When the number of sound circles is more than this, fibre groups are active. This theory has taken the help of the volley frequency in explaining sound or pitch. According to this theory, auditory actions depend, not on the frequency of nervous impulses through fibres, but on the volley frequency. When a great sound is produced, there are many spurts in the nervous impulse in the ear, in every one of which there is a sensation of a sharp sound because of the existence of an increased nervous impulse.

All the above three theories about auditory sensations have their own special importance. The place theory explains a sharp auditory sensation successfully. Volley theory is the refined form of frequency theory and explains the auditory sensation of the sound waves of an increased frequency. None of these theories is fully satisfactory. Some psychologists have, therefore, presented some other theories. No such theory in this direction could yet be presented as could be regarded fully satisfactory for lack of sufficient study and investigation in this field. Among modern theories, psychological theory of a psychologist, named Watt, about the auditory sensations is worth mentioning. In this theory, while keeping psychological point in view, physiological and physical facts have not been neglected. It is needless to say that in a satisfactory theory about the auditory sensations, psychological aspects, along with physical and physiological aspects, are very necessary to be kept in mind.

AESTHESIOMETRIC INDEX

Psychologists have made experiments to know the least distance which should be there between two points of tangency in order that the subject may feel both the points. Aesthesiometer is applied for this test. The least distance between two points of tangency, as discovered through this instrument, is called Aesthesiometric Index. Weber has called it difference limen. It has been found out through experiments that the difference is different in different parts of the threshold body. According to Volkman, aesthesiometric index depends on the movability of a particular part of body. It was discovered through Weber's experiments that, whereas there is a perception of two points of tangency on the tip of the tongue only from a distance of one millimeter : for a perception of two points on the back, a distance of 40 to 60 millimetres between them is sometimes required. Goldschider and Bonfray, through their experiments, found individual difference in aesthesiometric index. One individual gets a perception of two points in a short distance on the same part of the body, whereas another individual needs a greater distance for it. Even then, the psychologists, through various experiments, have reached a common result which clearly shows the aesthesiometric index of different parts of the body. It has also been seen that vertical aesthesiometric index is different from the horizontal aesthesiometric index. Then again, if a part of the body is touched at two points at the same time or is stimulated in turns, aestbesiometric index is different in both the situations. It is generally greater in the second condition than in the first condition. The habits of the subject also effect aesthesiometric index. Habits help to decrease it somewhat but this decrease is possible only to some limited extent after which no further decrease is possible, however much he may habituate. Besides this, the aesthesiometric index gets decreased also in other arts, similar to the part of the body, aesthesiometric index of which gets decreased by habituation. Physical conditions also have their effect on aesthesiometric index. It gets increased in conditions of being drunk or tired. In the same way, it gets increased in case of some physical injury, pain, disease or a low temperature. It decreases in hot atmosphere. The following list will indicate aesthesiometric index of different parts of the body :

Physical Part	Aesthesiometric Index
Tip of the tongue	1 Millimeter
Tip of the finger	2 M. M.
Outer part of the lip	5 M. M.
Nose	7 M. M.
Inner part of the lip	20 M. M.
Back of the palm	32 M. M.
Foot	40 M. M.
Arm and thigh	68 M. M.

Psychologists differ in their opinion about the basis of aesthesiometric index. As has been said before, Lotze has presented the theory of Local Sign. It has been accepted by most of the psychologists but it is not fully adequate.

QUESTIONS FOR EXERCISE

1. What is the nature of sensation? What are its attributes?
2. What is sensation? Illustrate its types, corresponding receptor organs and stimulus objects.
3. State fully the various characteristics of sensation. State also what you understand by local sign.
4. What are the main kinds of sensation?
5. Write short notes on organic sensations. Define sensation. Explain briefly the different kinds of sensations.
6. Describe the structure of the eye and explain how colour vision arises.
7. Describe the theories of visual sensation. Explain light and darkness adjustment.
8. State and explain the laws of colour mixture.
9. What is a contrast? Explain the determinants of achromate and chromate contrast.
10. Explain colour contrast.
11. Write note on visual constancy. Explain fully the phenomena of colour constancy.
12. Which of the theories of colour vision explains the main facts of colour vision satisfactorily? Explain how?
13. Examine critically the Young-Helmholtz theory of colour vision.
14. Write short note on Purkinje Phenomena.
15. Make a diagram showing the tympanic membrane, the ossicles, the semicircular canals and the cochlea in the apparatus of the ear and the particular functions of each of these parts.
16. Give an account of auditory sensations and their stimuli. How can we locate the source of sound?
17. Describe the attribute of auditory experience. Show that they are dependent on stimulus characteristics.
18. What are the various theories of audition?
19. Define aesthesiometric index. Describe the experiment performed by you to determine aesthesiometric index.

10
NERVOUS SYSTEM

CENTRAL NERVOUS SYSTEM

Central nervous system is a very important structure of our Response Mechanism. It can be divided into two main parts — (1) Spinal cord and (2) Brain.

Spinal Cord

Spinal cord is situated in the body case of spinal column. It is a soft structure like a rope. Its outer surface is made up of white matter. This outer matter has a thick layer. Two types of nerves join the spinal cord — (1) Sensory or afferent nerves and (2) Motor or efferent nerves. These nerves connect spinal cord with the receptors and effectors. Sensory nerves carry the sensations from receptors to the spinal cord and motor nerves carry the information from the spinal cord to the muscles. Receiving of sensations and sending out of motor impulses are mediated by the gray matter on the inside of the spinal cord. In the 50 per cent portion of the spinal cord is gray matter and the rest contains white matter. In the middle portion of the spinal cord are cell bodies, whereas conduction paths are found in the peripheral portion. Ascending and descending tracts are found in its white matter. Associative neurons lie in the gray matter of the spinal cord.

Functions of Spinal Cord

Spinal cord is the centre of integration of reflex action. In reflex action sensory nerve carries the sensation to the central nervous system and motor nerve brings message from the central nervous system to the muscles and muscles do the activity. This action happens so quickly that it takes only a very brief time. Besides integrating reflex actions spinal cord connects the outer organs of the body with the brain. 31 pairs of spinal nerves join the spinal cord from the outer organs. Each pair has one sensory nerve and one motor nerve. These nerves connect the spinal cord with the outer parts of the body. Thus, the activities of outer organs of the body (below the head) like hands and feet are controlled by the spinal cord. Many learned activities like writing, typing, playing on a harmonium, wearing clothes, walking etc. are controlled by the participation of spinal cord.

Besides the spinal cord, the brain is the second principal part of the central nervous system. Position, size and different parts of the human brain have been shown in the figure given below.

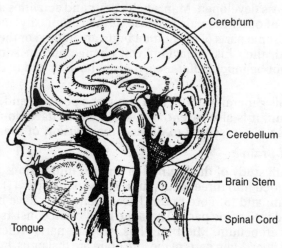

Fig. 27. Different parts of Brain

Brain has very important functions in human behaviour. This part of the central nervous system is an important and higher centre for various connections in the body. Some nerves do not enter the spinal cord. These nerves enter the central nervous system through the brain. Some impulses travel between the spinal nerves and cerebral cortex. Conduction of these impulses also takes place through the brain. Thus, there are many higher centres in the human brain which control and integrate various activities of the body.

Position and Structure of Human Brain

The position of brain in human body is specially protected. It is situated in the bony case of the skull. Below it lies the spinal cord. The structure of the brain is highly complex. Various types of neurons in their groups lie in this region of human body. If seen from above, it looks like a pea nut.

Its upper surface has deep lines on it called fissures. Because of these fissures the outer surface becomes convoluted. Generally, the weight of the human brain is about one pound. Its colour is white and gray. These two colours are because of two different substances in it. In the gray matter of human brain are mainly the cell bodies whereas in the white matter are present the nerve fibres.

It has been stated above that the structure of human brain is very complex. In fact, this high complexity of human brain makes a human being different and higher than other animals. This complexity of human brain is responsible for the typical intellectual activities of a man. Human brain is not only complex but also highly developed. On the other hand, brains of birds and other animals are relatively simple and much less developed. Man's behaviour and activities are different from those of other animals because of the complexity and growth of his brain. If some parts of the human brain are injured or their functions are blocked, then his behaviour will change and in some respects there will not be much difference in his behaviour and in that of other animals.

After this general introduction about the position and structure of human brain, it is also essential to know about its various parts. For this purpose it is essential to discuss the division of brain.

Division of Brain

For a full study of the brain, it is divided into various parts. Brain may be divided into three main parts. These parts are : (1) Hind brain, (2) Mid brain and (3) Fore brain. These main parts have been further sub-divided into some parts. Thus, the hind brain consists of medulla, pons and cerebellum. Mid brain has two sub-parts which are called rectum and floor. Main parts of the fore brain are thalamus, hypothalamus and cerebral hemispheres.

In a second type of classification the brain has been divided into five parts. This classification is based on embryology. Morgan and Stellar have given this classification. These authors have divided the three parts mentioned earlier into five parts. The aim of this classification is to simplify the study of brain. In this classification, each of the two parts in the first classification — Hind Brain and Fore Brain — have been further divided into two parts. Thus, in total there are five parts of the brain whose names are as follows : (1) Myelencephalon, (2) Metencephalon, (3) Mesencephalon (Mid brain), (4) Diencephalon and (5) Telencephalon. In this classification, the first two are the parts of the hind brain and the last two are the parts of the fore brain.

The myelencephalon, major part of the hind brain, is known as medulla oblongata. The second part of the hind brain, the metencephalon, has three sub-parts whose names are — (1) Pons, (2) Parts of the fourth ventricle and (3) cerebellum. The third part of the brain is the mesencephalon which is the mid brain. The fourth and fifth parts of the brain are concerned with the fore brain. The first of these two parts is diencephalon. This part has many structures whose names are : third ventricle, mammillary bodies, thalamus, hypothalamus, pituitary body, and optic tracts and the retinae of the eyes. The fifth part of the brain is called the telencephalon. Its parts are : olfactory bulbs, olfactory tracts, cerebral hemispheres, lateral ventricles and basal ganglia.

Outline of the classification becomes clear from the above description. Now it is essential to give a detailed description of these various parts. Structure and functions of these various parts will be given in this description :

HIND BRAIN

(i) Myelencephalon, (ii) Metencephalon

1. Myelencephalon

Major part of the hind brain in the classification of the brain is called the myelencephalon. Generally, this part is known by the name of medulla oblongata. The structure of this part is quite simple but its importance is great. For a complete knowledge of this part it is essential to know its structure and functions.

Structure of Medulla Oblongata

The position of medulla oblongata in human brain is between the spinal cord and pons. Spinal cord lies below it and the pons above. Cerebellum lies behind it. Thus, medulla is connected with these three structures — spinal cord (below), pons (above) and cerebellum (behind). It is about one inch in length. Many groups of nerve cells are connected together through this structure. Besides higher centres of the brain are connected with the spinal cord through conduction paths going through it. Many cranial nerves are connected with the brain through the medulla. Thus, medulla is considered an important structure of the brain.

In order to understand the structure of medulla fully, it is essential to look at its dorsal side. This side of the medulla is like an enlarged part of the spinal cord. Two centres — fasciculus gracilis and pasciculus cuneatus meet with each other on this dorsal side. A V-shape is formed on their joining point. On the other side (ventral side) of the medulla are cerebrospinal or pyramidal tracts. Beside this, in the lateral portion of the medulla are found two structures which are called thapezoid and restiform body.

Functions of Medulla Oblongata

Medulla has many important functions in behaviour. A brief description of some of its major functions are given below :

(1) The most important function of medulla is to establish connection between the spinal cord and higher centres of the brain.

For this purpose it provides many conduction paths between the spinal cord and higher centres like cerebellum, thalamus and cerebrum. It is through these paths that nerve impulses travel between the spinal cord and brain.

(2) Various nuclei associated with the cranial nerves lie in the medulla. In this position medulla sends various functional units of the cranial nerves from the higher centres of the brain to the parts of the body connected with these nerves.

(3) Inner side of the medulla contains gray matter. This gray matter is concerned with various main organs of the body like heart, blood

vessels and lungs. Because of this connection gray matter controls heart beating, blood pressure and activity of the lungs etc. Thus, this part of the brain is important for the whole body. If medulla is injured or destroyed, blood pressure falls considerabely and respiration is slowed as a result of which the person may die.

(4) Many essential activities of the body like coughing, blinking, and sneezing etc. are also concerned with this part of the brain. Medulla regulates these activities.

(5) Digestive activity of the body, blood circulation, respiration and phonation are also controlled by this part of the brain. Besides controlling, the medulla also regulates these activities as a result of which homeostasis is maintained in the body in normal circumstances.

(6) This part of the brain produces neural energy for the activities connected with respiration and blood circulation. Medulla also conducts sensations received from different parts of the body to the brain.

2. The Metencephalon

Second major part of the hind brain is called the metencephalon. Three sub-parts of this division of the brain have been accepted. Their names are : (a) Pons, (b) Cerebellum and (c) Part of the 4th ventricle. Structure and functions of these three parts of this division will now be given.

(a) **Pons.** Pons is situated in the ventral part of the brain above the medulla. It is directly connected with the medulla, cerebellum and cerebrum. In fact, pons is connected with both lobes of the cerebellum. It works like a bridge. Internal structure of the pons is similar to that of the medulla. There are many complex nerve centres in the pons. These centres are situated in the transverse fibres. These transverse fibres connect the two lobes of the cerebellum. Besides these there are other neural tracts in the pons which connect the various higher and lower parts of the central nervous system.

One function of the pons is to maintain balance in various movements of the body. Another major function of the pons is to integrate the activity of muscles. In the pons are found nuclei of the cranial nerve which is concerned with the sensations and movements of the mouth and face. Thus pons has important functions in connection with the sensations and movements of the mouth and face.

(b) **Cerebellum.** Cerebellum is situated just above the medulla at the level of pons. Cerebellum is connected with the rest of the brain through the pons. Cerebellum in human brain is of relatively smaller size. In birds and other animals, cerebellum is bigger than other parts. In the human brain cerebellum lies between the occipital lobes of the cerebral cranial cavity. Many tracts from the spinal cord enter the cerebellum. Similarly, it receives fibre tracts from the cerebral cortex also. Besides this, cerebellum has connections with corpus striatum, a part of the fore brain.

Structure of the cerebellum is quite complex. Generally, it is divided into two parts : (i) Hemisphere and (2) Vermis. The outer part is hemisphere and it is grey. It is covered with thin membrane of grey cells. The inner part of the cerebellum is called vermis and it has white colour. It is made up of white fibres. There are four types of nuclei in its inner surface. These are respectivelly called globose, dentate, postigii and emboliform nuclei.

We know that cerebellum is a part of the brain. It is connected with other structures of the brain through three pairs of fibre tracts. These are inferior tract, middle tract and superior peduncle tract. Cerebellum is also connected with other structures of the central nervous system through these fibre tracts.

Functions of Cerebellum

Functions of the cerebellum have not yet been definitely determined. It is a problem to determine its functions. G.L. Freeman has described the functions of cerebellum in these words : "Cerebellum meets the need of the organism as a whole and regulates the movement of the entire body. It maintains muscle tone which largely determines postures of the body. It also maintains the excitation of voluntary movements." Thus, it is clear that cerebellum regulates the activity of various muscles of the body. Besides this, a description of some specific functions of the cerebellum is given below :

(1) Cerebellum is often called an organ of motor co-ordination. Cerebellum co-ordinates many reflex actions of the body. Flying of the birds, swimming of the fish and walking of human beings etc. are regulated by the cerebellum.

(2) Another function of the cerebellum is the maintenance of balance of the body. For this purpose it controls all those movements of the body which are essential for body balance. If the cerebellum of a man or other animal is destroyed, it is not possible for that person or animal to stand straight or walk normally. The famous psychologist N.L. Munn has described this function of the cerebellum in these words : "If a bird's cerebellum is destroyed, the bird can still move but it cannot fly. This is because the separate activities required for flying are inappropriately patterned and timed. Similarly, a man with his cerebellum seriously injured is unable to walk normally. When he walks, he does so with a jerky, in co-ordinated movement." Thus, it is clear that cerebellum regulates and co-ordinates bodily movements.

(c) **Part of Fourth Ventricle.** The third sub-part of the metencephalon is called part of fourth ventricle. It runs through the brain stem having pons and cerebellum on its left and right side respectively. In fact, IVth ventricle is connected with the third ventricle. It is also connected with the front portion of the medulla.

MID BRAIN

The second main division of the brain is called mid brain. It is called mesencephalon according to a second basis of classification. In order to obtain a complete knowledge of this part, it is essential to know its structure and function.

Mid brain lies mid way between the fore brain and hind brain. Its position is like that of a bridge. Size of the mid brain in man is about 3/4 inch. Its internal structure is similar to that of spinal cord and pons. Mid brain connects the hind brain with fore brain.

On the dorsal side of the brain, mid brain can be divided into two parts. These are respectively called floor and tectum (roof). Functions of these two parts are different. Tectum has mainly sensory functions. Tectum is sometimes also called colliculi. There are two pairs of sensory centres in the tectum. These are called superior tectum and inferior tectum. Inferior tectum is concerned with hearing. It is concerned with the receiving of various sound sensations. The second centre is superior tectum. It is concerned with vision. Besides the tectum, the second part of the mid brain is floor. Its main function is to connect the higher centres of the central nervous system with the lower centres. Floor also regulates some motor reflex actions like blinking and head movement.

Ventral part of the mid brain is covered with cerebral peduncles and various nerve tracts. It is these tracts which join the cerebrum with lower centres like spinal cord, medulla and pons etc.

Thus, we see that the mid brain has two surfaces — dorsal and ventral. In both these parts various fibre tracts and nuclei are found. These are called fegmentum. Various sensory and motor tracts pass through it and connect it with the hind brain and fore brain. Some of the main tracts are pyramidal tracts, ventral tracts, rubrospinal tracts and fectyspinal tracts. Thus, it is clear that the mid brain is like a bridge between fore brain and hind brain and it has a close relationship with both these.

FORE BRAIN

The third major division of the brain is fore brain. It is further divided into two parts. These are respectively called diencephalon and telencephalon. There are various structures in these parts. A discussion of these structures will be presented below.

1. Diencephalon

Diencephalon has many structures. Following are the main structures in it : (1) Thalamus, (2) Hypothalamus, (3) Optic nerve tract, (4) Retinae of the eyes, (5) Pituitary body, (6) Mammillary bodies and (7) Third Ventricle. Now these structures will be discussed separately.

(1) Thalamus. Thalamus in human brain lies between the mid brain and cerebrum. Thalamus is intimately connected with the cerebral

cortex. A cross section of the thalamus is prepared for looking at its structure clearly. It is known by observing the cross section of thalamus that it has connections also with the lower centres of the brain and spinal cord.

The major characteristic of thalamus is that it works as an effective relay station of the brain. For the sake of convenience in study thalamus is divided into two parts : (1) Dorsal thalamus and (2) Ventral thalamus. Dorsal thalamus is concerned with groups of sensory nuclei whereas groups of motor nuclei lie in the ventral thalamus. There are three motor nuclei and these are concerned with the cerebral hemispheres and lower centres of the brain. Shape of the dorsal thalamus is like two joined eggs. The function of this part of the thalamus is to receive various sensations and then to relay them to different areas of the cerebral cortex. On the other hand, various motor nuclei are found in the ventral portion of the thalamus. These motor centres control various metabolic reactions in the body and help maintain homeostasis. A description of the major thalamic nuclei is given below :

(1) **Relay Nuclei.** Sensory nuclei of the thalamus are of great importance. These relay nuclei are also called Thalamocortical Projection nuclei. Two major nuclei in this group are lateroventral nucleus and posteroventral nucleus. Its main function is the coordination of the activities of the cerebellum and the frontal lobe. Thus, it helps in controlling muscular movements. The posteroventral nucleus is the relay station for sensory fibres representing the skin and the muscle sense.

(2) **Association Nuclei.** Association nuclei are also of great importance. These nuclei receive impulses from within the thalamus and send projections to the association areas of the cerebral cortex.

(3) **Sub-cortical Nuclei.** These nuclei have connections only with the structures below the cortex. They connect with the basal ganglia or with other parts of the thalamus.

Functions of the Thalamus

A brief description of some main functions of the thalamus is given below :

(1) Thalamus regulates various metabolic activities of the body. Along with these it helps maintain the homeostasis in the body.

(2) Thalamus acts as a relay station of the brain. Sensory impulses from various receptors are received in the nuclei in the dorsal thalamus and they are projected in the respective areas of the cerebral cortex. In other words, it works like a switch board.

(3) Motor nuclei in the ventral thalamus have connections with the sympathetic nervous system.

(4) Various learning activities of the organism also depend upon the thalamus. It also extends the centres for temperature pressure and audition in other structures.

(2) **Hypothalamus.** The position of the thalamus in human brain is in the dorsal part of the diencephalon. It is situated below the thalamus. Hypothalamus is also connected with pituitary gland. Like the thalamus, hypothalamus has various nuclei in it. Of these one group controls sympathetic functions. These are posterior and lateral nuclei. The second group of nuclei controls parasympathetic functions. These are mainly the medial and anterior nuclei. Both these groups of nuclei influence many bodily activities.

Functions of Hypothalamus

Hypothalamus has important functions in relation to the autonomic nervous system. If posterior and lateral group of nuclei are active, the following effects are seen. Heart activity is increased. Blood pressure is elevated. Stomach and intestinal activities are interfered and pupils of the eyes are dilated. Because of the influence of the second group of nuclei the heart is slowed, blood sugar is lowered and pupils of the eyes contract.

Hypothalamus has important role in many bodily functions. Its functions are concerned with motivational, emotional and behavioural activities of the person. It regulates various visceral reactions in the body and maintains balance in the internal environment. Hypothalamus has a unique function in emotional expression. It integrates the emotional behaviour of the organism.

Besides these major functions hypothalamus regulates metabolic processes in the body. It influences the activity of the pituitary gland. Hypothalamus also regulates and controls hunger, thirst, blood pressure and sexual functions.

(3) **Pituitary Body.** Another structure of the diencephalon is the pituitary body. It receives its fibres from the hypothalamus. It is in fact, connected with the hypothalamus.

(4) **Third Ventricle.** Third ventricle, a structure in the diencephalon, is situated between thalamus and hypothalamus. Third ventricle has relationship with lateral ventricles and the fourth ventricle. It is connected with these ventricles. Third ventricle divides the mid brain into tectum and floor.

Besides the above described structures, diencephalon contains mammillary bodies, optic tracts and retina of the eyes. They have their own importance in body functions.

2. Telencephalon

The second main division of the fore brain is called telencephalon. This division has many structures. It has a quite large area in the human brain. Telencephalon receives tracts from other structures of the brain. It is connected with the other parts of the brain — diencephalon, metencephalon and mesencephalon. Following are the main structures in the telencephalon :

(1) Cerebrum
(2) Olfactory bulb
(3) Olfactory tracts
(4) Basal ganglia
(5) Lateral ventricles

A discussion of these structures is presented below :

(1) **Cerebrum.** This structure of the brain is the most developed of the parts of the central nervous system in human beings. It occupies a greater area than other parts. Various receptors and effectors in the body have connections with the cerebrum.

Structure of Cerebrum

The structure of cerebrum is very complex. This part is highly developed in the human brain. It is this part which differentiates the human brain from the brains of other animals. There are various types of cells in the cerebrum. Its position in the brain is just below the skull. Structure of the cerebrum is of a special type. Its outer surface is not plane. It has many deep curved lines on its surface which form many convolutions on it. Some thinkers believe that these deep lines and convolutions have relationship with the intelligence of the organism. The organism having a cerebrum with greater convolutions possesses higher intelligence. In fact, cerebrum is concerned with various mental activities of the person.

Cerebrum has two parts. These are respectively called right hemisphere and left hemisphere. Each hemisphere is made up of nerve centres and connecting fibre systems. These fibre systems are of white colour. Nerve centres are made up of grey matter. There are three main types of fibres in the cerebral hemispheres. First type of fibres are association fibres. Association fibres connect different areas of the cerebral cortex with one another. Second type of fibres are commissural fibres. These fibres connect left and right hemispheres with each other. Third type of fibres are called projection fibres. Their function is to connect the cerebral hemisphere with the lower centres of the central nervous system. Of these thalamocortical projections are very important. These fibres connect various sensory areas of the cortex with the nuclei of the dorsal thalamus.

Cerebal hemisphere has three structures. These are : (a) Olfactory bulb, (b) Corpus striatum and (c) Cerebral cortex. Design of these three structures is presented below in brief :

(a) *Olfactory lobe* : Generally, it is believed by scholars that olfactory lobe is the most primitive part of the cerebrum. Cerebral cortex in the human brain has evolved out of the olfactory bulb. Various connecting fibres have developed out of this part of the cerebrum. Olfactory lobe is connected with the olfactory bulbs in the fore brain through olfactory stalk.

(b) *Corpus striatum* : Second part of the cerebral hemisphere is corpus striatum. Basal surface of cerebral hemispheres is made by it. If we see a cross section of the corpus striatum, its internal structure appears like two grey nuclear masses. These two nuclei are separated from each other by two types of tracts. These are cortical radiations.

(c) *Cerebral cortex* : The third structure of the cerebral hemisphere is called cerebral cortex. Structure of the cerebral cortex is very complex. Its colour is grey. There are many nuclei in it which control and regulate various bodily and mental activities. The structure and functions of cerebral cortex will be discussed in detail in the following page.

(2) **Olfactory Bulb.** Olfactory bulb is the second sub-part of the telencephalon. Its position in the human brain is in the region of cranial cavity. This structure is situated above the olfactory receptors. Its structure is made up of the olfactory nerve. In the human brain this structure is relatively less developed and less sensitive as compared to the lower animals.

(3) **Olfactory Tracts.** Olfactory tracts lie in the ventral portion of the cerebral hemispheres in the human brain. Nerve impulses from the smell receptors in the nose travel through these olfactory tracts to the smell area of the cerebrum.

(4) **Basal Ganglia.** Basal ganglia are considered the oldest parts of the telencephalon in the brain. Corpus striatum is also a part of these ganglia. These ganglia are a mass of grey matter lying above the thalamus and below the cortex. The Basal ganglia have important functions in connection with the posture of the organism and the coordination of movements. In lower animals these structures are relatively more sensitive and more developed.

(5) **Lateral Ventricles.** There are four ventricles in the brain. The first two are called lateral ventricles. Lateral ventricles are situated in the cerebral hemispheres. The two lateral ventricles are connected with each other and also with the third ventricle which lies below the thalamus.

CEREBRAL CORTEX

The cerebrum is bigger than the cerebellum or the mid brain. Hence, it is known as cerebrum or the bigger brain. Beginning from the eye brows, it extends to the middle of the skull. Thus, it is the frontal part of the skull. It is the highest part of the brain. In it the arrangement of the white and the grey matter is exactly opposed to that of the spinal cord. Its upper surface is made up of grey matter while the internal part is made up of white matter. As has already been pointed out, in the spinal cord the upper surface is made of white matter while the internal part is made of grey matter. The upper grey part of the cerebrum is known as cortex. In it there are clusters of nerve cells which make the sensory area and the motor area of the brain. The white matter forms the nerve fibres. The grey matter forms the nerve cells.

In the cerebrum, there are two hemispheres separated from the fissure known as the right and the left hemispheres. Most of the part of the right hemisphere is linked with the left part of the body. The left hemisphere is linked with the right part of the body. Thus, between the hemispheres of the cerebrum and the body there is a crossed relation. On the surface of the cerebrum there are small convolutions or gyre. These convolutions are separated from each other through the fissures. The fissures go deep into the matter of the cerebrum. But the brain is not actually divided into these fissures because under the surface of the brain various parts are connected with each other. In the cerebrum, there is a fissure in the centre which is known as central sulcus. It is also known as fissure of rolando. Besides this, there is also a fissure situated horizontally. This fissure is known as fissure of silvious or lateral sulcus.

The big portions of the cerebrum are known as lobes. These lobes are connected with each other. Thus, the cerebrum is divided into four parts, as given below : (1) Frontal Lobe, (2) Parietal Lobe, (4) Occipital Lobe and (5) Temporal Lobe.

All these four parts of the brain are connected by sensory projection fibres. These fibres enter one lobe from another.

These different parts of the cerebrum are connected with different types of sensations. For example, the frontal lobe is connected with thinking. In complex thinking, it is this frontal lobe of cerebrum which works. In the central part on the one side of the central sulcus there is a motor area. This is situated in the frontal lobe. In the parietal lobe there is a somaesthetic area where the sensations from the skin and muscles are received. In the upper part of the temporal lobe, there is auditory area where the sensations of seeing are received. Near the lateral sulcus there are areas of taste and smell.

Several experiments have been conducted regarding the value of these different lobes in the behaviour of man. Of these it will be relevant to describe here a case related with the importance of the frontal lobes in human behaviour.

A successful agent of the New York stock exchange used to have headache at the age of 40 years. This headache was very severe. Due to this his memory weakened and after sometime the pain became so severe that he lost his consciousness. An examination through X-Ray revealed that both the frontal lobes of the brain were swollen. An operation of the skull was made and the frontal lobes were removed. Care was taken that the motor speech area should not get any injury.

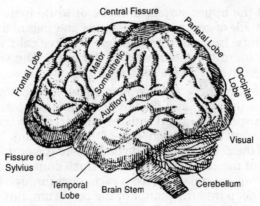

Fig. 28. Lobes, Fissures and areas of Cerebrum.

After this operation, the patient became healthy and his headache was cured. But in some respects he was entirely different now. He left the idea of working as an agent. He did not bother about the feelings of his friends. He could not seriously work on anything for a long time. When he was put under the care of some doctor, his behaviour improved a bit, but he could not take interest in his business. He did not like to sit peacefully. He used to walk or dance in the room. Singing, whistling and making noise became his habits. He had no control over his sex impulse and the impulse of self-aggrandisement. He openly used to take part in sexual jokes and was interested in them. He cracked jokes with other women, but did not try to exceed this. Whatever work was mentioned before him he used to boast of his ability in it. Often he threatened persons, but never indulged in physical violence.

When taken to the chamber of the psychologist, he appeared to be over active, factious and distractable. It was with some difficulty that he could complete the test. The test revealed that his intelligence was normal. He appeared to be weak in construction of the sentences and the pictures etc., in which there is a need to keep things together. But it appeared that he could never use his full intelligence. Before operation, he used to employ his faculties of observation, attention, memory, logic etc. But after operation he did not use them at all. Thus, it was concluded that his synthesizing and combining powers were lessened. He lost control over his impulses. Thus, he appeared to be impulsive and distractable.

From the above example, it is clear that the frontal lobes have an important part to play in human behaviour. Several experiments on animals have also been conducted regarding their importance. Their effect in learning activity was noted. When the frontal lobes of animals were removed, it forgot the learned activity, but learned after some training. In the experiments on chimpanzees and monkeys, it was seen that they could remember as to which cup contained food. Though some part of the frontal lobe was destroyed, the memory was not completely destroyed.

Functional Areas

The functional areas of the brain have been already referred with the description of different lobes. A survey of these different areas will also be helpful to understand them fully well.

1. Motor Area. This is the pre-central gyrus. This precentral gyrus is a part of the cortex, just in front of the central sulcus. This part is known as motor area, due to the following reasons :

(*a*) A shock to any part of this area results into paralysis of some part of the body.

(*b*) Application of electric current to any part of this area results in the movement in different organs of the body.

Hence, this part can be rightly called motor area. But this part does not govern the motor activities of the body. The cortex which is in front of this area also takes part in the movements of the different parts of the body. This part is known as pre-motor area. The motor area governs the single movements while the promoter, area governs the complex movements.

2. Sensory Areas of the Cortex. This is connected with the lower parts of those sensory organs which are situated near one another at the upper end of the cerebellum. The fibres from the eyes, ears and other sense organs meet at this place. The relay fibres also go to meet sense organs from here. It is through this area that the sense organs are related with the cortex.

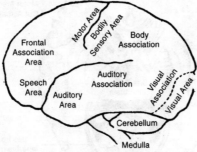

Fig. 29. Functional and Associative areas of the Cerebrum.

3. Somaesthetic Area. This is also called central gyrus. It is just behind the motor area. It is here that there is the main cortical centre for sensation from the skin and muscles. A shock in this region destroys sensitiveness of the skin of muscles.

4. Auditory Area. The auditory area in the brain is situated in a small part of the temporal lobe. It is here that the sensations from the ears are received. The relay fibres reach the ears from here. A shock in this region results in the destruction of the capacity of hearing.

5. Visual Area. The visual area is situated in a part of occipital lobe. It is here that the sensory fibres from retina are received. The relay fibres to the eyes also go from here.

Associative Areas

The associative areas are those parts of the cortex which would be included in the motor area. The associative area appears to be divided into two big parts. One associative area is situated in occipital, temporal and parietal lobe between several motor areas. Another associative area is situated in the motor areas and cerebrum in the front part. The associative areas are separated by the association fibres. If these fibres are damaged, some sensitive part of the brain is also damaged, *e.g.,* with the destruction of the association fibres of the cortex everything learned is forgotten. With the destruction of the areas near the motor cortex, the capacity to speaking and writing is destroyed. With the destruction of the visual area, it becomes impossible to understand language and the man cannot understand words even while seeing them. Some severe damage to the areas of the front part of the brain results in forgetting of something immediately learned, though one can remember something of childhood.

Inner Structure of the Brain

If the brain is cut transversally or horizontally two types of matter are observed in it — white matter and grey matter.

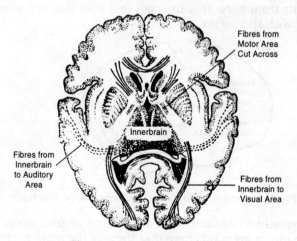

Fig. 30. Inner Structure of Brain

In the diagram given above the cerebrum is shown cut across in two parts. In it, the white matter is shown by white, the grey matter with dots while the liquid matter with black colour. The fibres shown in the diagram represent several thousands of fibres. These fibres show some main paths, auditory path, sympathetic path and crossing in a collosum.

If the tissue is observed by applying some colour with the help of microscope, innumerable nerve fibres are observed with white matter which go in various directions. In the grey matter there are cells with dendrites and axons entering and ending. In the lower part of the spinal cord and brain, there is grey matter. Some 60% part of the spinal cord and brain is constituted by white matter and the rest by grey matter. In the white matter there are nerve fibres which can be clearly distinguished from the grey matter. Even the eye can distinguish as to which parts of the nervous system are constituted of nerve fibres and which by nerve cells. The collection of nerve cells is known as ganglia. The collection of nerve fibres is known as tracts. The structure of the cerebrum and the cerebellum is of the same type.

Brain Fibres

In the brain three types of fibres are observed : (l) Commisural fibres, (2) Association fibres and (3) Projection fibres.

1. Commisural Fibres. The commisural fibres extend in one hemisphere of the brain by the white sheet and reach another hemisphere. Thus, they assume the form of corpus collosum. It is this corpus collosum, as has been pointed out earlier, which establishes relation between both the hemispheres of the brain.

2. Association Fibres. The association fibres establish contact between the two parts of cortex. Previously, it was held that different activities of the cortex are integrated by association fibres. But it has been discovered that the association fibres do not extend lengthwise. Thus, now it is established that the connection between the various parts of the cortex is not established by association fibres.

3. Projection Fibres. These are most important fibres. It is through these that the messages go out of and come in the cortex. Such projection fibres are of two types : (A) Afferent projection fibres, which send impulses to cortex from thalamus and sub-cortical centre, (B) Efferent fibres, which proceed from cortex and reach thalamus or spinal cord and carry the message to them.

Grey Matter

Most of the parts of the grey matter are found on the upper surface of the brain. This part is known as cortex. Cortex extends round about the fissures. In the brain there are even bigger particles of grey matter. The inner brain is entirely made up of grey matter. There is grey matter also in the depths and fissures of the brain.

If the grey matter is seen with the help of microscope, it shows nerve cells, dendrides and axons. The total number of the cells in the cortex of the cerebrum is estimated as 14,000,000,000. Of these, many are very small and undeveloped which are not used and kept safe in the brain. Along with nerve cells there are dendrides, axons and cell bodies. While seen with the microscope they appear to be innumerable.

It is in the grey part of the brain that all the conscious centres and fields of consciousness of the brain are found. Thinking, reasoning, imagination and other intellectual functions are found in the grey part. In it, there are the areas of sensations, associations and motor areas. In it, there is the field of physical activities and tactual sensations. If this field is injured, the sensations are not felt in hands, feet and skin. Thus, the consciousness of the man very much depends on the grey part of the brain.

The importance of grey matter is in brief, as follows :

(1) The conscious fields and the conscious centres of the brain are situated in the grey matter. Thus, all the intellectual and conscious functions start in it.

(2) The motor areas of the brain are in the grey part. Hence, it is from this part that the motor functions begin.

(3) The association areas of the brain are situated in the grey matter. Hence, it is the grey matter which keeps the different activities of the brain related to one another.

(4) The physiological activities and the tactual sensations are directed from the grey matter because their areas are situated in it.

Importance of White Matter

The importance of the white matter in the structure of the brain is as follows :

(1) The white matter helps in separating the nerve fibres from the nerve cells, because on the nerve fibres there is a white sheath of myelin.

(2) The white matter helps in connecting most of the subtle fibres and keeping them in the sheath.

(3) The white matter keeps the different parts of the cortex related.

(4) The white matter connects the two spheres of the brain.

(5) The white matter includes corpus collosum.

(6) The white matter sends sensation from the thalamus or subcortical centres to the cortex, and connects it with ganglia and spinal cord.

Localization of Brain Functions

The study of the localisation of brain functions has its own story in the history of psychology. The problem of localization is whether different areas of the brain activate different functions or not. This discussion was started in 1800 by the theory of phrenology advanced by the famous anatomist Gall who tried to relate the external elevations in the skull to mental specialties or peculiarities. He said that these elevations indicated mental peculiarities. According to the theory of phrenology, mental faculties are situated behind the forehead in the forefront of the brain. Thus, middle brain constitutes the localisation of the ethical qualities while the rear end is for the animal tendencies. The sex instinct is in the medulla oblongata while the quality of faith finds itself in the stem.

Experiments of Flourens

In 1925 or thereabout, Flourens concluded from his experiments that the cerebrum worked as a unit. Thus, he refuted the localisation of the various functions in the brain and challenged against the theory of phrenology, that the cerebrum works as a whole. Thus, some one hundred years from today it was believed that one part of cerebrum could not be distinguished from another. The cerebrum is a collection of many parts which can perform many activities but each part of which is capable of performing every one of those activities.

Proofs of Localisation

This theory advocated by Flourens was credited till 1860. After this, Paul Broca showed that when a particular area of the cortex was injured, a difficulty in speech was experienced. After Broca's experiments, Frish and Hitzig found that electrical sensation in specific parts of the cortex caused motion in various parts of the body. These experiments highlighted the theory of localisation for the second time. The expert physiologists supported the notion because they found substantial difference in the structure of the various parts of the brain. Surgeons also supported the theory of localisation because they wanted to explain the different physiological changes caused by injury to different parts of the brain. Thus, fifty years ago, the theory of different centres for different activities in the brain, of course, was being supported and these centres were being further subdivided. Psychiatrists were establishing relation between specific mental illnesses and the conditions of specific parts of the brain.

Current Situation

But now the emphasis laid in favour of localisation is losing its strength. Some localisation of function and structure in the cortex is still believed but great care is taken before a certain area is pronounced as the centre of a specific type of activity. The cerebrum is popularly believed to be an adjuster part. It is understood that its function is not to perform diversified and unrelated activities but to direct the creature to mould its behaviour in conformity with the environment. Many experiments have definitely proved that information of different kinds of changes reaches different areas of the cortex. The existence of somaesthetic area, pre-motor area, auditory area and visual area and different centres has been indicated by experimental administration of electrical sensations to various parts of the brain. Thus, this kind of cortical localisation is no longer in doubt.

The boundaries of different activities, however, cannot be decided by having them centred in the cortex. For example, we accept one somaesthetic or sensation area but in 1916, Dusser de Barenne showed at Oxford that in spite of the localisation of a sensation area, it extends over a large area of the cortex and its boundries are not established. From this, it is concluded that though the area of reception and projection of sensations may be localised, the localisation of areas for converting sensation signals into sensations is not possible. The direct paths of the entrance of visual sensations to the cortex of the brain can also be determined but they cannot be accepted to be completely unrelated to the areas surrounding them. The signals received in the motor area do not convey any thing and any knowledge is due to shock or injury. In fact, the first attempts at localisation were made in the direction of the motor area, but as the experiment at Oxford proved, there is a lot of scope in this direction. Nothing definite can be said whether the area for the assimilation of information from different organs of the body is definite or not. Nothing definite can be said about the location of mental functions or the limits of their areas and centres. Further research in the future may make it possible to say something with authority upon the subject.

Methods for the Study of Localisation

Many methods are employed for the discovery of localisation of different activities in the brain. The major methods are as follows :

1. Method of Electrical Stimulation. The exposed part of the cortex is subject to weak electrical stimulation and the resulting motion in the body serves the purpose of establishing the relation of the specific activity to a specific area in the brain. The method of the study of localisation is the most famous.

2. Pathological Method. The disturbed activities and behaviour of a diseased person are noted following which the person is cured by the surgery or otherwise removal of the diseased part of the brain. The effects are again observed.

3. Method of Extirpation. Some part of the brain is removed and the effects on the behaviour and physiological activities are observed. The area which is extracted is taken to be the centre of those activities or functions which either become absent or are affected in any way. These experiments are usually carried out on animals.

4. Fibre Tracing Method. This method traces the fibre which connects the cortex to the lower centres and finds the relation of the various parts of the body to some specific areas in the cortex. Though the method is satisfactory yet the tracing of fibres is no easy task.

When the above methods succeed in localising a particular activity in the brain, the research is credited and accepted in the absence of any evidence to the contrary. These methods are employed in the location of functional areas in the brain.

Localisation of Combining Areas

Besides these functional areas there are two sizable combining areas, one of which is situated in the midst of many sensation areas in the parietal, temporal and occipital lobes, while the other is found in the motor area and in front of the frontal lobes. The knowledge of the localisation of these areas originates from any injury to the brain. The result of these injuries is manifested in the form of Aphasia, Agnosia and Apraxia, and they are the ones to establish the localisation. Thus, it will be in keeping with the subject to make a brief description of them.

1. Aphasia. In this illness, speech and language cannot be used or can be used with difficulty. A connected and meaningful, comprehensible sentence cannot be spoken and neither can the meaning of such a sentence be understood. The cause of this difficulty is not paralysis but rather injury to the area surrounding the auditory area.

There are two kinds of aphasia — speech aphasia and motor aphasia. In the later kind, the difficulty lies in emitting or ejecting words from the mouth and the difficulty, too, takes various forms. Some patients can pronounce separate words but not sentences, even when written. Other patient's capabilities extend to the pronunciation of simple words like yes and no only. The lower motor area is usually injured.

2. Agnosia. The ability of perception is undermined in agnosia. The person hears and sees all right but he cannot utilise the sensory data in the form of specific, concrete signals. In visual agnosia, the result of injury to the occipital lobe, the person loses his ability to recognise and distinguish colour and form. He cannot recognise sounds. If the injury is just behind the somaesthetic area, the patient cannot recognise an object placed on his hand and neither can he, on the other hand, metaphorically speaking, make any guesses about its weight.

3. Apraxia. The ability of work or effort is adversely affected. An apraxia patient cannot light a cigar and smoke it. He can perform singular activities but the relating of many activities is beyond his capabilities. Generally, the appearance of apraxia is the consequence of injury to an area in the vicinity of the motor area.

Intelligent behaviour is absent in aphasia, agnosia and apraxia. Symbols and skilled efforts are of great importance in intelligent behaviour and skilled efforts or motor activities depend on specific areas of the cortex which, if injured, loses the combination of these parts. The loss of this combination and the loss of intelligent behaviour in the individual both are determined by the extent of the injury.

Types of Combination in the Brain

The work of combination in the brain is effected in two ways :

1. Internal Combination. In this, the stimuli are many while the activity is solitary. This combination finds expression in the unitary response to an object. For example, when we see a film, a stream of various stimuli falls on the retina with the result that we see an undivided scene. Similarly, though the noise enters the ear in a succession of sounds it is heard as music in the combined form. Thus, in internal combination there is a type of collective activity which necessitates specific nervous behaviour. Possibly, the area for the collective internal combination is the adjuster area of the posterior end, located in the midst of various sensation areas.

2. External Combination. Many results are caused by a unitary antecedent. For example, you have to get up from the chair, go to the door, turn the key in the lock, remove the bolt etc., in order to open the door. A distribution mechanism is needed for this. It is formed by the branches of an axon and the stimulating of many nerve cells by these branches. The area for distributive external combination is quite possibly the front part of the brain.

Localisation of Combining Activity

Undisputed evidence has not been found on the subject of the brain taking part in these combining functions. In fact, a large part of the brain takes part in these combining functions, a fact mentioned once before. Thus, it is difficult to localise it. There are many activities like learning or memorising of which the whole cortex partakes. In an experiment it was seen that a monkey forgot all learned actions when the frontal lobes were removed from the brain, but learnt it when taught again. Many experiments along these same lines made it apparent that different parts of the cerebrum assist in the learning of an action. Thus, the diminution in the ability of learning depends upon the percentage of the cortex removed. The difficulty in learning and the disturbance or disorganisation of activity depends upon the corresponding damage to the cortex.

Conclusion

The above treatise on the localisation of brain functions makes it clear that the localisation of the areas of various functions is accepted now a days. But the boundaries of these areas are as yet undefined and nothing can be said definitely about them. No indisputable statement can be made on the subject of localisation of the combining areas. Many activities are incapable of being localised because of their dependence on the whole cortex. The truth of the matter is that this problem of localisation is still in the experimental stage and more experiments must be carried out before any authoritative statements can be issued. Future experimentation will be the basis on which any conclusions will be founded. But till then, it can be believed that there are specific areas for dissimilar activities whose boundaries are not demarcated.

AUTONOMIC NERVOUS SYSTEM

Like the central nervous system, autonomic nervous system is also an important part of the nervous system. It is essential to discuss it while describing the response mechanism. It is called autonomic nervous system because it functions independently of the central nervous system. Central nervous system does not interfere in the activities controlled by this system. For example, many internal physiological changes take place in the state of emotion. These are regulated by the autonomic nervous system and the central nervous system does not act in their regulation. But this does not mean that autonomic nervous system has no relationship with central nervous system. In fact, spinal cord, which is an important part of the central nervous system, also has important role in the autonomic nervous system. Therefore, it can be said that the brain does not take part in the regulation of those activities which are controlled by the autonomic nervous system. The activity of this system cannot be stopped by volition. It functions in an independent way.

The main function of the autonomic nervous system is concerned with the internal adjustments of the organism. Many of its nerves come from the spinal cord and brain and go to various internal organs like glands, liver, blood vessels and smooth muscles of the viscera. It is mainly a motor system and regulates the activities of various organs like lungs, heart, liver, stomach, intestines etc. Many of its ganglia and synapses lie outside the central nervous system and the central nervous system has no part in their activity.

As it appears from the following diagram, autonomic nervous system is, in fact, a network of mutually related nerves.

In the Fig. 31 of the autonomic nervous system the upper-most portion shown is cranial. Nerves associated with this portion are called cranial nerves. Below it is the spinal cord. Nerves coming from this part are called spinal nerves. As has been shown in the figure, portion from the medulla to the upper part of the sacral region is called the middle or thoracico lumber autonomic nervous system. This is called thoracico lumber because nerves of this division come from the thoracic and lumber regions of the spinal cord. The portion below it, coming from the end of the spinal cord is called sacral division. Thus, the autonomic nervous system is divided into the three divisions : (1) Cranial, (2) Thoracico-Lumber or middle and (3) Sacral.

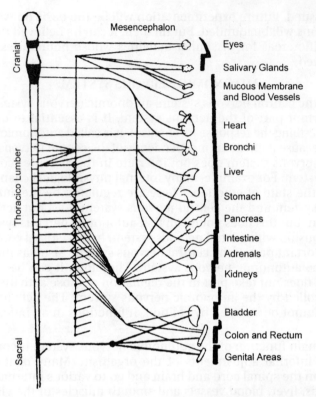

Fig. 31. Autonomic Nervous System

In the above Figure, autonomic ganglia, autonomic nerves and various organs of the body associated with these nerves have been shown. Thus, autonomic nerves go to the eyes, salivary glands, mucous membrane, blood vessels, heart, bronchi, liver, stomach, pancreas, intestines, adrenals, kidneys, bladder, rectum and genital organs. Besides, these nerves are also distributed to the sweat glands and cutaneous vessels. Nerve fibres from the middle portion of the spinal cord go to the ganglionic chain and connect the cord with it. There are 22 sympathetic ganglia in the ganglionic chain. In the figure, this ganglionic chain has been shown parallel to the spinal cord. In the ganglia of this chain terminate the fibres coming from the spinal cord. These are called preganglionic fibres. As they are covered with white myelin sheath, their bundle is called white ramus. Axons from the cell bodies in the chain go back to the spinal nerves. As they are not myelinated, their surface is grey and their bundle is called grey ramus.

Autonomic nervous system is divided into two main divisions — (1) Sympathetic nervous system and (2) Parasympathetic nervous system.

1. Sympathetic Nervous System

Sympathetic nervous system is also called thoracico lumber nervous system because its fibres originate from the thoracic and lumber regions of the spinal cord. This system is made up of ganglia and nerves. There are 22 pairs or sympathetic ganglia in it which are arranged to form a chain parallel to the spinal cord. This chain is called sympathetic chain or ganglionic cord.

Sympathetic nervous system has two types of fibres — white and grey. White fibres make what is called white ramus. It consists of preganglionic fibres coming from the spinal cord and entering in the sympathetic chain. Cell bodies in the ganglionic cord send axonal fibres back to the spinal nerves. Their bundle is grey ramus. Thus, there are two types of fibres in the sympathetic nervous system : (1) Preganglionic fibres and (2) Postganglionic fibres.

1. Preganglionic Fibres. Cell bodies of these fibres are situated in the lateral part of the grey matter of the spinal cord. Not all the preganglionic fibres terminate in the ganglia of the sympathetic chain. Some of these pass out through the ganglia and end in the ganglia located in the vicinity of the internal organs which are activated by them.

2. Postganglionic Fibres. These fibres originate from the ganglia of the sympathetic chain and go to the blood vessels, smooth muscles of the hollow organs, iris, sweat glands, liver and heart.

Sympathetic system has been further divided into two parts on the basis of structural characteristics :

1. *Thoracicolumber Region.* This region consists of fibres distributed to the liver, heart, stomach, intestines and adrenal glands.

2. *Cervical Region.* This region consists of fibres from the cervical ganglia in the region of the neck. Fibres of this region innervate the blood vessels and sweat glands of the head and pupils of the eyes.

2. Parasympathetic Nervous System

The second division of the autonomic nervous system is called parasympathetic nervous system. On the basis of its structure it is also called cranio-sacral system. It consists of preganglionic fibres, postganglionic fibres and ganglia. Its preganglionic fibres are much longer and they originate from the brain and sacral portion of the spinal cord. They extend to the parasympathetic ganglia which are close to the organs which they serve. Their postganglionic fibres are small and start from the ganglia to the organs which they serve, like smooth muscles and glands. Unlike sympathetic system, there is no chain of parasympathetic ganglia. On the other hand, each of its part is able to work independently.

Parasympathetic system is subdivided into the following two parts :

1. Cranial Region. Cranial part consists of all those cranial nerves which are associated with the head and brain. This part also serves eyes, sweat glands and the heart. Vagus is the most important nerve of this part.

2. Sacral Region. This part of the parasympathetic nervous system comes from the lowest region of the spinal cord. Its fibres go to the bladder, colon and the genital organs. Pelvic nerve is the major nerve of this part, whose fibres serve the above organs.

Functions of the two main divisions of the autonomic nervous system are opposite to each other. These are described below :

Functions of the Sympathetic Nervous System. Sympathetic system, in general, prepares the resources of the body for work and emergency. Thus, it saves the body from danger. Because of its activity in emergency, pupils of the eyes widen, blood vessels send more blood to the muscles and brain instead of sending it to the stomach for digestion of food. As a result, digestive activity in the stomach is stopped and the person does not feel hungry. Muscles and brain work speedily. Activity of the intestines is stopped and glands of gastric secretions stop their function. Throat and mouth become dry because salivary glands in the mouth stop salivation. Heart pumps out blood more quickly and its rate of beating increases. Adrenal glands secrete more adrenaline hormone in the blood. As a result, blood sugar level is increased. Because of increase in the amount of sugar in the blood the person feels more energetic. Rate of breathing is increased so that more oxygen is inhaled. All this increases the tissue metabolism. All these effects are produced in the body in fear or anger or at the time of quarrel and fighting. This is because sympathetic nervous system is active in emotional states of the person. In strong emotions electrical resistance of the skin is reduced and galvanic skin response becomes higher. One reason for this is that sweating is increased from the sweat glands in emotional states because of sympathetic activity.

Because of the difference in the structure of sympathetic and parasympathetic systems, their functions also differ. Parasympathetic system is concerned with the cranial and sacral regions. In sympathetic system, ganglia are either situated in the sympathetic chain or near the organs which they activate. But in parasympathetic system, ganglia are found only near the organs of innervation and there is no chain to interrelate its fibres. Thus, whereas sympathetic system acts as a unit, different parts of the parasympathetic system are independent in their action.

The major function of the parasympathetic system is conservation of bodily energy and building up of various organs of the body. This is called activity of anabolism. As has been stated earlier the function of this system is opposite to that of the sympathetic system. Parasympathetic activity reduces heart beating and the blood pressure falls. Body consumes lesser amount of energy under sympathetic influence, salivation from salivary glands is reduced and pupils of the eye are dilated. But in parasympathetic activity, salivation from salivary glands is increased which helps in the digestive process and as a result body weight is increased. Pupils of the eyes are constricted which allows lesser light in the eyes. It is useful for the eyes. Secral division of parasympathetic system removes unwanted waste products and other poisonous substances from the body by stimulating the activity of bladder and colon.

DIFFERENCE BETWEEN SYMPATHETIC AND PARASYMPATHETIC SYSTEM

Following difference between sympathetic and parasympathetic nervous system becomes clear from the above description :

1. **Difference Concerning the Position.** The position of the two systems is different. Whereas the sympathetic nervous system is situated in the thoracic and lumbar regions of the spinal cord, fibres of the parasympathetic system originate from the brain and sacral region of the spinal cord.

2. **Difference in the Position of Ganglia.** Sympathetic ganglia are mostly situated in the sympathetic chain near the spinal cord, on the other hand, parasympathetic ganglia are situated near the organs activated by them.

3. **Difference Relating to Emotion.** Whereas sympathetic system is stimulating in its effect, parasympathetic nervous system has mainly inhibitory effects.

4. **Difference Relating to Reflexes.** Sympathetic nervous system works diffusely as a unit in all reflexes. Parasympathetic system, on the other hand, takes part only in local reflex actions.

From the above discussion, it should not be understood that there is no relationship between the sympathetic and parasympathetic nervous systems. In fact, despite their opposite functions, the two systems work in a co-ordinated way. They do not function independently of each other. They cooperate with each other in various degrees depending upon the need of the organism. This equilibrium is maintained in the body both in work and rest because of the co-ordinated action of the two divisions of the autonomic nervous system. Morgan has written that these two nervous systems act independent of each other but are brought into correlated activity in varying degrees according to the circumstances. For example, if the organism has to struggle in the environment, sympathetic system becomes more active, whereas parasympathetic activity is decreased considerably. In everyday living in a normal environment, parasympathetic system becomes more active and sympathetic activity is reduced.

QUESTIONS FOR EXERCISE

1. What is Autonomic Nervous System? Discuss its parts and functions.
2. Explain spinal cord and discuss its functioning.
3. Describe the position and structure of human brain. Describe the functions of its parts.
4. What do you understand by cerebal localisation? Explain.

11

PERCEPTUAL PROCESSES

What is Perception?

Perception is the interpretation of the meanings of sensations. In seeing a rose the various sensations of colour, smell, touch etc., are aroused. We are given to understand by these sensations that there is an object in front of us. We know from past experience that an object of this nature is a flower of rose. We, therefore, conclude that we are beholding a rose.

Perception is a mental activity which acquaints us with the situation by giving us direct knowledge of it. The sensations are viewed as a whole, in perception. In perception, there is not just a perfunctory acquaintance with the object, there is a knowledge of it too. Whereas, in sensation, the individual does not know the object. The sensation of pink colour may have been excited either by some paper or some cotton wool or any thing else. The sensation of colour alone is not a sufficient proof of the identity of the object, and it is, consequently, not possible to say on the basis of the colour sensation that the pink object is a rose. The real meaning of the sensation is understood or revealed in the perception. Only then, it is known that the sensation originates from the rose. Accordingly, sensation precedes perception. Woodworth expresses it in this way : "In general, when we speak of sensation we are thinking of stimuli and investigating the relationship of the individual's experiences to various stimuli which reach his receptors, and when we speak of perception we are thinking of objects and are investigating how well the individual experiences correspond with the objective facts."

The Value of Past Experience in Perception

Sensation is not the only constituent of perception. Perception is caused by recognition based on past experiences. The perception of the rose is a recognition of it, as such by the perceiver. In this way, perception is an assimilation of recognition and sensation. Perception is the understanding of the sensory signs. This account should not create the impression that these processes of sensation and recognition take place step-by-step. In fact, all processes take place at such high speed that there is no knowledge of them. It appears that the perception takes place immediately the flower enters the line of vision. As Ward very aptly and truthfully says : "Pure sensation is a psychological myth." Even the presence of sensation is known upon an analysis of the perception. The understanding of the sensation in perception does not depend exclusively upon past experience. Time, environment, mental set, local signs, muscular sensations and unconscious traces, all play an important part in the process.

Perception and Sensation

The distinction between sensation and perception is similar to the one between a whole and its part. Neither of the two is possible without the other. Sensations are the constituents and raw materials of perception. The perception of the external world depends upon the sensations of colour, form, sound, taste, smell, heat, cold, density, amplitude etc. Just as the whole cannot exist without its parts, in the same way, perception is not possible in the absence of sensation. For example, the perception of the rose involves the experience of the sensations of the colour, smell, touch etc. To put the same more scientifically, the analysis of the perception of the rose yields these sensations. Sensation is a presentative process.

The second difference between sensation and perception is that while the former is a rudimentary and simple experience of life the latter is the complex of these simple experiences. It includes a memory of past experiences too. For this reason perception has been termed a "presentative-representative process". In the opinion of Woodworth sensation is the first response of the brain while perception is the second. Sensation is the first or at least the first conscious response born of the stimuli. Perception is the second response after sensation and in more appropriate words it is the direct response to the sensation and only an indirect response to the physical stimulus. The order of events is stimulation, response of the specific sense organ and sensory nerve, first cortical response which is the sensation, and second cortical response which is the perception. Using the old example, the presence of the rose first stimulates the specific sense organs. The sensory nerves convey this experience to areas of the cortex concerned. The sensation arises. The third difference between the two is that sensation precedes perception.

Characteristics of Perception

Prof. Stout has enumerated the characteristics of perception as follows :

1. Unity and Continuity.
2. Attention.
3. Persistence with varied efforts.
4. Free adaptation to varying conditions.
5. Learning by experience.
6. Reproduction in perception.

1. Unity and Continuity. The sensations are not scattered in perception. Perception is not possible if the sensations are scattered because they would, in that case, lack meaning. The perception of an orange includes the sensation of colour, taste smell etc., which are unseparated. There is a unity and continuity in the sensations which enable us to perceive an orange.

2. Attention. Perception is the understanding of sensations. Thus, the proximity of the sense organ and the object does not bring about perception, if there is no attention. You may not have noticed the building you pass by daily though it crossed your line of vision, because you never paid attention to it.

3. Persistence with Varied Efforts. The observer has constantly to change his efforts for complex perceptions. If, for example, a novel fruit, with which you are unfamiliar, is placed upon your palm then you do not rest content with a mere glance at it but, rather, you turn it over in your hand, smell it and, if it is innocuous, taste it. These changing perceptions have a unity and persistence.

4. Free Adaptation to Varying Circumstances. In some cases of perception, the sensations are constantly changing. The wrestler keeps an eye on the tricks his opponent uses. In this perception the sensations are changing. The wrestler has to adapt himself to the changing behaviour of his opponent.

5. Learning by Experience. It is difficult to perceive an object with which one is totally unfamiliar. A person who has never seen a kite flying cannot make anything out of the sensation of a patch of colour in the sky. Of course, if he once sees a kite, he will be able to recognise the sensation of colour in the sky and identify it as a kite.

6. Recollection. The above example shows that there was a recollection of past experience concerning kite and that the assimilations of present sensations and recollected past experiences resulted in the perception of a kite. Recollection is, thus, a speciality as well as a sign of perception.

7. Ambiguous Signs. Perception does not make it mandatory that the complete object be present. You perceive a friend on hearing his voice. This is because the sound is an ambiguous sign of his presence. Mostly, objects are seen in the form of signs. The bell was an indication of food in Pavlov's experiments on dogs, while the reaction was the same as in the case of a perception of food.

8. Reduced Sign. These are, as their title conveys, incomplete or reduced indications of the presence of an object. The dronning in the sky is a reduced sign of the presence of an aeroplane. The result is an indirect perception of the approaching or present aircraft.

Thus, besides the characteristics mentioned earlier, signs and indications have their importance in perception.

Perception, being a complex process, reveals four processes on analysis :

(1) **Receptor Process.** The first process in perception is the receptor process. The rose, by virtue of its presence, stimulated three different receptor cells thus activating three different receptor processes.

(2) **Unification Process.** This is the second step in the main process. For a perception of the rose, a unification of the different sensations is necessary. Even if the flower were to be seen or rather experienced by the eye, a unification of all the sensations from the different parts of the flower is a must.

(3) **Symbolic Process.** This process is the next, the third process in perception. From our daily life, we know that most things have a feeling or an experience attached to them. A rose reminds us of the friend who created in us the interest for roses. The flower symbolises the friend. Thus, every time we perceive a rose, this symbolic process makes it much more than just a rose.

(4) **Affective Process.** This too is attached to perception, because a flower may arouse a happy memory of a friend or a feeling of sorrow at their separation. Besides being pleasant or unpleasant, the process may also be indifferent.

The above detailed analysis of the processes of the perception will make it clear that it is a complex process and not merely an aggregation of sensations. But even though it is a complex process involving many processes, its basic constituents or components are still sensations and past experiences.

Perceptual Grouping

The Gestaltists opined that perception is not the mere aggregate of sensations and past experiences. It cannot be elaborately explained on the basis of past experiences. The real form of the object is to be taken as a whole. In German, the word for form is Gestalton, while in English it is Gestalt. This gestalt is very important in perception. A face is beautiful because of the effect of this gestalt. This theory on the subject of perception was first introduced in psychology by the gestalt psychologists. In 1912, Wertheimer announced on the basis of his experiments, that the perceptions by the various sense organs, eyes, nose, ear, tongue etc., take place as a whole. The tune issuing from the harmonium is very pleasant, but if this tune is analysed into its notes, the tune vanishes.

According to the gestalt theory, perception is fixed or controlled by the psychological activities in the nervous system which result from the stimulation from physical objects. Whatever the person sees, depends to a great extent, upon the sensations from the perceived object.

The orchestra in film music is very attractive, because the sound of many instruments is incorporated in it. If the basic constituents of a scent are smelled the odour may be detestable, in contrast to the delightful smell of the scent in the form of a compound in its finished state.

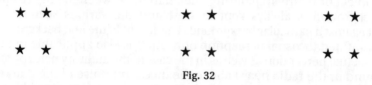

Fig. 32

The flowers illustrated above are nothing strange, because you must have seen them in many books. But do you notice anything special about them? Of course you do, as you notice that they are divided into 3 groups of four each. Obviously, the physical position and the spatial relation of the object influence their perception. The spatial relation depends not on the perceiver but on the perceived object. These independent sensations which, in the field of knowledge, establish the specific organisations, are known as the constructive organs of the process of perception. The gestalt psychologists have derived some laws of organisation based on these. The major laws are the following :

Laws of Organisation

(1) **Law of Whole.** The law so entitled is the most important among the laws of organisation and this is the opinion of its discoverers, the gestaltists. This law states that the total situation is perceived simultaneously. The collection of all the sensations impresses itself on the brain of the creature as an organised structure. The word Gestalten in the German language implies this organised structure.

The first thing that attracts your attention in the following figure is the organisation of the material, whence you observe that some asterisks have been arranged in pairs. You then turn your attention to the number in the figure and it is doubtful that you pay any attention to some particular flower. You hardly notice a solitary asterisk.

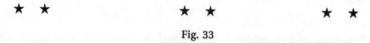

Fig. 33

The law of whole means that the whole is noticed first in perception. This is the reason why a person sometimes overlooks minor and insignificant defects in the picture. If we make an effort, we will find that we are unable to remember the individual peculiarities of the eyes, nose etc. of persons we know very well, unless we have paid conscious and deliberate attention to him. The reason attributed to this is that we have perceived the face as a whole and not attended to the different parts. The law has been proved by the gestalt psychologists with many examples of illusions.

(2) **Law of Figure and Background.** This is the second law of organization. The perception of a sensation is always based on something. The background affects in no small measure the perception of the object or figure. In painting, the relation between the figure and the background is always kept in view and the various scenes are present against a particular background. This law of figure and background is not confined to visual perception only but it is also applicable in the case of tactual perception as well as in the case of the auditory perception. The sound of the radio heard above the incessant noise of the market place is set in the noisy background. The background provided by an orchestra for film song is such as to increase the melody of the song.

Determining Laws of Figure and Background

The Gestalt psychologists did not rest content with the laws of organisation but they also provided laws, based on experimental findings, which determine the figure and background. These laws are as follows :

(1) **The Law of Similarity.** This is the first law. Two parts similar in any way, *e.g.,* colour, figure, extension, etc., have a tendency to become organised.

When we direct our attention to the asterisks in the Fig. 34 we see organised framework of three perpendicular and five horizontal lines. Similarly, if our attention is focussed on the circles we see an organised figure in the form of four perpendicular and two horizontal lines. But, ordinarily we do not see the square drawn on the right, and even if we do, it stands out by itself a solitary figure. It is not organised either with the circles or with the asterisks.

It is clear from this description that similar parts become organised and are viewed as wholes.

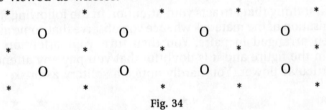

Fig. 34

(2) **The Law of Proximity.** The second determinant law is the law of proximity which states that objects in close proximity in time and space exhibit a tendency to organise with the result that they are perceived as wholes.

Fig. 35

(3) **The Law of Symmetry.** This is the third law. When placed in an order or symmetry, the various parts become organised into a whole and they are then perceived as such. This is more effective than either similarity or proximity.

(4) **The Law of Homogeneity.** The fourth determinant of figure and background is the law of homogeneity. Two parts of equal intensity or brightness are easily assimilated. In a given figure in one there were two concentric circles while in the other space in between the same circles was coloured. They were, therefore, organised and gave the appearance of a ring, instead of two circles.

(5) **Continuity.** This too, has an effect on organisation. The law of constancy was enunciated on the basis of continuity.

(6) **Closure.** This too, when compared to continuity, has an effect on the organisation of parts. See the Fig. 36. On first seeing it one observes, a triangle, a circle, a square, another circle and a hexagon. If the eye is not moved along the lines of each figure, nothing is visible. Three lines are, of course, visible but they do not make any angle because they do not meet. A careful observation, similar to the preceding one, of the two circles, the square and the hexagon will reveal that there is no figure in the picture. The illusion of figures in the first case was caused by closure which did not allow the attention to dwell on the gaps, so that the figures appeared organised.

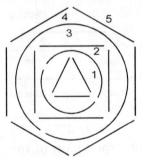

Fig. 36

Besides the six peripheral factors, mentioned; Wertheimer and other Gestalt psychologists suggested some central factors which are in the person, in contrast to the peripheral factors which are outside him. They organise the sensations received by the person in a certain way. They are :

(1) **Familiarity.** The organisation with which the person is acquainted is perceived easily and with alacrity. Seeing a familiar picture quiz we at once understand its reality and solution and the remaining figure forms no obstacle in this. If the picture quiz is presented to some uninitiated person he will be unable to fathom its secret. But if the acquainted person is affected by some other part of the picture, he will

be incapable of recognising it, notwithstanding his familiarity. Therefore, the Gestalt psychologists give it as their considered opinion that familiarity may or may not affect perception.

(2) **Mental Set.** This is the second central factor. Mental set has, by no means an insignificant effect upon the organisation of the sensations. One of the causes of mental set is habit. For example, a philosopher looks at the truths of the universe while a trader is always involved in worldly things, because they both need this for their differing occupations. Mental set may also be created by a situation as a person finds himself exasperated at the slow speed of a carriage. This is in spite of the fact that it is the fastest carriage. It is because of his hurry to get to his destination. The differences in mental set are the cause of the varied perception of the same thing by different people at the same time or the same people at different times.

Reinforcing Factors

The Gestaltists believed in reinforcing factors, besides the other two. These include pregnance and good figure. The supplementing of the incomplete is a mental tendency, which diverts our attention from the gaps and presents a circle. The idea of good figure is explained by the picture in the description of closure.

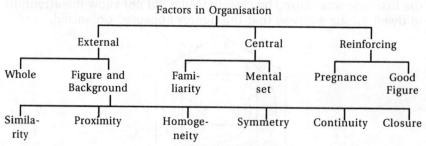

ILLUSION

An illusion is a misinterpretation of the correct meaning of a perception. It is not a dream because the perceived object is present and it is not imagination because the object of perception is not a creation of the mind of the individual. An illusion is a wrong or false perception. A stick appears crooked when held partly under water. This is perception, of course, but not in keeping with the situation of the perceived object as it is falsified due to some reason.

HALLUCINATION

Hallucination is dissimilar to illusion. The vision of an oasis at a distance in a desert is a hallucination. Some people see a ghost in the dark. This is another example of a hallucination. Some people relate strange incidents of hallucination *e.g.*, a woman dressed in a white saree came at midnight and sat down on my bed and she massaged my feet etc. These are examples of hallucinations.

There are the following differences between hallucination and illusion :

1. In illusion, there is a distinct external stimulus, while in the case of hallucination the external stimulus is often absent, as exemplified by the example of the white-robed woman.

2. While illusion often happens to very ordinary people, hallucination befalls the lot of mentally afflicted, tired or intoxicated people.

3. In illusion the stimulation is usually external while the stimulations in hallucination are in the person himself, which make the latter a kind of subjective perception.

4. The perception of the same situation is identical to every person in the case of illusion. The stick in the water appears bent to every observer. The illusion is, thus, a primitive organisation. On the other hand, in a special condition different people have different types of hallucinations due to diversified intoxications. Some people see ghosts, others snake while still other people see giants with swords when in an uncommonly intoxicated condition.

Distinction between Illusion and Hallucination

Illusion	Hallucination
1. The stimulus is explicit.	1. The stimulus is not clear.
2. Happens in a normal condition.	2. Happens in an abnormal condition.
3. The stimulus is external.	3. It is in person himself.
4. The experience is identical for everyone, in the same situation.	4. The experiences vary in different people in the same situation.

Types of Illusion

A comprehensive classification of illusions is made under two heads — personal and general. The personal illusions are those which differ from individual to individual. In the dark, some people mistake a rope for a snake but a person unfamiliar with a snake cannot make this mistake. On the contrary he is more likely to mistake a snake for rope. The common illusions are of a universal kind and are similar in the case of every person. The railway tracks appear to meet at a distance which is an experience common to all. Geometrical illusions are similar in appearance to everyone. A famous example of an illusion,

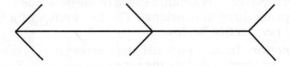

Fig. 37

is Muller Layer Illusion. The straight-line is divided into equal parts at the apex of the middle angle but the left part appears longer.

Causes of Illusion

There are many theories which were advanced to explain the phenomena of illusion. The following is a collection of the causes according to the various theories :

(1) **Confusion.** One of the major causes of geometrical and similar illusions is confusion. Confusion means the impurity or inaccuracy of perception of the various parts of a picture. Often a beautiful form tends to cause illusion by confusing. While looking at a picture, the person becomes so engrossed in it that he does not notice the peculiarities of the parts or the merits and demerits of the picture.

(2) **Eye Movement.** The movement of the eyes has a lot to do with the creation of illusions. In the given figure, there is a greater strain on the eyes in viewing the perpendicular than the horizontal line with the result that the former appears longer.

In the Muller Layer Illusion (Fig. 37) the lines AB and CD are of equal lengths, though AB appears longer due to eye movement. AB is the feather headed line while CD is the arrow headed line. Comparatively, there is more movement in perceiving the feather headed line than in perceiving the arrow headed line. Therefore, the former appears longer than the latter. Actual eye movement is not necessary, because even an equivalent tendency to it will be sufficient to cause an illusion.

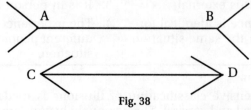

Fig. 38

(3) **Tendency Towards Wholes.** This is another cause of illusions. This theory of illusions is the creation of the Gestalt psychologists. In perception there is a tendency to view the whole. This tendency towards whole is also known as the tendency towards the perception of Good Figure. The tendency to the perception of good figures or wholes leads sometimes to the perception of angles in the triangle which are not there.

(4) **Perspective.** It is another cause of illusion, due to which every object appears three dimensional. The perception of a figure in the context of perspective is illusory.

(5) **Emotion.** In an emotional state perception is often false and this causes an illusion. In fear the rope appears in the form of a snake

while the scraping noise created by rats feels like the walking of thieves.

(6) Contrast of Stimuli. Yet another cause of illusions is the contrast of stimuli. A fair face looks more fair if viewed next to a dark face due to the sharp contrast.

In the following Fig. 39 the two circles A and B are of equal diameter, but because A is surrounded by asterisks while B is surrounded by circles, B appears smaller than A. Many of the above mentioned reasons are at work in this illusion. A looks bigger in contrast to its surrounding asterisks but B looks smaller due to an unavoidable comparison with its surrounding circles, so that, on the whole, B appears smaller than A. B also looks bigger than A because we tend to observe the whole picture with the result that the tendency towards wholes or perception of good figures comes into play. The perception is illusory due to an imperfect isolation and also due to eye movement and confusion.

(7) Preconception. This, too, causes illusions. If for example, a person is daily visited at a fixed hour, the person may feel that he has heard his name pronounced, on a day when the friend has not actually put in an appearance.

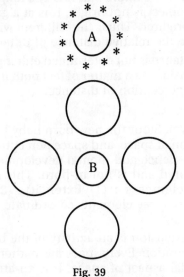

Fig. 39

(8) Habits. Habits also cause illusion as is exemplified in the mistakes of the inexperienced proof readers.

(9) Defects of Sense Organs. Defective sense organs cause incorrect perception and consequently an illusion. A person running a temperature finds sugar tasteless.

(10) Imperfect Isolation. There is a possibility of deception due to imperfect isolation, an example of which is the Size-Weight Illusion.

Two boxes of equal weight but of very unequal size are taken. A person lifting them will report that the smaller is infinitely heavier.

The above description includes all the major causes of illusion.

Perception of Distance

The relative distance of the different objects is known through active touch and movements. By active movements there is a direct perception of the distance. This perception of the distance is constituted by two elements : (1) Tactual sensation and (2) Muscular or movement sensation. Thus, by extending the hand or the leg, one has the perception of short distances. Long distances are however perceived through walking or running. The distance is not directly perceived through the vision. Perception of the distance through the vision depends on visual signs. These visual signs are not innate or inborn, but acquired. They include various types of shades, the differences of colours, relative motion, the definiteness or indefiniteness of the outlines etc. *e.g.*, if a tree is clearer than another, it will be perceived nearer than the other. Thus, clearness is a visual sign of the distance. As a general rule things nearer to us are seen clearer than those which are at a distance. Again, if a big thing is perceived as small, one infers that it is at a long distance. Similarly, if the colour of an object is not bright, it is at a greater distance than when it appears brighter. Thus, the different visual signs help the vision to determine the relative distance of different objects.

The relative distance is not determined either purely by movement or purely through vision. As a matter of fact both movement and vision co-ordinate in the perception of distance.

Perception of Space

According to Prof. Stout the new born baby has only a vague and indefinite perception of space, and space perception becomes definite and clear with experience and mental development. Thus, the space perception is acquired and is not in-born. This is acquired through these important elements : (1) Extensity, (2) Local signs and (3) Movement. These three elements co-ordinate in the perception of space.

(1) **Extensity.** Extension is an activity of the body while extensity is an attribute of sensation. Every space has matter and form. Extensity signifies the material aspect of space. It is an attribute of spreading out, possessed by sensation *e.g.*, the pressure of a needle on the skin is very little extended in comparison to that of a coin. If you put your finger in the water and again the whole hand into it, the later sensation is far more extended than the former one. The sound of a clock is definitely less extended than the sound of a shot, just as the light of a candle has less extensity than the glare of lightening. All these examples make it amply clear that different sensations have different extensity. Thus, extensity is not an attribute of the objects, but of the sensations.

According to Prof. Stout, extensity forms the material part of extensions while space the formal part of it.

Thus, the perception of space starts with extensity in sensations. But this alone is not sufficient since, as has already been pointed out, it is only the material part of the extension while the space is the formal part. Hence, extensity requires space for its form. This space perception is not in-born, but acquired. It is acquired by learning the position, distance and direction of the different parts of an extended substance.

(2) **Local Sign.** The second important element in the perception of space is local signs. It is through these that the local parts of a space are distinguished. "Local signs are qualities, which vary, independent of the nature of stimulus, according to the nature of stimulus, according as this or that part of the surface is effected." Thus, the same stimulus creates different sensations on the different parts of the body. Local signs are not a quality of the stimulus. It is because no two parts of the body are identically the same. Hence, different parts have different sensations from the same stimulus e.g., the sensation of the touch on the cheek is very much different from the sensation of the touch on palm. If one touches the tip of one's nose one experiences a different sensation than if the bridge of the nose is touched. Thus, sensations of different parts of the same hand are different. The sensation on the palm is different from the sensation on the hand. Again, different spots of the retina have different sensations of the same stimulus. The difference in sensations causes difference in local signs, by knowing which the precise position of a sensation can be determined e.g., in a pin pricking the back of hand the local sign is different from the pricking of the pin on the palm of the hand. By this difference in local sign, the perceiver can determine whether the pin is pricking the back or the palm of the hand. Thus, the local signs differentiate the whole into the parts of which it is composed, because different parts of the whole come in contact with different parts of the body of sense organ.

(3) **Movement.** But the space perception is not possible by mere differentiation of the parts, since a space is a whole and not merely a sum of parts. Hence, these parts should be spatially related. This is done through active movements. To give an example, when a blind man or a man with closed eyes, perceives a table through touch, he moves his fingers gradually, from point to point on the whole table. Through these subsequent movements the fingers pass through many points and hence different local signs. Thus, the movements relate the different points on the table and a definite arrangement of different parts is established. Along with tactual experience in the movements, there are muscular sensations due to the movement of muscles etc. The series of positions on the table and the series of muscular sensations are experienced together and so they get closely related.

The space is perceived through extensity, local signs and movement. In this spatial perception the role of eyes is most important. It supplements touch and sometimes even supersedes it, though space perception starts with touch. As a matter of fact space is perceived through the co-operation of both touch and vision unless the person is blind.

QUESTIONS FOR EXERCISE

1. What is perception? What light does study of illusions throw on perception?
2. Define perception and analyse the factors involved in it.
3. What are the various factors that influence perception? Explain with illustrations.
4. Explain principle of perceptual grouping.
5. What is perception? Discuss the role of Figure and Ground in determining perception?
6. Distinguish between sensation and perception. What are the laws of sensory organisation?
7. "A perception is nothing more than a sensation." Evaluate this statement in the light of Gestalt theory.
8. What are illusions? Explain with the help of examples the illusions caused by various factors.
9. Write note on Geometrical illusion.
10. Distinguish between an illusion and a hallucination.
11. Explain perception of distance.
12. Explain visual space perception. Explain fully the binocular determinants of perceived distance.

12

ATTENTION AND DISTRACTION

Attention is a selective process. Man lives in an environment. The stimuli from the environment are always affecting him. But these stimuli do not affect him equally. It is a common place observation that some stimuli affect us more than others. This shows that man selects out of environmental stimuli. This tendency of selection shows that there is a motivational process in him which is known as attention. This attention is affected by interest, attitudes and set. It is a selective process which includes motivation, set and selection. The cat will attend to the mouse, one can see a definite set in it. This set is both physical as well as mental. To take an example from human beings, if a student is motivated, he will attend to the class lecture. Again, while a professor is delivering a lecture in the class, there are several other sounds being made in other rooms and the surroundings. The student who hears the lecture selects professor's voice out of the noise in the surroundings. While a student is attentively hearing the lecture, one can very well note his physical set which is also symbolic of his mental set. Receptor adjustment, postural adjustment, muscle attention and central nervous adjustment are typical of bodily attitude in attention. Thus, in brief, attention can be defined as a process which compels the individual to select some particular stimulus according to his interest and attitude out of the multiplicity of stimuli present in the environment.

DETERMINANTS OF ATTENTION

As a selective act of the mind, attention depends upon several conditions. These conditions may be of two types — external or objective and internal or subjective. External or objective conditions are related with the environment. In the environment or surrounding of the individual there are several stimuli, but he does not attend to all of them at the same time, because some stimuli are stronger than others. The factors making these stimuli stronger than others, are known as external determinants of attention. Besides the external conditions the mental conditions, culture and heredity also influence attention. Due to these internal conditions some objects attract our attention more than others. These internal factors are internal determinants of attention. The methods of achieving attention are based upon these external and internal determinants of attention.

External Determinants of Attention

The following are the most important external determinants of attention :

(1) **Nature of Stimulus.** Nature of stimulus means its type, *i.e.*, whether it is visual, gustatory, auditory, olfactory or tactual stimulus. It has been found by experiments that in comparison with other sensations, form, colour and sound attract more attention. Among the pictures, the pictures of human beings attract more attention than those of animals or objects. Among the pictures of human beings those of beautiful women attract more attention. Besides these, the coloured pictures attract more attention than black ones. All these factors are important in advertisement. In the auditory stimulus, the melodious voice attracts more attention than other voices.

(2) **Intensity of the Stimulus.** The intensity of the stimulus is a helpful condition in attention. In comparison with the weak stimuli the intense stimulus attracts more attention of the organism. High sound, excessive pressure and acute pain attract our attention. In the market there is always some buzzing sound and yet the pedestrians hear the horn of the motor car, since the sound of the horn is louder than other sounds. But it is not always necessary that one should attend to the intensity of stimulus. Sometimes while walking on the road, calling of our name attracts so much attention that we fail to hear even the loud sound of the motor horn. As a matter of fact, the attraction of the attention does not depend on any single factor, but on several factors interconnected with one another. Hence, it can be said that other things being the same, the more intense stimulus will attract more attention.

(3) **Size of the Stimulus.** In the visual stimuli the size of the stimulus is also a determinant of attention. As a general rule the bigger size attracts more attention but a small advertisement of a very wide background also attracts attention. Thus, the attraction of an object does not depend upon its size alone, but also on its background. To illustrate, a big black spot on black face will not attract so much attention as a very small black spot on a white face.

(4) **Location of the Stimulus.** The location of the stimulus also affects attention. In the visual stimuli, the most effective location is just in front of the eyes. The role of different pages in the newspapers or the magazine and the different places on the same page, is important in advertisement. It has been found by experiments that advertisements given on the front page or on the upper half of any page attract more attention.

(5) **Contrast of the Stimulus.** The contrast of the stimulus is also an important determinant of attention *e.g.*, the presence of a woman among men and that of a man among women definitely attracts more attention.

(6) Change of the Stimulus. Attention cannot be concentrated for a long time on some particular object. Hence, the change of the stimulus affects attention. Attention is sustained by change of the stimulus. The advertisers change their advertisements from time to time lest they may cease to be attractive.

(7) Isolation of the Stimulus. A man sitting alone in some corner of the park, hotel or club attracts more attention than others. A student sitting alone at the far corner of the class, is seen first. Thus, isolation is an important external determinant of attention. This fact is based upon the reason that the isolated individual is not mixed with other individuals and hence seen separately in his own background. By experiments in advertisement it has been found that only the fact of isolation attracts 30% more attention. In the *British Journal of Educational Psychology* of August 1951, D.B. Berlyne points out the following principles based upon latest experiments :

(a) In comparison with the unchanged stimulus the stimulus changed in the near past has more possibility of attracting attention.

(b) The effect of the change goes on diminishing with the passage of time.

(c) Whenever stimuli are changed together and in which one is left unchanged, the effect of change is not noticeable.

(d) If change goes on in the changed stimuli, the process of attention is rather permanent and strong.

The modes of change also influence the process of attention. If there is a change absolutely opposite to the present stimulus it will definitely attract more attention. While studying one does not hear the sound of the clock or that of electric fan but if either of these suddenly stops, one cannot fail to attend to it. Man becomes used to regular changes and does not pay much attention to them. But if some irregular change or any sudden change occurs, it at once draws attention.

(8) Duration of the Stimulus. As a general rule, the stimulus having more duration, attracts more attention. The duration of the stimulus is an important determinant of the attention. But sometimes the smallest flashing of a movement attracts more attention than the bigger stimuli, *e.g.* a sudden flash of light for several seconds will attract more attention in a dark night than a continually burning lamp.

(9) Repetition of the Stimulus. Along with duration, repetition of stimulus is also an important determinant of attention. It is a common-place observation that when the teacher has to attract the attention of students towards a particular phenomenon, he repeats it several times. But sometimes, man ceases to attend a phenomenon simply because it is repeated many times, *e.g.*, if a man says some thing about him, we take interest in it once or twice, but if we find that he always repeats the same thing, we cease to pay attention to it.

(10) **Movement in the Stimulus.** In comparison with the static, the moving stimuli attract more attention. The position of stimulus changes due to movements. An object lying in some corner of the room will not attract our attention, but even if there is some illusion of movement in it we cannot help attending to it. The influence of movement in stimulus is widely used by the shopkeepers and businessmen, who advertise through moving electric lights.

Internal Determinants of Attention

The conditions of attention as described so far are the external determinants of attention. They can also be called external laws of attention. The presence of these conditions in the environment is helpful for attention. Besides these external conditions, some internal conditions are also helpful in drawing attention. These conditions are related to motives. As a matter of fact, the influence of conditions depends on these internal conditions to a very great extent. The hungry man will attend to the form and stimuli of the food. A man with a full belly will not attend to food, however nice it might appear. In the advertisement, those demonstrating the naked organs of the women have the maximum power of attraction of attention. Those interested in cinema look to the advertisements of cinema at first sight. It is difficult to describe all the internal conditions helpful in attention. Hence, only the most important will be enumerated here :

(1) **Interest.** Innate and acquired interests draw the individual's attention to a particular object. Doctors, engineers, professors, all attend to the objects of their own interest. Even among the professors an object attracting the attention of a professor of geology need not attract the attention of a professor of philosophy as well. Thus, the innumerable differences in interests create innumerable determinants of attention of different men. The stimuli influencing innate tendencies attract more attention than those influencing acquired interest.

(2) **Basic Drives.** The basic drives or instincts of the individual are also important in drawing his attention. The animal attends to a particular stimulus when driven by the basic drives of hunger, thirst, sex, etc., e.g., a normal man motivated by sex will naturally attend to individuals of opposite sex. We all know by experience that when hungry we may attend to even a distasteful object, but while our belly is full, we may not attend even to the most tasteful food. Among the instincts, the fear has got a definite influence upon attention. All men who fear snake will attend to all things resembling the snake. Like fear, curiosity also influences attention. We attend to even the smallest details of the object about which we have any curiosity.

Innate need also is very important in attention. The influence of sexual need in attention is very much exploited in the advertisements. Normally, the sexual need in human beings can be easily evoked. Hunger, thirst etc., are felt occasionally and the means to satisfy them are also readily available, but neither the sexual need is ever fully satisfied nor are the means of satisfying it available to all persons all the time. Hence, most of the advertisements draw attention by stimulating the sexual need in human beings.

(3) **Mental Set.** Mental set is one of the most important internal determinants of attention. Mental set means the tendency or attitude of the mind. A man will attend to those objects towards which his mind is set. In the days of examinations, the mental set of students is generally towards the examination and hence even the smallest thing concerning the examination will attract their attention.

(4) **Aim.** Aim also influences attention. Every man has some immediate and some ultimate aims *e.g.*, the immediate aim of the student is to pass the examination while the ultimate aim may be to get a job to earn living or any thing else. The man whose aim is not to pass the examination will not be concerned with textbooks or notes etc., but one who has the aim to pass the examination will at once attend to them.

(5) **Meaning.** In comparison with meaningless things, meaningful things and talks attract more attention. A man will not attend to a thing which has no meaning for him. Men do not like to hear meaningless talk. If some persons are talking in Tamil, the Punjabi will not like to hear it since for him it has no meaning.

(6) **Habit.** Habit is also an important determinant of attention. If a man is habituated to rising early and winding his clock early in the morning, he must attend to the clock as soon as he gets up. It has been rightly pointed out that man learns as to which object he should attend to and to which he should not, and thus develops habits of attending and not attending to things. Thus, habit has two aspects in relation to attention. On the one side, man develops a habit of attending to necessary desirable things and on the other side he develops the habit of not attending to unnecessary and undesirable things. Both these kinds of habits help man in his daily routine.

(7) **Disposition and Temperament.** Both disposition and temperament are important internal determinants of attention, *e.g.*, a man having a religious disposition and rational temperament will attend to religious matters, while another person having a sexual disposition and passionate temperament will attend to matters concerning sex or crimes etc. William James has rightly pointed out that it is our tendency to take interest in particular things, a result of our innate disposition and mental development, that determines as to which among the crowd of sensations, should attract our attention.

(8) **Past Experience.** Past experience also affects attention. If we know it by our past experience that a particular person is sincere towards us, we shall pay attention to whatever he advises us. If we

know by experience that he is not sincere to us, we shall not attend even to his most serious advices.

(9) **Emotion.** Emotion is also an important determinant of attention. It is a matter of everyday experience that we attend even to the smallest fault of the person whom we hate while we do not attend even to the greatest blunder of a person whom we love. A mother seldom finds faults with her child. The lovers find the whole world singing and dancing and immersed in romance.

(10) **Social Motives.** Social motives are very important determinants of attention. In advertisements the human figures attract more attention than figures of animals and things. The reason is that man is guided by his social motives. The news about altruism, bravery and saving another's life by putting oneself in danger attracts our attention because we praise these qualities. Men attend to things concerning their duties because of social motives.

Besides the conditions described above, many other factors influence attention. Heredity, education and training have a wide influence on attention. The family, school, club, class and society of which an individual is a member, do have some influence on his attention. The physical condition, desire, purpose of the person concerned also affect his attention. Thus, all the factors affecting the personality of a man affect his attention as well. As a matter of fact, it is difficult to describe all direct and indirect determinants of attention. The description given, however, includes the most important of such factors.

KINDS OF ATTENTION

(1) **Voluntary Attention.** Voluntary attention (its name is indicative of its nature) is that attention which is willingly directed to an object. If, for example, a student attends to his studies of his own account and not as a result of any external pressure, his attention will be called voluntary attention. An analysis reveals elements of desire and interest, aim and social adjustment in this voluntary attention. In the foregoing example the student directs his attention because of particular aim like the passing of an examination, acquiring knowledge or one of a number of other goals. He takes an interest in studying. By passing the examination or acquiring knowledge he may be able to support a family or gain social standing and status. Like other activities, sensation is just another form of adjustment. The difference between the voluntary and involuntary attention is that while the former is secured by the motivating elements in the individual, the motivating elements exist outside in the later case. Thus, when attention is suddenly attracted by a song, the attention is called involuntary.

(2) **Involuntary Attention.** As has been explained above, involuntary attention is not only directed by the individual's desire of motivation, it may even be against it. It hinders the process of goal seeking sometimes, not always. If, for example, your attention is attracted by a song while

you are studying, your studies will be hindered. Social adjustment is similarly obstructed by involuntary attention. The proper adjustment of a student can be the outcome only of an undisturbed attention to his studies. On account of the fact that one can pay attention to only one thing at a time, the student will not be able to attend to his studies if his attention continually wanders in other directions. Obviously, a person forgets his goal owing to involuntary attention and cannot effect his adjustment.

(3) **Habitual Attention.** Besides the two types of attention mentioned above, there is a third type, the habitual or non-voluntary attention. The difference between non-voluntary and involuntary attention is that the former type is the result of some habit or practice and the motivation is in the individual but the reason or attention in the later type is in the object. Habitual attention is different from voluntary attention because habitual attention has no need for a desire as the latter does. But continued application of voluntary attention converts it to habitual attention. For example, a student pays voluntary attention to study in the beginning but it is gradually transformed into habitual attention towards reading or writing. Thus, the position of habitual attention is in between voluntary and involuntary types of attention.

Actually, the above distinctions made in attention are not very clear. The difference between voluntary and involuntary attention is often only just discernible. No attention can be said to belong to any one of the three types completely. A scholar has to exercise his desire in spite of his involuntary attention in reading. There is an unconscious desire to pay attention to an object which involuntarily draws your attention. In this way, the difference in the types of attention is small though it is of great importance from the psychological viewpoint.

The nature of attention permits of its concentration in only one direction at one time. Direction of attention to two or more objects means either their acceptance as one or such an oscillation of attention between all of them as gives the impression of simultaneous attention. But experiments have proved, beyond doubt, that a person can pay attention to only one object at a time.

Distraction

Distraction means the dividing of attention or some interference in attention. For example, when one is studying, the sound of a song or noise breaks in upon attention. The object which causes the distraction is called the distracter. In fact, broken attention is not absence of attention because the distracter is associated with the activity, often, though not always, and it no longer interferes with the activity.

Thus, the notion that distraction invariably hinders work is misleading, it being seen, for example, that the labourer produces more when there is music. Some labourers, men and women, sing at work in view of this fact. Not a few people do their reading and writing while the radio is playing. Some people work better in a noisy environment than in a peaceful one. Experiments conducted by Morgan indicated that at first distraction caused a drop in the speeds of typewriting but it later became constant. Pursuing the work in the disturbed condition increased the speed and it again dropped when the distraction was removed. But distraction in some experiments by Weber caused harm. Though it cannot be definitely said that distraction increases the speed of the work, it is possible to say with some degree of confidence that a decrease in speed due to distraction is not inevitable. Actually the effect of a distraction on some work depends in no small measure upon the capacity, interest, practice, skill and mental set of the worker. If the distraction is suitable the speed will be increased but if it is unsuitable the speed will drop. Roughly, distraction can be divided into two forms :

Form of Distraction

(1) **Continuous Distraction.** As the name suggests, it is the continuous distraction of attention. Some examples of it are the sound of radio or gramophone played continuously, the noise of the market place etc. Experiments have led to the conclusion that adjustment to continuous distraction takes place quickly.

(2) **Discontinuous Distraction.** This type is irregular, being interspersed with intervals e.g., the hearing of somebody's voice every now and then. It interferes with work because of an impossibility of adjustment.

Means of Removing Distraction

Some major means of removing distraction are :

(1) **Being Active in Work.** Work in distraction calls for more energy, so that one way of adjusting to it, or removing it, is to become more active in work.

(2) **Disregard of Distraction.** The presence of a distracting factor while a man works is no extraordinary condition, and so, the best way to remove this element is to disregard it. The distraction is effective only when attention is directed to it, so that in attention, even the most serious distraction, will keep that activity from being interfered with in any way.

(3) **Making the Distraction a Part of the Work.** Distraction is an obstacle only when it is distinct from the activity or against it since attention can be focused just on one object at one time. Therefore, another method of making a distraction ineffective is to make it a part of the work. Some people work better when listening to a song because they make it a part of their work. But this approach is very difficult because in this the interests, nature and capacities of the person are involved. It is very difficult to make an uninteresting and contradictory distraction a part of the work.

Attention and Perception

Attention is the selective activity of the mind. Perception is the understanding of the meaning of sensation. The perception of any one particular object in the midst of many depends on attention. Often you do not see it. You frequently pick out one voice or sound from among many because you attend to it before you attend to others. On the other hand, perception is not possible without attention. Attention is a selective activity but selection will take place only if many objects or activities are present in the conscious area. Therefore, attention is possible only after perception. Perception is inevitable after attention but attention does not necessarily follow perception. The two are, obviously, intimately related.

Fluctuation of Attention

Attention is a mobile or dynamic activity, and it is difficult to attend to one particular object for any great length of time. When attention moves from one object to another, it is called the shifting of attention. But even when the attention persists with one object, it grows more or less. This is called the fluctuation of attention.

The causes of fluctuation of attention were, in previous times, attributed to the temporary slackness in the mental activities and sense organs. Some psychologists found the fluctuation even when the muscles had been numbed. The fluctuation was then believed to be due to the changes in adjustment or adaptation. Though nothing can be said definitely about the matter still the importance of the senses, mind, psychological state and environmental factors in fluctuation of attention is undeniable.

Attention and Interest

Attention is selective act of the mind. To attend to a thing is to concentrate on it by removing attention from other things. The mind can attend to one thing at a time. Hence mind has to select. In the selection it is natural that the mind should select such objects in which it is interested. This is amply demonstrated in our daily life. The boy whose interest is in playing will attend to play while one who is interested in studying will attend to study. Hence, one cannot attend to the studies by forcibly sitting for it. One can attend to the studies only when one is interested in it. Hence, the successful teacher tries to make the students interested in their studies.

Interest is affective disposition which evokes attention and maintains it. Interest is not activity. It is a permanent tendency or a mental structure which supplies sufficient motivating power to motor activity. Interest is sometimes innate and sometimes acquired. In the fulfilment of instinctive needs, the animal naturally shows interest. Thus, the individuals of different sexes are naturally interested in each other. The herbivorous animals are interested in grass while the carnivorous are interested in meat. Lion is interested in goat while goat is interested in green leaves. Besides the instinctive interest, there are some acquired interests as well, *e.g.*, the scientist is interested in the instruments of his laboratory while they are of no interest to the ordinary layman. Thus, individuals develop different interests according to their disposition, attention, economic, social and political status etc. Attitudes towards those things are mostly acquired. The acquired interest depends upon experience. The interest is directly related with the emotions and desires. The thing or the individual in which we are interested finds a place in our inner life and develops it through our emotions towards it. It is not necessary that the interest should be permanent. Things which do not fulfil any permanent need evoke only temporary interest. As the need is fulfilled, the individual ceases to take interest in such subjects, *e.g.*, if a man has to cross a river, he will be very much interested in the boat, but after he crosses the river his interest in the boat will also come to an end. Permanent interests are related with emotions and sentiments. They are permanent mental conditions. According to Drever interest is a disposition in its dynamic aspect. Interest is not an affective experience, but affective tendency. It is not mental process, but mental structure.

According to McDougall "Interest is latent attention, attention is interest in action." As it has already been pointed out, interest is mental structure and it is expressed through attention. When the individual is not attending to a particular object, his interest in it is in a dormant form, *e.g.*, suppose a man is interested in seeing a tennis match. Whenever there is a tennis match, he always goes to see it. He reads news about tennis very attentively. But neither a tennis match is played daily nor news about it is heard everyday. Hence, when this particular man is busy in the activities other than seeing the tennis match or hearing news about it, his interest in tennis remains latent. When we attend to an object, our interest in the object is manifested. If we are interested in a certain thing we must attend to it. A man interested in national progress will attend to every national issue. A man interested in women will normally pay attention to them.

Interest is a mental cause of attention. It is not necessary that all men should be acquainted with their interests. Sometimes when we attend to a thing, we wonder how we came to be interested in it. Sometimes we do not know as to in which things we are interested. Sometimes we are not prepared to accept that we are interested in a certain particular thing.

But the innate relation between interest and attention should not mean that one cannot attend to an object in which he is not interested or if one attends to a thing it necessarily means his interest in it. Very few persons are interested in studies. Mostly, the students study with the purpose of getting a degree or finding a job by passing through the examination. But this need not cause any deficiency in their attention.

Even when one is not interested in his studies, he can attend to it. There is no correlation between the degrees of interest and attention. As a matter of fact neither interest and attention are identical nor there is a positive correlation between them. Interest is a cause of attention, but attention is not a result of interest. By saying that there is innate relation between interest and attention, it is meant that interest is a very helpful factor in attention.

QUESTIONS FOR EXERCISE

1. What do you understand by attention? Give analysis of its nature.
2. Write short note on Determinants of Attention.
3. Describe the nature of attention and also its principal varieties.
4. Explain fully what is distraction and how you can overcome it.
5. Write a short note on Distraction.
6. What is the relation between attention and perception?
7. Can attention be identified with interest?

13

STUDIES OF ACTION : MOTIVATION

In the words of Guilford, "A motive is a particular internal factor or condition that tends to initiate and sustain activity." Thus, motivation includes all those internal conditions which begin an activity or sustain it. Motive is different from stimulus because it is there even before the stimulus. In the absence of internal motive there cannot be any response, however intense the external stimulus may be. The word motive includes all the internal and external factors that initiate an activity. But in psychology motive includes only those factors which control the activity of the living being. It does not include mechanical or reflex actions because they depend on the physical structure and the external environment. Such mechanical behaviour is observed in less developed animals. On the other hand, in the developed animals their changing physical and mental conditions control their behaviour. It is said that the horse can be taken to the water, but no amount of effort can make it drink. In spite of the presence of water, the horse will drink only when it feels thirsty. The motives depend on the changing physical conditions and past experience. A burnt child dreads the fire because the memory of burning is always present in his mind. Thus, it is clear that motivation explains the 'why' of behaviour. Why a certain animal or man behaves in a particular way can be known by an inquiry into his internal motivating factors. Sometimes this "why" can be inferred from external behaviour also. The influence of the sex motive can be inferred by a particular behaviour of a pair of pigeons. The cause of a particular behaviour towards the child shows tender motive in the mother. There can be one motive behind different actions and different motives behind the same action. A man can throw a rupee towards a beggar due to disgust and also due to pity. A soldier can save a person from drowning due to altruistic motive and also to take him to gallows. Psychology explains the real motives behind the behaviour and experience of the individuals and living beings.

Motivation in Learning

The motivation has much effect on learning. In the absence of motivation either there will be no learning or very little learning and the learned activity shall be forgotten very soon. On the other hand, sufficient motivation will release energy in the process of learning.

The motive gives energy for the continuation of the process of learning. It is due to motive that the student goes on studying attentively for weeks, months and you can very easily see the fact of motivation in his activity. He tries to learn cycling with perfect attention and with all his energy. He fails several times and gets cuts and bruises, but he does not cease to make effort. If he does not succeed one way he adopts another way. So long as he does not learn cycling, a restlessness is seen in him so much so that he often dreams of cycling. After he learns cycling, he seems to be very happy and is seen cycling now and then, here and there. This importance of motivation in learning has been widely utilised in education. A good teacher tries to excite motives in the students before beginning some new chapter or before asking them to learn some new work. As he succeeds in doing so, half of the work is over, because now he has only to guide the child, the rest the child learns himself. Learning is a voluntary activity. The more difficult a subject of learning is the more power will be required to learn it and consequently the more motivation is required for it.

Motivation is not only required in teaching, but also in learning for oneself. Hence, an intelligent student develops motivation in his studies. By motivation the learning becomes active. In it, the interest and attention are spontaneous, more work is done in less time and a thing learnt once is remembered for ever. Motivation has the same place in learning as energy in mechanical function.

CLASSES OF MOTIVES

Different classifications of motives have been effected from different viewpoints e.g., physiological, innate and acquired, personal and social. They have been given different names also e.g., needs, motives, propensities etc. The theory of instinct is included in this. Two types of motives are the most popular — logical and psychological needs and personal propensities while the acquired needs account for the social and the learnt personal needs.

Woodworth has divided motives into the following three categories :

(1) **Organic Needs.** Those motives which are aroused by the bodily conditions, e.g., hunger, thirst etc.

(2) **Emergency Motives.** Those motives which are aroused when the condition of the environment demands a strong and quick reaction, e.g., the motive to escape.

(3) **Objective Motives.** The object of these motives is impressionistic behaviour with people and the objects in the environment. This class of motives is quite comprehensive.

Other psychologists have classified motives under primary and secondary needs, while some classify them as innate and acquired. The later classification will be the one on the basis of which the following description will be made, because it is the simplest classification.

Internal Motives

Internal motives are not learnt, they are natural. They are the primary, vital, physiological and biological needs, which the person brings with him upon his entry into this world. Their fulfilment is indispensable and of prior importance. They are also necessary for the protection of life. The equilibrium of the body and the mind is disturbed if they remain unsatisfied and it can be restored only when these needs are satisfied. The microscopic cells or fibres of body led the psychologists to the hypothesis of drives which are internal motor activities.

Specific Organic Needs

First, mention will be made of the specific organic needs which may be described as animal drives. They are found both in men and animals, the only distinguishing feature being the mode of their fulfilment. Some of the major ones are :

(1) **Homeostasis.** This is specific organic need, in which the body tries to keep the condition of blood under control, because the equilibrium of the body is disturbed if quantity or proportion of water, salt, oxygen, carbon-dioxide, acid, sugar, protein, fat and glandular excretions is, in any way, altered. The body is anxious to maintain the normal balance. This balance needs water, oxygen etc. from the environment. Thus, homeostasis is the origin of many activities, in which the nervous system takes part. Many psychological motives are also conceived in homeostasis. The individual knows the means of satisfaction of some needs while knowledge of other means is supplied by experience and learning. When the person feels hungry due to some biological inefficiency, for the first time, he has not the least inkling of the sense from which the satisfaction is to come. But, when once his hunger is satisfied some way or the other, he discovers the means by which he may allay his hunger in the future.

(2) **Regulation of Temperature.** This is the second specific need of the body. The hypothalamus in the brain is an automatic machine which regulates the body temperature so that there is never any very substantial difference. Perspiring, trembling, lighting a fire, donning clothes, fanning oneself, installing cooling systems etc., are all perceptible or imperceptible activities caused by the hypothalamus.

(3) **Sleep.** This is the third specific need of the organism, the importance of which cannot be denied. The activity of sleeping consumes the individual's greatest share of time. Sleep is the natural reaction of the organism to fatigue and an absence of stimuli. Its centre, too, is the hypothalamus which induces sleep, when acted upon chemically. Experiments indicate that a person is not completely inactive in his sleep. Generally, he alters the posture of the body every twelve minutes or so. Sleep is deepest during the first few hours. It gradually becomes lighter as time passes. Every person has individual and unique habits

of sleep but this does not mean that sleep is a habit. If a person stays awake indefinitely his interest and energy become lax even though he may complete many of his activities as usual.

(4) **Hunger.** The stomach makes some motions when it is empty, which may vary in frequency from 10 a minute to 20 or 25 a minute.

Detailed investigations and experiments have shown that there is a close relation between blood chemistry and hunger. The reduction of the sugar in the blood starts hunger-sensation, while its excess reduces the hunger. If blood is transferred from a hungry dog to another dog, the latter starts feeling hungry. But it cannot be said that blood chemistry is the only factor upon which hunger is dependent, because the deficiency of proteins, fat, carbohydrate also results in hunger. Mostly, man or animal demands some particular type of food and not just food, when he is hungry. The choice is regulated by the deficiency in the body. During pregnancy, a mouse needs about twice the normal quantity of salt. It has been adequately demonstrated by experiment that the animal has not to be told the type of food to be consumed by it. When the feeding was done by the Cafeteria Method, in which the child may eat anything he likes, in any way which he may prefer and as much of it as he likes, the children soon started to pick out the food by mere vision or by smelling. This experiment proves that children develop properly if only they are fed in accordance with their wishes. Generally, there is no difference between the food suggested by doctors and food individually selected. The animals, *e.g.*, rats have individual preferences which change with alterations in bodily conditions. The choice of food is neither by trial and error only nor by the motivation of bodily needs exclusively. The physiological needs furnish a motive for the selection of food by trial and error. Human beings as well as animals eat more if they eat in a collective group. The taste, smell and shape of the food have a marked effect on its selection by human being. As a general rule habits are important in eating though these habits may be violated under certain circumstances. There are many harmless things which people do not like to eat. The rejection of a particular food by some individual does not indicate that it is harmful for him. In animals too, the hunger may be due to causes other than the biological needs. In experiments on hen it was found that she starts eating merely on the sight of a heap of grain, she stops eating but starts again if the grain is first removed and then replaced. She also starts eating if she sees other hens doing so, even when she has no appetite. A similar type of behaviour may be seen in human beings.

(5) **Thirst.** Thirst, too is a specific organic need, similar to hunger. A person is very restless and active if he is denied water for any length of time, even though every other need is satisfied, and this is an unmistakable sign of some deficiency. The throat and the mouth become dry due to the diminution of water in the salivary glands which is the result of a reduction of water in the blood. Consequently, there is a

strong desire to imbibe water or some liquid. Due to some social reasons, man does not feel restless even when extremely thirsty. Thirst cannot be definitely or indefinitely quenched by a mere wetting of the mouth and throat. This proves that the cause of thirst is not the drying up of the mouth and throat but rather the decrease in the normal quantity of water in the blood. The dogs, in experiments, drank the water they needed. This ratio seems to be the result of the balance maintained by the pituitary hormones.

Besides the specific organic needs mentioned above, the excretions of the waste products in the form of perspiration, urea etc., and the need for physical exercises is felt in men as well as in animals. They are both important for the body. The physiological needs mentioned so far are of vital importance for the life of creatures and are consequently vital physiological motives, and they have their origin in some organic condition or the other.

Some physiological needs will now be described whose stimuli and the resulting reaction may take many varied forms. A delay in their satisfaction, or incomplete satisfaction need not be of fatal significance for the individual. In case the natural means of satisfaction are not available other means may be adopted. Some of the more important among the less specific needs are :

(1) **Sex.** Being related to the sex glands, it is an organic need. It is a means of giving birth and sustaining the species. It is known by the seasonal menstrual changes in the female mammal. The manifestation has become very complex in view of the restrictions placed upon men by the society, though its importance cannot be denied. Sigmund Freud, the founder of the school of psychoanalysis, believed the sex motive to be the most important and comprehensive motive of all.

The inception of the sex motive is due to the excretion of a gland. In the male it is caused by the excretion of the sex glands, while in the female due to the ovaries. The circulation of the blood carries it to the brain, the resulting behaviour being of a type not normally observed. The normal activity due to this motive is an interest in the members of the opposite sex, and a particular type of behaviour towards such, the goal being the mating of the male and the female. In the lower species, the sex activity is related to the seasons, being the highest in spring when the daylight is of a longer duration. The light has an effect on the brain via the eyes and it excites the excretion of the pituitary. This excites the sex instinct.

(2) **Maternal Behaviour.** Maternal behaviour is a symbol of the love and affection a mother has for her child. It is believed that this form of behaviour is the consequence of a pituitary excretion, the prolactin which affects the brain and causes specific type of behaviour in the mother towards the child. She makes many and varied attempts to protect and lookafter her children, to get near them when they are

separated from her. Prolactin, when injected, created, maternal behaviour in a hen who had no chicks of her own. It is seen sometimes that the behaviour of the female towards her children is not exemplary. She deserts and sometimes even devours them. It cannot be concluded from this that the maternal drive is completely absent but all that this indicates is that there is a more powerful motive at work in the female at the time. Another reason for this extraordinary behaviour on the part of the mouse may be the deficiency of some material, a definite capable of being removed by the eating of the offspring. A mother, fearing disgrace or pursuing some other motive of prudence, may abandon a child without it being essentially assumed that she has no maternal love or that she is indifferent towards the parting.

The maternal behaviour in animals as well as birds presents many complex activities. Maternal behaviour, being similar to sexual behaviour in as much that it is innate and that it has a definite pattern in the species, is not the only aspect because the existence of the maternal instinct may also be accepted. The maternal behaviour becomes more specified with every increase in the level of development in species.

Maternal Behaviour in Human Beings

Maternal behaviour is compared with sexual behaviour because the presence of the maternal instinct is as unacceptable as the existence of the mating instinct. Besides, the existence of such an instinct is not clearly proved. A desire for children before they are born is one thing and their care and a love for them after they are born is another. In the present age, many educated, prosperous women consider children a mere burden. And if, in some way, a desire to give birth to a child is conceived the care of the child is entrusted to a nurse. Consequently, the desire for children, in women, is not universal and neither is the desire for their care. Nearly 75% of the 87 pregnant women, who were subjects in an experiment in U.S.A., replied in response to a question that they were not happy at the prospect of having children. About 60 per cent of another group of 66 pregnant women confessed that they had no plan about their children. The very substantial dissimilarity between the Indian and the American culture does not admit of the application of these experiments in identical form in Indian conditions. But if the westernized Indian ladies are the subjects of the experiments, the results will not differ to any great extent. If the element of culture is eliminated, it is unbelievable that the maternal behaviour is innate or instinctive. This fact is further strengthened by the fact that there is an intimate connection between maternal behaviour at an adult age and doll playing in the childhood. Many women have children because their husbands want them to other because they feel it is necessary, while other women feel that a childless woman is looked down upon by the society. Some women procreate because they feel that it is conventional. Those women who have children purely because they were motivated by the maternal instinct are not many. Another proof of the absence of the maternal instinct in woman is the fact that many children are devoid of the indispensable love of their mothers. On this point, there is a great difference among them. The patterns of maternal behaviour vary with the culture and the individual, a major part of which is learned. The girls learn their maternal behaviour by observing the behaviour of their parents and by playing with dolls, and even then there are very few successful mothers. In reality, the maternal behaviour in human beings is learned to so great an extent that it is difficult to accept it as motivated or instinct originated.

General Needs

Apart from the needs detailed above, there are some internal needs which are common to living beings. Woodworth calls them emergency motives, but they are also called general needs. The major ones are — Escape, Combat, Mastery motive etc.

(1) The Urge to Escape. The urge to escape is natural in danger when there is a possibility of physical damage. This urge is active in a dangerous situation. We jerk our hand away when it is pricked and similarly, an animal shrinks his foot if steps on a thorn. The tortoise withdraws its neck back into its shell on the slightest noise. The natural reaction to danger is the preparation for protection against it.

The signals of approaching danger are of importance in the urge to escape. These signals are different for different animals and are received from diversified sources. They are innocuous and the danger lies in the comprehension of their meaning. An interesting experiment was carried out to test this. A non-poisonous snake was given to people to touch. Children below two years did not show any fear while three-to-four-year old ones tried to get away from it. Older children ran away from it and college students definitely exhibited fear. In this way, children do not fear many things of which the elders are afraid.

The meaning of these indications is learned either by association or by controls. Besides association, children feel frightened if they see their elders similarly affected. There is a famous experiment conducted by Watson on this subject. A one-year old lad named Albert played with white rabbits, dogs or rats fearlessly. The boy was frightened by the noise of a hammer striking an iron rod just as experiment. The boy stepped back in alarm. When this process was repeated over and over again the child became frightened of the white rabbit, and started running away from it. He was so much affected by this incident that he started running away from the dog too. The conditioning in understanding the meaning of the danger is quite obvious. The child associated the noise with the animals and took the animals to be the signs of the danger. Comparatively more intelligent children did not associate the two. The hen screeches loudly on perceiving the kite and hen chicks are scattered. In the human beings too, a similar phenomenon may be observed. It is amply illustrated by the crying of the child who has seen his mother crying and screaming. The children learn to be frightened by lightening, rain or storm from their frightened elders.

The fear so learned gradually takes root in the mind of the child and becomes difficult to eradicate but sometimes it is the same conditioning that is used to remove these groundless fears. For some unknown reason a small boy, Shiboo by name, was frightened of rabbits. The fear was removed by conditioning. The experimenter placed a caged rabbit at a distance which did not disturb the tranquility of the boy and induce him to abandon his supper. The cage was gradually pushed nearer till the cage was very near the boy and when he got used to the spectacle the cage was dispensed with. Then the boy started playing with the rabbit, even when he was not eating. The boy thus ceased to associate the rabbit with the interesting condition of eating and forget his fear. This activity of fearing due to association is comparatively more in the young than in the adults because they do not associate any and every object with fear. An adult does not run away at the sound of an engine and neither does he associate, like a child, any noise with any object. But on the other hand, an educated and grown up person, by virtue of his understanding sees danger in objects appearing harmless to the uneducated or the child. There is no organ or gland which may give birth to fear. Some parts of the brain, do, of course, act in a fearful situation but the stimuli are generally external. These stimuli include the possibility of pain, injury or some other damage.

The means of escape to which a person may resort are not the same. To take an example, some people daydream in order to escape from danger, and they do so through the medium of imagination. The person afraid of other people in society begins to love solitude. Some people become ill when they want to avoid some stern duty. This method of escape is employed by soldiers, because some of them become ill as the danger of proceeding to the war makes itself manifest.

(2) **Combat Motive.** This motive is universally applicable. Its strongest stimulus is resistance. Commonly it is a normal experience that if you approach a cat, she runs away from you, but if all the avenues of escape are blocked she will bare her teeth and prepare to attack. If you restrain the movements of a child by holding its hands, legs, head, etc., it will go red in the face, screaming and struggling. Remove a chick from the hen, make fun with an irritable person or obstruct the culmination of the motive in an animal and the struggle will start. Usually the struggle is a reaction to the obstruction in the fulfilment of the motive.

The aim of combat is to remove or overcome the obstacle. An internal, physical and emotional confusion persists till the person either gets rid of the obstacle or overcomes it. The pattern of the struggle or combat does not conform to any rules and is therefore dissimilar in people. The same rule applies to the instruments used in action. The animals with long nails find in them admirable instruments or weapons for attack or defence. Usually, it is the male who does the fighting. He fights with members of other species and fights with members of his own group for the female or for his own food. The excretions which are the specialities of the feminine, probably suppress the element of combat. Some animals and men threaten before they fight. The monkey's threat is famous. Some animals achieve this by showing their teeth, others by screaming, while still others do it by thumping on the chest. Age, intellect, social and cultural factors alter the methods of combat. A civilized man manifests his combative tendencies indirectly. His enmity continues over the years and he adopted indirect methods in revenge. One form of combat, which is very popular or common in civilized societies, is the fighting of cases in law-courts. It is difficult to accept combat as instinct, drive or an internal motive whose sole aim is fighting. The tendency of competition may be innate but combat is usually seen actively when the fulfilment of a motive has been hindered. Combat is the result of anger but sometimes anger is expressed in some other way. An employee, rebuked by his senior cannot talk back to him for fear of loosing his job, so he gives vent to his anger on his wife or children. Our tendency to combat is sometimes excited by the sight of others fighting. Playing or watching a game in progress or boxing in films are all outlets for the tension of combat. In the family, the parents restrict many tendencies of children thus generating a feeling of ill-will in them, due to which the children worry the parents who feel disgusted with their children. Brothers and sisters compete with each other for the love of their parents. In the same way, the husband and wife also quarrel on some point or the other. A harmless outlet for these tensions is necessary to preserve the peace of the family. Play is adequate for the children. The elder people should be given an opportunity to have their say because it is better to get it off their chests.

Besides in motives mentioned above curiosity, play, humour etc., is innate behaviour.

Other Innate Motives

(3) **Curiosity.** This is a fundamental motive which has no particular bodily base. When a creature is confronted with an unfamiliar object, a desire to know or understand is naturally generated. In human beings, besides the tendency towards curiosity a feeling of surprise or curiosity is also observed. Everybody has a desire to know new things and see new places. A child, given a new thing, will turn and twist it to gain some knowledge of it. A child is always ready to ask questions which are endless. You may reprove him because you are tired of his questions but he will never be exhausted on this account. If the child's curiosity is not repressed, he will continue his search till he has acquainted himself with his surroundings. These are the children who

become great inventors, scientists and explorers if they preserve their curiosity tendencies to adult age. This is an important motive from the biological point of view. It makes the creature become familiar with his environment.

(4) **Urge to Play.** As a general rule, the urge to play is present in almost everybody. It is an innate tendency which has no specific centre in the body though it does depend upon the general condition of the body. A tired or convalescent person does not relish the idea of engaging in a game. The desire to play is felt only when the person has adequately rested and is healthy. A game is played when the person has enough energy and is not forced to spend it on some activity related to his livelihood. Children like to play more than the problems of life to struggle with.

The pattern of playing varies with the culture or the race and with the individual in the race. Some of the forms which playing takes are jumping, chasing, catching, fighting, sexual behaviour, construction and turning and twisting objects. Often, children are seen copying their elders at play. It is incorrect to interpret this to mean that games are a means of preparation for older life. Games definitely assist the activities of older life by strengthening the tissues and making them efficient to carry on some activities. But it cannot be accepted that games aim at the preparation for the life in future. The fundamental motive is the need for physical exercise and it may be expressed in any form, being directed by the environment in its expression. The tendency to gain superiority or the sex drive may be the alternative causes for the urge to play.

(5) **Humour or Laughter.** The tendency to laugh is nearly universal in people, and it is a special tendency present in human beings only. The action of laughing in people does not vary very much but the mirth raising situations do vary with the individual. No rule can be laid down to state the incident capable of raising laughter in a certain person. Some people are amused if they see some person slipping on a banana skin or people falling in a cycle accident or horse-carriage overturning, while other people may see nothing funny in these incidents. But leaving aside individual perversions, there are some things on which people generally do laugh. For example, we laugh at another person's mistakes, or we are amused on perceiving another in an embarrassing position. It is not uncommon that boys laugh when they talk of girls who, in their turn not harbouring any charitable feelings for the boys, laugh at the expense of the boys. Grownup boys and young people are vastly amused by sexual jokes. It is seen sometimes that people laugh more at broad and indecent jokes. Psycho-analysis give it as their considered opinion that such type of talk being prohibited and suppressed by society a tension is created the slackening of which on hearing such talks, leads to laughter. This does not lead on to say that every type of humour is a safety value for the evacuation of

suppressed elements of the sexual tendency. It is of course, established that there is a lessening of tension in laughter, and due to this view-point, the safety value theory is the best. Laughter is a tendency, similar to games, to get ride of tensions. It is natural to feel light and delighted after laughing.

ACQUIRED MOTIVES

So far we have treated of innate motives which are also called primary motives because they are directly related to the biological needs of the creature. These motives are active almost throughout life though the methods of satisfying them are modified with age and experience. These motives are universal because they are the creatures' heredity. A major share of them is directly or indirectly related to the physiological conditions of the creature. Though most of motives rely upon the physical condition of the creature it is not correct to conclude that all his motives are physical or internal. The internal motives are connected with the creature but there are some motives which are related to objects outside the creature. Woodworth called them objective tendencies. Many motives are the result of social effects. Gregariousness is a social motive. A child is unable to fulfil his physiological needs unaided. He learns the ways of their fulfilment from others. Thus, a developed individual fulfils his needs in accordance with the laws of society. This leads to a socialization of his needs, an activity in which the individual develops many needs and motives the physiological causes of which are difficult to trace. An example of this is the difficulty in identifying physiological causes with the lust for money, search for fame, literary and aesthetic tendencies of the modern man. It is apparent that many of the motives and needs of individuals are learned in society. They may be called secondary and non-vital motives. Some learned motives, which are found in most people in a greater or lesser degree, are now described. These being numerous, only the major ones will be dealt with here.

(1) **Praise and Blame.** The tendency to win the praise and avoid blame motivates human behaviour in nearly all societies. Every person wants to be praised by other people even though he may not like to be praised by them directly. Similarly, no one likes to be defamed or humiliated by others. Generally, the thought or right and wrong is linked with praise and blame. A person learns praise worthy behaviour and avoids a detestable one from his childhood. A child fights shy of punishable behaviour but gladly adopts behaviour which may earn him the love of his mother. Later, this tendency takes the form of praise and blame because praise is fruitful and blame is harmful. Even a person indifferent to the derogation or flattery of the society pays great attention to the praise or blame accorded to him by his own conscience which is the product of thoughts of the socially proper and improper. The experiments carried out to study the effects of praise or

blame establish that they definitely effect the person. The effect of praise is comparatively more than the effect of blame.

(2) **Mastery Motive.** Alfred Adler has accepted the mastery motive to be the most important motive in human life. According to him man tries to master others, in every field of life. Neitzsche believed the *'Will to Power'* to be the major motive in life. According to Darwin there is a struggle for existence at every step in Nature and it is the fittest who survives. It follows that every creature tries to attain power. Creatures living in groups have a leader who maintains his masterly position by force. Besides the leader there are people who are situated at different levels. The person who will replace the leader is also decided upon. Mastery may be ascertained by age, power or intelligence and these criteria of mastery change with the time and place. In animals, usually, it is the power which is the criterion of mastery.

As a consequence of the mastery motive a competitive tendency and a tendency to rivalry is found in most societies. When competing, a person invariably puts in greater efforts, and even more so when the competition is personal rather than in groups.

But these facts cannot go un-contradicted. The mastery motive, being acquired, it is not inevitable that it be found in every society. The tendency of self-assertion is so rare in Arapesh of New Guinea that it is an abnormality there. This tendency is uncommon in Zuni and Hopi Indians. Among these people the best man is not allowed to participate along with the other competitors. In observation it was seen that the Zuni children do not try to get ahead of others in a question competition and hesitate in showing results better than the others. Why are they so different from other societies in this respect? The elderly people in their society discourage the tendency of self-assertion in infancy whereas this tendency is encouraged right from the start in other societies. In comparison with the western society, the Indian child is taught to live peacefully, believe in God and depend on luck. Therefore, an Indian is comparatively less active than a member of the western society.

(3) **Aggressiveness.** This is an expression of the mastery motive. There is a great diversity in this tendency which is the result of the different existing ideals and rules in a society. In India, for example, the Nagas are a blood thirsty tribe who are called Head-hunters while many other Himalayan tribes are very peaceful. In a civilised society murder is considered a wrong and no woman marries a murderer but among the Nagas it is that person who does not cut heads who finds it difficult to find a bride. The Arapesh tribe of New Guinea discourages the aggressive tendencies, while on the other side, the Mundugumors encourage it from childhood. Therefore, the aggression tendency, like the mastery tendency, cannot be accepted to be innate and universal. They are acquired tendencies whose existence depends upon social conditions.

(4) Self Submission. Some people have accepted as natural the tendency of self submission, as opposed to that of self-assertion. Undoubtedly, the child has many occasions for self submission, being helpless before his elders. These childhood impressions are important and lasting but it is correct to call the submission tendency a learned tendency because it is usually learnt in the family or the society. Being comparatively weaker, women have a greater tendency to self submission but in some South America sea islands the women are the leaders and the men follow them in political and economic matters. Thus, this tendency depends on the social pattern. It varies in degree in different persons, and it may even be completely absent.

(5) Gregariousness. This tendency makes a person want to live in a group with the rest of the tribe. This tendency is expressed in the form of herd behaviour in animals. For this reason, goats and sheep live in flocks, though this tendency is not present in all animals. Thus, it is neither internal nor universal, and also not self-generated. This gregarious tendency is not found in every person. While many people live in group there are some who detest. This tendency is in reality, learnt which includes the advantages of a society. The person gets food, drink, accommodation easily, in a group, and he is enabled to satisfy his many tendencies.

(6) Imitation. Though imitation is seen very much in the human beings it is not compelling. Even, if the existence of any such instinct is given credence its field is very limited. It is common knowledge that a child learns his activities, habits and behaviour by imitating others, sometimes imitating grownups without a knowledge of what he is doing. The power of imitation is stronger in humans because they can make more minute distinctions. It is not necessary that he may observe all the details or that he may imitate immediately but imitate he does. Imitation is very important in human learning. Some birds give a very good imitation of voice but others do not have this quality. This tendency varies with the power of imitation in the animals.

(7) Sympathy. This is an experience of another person's emotional response. Seeing another person in serious trouble a sympathetic person experiences a similar, though less intense feeling. Some people cannot keep back their tears when they see another crying. Some people are seen crying for hours upon seeing a tragic story on the cinema screen. Take a look at the ladies coming out of the picture house after seeing a tragedy and you will see marks of crying on most faces. But this reaction is not seen in every one. Some people laugh, not only at people in pain but even when they are causing grave pain to others. The news of the death of hundreds of people in Germany makes you curious but even the death of a distant relative makes you unhappy. Why is it so? Actually, sympathy cannot be said to be innate. A major part of it is conditioned response while the remainder, too, is in some way a learned motive.

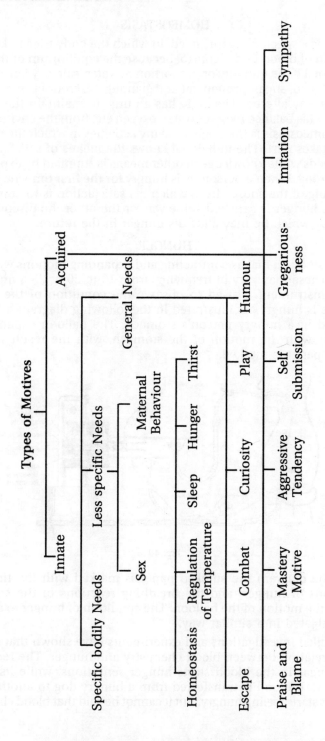

HOMEOSTASIS

This is a specific organic need, in which the body tries to keep the condition of blood under control because the equilibrium of the body is disturbed if the quantity or proportion of water, salt, oxygen, carbon-di-oxide, acid, sugar, protein, fat and glandular excretions in the blood is in any way altered. The body has an urge to maintain the normal balance. This balance requires water, oxygen etc. from the environment. Thus, homeostasis is the origin of many activities in which the nervous system takes part. The individual knows the means of satisfaction of some needs while knowledge of other means is supplied by experience and learning. When a person feels hungry for the first time, he has not the inkling of the source from which his satisfaction is to come. But, once his hunger is satisfied some way or the other, he discovers the means by which he may allay his hunger in the future.

HUNGER

The stomach makes contracting and expanding motions when it is empty. These may vary in frequency from 10 to 20 or 25 a minute. A special instrument is used to observe the condition of the person when he is hungry. As illustrated in the following diagram a balloon is placed in a hungry person's stomach. The balloon expands and contracts with the motion of the stomach, with the result that the smoked paper is marked.

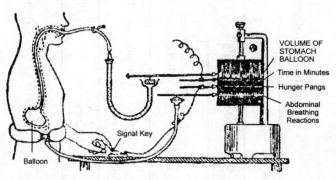

Fig. 40

In the diagram the smoked paper is marked with the time, the sensations of hunger, and the breathing reactions of the stomach, besides the motion of the balloon. The condition of hunger in animals is investigated in a similar way.

Detailed investigations and experiments have shown that there is a close relation between blood chemistry and hunger. The reduction of the sugar in the blood starts hunger sensations, while its excess reduces it. If blood is transferred from a hungry dog to another dog, the latter starts feeling hungry. But it cannot be said that blood chemistry is the only factor in hunger because the deficiency of proteins, fats and carbohydrates also results in hunger. Mostly, men or animals demand some particular type of food and not just food, when hungry. The choice is regulated by the deficiency in the body. During pregnancy, a female mouse needs about thrice the normal quantity of salt. It has been adequately demonstrated by experiments that the creature has not to be told the type of food to be consumed by him. When the feeding was done by the cafeteria method, in which the child may eat anything he likes, in any way which he may prefer and as much of it as he likes, the children soon started to pick out food by mere vision or by smelling. This experiment proves that children develop properly if they are fed in accordance with their wishes. Generally, there is no difference between the food suggested by doctors and food individually selected. The animals *e.g.*, rats have individual preferences which change with alterations in bodily conditions. The choice of food is neither by trial and error nor by the motivation of bodily needs exclusively. The physiological needs furnish a motive for the selection of food by trial and error. Human beings as well as animals eat more if they eat in a group. The taste, smell and shape of the food have a marked effect on its selection by human beings. As a general rule, habits are important in eating though these habits may be violated under certain circumstances. There are many harmless things which people do not like to eat. The rejection of a particular food by some individual does not indicate that it is harmful for him. In animals, too, hunger may be due to causes other than the biological needs. In experiments on hen, it was found that she starts eating merely on the sight of a heap of grain. She stops eating but starts again if the grain is first removed and then replaced. She also starts eating if she sees other hens doing so, even when she has no appetite. A similar type of behaviour may be observed among human beings.

SEX MOTIVE

Being related to the sex glands, sex is organic need. It is a means of giving birth and sustaining the species. It is known by the seasonal menstrual changes in the female mammal. Its manifestation has become very complex, in view of the restrictions placed by the society, though its importance cannot be denied. Sigmund Freud, the founder of the school of psychoanalysis, believed the sex motive to be the most important and comprehensive of all.

The inception of the sex motive is due to the excretion of a gland. In the male it is caused by the excretion of the sex glands, while in the female due to the ovaries. The circulation of the blood carries it to the brain, the resulting behaviour being of a type not normally observed. The normal activity due to this motive is an interest in the members of the opposite sex, and a particular type of behaviour towards them, the goal being the mating of the male and the female. In the lower species, the sex activity is related to the season, being the highest in spring when the daylight is of a longer duration. The light has an effect on the brain via the eyes, and it excites the sex instinct.

A distinction between sex drive and lust, similar to the one made in the case of hunger and appetite, must be made. While the drive for sex is based upon the sex organs; lust is kindled by either the beauty or femininity of the female or the masculinity and strength of the male which act as stimuli besides the organs. The proximity of a member of the other sex may also create lust. In human society cinema, colourful clothes, make-up, etc. elements which excite lust.

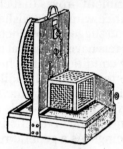

Fig. 41

Sex activity in human beings is very complex. Hence, in order to ascertain its natural or real form, it has been studied among animals. Rats were experimented upon in this connection. A rotating drum was attached to the rat trap. There is a board in the drum which records its rotation in any direction. The rotation of the drum is a measure of the distance travelled by the mice. The instrument is shown in the above.

Experiments with this instrument proved that male rats show less activity without any particular pattern of change. The female rat runs a mile in the first three or four days, but on the fourth and fifth day her activity is very much increased. When extremely active she covers a distance of 15 miles in a day. The effect of the ovaries should be investigated because the absence of the sex organs does not alter this behaviour. It seems that this behaviour is due to the excretion of the ovaries. The level of sex activity is reduced by castration but not completely stopped. An injection of testosterone steps up this activity. Thus, the effect of the glandular excretion is unmistakable. Besides the sex glands, other glands such as the pituitary and the adrenal, also affect the sex activity. Though the individual analysis of the effect of the three glands has not been made, it is definitely established that they do play a part in sex behaviour.

Seasons do not affect the sex activity in humans as much as they do in animals. The excretions of the sex glands have a specific effect.

With the extraction of the ovaries a development of the signs of femininity in a girl is stunted. But the removal of the sex glands does not substantially affect the sex activity in developed people. Quite possibly, this is the result of the habits formed in the presence of the glands. The sex activity can be restored by an injection of glandular extracts, at a late age, if it is impaired in any way.

The sex motive is not equally intense in every man and woman. The intensity of the motive and the means of its fulfilment vary from individual to individual. Quite a few people are abnormally sexual either due to excessive glandular excretion or social stimulation. The famous Kinsey report has thrown adequate light on the vast differences in human sexual behaviour. Excessive repression leads to the reduction of lust in a normal person. Abnormal sexual practices start in childhood because the child tries to satisfy his sexual motive in some way. These result in many perversions concerning sexual behaviour in adults. These perversions are far more numerous in human beings than in animals due to the social restrictions imposed on the sex motive in human society.

But is there some mating instinct in humans and animals? As has been mentioned earlier there is undoubtedly a mating instinct in animals like rats belonging to the lower species. The experiments on rats have shown that a two months old rat reared separately from the female shows an abundance of activity indicative of the sex instinct, and if released with a female ready to mate, he very soon mates like a normal rat. Even in the absence of previous experience, the rats exhibit a definite pattern of sex behaviour and mating activity when they attain adulthood. Apparently, mating is instinctive in rats because they do not have to learn it. In the higher species the pattern is not so well established. Experiments on chimpanzees, carried out at the Yale University, show that these animals learnt sexual behaviour by trial and error over a long period of time and that the pattern is different in each. Though experiments have not been carried out on human beings, it is obvious that the patterns of sexual behaviour are mostly acquired and learnt by seeing trial and error or other methods. Therefore, it is difficult to say that there is a mating instinct in men similar to the sex instinct.

Cycles of Sexual Motivation

Sexual behaviour runs in cycles, *i.e.*, it becomes intense and it disappears. These cycles are of three main types :

(1) **Life Cycle.** In this cycle sexual behaviour is seen more clearly in a major period in the life of the organism. For example, youth is such a period.

(2) **Seasonal Cycle.** In this cycle intensity of sexual behaviour in males and females is high in some specific seasons.

(3) **Estrous Cycle.** This cycle depends upon the secretion of endocrine glands. For example, in mammalian females changes in intensity of sexual behaviour is seen in different phases of menstrual cycles. There is a low beginning period, a peak period and again a low end period of sexual activity in this cycle. In the human beings and other mammals extensive studies have been made on the above three phases of sexual behaviour. It has been found that many endocrine secretions affect the sexual behaviour of the organism. These are Estrogens, Prolactin and hormones from the anterior Pituitary. Useful information about sexual behaviour has also been gathered by many studies of pregnancy. For example, it has been seen from the studies on rats that once pregnancy occurs, there is no sexual drive in the female rat till she gives birth to the babies. But a few hours after the birth of the babies, sexual drive again becomes intense in the female.

Influence of Environmental Factors

Besides the endocrine secretions, the influence of environmental stimulation on sexual behaviour can be seen on almost all animals. Learning and experience of the organism has also a great influence on it. No generalization can be made about the influence of environment for all the species. But the influence of light is seen in almost all animals. Greater length of the day in winter and spring is an important cause of greater intensity of sexual behaviour in fish, birds and mammals. Light also affects estrous cycles. This is supported by the experiments on rats. Besides light, the effect of temperature on sexual behaviour has also been established. Influence of olfactory stimulation is also well-known.

Influence of Physiological Factors

Influence of various hormones like androgens and estrogens on sexual behaviour has been established. Giving these hormones to many animals makes them sexually active before the age of maturity. Similarly, sexual behaviour can be induced off season by injecting these hormones. It has been observed that sexual potency declines in old age in man and other animals. In lower animals like rats, injection of hormones in old age brings back sexual potency. This has not been successful in the case of man. Physiological factors, besides old age, are more important in human beings than in lower animals.

It is clear from the above discussion that sexual behaviour of the organism is affected by sex hormones on the one hand and experience and learning on the other hand. These two influences work through the nervous system. As is clear from the Fig. 42, beside the normal factors sexual behaviour of the organism is also controlled by the neural factors like spinal cord and other brain structures. Sensory stimulation has a special importance in arousing sexual behaviour. Androgens influence the sexual behaviour of male whereas Estrogens influence female behaviour. Spinal cord integrates genital reflexes of males and females. Hypothalamus acts as an integrative centre and organizes the patterns of sexual activity. Various factors influencing sexual behaviour can be seen in the Fig. 42.

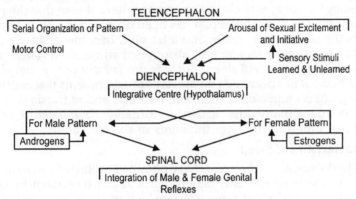

Fig. 42. Factors Regulating Sex Behaviour.

Influence of Sensory Factors

As has been said earlier sensory factors have important role in arousing sexual behaviour. One or more senses may contribute in sexual arousal. Substances having characteristic smells secrete from the genital tract of the female rat or dog; specific type of sounds are given by the cat; skin of the sex organs of monkeys becomes red; and many signs are seen in the birds. Beside these, tactual and kinaesthetic cues have important contribution in the total sexual behaviour. In the absence of these stimulations, change in sexual behaviour may occur. Even, if the sensory contributions of other organs are not essential, smell, hearing or vision have important influence in sexual behaviour. But it cannot be said that sexual behaviour of the organism depends totally on the sex organs. Female rats showed normal mating behaviour after removal of the uterus and vagina. This finding was also confirmed by the studies on cats. Thus, taken together, it can be said that sexual behaviour is not aroused by any particular kind of stimulation but on the total amount of relevant sensory stimulation. In some instances it has been seen that hormones have a special contribution in sexual arousal. Besides this the influence of various structures of the brain is also important. The most important neural structure is cerebral cortex. Hypothalamus is another important structure which acts as an integrative centre. Spinal cord mediates in the control of genital reflexes. These findings have been confirmed by the experiments on rats and cats.

It is clear from the above discussion of physiological aspects of sexual behaviour that stimulation from various senses, hormones and neural structures like hypothalamus and cerebral cortex have important influences in the sexual behaviour of the organism.

SLEEP

Sleep is a state of the organism which takes his maximum time. The person in the state of sleep usually lies down and there is a tendency for the eyes to close. Experiments have shown that the person is not totally inactive in sleep. It has been observed that in the first few hours the sleep is very deep; and later on it becomes light. Sleep is a natural reaction to fatigue and absence of stimulation. Each person has individual habits of sleep. But it is not correct to say that sleep is only a habit. It has been seen on the basis of experiments that continuous waking affects a person's attention, interests and enthusiasm though he may do his many other activities normally. Neural centre of sleep has been found in the Hypothalamus in the fore-brain.

Characteristics of Sleep

Physiological psychologists have obtained useful information about sleep on the basis of many experiments. It can be known by several characteristics whether a person is asleep or is awake. Among them the main characteristics are : (1) Bodily activity is greatly reduced; (2) thresholds of many reflexes are increased and responsiveness of many types of stimulation is decreased; (3) in man, consciousness is lost and therefore the sleeping person is neither aware of stimulation nor able to remember the events occurring during sleep; (4) the sleeping organism can be awakened by strong stimulation. This characteristic differentiates sleep from other states of unconsciousness.

Two changes can be seen mainly in the body of the organism going to sleep : (1) The muscles supporting the body relax and the organism usually lies down, (2) There is a tendency for the eyes to close. Generally, both these changes are taken as sign of sleep. When the person is asleep, he remains relatively quiet. But this does not mean that there is no activity during sleep. In fact, during sleep some changes in body position do take place every twenty or twenty-five minutes.

Autonomic Activity During Sleep

Beside somatic activity the following autonomic changes can be seen during sleep : (1) Heart rate is significantly reduced, sometimes by about 20 beats per minute, (2) Blood Pressure also comes down in sleep by 20 or 30 millimeters. Usually, the blood pressure reaches a minimum in the fourth hour of sleep and it begins to rise gradually afterwards. It rises abruptly upon waking, (3) Respiration is also relatively slower and as compared to waking its depth is greater in sleep. It is also more regular in sleep. (4) Body temperature is lower in sleep than in waking. Activities of the stomach and intestines in sleep go on as it is in the normal state. Sometimes it is increased during sleep. In fact, the above described autonomic changes are not caused by sleep. These changes can also be seen in the state of prolonged rest. As these changes show less energy is required in sleep or resting state as compared to waking or active state of the organism.

EEG Studies

The most useful and successful studies of sleep in Psychology have been done through Electro-encephalogram or EEG. Differences between sleep and waking states are clearly reflected in it. It is known by the use of EEG, whether a person is really sleeping or feigning sleep. EEG records taken from the human skull during different states show three indexes : (1) Amplitude, (2) Frequency and (3) Regularity of the waves. In relaxed waking state in man, EEG record shows regular Alpha waves of moderate voltage. These occur at a speed of about 10 waves per second. As the person becomes drowsy, the amplitude of these waves is reduced, and slow Delta waves of low amplitude are seen. In light sleep, the Alpha waves disappear totally and Delta waves of 1 to 4 per second are seen. Along with this spindle bursts of 14 per second appear. In fact, this bursting of spindles is a sign of light sleep. One hour after going to sleep, the sleep becomes deep. In deep sleep, large and slow Delta waves can be seen. From EEG records it has been known that there are significant differences in the brain waves during wakefulness, and deep sleep. The main advantage of using the EEG to study sleep is that it does not affect the sleeping person in any way. An easier method for determining the depth of sleep, used before the EEG came into use, was to find the intensity of sound required to awake a person. In the Fig. 43 is given the intensity of sound required to wake a person according to the variation in the depth of sleep throughout a whole night. It has been found through these experiments that a person does not sleep uniformly throughout a night or a long

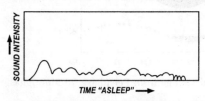

Fig. 43. Diagram of a variation in Depth of sleep throughout a night, as measured by the intensity of sound required to wake the individual.

period of sleep. On the other hand, a person passes through cycles of deep and light sleep. These cycles are about 10 to 30 minutes length, but they vary in different individuals and even for the same person they vary for different nights. No generalized principle can be stated in this connection. However, it can be definitely said that there is continuous variation in the depth of sleep.

Monophasic and Polyphasic Sleep

Most adult human beings sleep for one long period daily. But the human life does not start in this way. New born babies sleep five to seven times a day and they take asleep of three to four hours each time. In other words, the sleep of an adult is Monophasic and that of a baby is Polyphasic. After the age of some months, the human baby gradually changes from a polyphasic to a monophasic pattern of sleep, although this process of change is not complete till the nursery school age. In the Fig. 44 is shown the diagram of the change from polyphasic to monophasic pattern of sleep from birth to adulthood. As is clear from the figure, the new-born baby is polyphasic and the individual becomes monophasic at the age of ten years though the duration of monophasic sleep is much more than that of the adult. In this diagram are shown the sleep cycles and duration of these cycles in 24 hours for the new-born, one year, 4 year, 10 year and adult human being. Thus, for the adult, sleep starts around 9 or 10 P.M. in the night and continues till 5 A.M. For the 10 year child this period is from 9 P.M. to 7 A.M. The period of sleep is more for the individual below ten years. There are 2 cycles for four years old, 3 for one year old and 5 or 6 for the new born baby. As is clear from the figure, the new born baby remains sleeping with a break of an hour or half between the cycles.

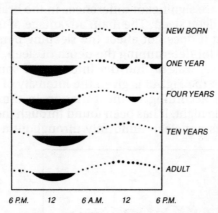

Fig. 44. Cycles of sleep and change from Polyphasic to Monophasic sleep with age.

Beside human beings some animals are monophasic and others are polyphasic. For example, snake is monophasic whereas, rats and rabbits are polyphasic. Activity of sleep and waking is also controlled by the light and darkness cycle. Organisms that are more influenced by light are generally monophasic, whereas those organisms which readily hide from the light, sleep many times a day.

Evolutionary Theory of Sleep

In 1939, Kleitman collected the facts concerning sleep and proposed an evolution theory of sleep. This theory was called evolutionary because according to Kleitman, the patterns of sleeping and waking in animals are dependent on the evolutionary development of the cerebral cortex, particularly in animals. Whereas in some animals waking state comes because of necessity; in other animals with more developed cerebral cortex wakefulness is a matter of choice. This evolutionary theory of sleep and wakefulness has been supported by modern studies. If the cerebral cortex of a dog is removed, the characteristics of 'wakefulness of necessity' are seen in that dog. The same characteristics are seen in the new-born baby because his brain is relatively less developed. In the animal with a highly developed cortex, sleep and wakefulness are a joint function of both subcortical and cortical structures. Wakefulness of necessity is maintained subcortically, whereas wakefulness of choice is maintained by the effect of cortical activity. This is also influenced by the learning of the organism. Once the time of sleep is fixed, it becomes a natural rhythm of the brain and remains more or less permanently. This has been confirmed by extensive studies of prolonged wakefulness. Whether a person sleeps or remains awake, the body temperature and activity drop at night and go up in the day time. Similarly, a person is more awake in the third quarter of the night as compared to the second quarter of the night. Thus, symptoms of sleep appear in a person in his normal period of sleep even if he is forcibly kept awake.

Many theories of sleep were prevalent about twenty years ago. None of them satisfactorily explained all the above facts. Chemical theory of sleep believed that various toxins accumulate in the body during waking hours and these toxins are the cause of sleep. Experiments by Kleitman rejected the chemical theory of sleep and it was demonstrated that the cause of sleep lies in the brain structures. It had been observed that Siamese twins possessing two brains may sleep independently. As has been stated earlier, modern researches have confirmed the evolutionary theory of Kleitman. Experiments conducted on this subject have shown the role of the following brain structures in sleep — Cerebral cortex; Thalamus, Hypothalamus, Reticular activating system etc. Experiments on Reaction time and Attention have also confirmed these findings.

MEASUREMENT OF NEEDS

Needs are not only qualitative but they have an aspect which makes it possible to measure them by various techniques. These techniques provide indirect measures, as needs cannot be measured directly. Indirect estimates are obtained by measuring the effects of need upon behaviour or consciousness. There are two main types of methods for the measurement of need : (1) Observation method and (2) Learning method.

(1) **Observation Method.** In this method, as is clear by its name, the strength of a need is measured by the type of obstruction or the number of obstacles overcome to reach the goal. For example, the need which motivates the organism to overcome a greater obstacle is

certainly more strong. Similarly, that need is considered stronger which drives the organism to overcome more obstacles. Generally, this method is employed for measuring the needs of animals. Many experiments with this method have been done on rats. An obstruction box used in experiments on rats is shown in the Fig. 45. In this diagram the middle portion 'B' which is blackened with lines, shows an ally through which the rat has to pass and flowing a current through its floor electric shock

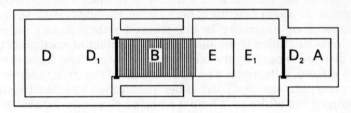

Fig. 45. Obstruction box used in experiments on rats.

is given to the animal, 'D$_1$' and 'D$_2$' are two doors. Door 'D$_1$' takes the animal to the obstruction 'B'. After crossing the obstruction 'B' when the animal reaches on 'E$_1$' the door D$_2$ opens automatically. Experiments on the sex need of a female rat have been done with this obstruction box. The female rat is placed in the chamber 'A' and the male rat in the chamber 'D'. Driven by the sex need the female rat crosses the obstruction and reaches on 'E'. This opens the door of the chamber 'D' and the male rat is liberated. It has been found that the female rat driven by the sex need crosses the obstruction without hesitation frequently. Similarly, it has been found by experiments with obstruction box on other needs like hunger, thirst and maternal needs that the animal crosses the obstruction more easily and more frequently if the needs are strong enough. Actually, through this technique a particular need is not measured directly, but instead it is measured in comparison to other needs. Every animal has a natural need to avoid obstruction; but whenever other need like hunger, thirst or sex become strong the animal does not care for obstruction. In other words, when the animal does not care for the obstruction and crosses if frequently and without hesitation, then it becomes clear that the other need in him is stronger than the need to avoid obstruction. It is needless to say that the stronger the need in the animal is, more often and with more vigour the animal will cross the obstruction. It is emphasized here that the animal gradually becomes accustomed to the obstruction and he does not feel any difficulty in crossing it even when the other need is not much strong.

As has been explained above, psychologists have studied the relative strength of various needs in a particular animal. It has been found from these studies that maternal need is the strongest of the animal needs and after it come respectively thirst, hunger, sex and the exploratory need in rank order of strength.

Following points should be taken into consideration before reaching any conclusion regarding it :

(1) Every need of the animal is temporary, therefore, its comparative measurement cannot be totally true.

(2) Changing the apparatus for measurement may also change the results concerning the need.

(3) Different needs are interrelated. If one need becomes strong, second need is also affected. For example, prolonged hunger normally decreases the sexual drive of the organism. Similarly, we know from our own experience that if we are very thirsty we cannot eat much food. A thirsty rat eats very little food. It has been seen from experiments that an increase in the hunger of rat is accompanied by an increase in their need for exploration. When sex need is strong, need for food is greatly reduced. These types of interrelations are seen in human beings also. A mother is ready to make a great sacrifice for the comfort of her children. A person who falls in love, does not hesitate to make the greatest sacrifice. A fat girl in order to become beautiful and slim reduces the intake of food. Similar examples about other needs of human beings are common. It is a matter of common experience that a highly motivated person willingly faces great hardships to reach his goal.

(2) **Learning Method.** In this technique of measurement of needs, readiness of the organism to learn a particular activity under different conditions of motivation is observed. Strength of a need is measured in terms of the readiness to learn. Rate of learning and readiness change as a function of the degree and kind of motivation. Many experiments have been done on animals in this connection, as motivational tendencies in human beings are more complex than in animals. It has been found from experiments on learning method that the rate of learning increases with the strength of motivation. In one experiment, three groups of rats were taken. The first group was very hungry and very thirsty. The second was very hungry but only slightly thirsty and the third was very thirsty but only slightly hungry. In the first nine days of the experiments the rats were rewarded with food. During this period it was seen that the first group of rats which were motivated both by hunger and thirst, learned faster than the other two groups. This shows that two needs together have more motivating effect on learning than one need. In the last nine days of the experiment, only water was used as a reward for the rats. With this shift in reward, the first group was disturbed temporarily. At first, they showed an increase in the number of errors in learning, but at the end of the experiment they were again better than the other two groups. Thus, the shift in reward had little effect on the first group; but it had a notable

effect on the other two groups. The third group of rats, which were more thirsty and only slightly hungry improved their learning speed because water was given as a reward. On the other hand, rats of the second group which were more hungry and only slightly thirsty showed no improvement in learning because these animals has a great need for food than water. Following two conclusions are drawn from this experiment :

(1) Two needs together constitute a more effective condition for learning than one need.

(2) Learning is faster if the motivating need is appropriately rewarded.

The result of this experiment can be used very successfully with the children. A successful teacher increases the rate of learning of his students by giving various incentives. In one experiment with children it was seen that the offering of a reward of a chocolate bar increased the learning by 52 per cent above the usual level. When a number of incentives like candy, a definite goal, rivalry and praise were presented an increase of 65 per cent in learning was observed. In human activities, it is seen that an increase in motivation leads to an increase of performance.

It has also been found by experiments that the amount of reward also influences the rate of learning. For example, some chicks were given a grain of boiled rice as a reward for learning a simple maze. Other chicks who were rewarded with six grains of boiled rice, showed an improved rate of learning than the earlier group rewarded with only one grain. In human beings, the effect of the amount of reward offered can be seen on salaried workers. Workers do more and better work for more pay than for less pay. Not only is the amount of reward important in determining the rate of learning but also the kind of reward. An experiment on maze learning was done with two groups of rats. To the first group was given sunflower seeds, a less preferred food as a reward. The second group was given a more preferred food. As a result of the experiment, it was seen that the group getting more preferred food learned the maze more rapidly than the group rewarded with less preferred food.

QUESTIONS FOR EXERCISE

1. Discuss the role played by motivation in the learning process.
2. What are the major classes of human motives? Explain with illustration.
3. Explain the different methods employed in Psychology to measure needs.

14

FRUSTRATION AND CONFLICT

What is Frustration

Conflict with various factors in the environment in search of satisfaction for his desires is a normal condition of human life. No man in the world can entirely fulfil his desires. Failure in the satisfaction of some desire is normal in every person's life and the path of satisfaction of most of our motives is marred by obstacles and troubles. Naturally, our desire of motive remains unsatisfied on this account. Frustration is the natural consequence of such difficulty. It is a kind or state of hopelessness and disgust. It destroys the person's enthusiasm, his tension in life is increased, and sometimes he becomes the victim of complete despair. Hence, frustration is a mental condition which is resultant upon our failure to satisfy some motive or the other. Main features of a frustrated state of mind are — extremity of tension, sense of inferiority, lack of peace and various kinds of mental mechanisms.

Various Reactions of Frustration

Reactions to frustration also succeed in elucidating its nature. Main forms of reactions to it are the following :

(1) **Creation of or Increase in Emotional Tension.** A child is naturally and very strongly motivated and inclined to go out of the house and to play with other children of his own age. If he is prevented from doing so he evinces definite signs of labouring under great emotional tension, and this tension remains till the frustrated emotion or motive succeeds in finding some mode of release. And this expression can take the normal form or instead it can be manifested through different kinds of mental mechanisms.

(2) **Increase in Effort.** A healthy person's reaction to frustration is in the form of increased efforts towards overcoming the obstacle causing the frustration. For example, if a student fails to secure good marks at one of the terminal examinations, then instead of being completely discouraged and deprived of the will to try, he redoubles his efforts so that success in future may be made possible and often this does come to pass. Actually, when frustration falls to a person's lot in life, then he should think upon the causes of that frustration, since it is not essential that the frustration is inevitably the outcome of a low degree

of enterprise in the individual. It is possible that the work he is trying to perform is outside his capability, as not many students succeed in studying a subject that interests them not. But if the failure to attain a goal is the result of our lack of effort or enterprise, then the best one can do is to step up the efforts, in complete disregard of the frustration suffered.

(3) **Different Approach.** Another cause why frustration dogs our footsteps in life is often the choice of a wrong method of approach. For example, many of the students are not aware of the method of study that should be adopted for scoring well in an examination, as a result of which they fail to do it, despite their best, concentrated effort. If frustration is the outcome of such faulty orientation, then success can be had for the asking in the future by changing one's method of approach, and quite a number of people intuitively realize this fact. When a sensible man fails to attain his objective through one approach, he immediately tries another, and in this manner sticks to trial and error till he discovers the one correct method of action.

(4) **Change of Objective.** On the other hand, when some people fail to obtain their object, they avoid frustration in this line by changing their very goal. And the goal can be changed in the following ways : first, by reducing the objective and aiming at a lower level, and second by entirely adopting a different goal. For example, every student who chooses to study has not the capacity or ability to stand first in an examination; hence, if all of them have this object then frustration is only going to be naturally theirs. When this does happen, some students choose to aim at the second division while certain others aim still lower and choose only to succeed at the examination without talking in terms of merit. Frustration, is thereby avoided. Other students may even lose their interest in academic pursuit and turn to trade and commerce, where success may or may not meet them.

(5) **Feeling of Inferiority.** All the reactions to frustration mentioned so far are simple and straightforward, and can be seen in a large majority of individuals but there are certain other reactions that are more indicative of abnormal behaviour. For example, when frustration meets certain people they not only refuse to change their method but also their aim, in other words, they do not accommodate themselves, and instead, get into the habit of regarding themselves as very weak and helpless, hopeless and unfortunate. A tense mental state of this kind is called the feeling of inferiority. A person full of the inferiority feeling looks only to his own shortcomings and is always afraid of inviting criticism from and disregard of others. Mental characteristics such as suspicion, jealousy, criticism of others, anxiety, introvert tendencies, fear of competition, high emotional excitability towards criticism, very profound reaction to failure, etc., are to be seen in his life. This sense of inferiority is not caused by actual deficiency of interests and abilities in the individual. It has instead been seen that

many unintelligent students do not allow this sense of inferiority to step near them, and despite repeated failure continue to make gorgeous plans of the future, while on the other hand, many very actually intelligent students develop a sense of inferiority even on the slightest failure. Thus, the sense of inferiority is a concomitant not of capacity but of character. Very highly ambitious people have very many frustrations, and thus their sense of inferiority, once it is developed, is also strong. For example, when a student hopes to get a first division and gets a second instead, he is beset by the feeling of inferiority, whereas, other students feel very puffed up merely because they have succeeded in passing the examination.

Consequently, it can be reasoned that in order to avoid the sense of inferiority away from him the individual should first of all try to aim at something that is within his own capabilities to achieve, and secondly he should spare no effort to attain this end. There is a proverb : Know what you can do and do it like a Hercules. Success does not come easily when one does not know what one is capable of or one does not pursue an objective with all the ability at one's disposal, after one has become sure that it is within his capacity. It is this simple formula of success that led some common men to the most coveted and revered positions in the world. Ram Murti, a famous wrestler, was a learned and thin person in his youth, and it was through rigid application and continued effort that he became a great wrestler. Helen Keller was born blind and deaf but through her indomitable courage and unconquerable will, she became a wonderful writer and a fine orator, besides becoming a symbol of these qualities for all the world to look up to and emulate. It is evident from these examples that the sense or feeling of inferiority is not bad in itself since it can conceivably spur the individual to great and immense efforts which may bring him great success. But if this healthy reaction towards the inferiority feeling does not take place, then it develops into a very harmful mental complex as a result of which the individual becomes abnormal and a mentally diseased person.

(6) **Aggressive Behaviour.** Often, the reaction to frustration takes the form of aggressive behaviour. It is proverbially said that the bad worker blames his tools since he wants to transfer the blame for his failure to the tools. It is observed commonly that when people are scolded in office for their inefficient work, they work off their steam and charge in by being angry with the children at home. When in an aggressive mood, sparked off by frustration, an individual can, directly or indirectly, launch an attack on others, but in quite a large majority of people this wrath turns in upon themselves rather than on other people or objects. They take to beating their heads with their hands or banging it into the nearest handy wall, while the more disturbed go to the extreme of committing suicide. It is because of this close intimacy between frustration and aggressive behaviour which has been observed

that some psychologists have cited frustration as an important cause of war, and they have further suggested that if wars are to be eliminated from human society, then such conditions be created in which frustrations of every field of life be at their minimum possible. The most dangerous forms of aggressive behaviour are the consequences of sex frustration. Such a fact is born out if we study the life histories of notorious master criminals.

(7) **Mental Mechanisms.** Sometimes the reaction to frustration is evident in the form of mental mechanism, the main ones being fantasy, compensation, identification, projection, sublimation and rationalization. The following are their examples :

(i) **Fantasy.** Any motive of a person that is frustrated in the actual world is satisfied in an imaginary world through the medium of fantasy.

(ii) **Compensation.** When people are frustrated in their desires in one direction, they compensate for it by attaining success to a pre-eminent degree in other directions. An ugly girl, for example, becomes very learned and scholarly.

(iii) **Identification.** Many people who find no success in their lives at all, find satisfaction and pleasure in identifying themselves with different great people and with their children whose success brings them the sense of having themselves succeeded.

(iv) **Projection.** When frustrated, some people avoid its consequences by projecting their own shortcomings upon others, and by holding them responsible for their failure. Many students console themselves, for failing at examinations by blaming their teachers and the educational system in general.

(v) **Rationalization.** Again, the consequences of frustration are by-passed by certain other individuals who, instead of probing the cause of their failure, choose to put forward convincing reasons and arguments for their failure to succeed.

(vi) **Sublimation.** When frustration comes to the life of certain other individuals they choose to turn into directions accepted and credited by society, and thus find satisfaction for their motives. For example, the consequences of sexual frustration can be avoided by turning to the study of various fine arts.

Sources or Causes of Frustration

Having gained a fair working knowledge of the nature and consequences of frustration, it is now possible to pursue analysing its sources or causes. The main causes or sources are the following :

(1) **Objective Beyond One's Power.** As has been pointed out, for achieving success it is essential that the individual's objective should be within his power and capacity. Many people pose before themselves objectives that have no regard of their actual capability and are outside their reach. As a consequence their life becomes a tale of frustration

and woe, and they always appear disconsolate, anxious, irritable and disturbed. Here it is necessary to understand that according to psychology every individual cannot be made into anything. Hence, an individual should take care to select an objective and aim that is within his power, and having done so, should exert himself to the very utmost.

(2) **Lack of Requisite Effort.** But when frustration meets some effort of ours it should not be taken for granted that it is outside our power, since the failure may be due to lack of necessary effort, or due to a wrong approach and defective methodology. These difficulties can be overcome with ease.

(3) **Competition.** Frustration would have been an unknown phenomenon in human life if every pleasure and all the good things of life had been freely available, as are water and air. But this is not the condition with regard to most physical perquisites. There are very many things and qualities such as wealth, money, land, property, beauty, attractive personality, great character, fame etc., in which there is not enough of it to go round, as the saying is. The desire to possess them is present in every individual, and a degree of cut-throat competition exists between all people for them. Frustration and failure comes to many in this unequal struggle, and bliss only to a very few.

(4) **Social and Cultural Obstacles.** Another very fundamental cause of frustration consists in the taboos inflicted upon the manifestation of our motives by society and culture. In his book *Civilization and its Discontents,* Freud, the famous psychoanalyst, has shown how man has had to pay the price of civilization in terms of frustration and mental agony. And among the various social and cultural taboos the most effective and the most powerful is the one concerned with sex instinct and its manifestation, and Freud has indulged in a detailed consideration of the mental aberrations and abnormalities resultant upon such restraint. Anthropologists have found that fewer frustrations are to be seen in the population of ancient tribal people in which social and cultural taboos are fewer than in the allegedly more civilized societies.

(5) **Physical Causes.** Man exists in a physical environment upon the machinations of which he has little control; hence, such physical phenomena and events as floods, plague, earthquakes, excessive rain, drought, etc., are some of the sources of frustration in man.

(6) **Political Causes.** Every human individual is part and parcel of a political organization, and the manifestation of many of his instincts is controlled and limited by the state. Hence, the result of this control is evident in the frustration of numerous motives that would otherwise have been satisfied.

Frustrations arising from the above sources can be simple just as much as they can be complex. Simple frustrations are very much a part of every person's life, and are often a spur of one's activity since they increase our enthusiasm to achieve some end that is eluding us, but the arising of complex frustration can lead to a person becoming tendencious towards abnormality and mental disease. Such states and calamities can be avoided if we try to keep a sane and healthy outlook on these frustrations. And the first step towards such a healthy and sane outlook is the clear realization that frustration is a natural and inevitable part of human life. Many thinkers have gone so far as to opine that frustration is essential if success is to be attained and prosperity achieved. Secondly, when a frustration thrusts itself on our mind we should consider it with a cool mind, search for its causes, and make an effort to get rid of them. In this manner we can evade the worst consequences of frustration.

CONFLICT

What is Conflict

Most of man's activities result from motives. Often, more than one motives arise in the person simultaneously, which originate a doubt in his mind and cause tension. He finds it difficult to decide on the mode of action, the state being psychologically designated 'conflict'.

Causes of Conflict

There are two main causes of conflicts :

(1) **Environmental Obstructions.** Many hindrances in the environment create conflicts inside the person.

(2) **Personal Deficiencies.** The deficiencies of the character, nature, personality of the person himself create conflicts between the motives. In reality, the existence of conflict in life is indispensable, without which development is not possible, but when these conflicts assume abnormal proportions they become harmful.

Types of Conflict

The major types of conflicts are as follows :

(1) **Approach-Approach Conflicts.** In this type, both the motives engaged in the conflict are such that the individual accepts them both and would like to fulfil both, the conflict arising from the fact that both cannot be fulfilled at the same time. A person for example, wants both a pantaloon and a blanket but has money enough only for one.

(2) **Avoidance-Avoidance Conflicts.** In this case, both the motives are of such a nature that the individual would avoid them if he could. For example, neither does a person want to work nor would he appreciate being called a malingerer.

(3) **Approach-Avoidance Conflicts.** In this type the motives which conflict with each other are such that one of them the individual wants to fulfil while the other he wants to avoid. For example, a player would like to participate in a game but would also like to avoid injury.

(4) Double Approach-Avoidance Conflicts. In this class of conflicts although the person has come to a decision in one direction he still feels an inclination towards the other allurements, although he cannot alter his decision.

Excessive conflicts indicate weakness of determination. Strong will power is needed to avoid or to be rid of it.

QUESTIONS FOR EXERCISE

1. What is meant by Frustration? What are its sources and forms of reaction?
2. Write a short note on Mental Conflict.

15

REACTION TIME

What is Reaction Time?

After a stimulus presents itself before us, some action from our side follows and this after action is called reaction. The time taken by a reaction to follow after the presentation of stimulus is called the reaction-time. Practical fitness of a person depends on the speed of his reaction to a great extent. It, therefore, becomes important to know about the speed of reaction of a person in special circumstances as compared to that of other persons. At the same time, it shall also be important to know how far he can increase the speed of his reaction and his practical fitness through habitation and his interest in the work.

Importance of the Study

The aptitudes of the people in vocational selection have to be ascertained. Experiments of reaction-time are very helpful in ascertaining these aptitudes. For example, in selection of a telephone operator, it is necessary to find out the speed of his reaction and the number of mistakes he commits in it. In this way, in the selection of expert motor drivers and other machine operators, a test about their speed of reaction and their practical fitness is necessary. It has been seen that the taxi drivers, whose speed of reaction is very little, commit accidents more frequently. On the other hand, persons, whose speed of action is too high, also make more accidents. The selection of such drivers, whose speed of reaction is neither too high nor too slow, will, therefore, be advisable. Various other practical advantages have been derived from the study of reaction-time. A crime has sometimes been successfully traced through experiments of word-association reaction. In one experiment various words, connected with the crime, were included in the list of words placed before the accused. Now, this list was read before the accused and he was asked to speak quickly an associated word for every word given in the list. It is a matter of common experience here that when we are placed in such circumstances where our emotions arise easily, we, either hesitate to answer a question or give a foolish and irrelevant answer. In the above experiment, the person accused also did the same; either he reacted through very long words against the words related to the crime or atleast his reaction against these words was very different from his reaction against other words. The chief reason behind this was that the meaning of the words connected with the crime was different for the accused from that for an ordinary person.

Jung, Kent, Rosnauf and many other psychologists made use of this experiment of reaction-time to discover the various complexes. These complexes are unconscious and also work in one unconscious condition. The person, in whom complex arises against some object or person, gives expression to extraordinary reaction, when the name of that object or person is spoken before the person having complexes, and in this way complexes are recognized.

Kinds of Reaction Time

In the study of reaction time, various psychologists have thrown light on its kinds. There are two kinds of reactions in a material form, simple and complex, which are explained below :

(1) **Simple Reaction Time.** Among the simple experiments of reaction time, the subject has to react upon the sign made by the experimenter by pressing a telegraph key. It has been seen in these experiments that the speed of reaction, in different persons and in connection with different sense organs of one and the same person, is different. How much time a reaction upon the stimulus of a specific kind takes is shown in the list given below :

Kind of Stimulus	Reaction time (in seconds)
1. Visual	0.150 to 0.225
2. Auditory	0.120 to 0.185
3. Tactual	0.115 to 0.190
4. Olfactory	0.200 to 0.800
5. Gustatory	0.305 to 1.080
6. Pain	0.400 to 1.000
7. Cold	0.150
8. Warm	0.180

It can be known from the above list that the time of reaction to the stimuli of pain is the longest, because the distance between the stimulus and a feeling of pain is great enough. In the same way, in different parts of the tongue, a difference is seen in the time of reaction to different kinds of tastes. It has been found out through experiments that the time of reaction to a taste stimulus in case of something bitter is the longest, while in case of something salty is the shortest. In the same way, a difference in the reaction time is seen in the different parts of the body as well as in the different parts of the skin of the same parts of the body. It has been found out through experiments that the reaction of tactual stimulus in one hand is very quick in comparison to the circumstances in which tactual stimulus is given to the other hand. In the same way, reaction time of the tactual stimulus is greater in the forehead than in the hand. Even in visual sensations, a difference in reaction time is seen according to the effect of the light waves on different parts of the eye. It has been found out through experiment that the greater is the distance of a certain part of the eye from the central point of the eye lens, the greater will be the time of its reaction to light. In comparison to monocular stimulus, the reaction time in reaction to the binocular stimulus is less. In many experiments, a sign is given for preparation before reaction. By increasing the interval between this sign for preparation and a sign of reaction, a change in reaction time is seen. If that interval is very short, the reaction time is longer, and if the interval is enough for the preparation, the reaction time is shorter. In the same way, if the interval is lasting, the subject receives a lasting attitude to it and the reaction time is consequently short. But if a change continues coming in the interval, the reaction time also goes on increasing.

It has been seen in reaction-time experiment that the contribution of distraction in reaction time is also important. This contribution is against an ordinary hope, which means that as a result of distraction, the reaction time decreases in place of increasing, because, on presentation of an obstacle, the subject makes a great attempt to overcome it. It has often been seen that the people who are habituated more or less, to work in a noise, their reaction time increases in absolute absence of noise. In the same way, along with an increase in the force of the stimulus, a decrease in reaction time has been seen. It has also been found out through many experiments that, if the reaction time of some person is decreased about some special stimulus, it can generally be hoped that quick reactions will follow it even about the stimuli of other organs. Ludvig Lange has classified simple reaction time into the following three parts on the ground of the direction of subject's attention.

1. Sensory Reaction Time.
2. Muscular or Motor Reaction Time.
3. Natural Reaction time.

Many important things have been discovered about these three kinds of reaction times through various experiments. It has been seen that the functional reaction time is decreased as compared to sensational reaction time. Sensational reaction is complete, whereas a nervous reaction is incomplete. Besides Lange, Titchener also has made experiments about reaction time of different kinds. Besides Titchener, Cattell, Baldvin and Angell also have made experiments in this connection.

(2) **Complex Reaction Time.** Complex reaction time has been divided into two groups as explained below :

(a) **Choice Reaction Time.** Donders has called it B reaction time. In the study of choice reaction time, two or more stimuli are presented before the subject and an instruction, to react to those stimuli in different ways, is given. For example, red and blue sky was shown to a subject and he was instructed to make the reaction of the red with a finger of his right hand and of the blue with a finger of his left hand. The importance of choice in these experiments of choice reaction time has been very great.

(b) **Discrimination Reaction Time.** In a test of discrimination reaction time, the subject has to react to any one of the many presented stimuli. For example, he is asked to react to any one kind of light from among the many kinds of light stimuli presented before him. In this, the subject has to discriminate. It has been seen through experiments that the discrimination reaction time is less than the choice reaction time. A reduction, in both the kinds of complex reaction times through habituation, has been seen. Marked has made many important experiments in this direction. It has been found out from the experiments made by Hemmon and Lemmon that the reaction time changes with the equality of stimuli. Donders has called the discrimination reaction time by the name of C Reaction Time.

Factors Affecting Reaction Time

The factors which affect reaction time are made distinct from the above explanation of its different kinds. The main factors of this kind are given below :

(1) **Characteristics of Stimulus.** As has been said before, sharpness, shape and extension of the stimuli have an important effect on the reaction time. It has been found out from Berger's experiments that when the sharpness of a stimulus is reduced, the reaction time is greater than the reaction time when the sharpness is ordinary. Froberg has also approved it from his experiments, although, no proportionate relation between the sharpness of the stimulus and a reduction in the reaction time was marked. As has been said before, a difference among the reaction times of the stimuli of different sense organs is seen.

(2) **Group of Stimuli.** It has been found out from the experiments made by Poffenberger and other psychologists that the reaction time to a group of different stimuli is less than the reaction time to any one stimulus.

(3) **Fore Period.** Fore period means the time between a sign of attention and the stimulus. As has been said before, fore period has an important effect on reaction time. If the fore period is long, the reaction time is also long; and if the fore period is short, the reaction time is also short. But if the fore period is shorter than even one second, the reaction time increases. According to Cattel, an interval of one second is enough for reaction time. Others have maintained that this time should be from two to four seconds. Then again, as has been

proved from experiments made in Yale University, if the mode of reaction differs, it will also bring about some change in the reaction time.

(4) **Incentive.** It has been found out through experiments that there is an important effect of praise and other incentives or of their absence on the reaction time. The reaction time of the subject on his being encouraged, decreases; whereas the important reaction time of the subject increases if he is punished.

(5) **Conditions of Subject.** Besides the above factors, many other conditions related to the subject also throw light on his reaction time. Some of the main conditions are given below :

(a) **Age.** Reaction time of the children and old people is longer than that of adults, because in the former, their power of controlling attention and their readiness for reaction is less.

(b) **Physical Conditions.** The physical conditions of the subject such as temperature, tiresomeness, use of intoxicants etc., have an important effect on his reaction time. The effect of bodily temperature is very little and a moderate use of intoxicants have no special effect but their use in excess has a clear effect. Reaction time gets increased by drinking whereas it gets decreased by taking coffee or tea. Some mental abnormalities increase and others decrease the reaction time. Tiresomeness increase the reaction time.

(c) **Practice.** Reaction time in an expert subject is less than that in a new subject. On the basis of experiments, Cattel concluded that the effect of practice on reaction time is limited only to some experiments. It has been found out from the experiments of Cassel, Delanwak and Woodrow that a diversion of attention increases the reaction time but the reaction time decreases by keeping attention.

(d) **Attitude.** As has already been said, a favourable attitude reduces the reaction time, and an unfavourable attitude increases it.

(e) **Mental Set.** If the mental set is favourable, the reaction time is less; but if the mental set is adverse, the reaction time is more.

(f) **Attention.** As has been said before, attention and diversion of attention, both affect the reaction time. When the subject is attentive, his reaction time is less, but when he is inattentive the reaction time is sometimes more and sometimes less.

Measurement of Reaction Time

Kymograph drum is used for measuring action time. Hip-cronoscope has already been alluded to. Besides these, Bernier-cronoscope is also a good instrument for measuring reaction time. It has two pendulums. On the presentation of the stimulus, the bigger pendulum begins to swing and the smaller pendulum swings on reaction. The number of swings, which bring both the pendulums parallel to each other, is multiplied by 0.02 and the reaction time is found out in seconds.

QUESTIONS FOR EXERCISE

1. What is the meaning of Reaction Time? Describe an experiment for measuring reaction time.
2. Write short note on Reaction Time.
3. What is Reaction Time? Bring out the difference between simple, disjunctive and judgment reaction time?

16

FEELING AND EMOTION

The word 'emotion' is a derivative of the latin word 'emovere' which means 'to shudder'. Thus, emotion is that state of the individual which deprives him of his equilibrium. In fear his teeth are clenched together, his body shudders and signs of perspiration can be seen upon his forehead. Emotions shake a man violently. Even, when the object of his anger is no longer present, the person's arms twitch uncontrollably. Emotions stimulate the energies of the creature and assist him in dealing with emergencies. In an emotional condition he performs actions which he is incapable of performing in a normal state. But sometimes, though comparatively infrequently, a person is absolutely stupefied and fails to perform even the ordinary activities. These mutually contradictory results bear testimony to the fact that it is difficult to define emotion. Though psychologists have not differentiated between motive and emotion, everyday experience shows that there is some difference. Similarly, some psychologists do not find any difference in physical activities and emotion. But experiments reveal this difference which is by no means negligible.

P.T. Young has defined emotion thus : "Emotion is acute disturbance of the individual as a whole, psychological in origin involving behaviour, conscious experience and visceral functioning." In Woodworth's opinion, an emotion is a disturbed state of the body.

It is a disturbed glandular and muscular activity. Woodworth rightly says that "each emotion is a feeling, and each is at the same time a motor set." In this way emotion is that state of the individual in which the body is externally as well as internally upset. This can be clarified by an example of anger.

The emotion of anger is the painful aspect of the pugnacious instinct. Anger in the creature is aroused by any interference in the execution of an instinct generated activity, or by the failure of such activity. Therefore, anger is directed upon the interfering object or creature, though not always because sometimes anger is directed to oneself. For example, when angry, clenching of the eye brows, vociferating, kicking, attacking, trembling — these and other physical activities, or rather disturbances are apparent. The activities in an emotional condition of anger are the opposite of the activities of a person who is struck into fear. In anger a person becomes aggressive.

Emotion and Feeling

Both emotion and feeling are closely related to one another. They both depend on the brain stem in the nervous system. Pleasure pain, fear, anger, love and gaiety etc., involve feelings as well as emotions. Consequently, many of the emotions are linked with feelings. Feelings can be pleasant and can be painful too. Similarly, emotions may be caused either by happiness or by sorrow.

In spite of such a close relation between feeling and emotion they are not identical, this difference should not be lost sight of. Feeling is the reaction of pleasure or pain originated by the sense organs, which results from sensation. For example, the observation of a rainbow in the sky results in a feeling of pleasure. When a thorn pricks the foot, a feeling of pain is generated. Thus, feeling is sensory and simple, whereas, on the other hand, emotions are more complex. They can be aroused not only by the existing circumstances but also by a recollection of these circumstances. Players are excited by the imagination of decision of the failure in the game. We are filled with hatred when we are reminded of disgusting circumstances. Another difference between emotion and feeling is that while feeling is aroused by sensory reactions, emotion is activated by thoughts and imagination, not by sensation. It follows that there is a difference between emotion and feeling from the mental viewpoint. The difference between their mental qualities is the result of the contributory circumstances from which they originate. Emotion is evolved at a more complex level and new elements are introduced in it. The pleasure which we receive by listening to a good discourse or by reading a good book is not due to the words as such but due to the thoughts expressed by these words. The pleasure which arises out of listening to an oration by a famous leader is due not to the voice of the leader, but rather to his opinion. These are examples of emotion.

Another substantial difference between emotion and feeling is that the former is more comprehensive than the latter. Feeling is a part of emotion. Emotion includes feeling and, it is therefore something more than a feeling. This closeness of the relation of the two often causes people to forget the difference between them. In emotion some glands inside the body excrete some specific types of juices. But there is no excretion in the case of feeling. In feeling there is more neural excitement than in emotion. At a certain stage, even a tendency to become active is perceived.

Emotion is more vigorous than feeling and it upsets the whole body. The individual is divested of his stability and his control over the situation. Consequently, the necessary reaction is impeded in its execution and behaviour is disturbed. The derangement is present in feeling too, but not as much as in emotion. In reality slightly disturbed state indicates feeling and a greater disturbance points to emotion. In an emotional state the behaviour of a person is more excited, vigorous and disturbed than is feeling. Feeling is never as full of excitement as emotion is. In the grip of emotion a man sometimes transcends every type of limit, reason being completely paralysed. Feeling never attains such a frenzied stale. Pleasure is never as effective as anger is.

Physical Changes in Emotion

Emotion results in bodily changes which can be classified as external bodily changes and internal bodily changes.

External Physical Changes

Generally, emotion is identified with bodily changes. An emotion is guessed on the basis of external physical changes. If a person grinds his teeth we say that he is angry. When a person trembles it is remarked that he is nervous. In love our face lights up, in grief our eyes are filled with tears and in surprise our eyes dilate. In this way, a difference in the expression of the eyes, nose, mouth, forehead etc., is discernible in emotion. A person's voice is altered and he adopts a fresh posture. These are the external changes in the manifestation of emotion. These will now be described in detail.

(1) **Facial Expression.** When under the influence of emotion, the facial expression of the person is the first to be altered. It is easiest to read the emotion of love or hate from the face. No amount of effort can successfully disguise the facial contortions in strong emotion, from an experienced observer. In an emotional state the muscles of the face expand or contract. In pleasant emotion, it is said, that the face lights up with delight, this lighting up refers to the muscular expansion. Similarly, it is said that the face hangs down. The reference is to the contraction of the muscles. Prevalent saying such as blushing with shame or averting the eyes, expansion of the eyes in fear, elevation of the eye brows in anger are used to describe the changes in facial expressions in emotion. Many psychologists have experimented in order to determine the meaning of a variety of facial expressions. Some experiments seem to indicate that the facial expressions by themselves are insufficient to enable a distinction to be made between the emotions, but the data collected from these studies is insufficient.

1. It is difficult to get the normal emotion in the artificially created situation in the laboratory.

2. In different cultures the mode of expression of the various emotions is not uniform.

3. Even, if the normal emotion is produced in the laboratory it is necessary to photograph it at high speeds.

4. In the recognition of emotions, experience and instructions are indispensable.

In reality, it cannot be said with any degree of certainty that it is not possible to recognise emotion from the facial expression. Even after the effects and impressions of the culture, there is a degree of similarity in the facial expression of the emotions of the members of every society. It is easy to recognise the conflicting expressions of pleasure and pain in Leonardo da Vinci's sketches given in Fig. 48.

(2) **Vocal Expression.** Emotions can be expressed through the medium of voice and through this medium similar emotions can also be aroused in others. In expression of emotions the voice is influenced *i.e.*, the pitch and loudness of the voice changes. The voice of an angry person is hoarse and loud whereas a loving person's voice is rhythmical and sweet. Some of the stronger emotions can be thus distinguished by hearing the voice. Sometimes even language can successfully excite emotions.

Fig. 46

(3) **Postural Expression.** In an emotional condition, the posture is affected too. These changes are not similar in all societies and in all the members of society. When frightened a person is seen either running or standing still. In love, embracing, kissing, etc., may be observed but these show substantial changes in different societies due to the effect of culture. When angry some people use foul language, others pace about in a frenzy and still others attack. Rubbing hands, clenching fists, standing erect, sitting with a bowed head, hiding, flinging the arms about etc., all indicate emotion but identification of emotion depends upon the person and the society to which he belongs and is possible only after adequate research.

Internal Physical Changes

Besides the external changes mentioned above, there are some internal physiological changes too, in an emotional state. When surprised our breathing almost stops. Our heart beats faster when we are angry. But these internal changes can be known only when they are measured by instruments. Some major changes are detailed below :

(1) **Change in Heart Beat.** Generally, the heart beats faster or slower if the individual is disturbed. This fact is utilised by literary people, as they mention this fluctuation of the heart beat to show the presence of emotion. The face is flushed or blood shot in anger, because they alternate contraction and expansion of the blood vessels sends and excess of blood to that part of the body. This abnormal

activity is the result of the altered heart beat. The blood pressure of all those who were present rose when Scott, during his experiments, exhibited some sexually exciting photographs.

(2) **Blood Pressure Changes.** We saw above how the heart beat changes and effects the blood pressure; this change, being very prominent, is very noticeable and is generally considered to be a good indicator of emotion. It is measured with a plethysmograph. It can be used as a lie detector though its validity is restricted to the inexperienced deceiver because only such a person will be disturbed or upset at the prospect. Contradicting all that we have been asserting all along are some experimental results which prove that this change is not inevitable. Examining some soldiers injured in war, it was noticed that their blood pressure was not noticeably altered, in spite of the emotional experience of the war, while the visiting relatives were more severally affected, as was proved by their blood pressure.

(3) **Change in the Blood Chemistry.** This is not all, because in an emotional state some changes in the chemical conditions of the blood also take place. Another reaction to the emotion is the excretion of adrenaline from the adrenal gland, which puts more sugar in the blood and gives person a reserve of energy to rely on and face the situation. The effect of Adrenaline is felt in other quarters too. There is more sugar in the urine, blood pressure and heart beat increase and some capillaries in the skin start contracting.

(4) **Change in the Rate of Respiration.** It is a matter of common experience that when excited, one's breath comes in short, quick gaps. When a person is feeling sorry or depressed he breaths slowly. These changes are measured with a pneumograph. Commonly, emotion causes changes in the rate of respiration.

(5) **Change in Galvanic Skin Response.** A psycho-galvanometer is an instrument used for measuring the resistance of the skin to an electric current. A skin dampened by perspiration offers more resistance than usual. Previously, this state was supposed to be the peculiarity of emotion, but it has now been established that the same state will be the outcome of any physical or mental exercise. But still the response of the skin is present in emotion and is a definition of the emotional state.

(6) **Metabolic Changes.** Another important factor in the internal changes is the effect upon the process of digestion. But it has not been finally proved whether the change differs in different emotions or not. Burnswick's experiments on human beings showed that in fear, sorrow etc., the processes of digestion are interrupted or stopped but in surprise the process was apparently accelerated and happiness left the digestion indifferent.

(7) **Changes in Brain Waves.** The frequency of brain wave is affected in emotion. This change can be measured by instruments.

These are major internal and external changes but they do not include every one. There are some other psychological changes which are apparent in emotion *e.g.*, when a person is extremely frightened, he may excrete urine etc. This is a tendency present in every animal and bird. This comprehensive study of internal and external psychological changes must have made it very clear that in emotion there are changes, though it is not possible to determine with accuracy the connection of a certain emotion with a certain change.

These changes due to emotion will be clarified further from the following chart :

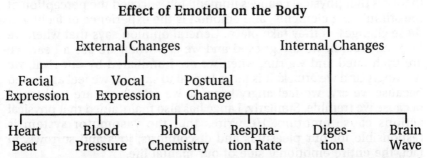

Effect of Emotion on the Body

External Changes   Internal Changes

Facial   Vocal   Postural
Expression   Expression   Change

Heart   Blood   Blood   Respira-   Diges-   Brain
Beat   Pressure   Chemistry   tion Rate   tion   Wave

Psychologists do not agree as to the importance of physiological changes in an emotional state. The behaviourists place much emphasis on the physiological changes due to emotion and do not give any credence whatsoever to the mental response. On the other hand, some psychologists lay and equal emphasis upon the mental changes. Looking at it realistically the physiological changes cannot be assumed to be everything, but then neither can they be neglected and considered insignificant. Similarly, the mental aspect of emotion can neither be neglected nor relied upon exclusively. It is necessary to understand both the aspects to understand emotion completely. As experiments are still being conducted in both these aspects, it is necessary to keep in view the psychological changes as well as the functions of the different parts of the brain while making a comprehensive study of emotions. A fully satisfactory theory of emotions can be evolved in the future only with a balanced viewpoint.

THEORIES OF EMOTION

James-Lange Theory of Fraction

In 1884, the famous American psychologist William James published his theory of emotions. In 1885, a Danish psychologist Lange, independently presented his theory of emotions. Due to many points of similarity between the two theories, this theory became famous as the James-Lange theory.

The James-Lange theory is the very antithesis of the popular belief about emotions. The theory states that physiological changes take place upon perceiving the circumstances and these changes make an emotion felt.

Thus, according to this theory, emotion is a pattern of organic changes. The external stimulus excites one or more sensory organs. The excitement is sensed and conveyed by the sensory nerve impulses, the cerebral cortex whence there is a knowledge of the specific stimulation. Next, the nervous impulse goes to the muscles and the viscera which are excited. The excitement is then conveyed to the brain via the sensory nerve impulses. And from this results arousal of emotion. James, in his book *Psychology*, has presented his theory saying that his theory is that physical changes immediately succeed the perception of the stimulating elements, and emotion is the experience or feeling of these changes as they take place. General opinion says that when we lose our wealth, we are grieved and we cry, when we see a bear, we are frightened and we run, when we are humiliated by our rival, we feel angry and we attack. It is more logical to say that we feel aggrieved because we cry, we feel angry because we attack, we are frightened because we tremble. Similarly, Lange has also maintained that physical actions cause emotion. He writes that the vasomotor system is responsible for our pleasures and discomforts, joys and sorrows, in fact, the entire emotional side of our mental life.

Arguments for James-Lange Theory

The following are the more important arguments in favour of the theory :

(1) **Perception Causes Bodily Changes without Arousing the Emotion.** According to James, if we see a mobile black image in the jungle, our heart stops beating and we start trembling before any clear idea of danger is conceived. Apparently in this case the perception and bodily changes precede the emotion.

(2) **An Emotion cannot be Imagined in the Absence of Physical Expression.** According to James, if we imagine as emotion and then try to remove the signs of its physical experiences from our consciousness we do not find any such thing which may constitute an emotion. Whatever is felt is only an immutable state of feelingless intellectual perception.

To experience an emotion it is necessary to adopt a suitable bodily posture. Without it, the emotion cannot be felt.

(3) **The Suppression of Physical Expression Results in the Suppression of Related Emotion.** If the emotion is not permitted to express itself, it is destroyed. One tries to amuse a person who is crying on account of sorrow because it is generally believed that if he ceases weeping, his sorrow will be reduced or that he will be happy if he laughs. In practice, it is seen that this is exactly what happens generally.

(4) The Artificial Creation of Physical Expression Creates the Related Emotion. Presenting the examples of actors, James said that, while acting, they experienced the emotions, the physical expressions of which they were enacting. When alcohol and other stimulating drugs are consumed, the manifestation of the various physical conditions results in the experiencing of various emotions.

(5) Some Bodily Abnormalities Cause Emotions. Giving an example of this, James says that the troubles of the liver cause a loss of appetite and touchyness while mental diseases cause fear and despair. In James' opinion, objectless emotions are the result of bodily infirmity.

In this way, this theory does not distinguish between emotion and physical sensation. Ward says that in this theory of emotions are a group of physical sensations and these sensations are emotions. They are not only complementary but inseparable too.

Criticism of the James-Lange Theory

This theory has been bitterly criticised. The following are the main points of criticism :

(1) Emotional Reactions are Possible even in the Absence of the Physical Correlates. Sherrington operated upon many dogs and severed the connections of the extremities and the brain by operating upon the spinal cord. But this did not affect their emotions in any way. Cannon and his assistants proved a similar thing in the case of cat. Dr. Dana proved it too, by observing the case of a forty-year old lady who exhibited and felt emotion even though she could not receive any sensations from the sympathetic nervous system.

(2) Contradictory Results have been obtained from Actors. Archer found that many actors do not feel any emotion when they are acting.

(3) Visceral and Internal Changes and Infirmities do not make Emotion Inevitable. Cannon and his followers administered injections of the excretion of the adrenal gland to common people and caused many internal and visceral changes. But nobody felt any emotion due to these changes. Vernon, Cantril and Hunt also achieved similar results from their experiments.

Even alcoholic drinks failed to arouse any emotion.

(4) The Absence of the Sex Organs did not Undermine a Person's Sexual Emotions. Maccurdy wrote that a person unaware of his sex organs, still expressed a sexual interest in the hospital nurses.

(5) The Emotions cannot be Differentiated on the Basis of Physiological Changes. If emotion is the result of physiological changes then the creation of one emotion by various changes or the presence of the same changes in different emotions cannot be explained, though this is noticed in daily life.

(6) Objectless Emotions are not in Reality Objectless. Titchener pointed out that the objectless emotions are unmotivated remnants of motivated emotions which result from old emotional tendencies.

(7) In different people, one emotion produces varied physical changes while the same changes may be observed as a result of different emotions. Therefore, emotion and physical changes cannot be believed to be inseparable.

(8) **James has not distinguished between Emotion-producing and Unproductive Physical Changes.** Stout says that undoubtedly, every bodily change is not emotion. Hunger and stomach ache are not emotional experiences.

(9) **If emotions result from a mere perception of the objects, then why is it that similar stimulants do not arouse similar reactions?** Ward says, "Let us suppose that at first James is faced with a caged bear and then with a free bear. In the first case he feeds it groundnuts while in the latter he runs away from it." Obviously, emotions are aroused not by objects but by circumstances. Woodworth opined that emotions are aroused when some instinct excited by the circumstances is not satisfied. Drever is also of the same opinion. McDougall has also stressed the instinct-originated elements in emotion.

The arguments against this theory of emotions prove its unscientific nature. Later on, James made some amendments in his theory and accepted that the perceptible object is influenced by the background. He went so far as to accept the presence of a feeling core between perception and the physiological changes. As a result of this change, emotion was no longer considered to be the result of perception nor was physical expression predominant in emotion. Consequently, the amended James-Lange theory confirmed the popular opinion. As a matter of fact, the importance of this theory in psychology lies in its emphasis upon physiological changes in emotion. Its elaboration upon the subject of emotions is, however, unsatisfactory.

CANNON'S THEORY OF EMOTION

Cannon's theory regarding emotions is also known as the Emergency theory or the Hypothalamic theory. According to this view the major part in emotion's reactions is played by the excretion of the hypothalamus. In this view, the cerebral cortex, is the centre of emotional feeling while the internal brain or Diencephalon, which is formed of hypothalamus, and thalamus is the centre of emotional expression. The nervous impulses reach the thalamus through the sensory nerves. The thalamus attaches to this an emotional quality and passes it on to the cerebral cortex so that the person experiences a specific emotion. While sending it on to the cerebral cortex, thalamus deflects a part of the nervous impulse to the viscera and the skeletal muscles. This results in a change in them which can be observed.

It is undoubtedly true that Cannon's theory is more appropriate than the James-Lange theory. It has been proved that the hypothalamus does have a hand in the control of emotions. The acceptance of this theory makes it possible to understand how the emotions remain unaffected by the severance of the spinal cord or by the mild reactions of the viscera. It also explains the failure of adrenaline injections to arouse emotion. But this point of view is limited and one-sided. As Lashley has shown by his experiments, every aspect of emotion cannot be explained by this theory. In reality, the other parts of nervous system have as much a hand in emotions as the hypothalamus. For example, the cerebral cortex has a greater part in the adjustability of emotions.

Motivational Theory

In presenting the motivational theory, Leeper made emotion completely motivational and proved this fact through experiments. According to this theory, every emotion has a goal which pilots and guides the emotional action. Leeper has proved that every bodily change assists in the adjustment of the individual. Rate of respiration, heart beat, blood pressure, perspiring and visceral functioning all help the individual to adjust himself to the contingency. The excretion of the sympathetic nervous system spurs him to greater efforts. Other sympathetic reactions keep the body safe.

Everyday experience makes it quite obvious that emotional actions have a goal and that they help in adjustment. For example, we run away from a snake because we are frightened and we wish to save ourselves. Thus, the motivational theory is true to some extent but only in the simple condition of emotion. If a person is extremely frightened he stays rooted to the ground and gets bitten by the snake. Similarly, in a state of extreme agitation, like extremely sexually excited situation, the person's adjustment to the situation becomes worse instead of getting better. In reality, the motivational theory is correct in common emotional states, but it seems to lose its value with the increase in intensity due to the fact that in such conditions the actions in emotion are not directed towards adaptation. A psychologist E. Mira disproved this theory by pointing out stages of development in fear. Mira's study indicates that in different stages the inhibition in emotion increases and the activities of the higher nerve centres are restricted.

Activation Theory

The most modern theory advanced on this subject is the Activation theory. It has accepted all the important aspects of the above mentioned theories. In keeping with the James-Lange theory, it accepts the importance of physical changes and expressions. It agrees with Cannon's theory on the importance of the hypothalamus. It accepts the part played by the sympathetic nervous system and the assistance of emotion in adjustment which is in keeping with the motivational theory.

The activational theory has emphasised the activities of the cortex because this theory originates from a study of brain waves. It is based on research in the physiological field. This theory propounds that in emotion the whole body and not any one part of it takes part. Consequently, it cannot be said that emotion is based on some specific part. The arrangement of emotional activities can be affected only by the adjustment of the activities of the various parts of the brain. Thus, an understanding of the internal activities of the brain is necessary for an understanding of emotion. Though the activation theory of emotions is superior to all the preceding ones, it is not the final theory. Some more experimentation is necessary to say anything definite about this subject.

QUESTIONS FOR EXERCISE

1. Describe the nature of emotion and consider how far it can be identified with visceral sensation.
2. Clearly distinguish between Emotion and Feeling.
3. Describe major bodily changes during emotion.
4. Discuss the James-Lange theory of emotions.
5. Give the different theories of emotion.

17
LEARNING

The following are some definitions of learning which should make it clear :

(1) Learning is Change in Behaviour. In J.P. Guilford's opinion, "We may define the term very broadly by saying that learning is any change in behaviour, resulting from behaviour." In this definition a distinction between change in behaviour due to maturity and change in behaviour due to learning is not clear though both these activities occur simultaneously. In the words of Woodworth, "Typically at least learning consists in doing something provided this something new is retained by the individual and appears in his later activities."

(2) Learning is An Organisation of Behaviour. According to Garrett, "Learning is that activity by virtue of which we organise our response with new habits." Thus, the element of organisation in learning is very much important. Guilford too, maintains that learning involves organisation of behaviour. Thus, in learning to ride a cycle we have to organise the activities of turning the pedal, balancing the handle, etc., in order to be reasonably safe with the vehicle. It is another matter that a person does not learn this organisation at the outset and that he may take much longer time to learn to balance the handle than the time he may take to learn to turn the pedal. But his learning of the activity of cycling will be complete only when he accomplishes this organisation.

(3) Learning is the Reinforcement of a New Activity. R.S. Woodworth maintained that the learning of a new act is an addition to the person's store of experiences. Clarifying the statement further, Woodworth says that reinforcement, too, is an indispensable element in the act of learning because it helps forming only successful responses and weeding out the unsuccessful ones. To quote Woodworth "An activity may be called learning in so far as it develops the individual in any way, good or bad and makes his environment and experiences different from what it would otherwise have been."

The psychologists who stress external behaviour consider learning to be a change of behaviour while those who lay emphasis on internal changes are convinced that learning is change in the perception of the individual. Combining these two views, Murphy writes : "From this point of view it would be legitimate to regard learning as a modification both of behaviour and of the way of perceiving." The following definition of learning given by Hilgard is an essence of all the foregoing definitions offered by other psychologists, "Learning is the process by which an activity originates or is changed through reacting to an encountered situation, provided that the characteristics of the change in activity cannot be explained on the basis of native response tendencies, maturity or temporary status of the organism."

LEARNING AND MATURATION

Learning changes behaviour and so does maturation. Thus, some times it becomes difficult to say definitely as to which of the subject's activities are the result of learning and which are the consequences of maturation. Automatic activity, random acts, reflexes and instincts and sudden expression of emotion can be accepted as unlearned actions and the result of maturation, but in most of the activities of human beings it is difficult to decide whether these activities result from maturation or learning. In fact, these activities develop both due to learning and maturation. Take the example of learning a language. It is true, of course, that a child is manifestly incapable of learning language until he reaches a certain stage or age in maturation, but it is also equally true that he does not learn the language just because he attains that stage. The language is taught to him.

An experiment on co-twins indicates the extent of the changes in behaviour caused by maturation and the extent to which changes may be affected by learning. The purpose of the experiment was to measure the extent of advantage of learning in such activities as climbing the stairs. Two twins were chosen for the experiment because due to the similarity in heredity, the speed of maturation is the same and any changes which may occur may be attributed to learning. One of the twins 'S' was not given the opportunity of climbing stairs for 53 weeks while the other twin 'T' was taught to climb the stairs from her forty-sixth

Fig. 47

week. On examination this twin 'T' failed to climb at all at the age of 46 weeks and had to be aided up all the 5 stairs. In the space of four weeks she climbed all stairs in 26 seconds.

When 'S' was placed on the stairs at the age of 53 weeks she climbed all the five stairs unaided but it took her some 45 seconds. After two weeks of practice 'S' at the age of 55 weeks, traversed the distance in 13 seconds. In this way, at this age 'S' was ahead of 'T' who, at a younger age had practised three times as much. 'S' was three weeks older than 'T'. Thus, in spite of all kinds of learning, T was left behind, due to a lack of maturity.

This experiment proves that learning plays an insignificant part in reflex and other physiological activities peculiar to one's species. Those activities which appear in all human beings at a certain age, are due to maturity. Those activities which do not inevitably appear in every person are affected by maturation to the extent that they can be learnt with ease at the age of maturity. Some examples of this type of activities are swimming, horse riding, climbing trees etc. The learning of these activities is made more facile by motor, sensory and neural maturation.

Conditioned Response Learning

As a general rule the higher the species of the animal, the more easily conditioning of response is achieved. The conditioning should be the easiest in the case of human beings. But man is a complex animal and hence the factors which distract his attention are larger in number than in the case of other animals. However, in spite of these distracting elements in conditioning of responses it certainly remains one of the most important methods of learning, especially in the case of children. In childhood, many of the responses of the child are conditioned to particular objects and even when the individual becomes an adult, his conditioned response continues *e.g.*, if a man behaves wrongly with us, we develop a kind of fear, abhorrence or hatred with every person resembling him.

Modern psychology does not admit the view that all learning is conditioning, but no psychologist denies that conditioned response is an important method of learning both in the case of animals as well as of human beings. A person can find hundreds of examples of conditioning of response in his daily life. In the case of the tamed animals the conditioning process is very much used to teach so many activities. The conditioning of response, as it is established, can also be extinguished. In the establishment of the conditioning the stimuli has to be repeated while in its extinction the stimuli is not repeated. Thus, in the example of Pavlov's dog, if the dog's response has been conditioned by the ringing of the bell, it will be de-conditioned if food is not served in spite of the ringing of the bell or food is served without ringing of the bell. Similar examples of de-conditioning process can be found in the case of human beings. Suppose a person is used to get out for a walk to a bridge with a certain friend, he will always remember his friend when he is absent. The sight of the bridge will make him recall his friend, because he always used to come with him to bridge. Thus, the bridge and the presence of his friend have been linked. Now, if the friend is absent and returns after a long time and the man has to go alone for a walk, he will forget his friend gradually and the sight of the bridge will no more awake the memory of him. In this example, one finds de-conditioning of a certain response to a particular stimulus. Just as a response can be de-conditioned, it is also re-conditioned. Conditioning, de-conditioning and re-conditioning of the response are governed by the same fundamental principles.

Trial and Error

The method of trial and error is used in the following circumstances :

(1) This method is used when the learner is completely motivated and can see the goal clearly. If the cat is not hungry she will not try to come out of the cage or leave the attempt after trying it without success for some time. The cat tries to come out of the cage simply because she is hungry and knows that there is food outside the cage. In the absence of the food outside the cage the cat will not try to come out of it. Thus, it is clear that motivation as well as the presence of the goal is necessary for awakening the response in learning through trial and error.

(2) The method of trial and error is used when perception alone or learned activities are not sufficient. If the cat could come out of the cage by merely moving in some direction, there was hardly any need of several trials and errors.

(3) The method of trial and error is used when the learner fails to find the solution of the problem. In Thorndike's experiment the cat used trial and error method simply because she did not know how to come out of the cage. In the case of human beings in such situations, if the subject knows the solution of the problem, there is hardly any question of trial and error. It is only when he fails to find out the solution of the problem that he proceeds blindly, tries in various directions, commits errors, eliminates them and finally arrives at the successful response.

Thus, the method of trial and error is widely used both by animals as well as by human beings. In the case of human beings, however, this process is somewhat different, because man has better powers of perception, understanding, intelligence and language etc. Man uses the method of trial and error, but he also takes the help of language and other instruments in the process of learning.

Insight

Insight is an important constituent in the solution of problems, and is found in the higher class of animals and human beings. It is the best method among the methods of learning.

According to the gestalt psychologists, a person can deduce the solution by insight if he perceives the situation as a whole. A German gestaltist Kohler, prepared some simple problems for experiments with dogs, hens, monkeys and chimpanzees. In an experiment, a hungry animal was released from the house while some food was placed behind the fence adjoining the wall. Both the dog and the hen trotted around in the vicinity of the wall but as soon as they found the way out, they made their exit and reached the food. This perception of the change in the meaning of the wall is insight. Before the insight the wall was an insuperable obstacle, but after insight it was no longer an obstacle but an object necessitating circumvention. The result of insight is the understanding of new relations, the discovery of new patterns and the formation of new organizations.

The most famous experiments conducted by Kohler, in relation to insight were those that were carried out on chimpanzees. Some bananas were placed outside the cage of a chimp, called Sultan, who was then given two sticks so constructed that they could be fitted together. Sultan tried to pull the bananas with the sticks, an effort which he kept up for an hour, but he got tired of the attempt and gave it up for playing. While playing he brought the two ends together and suddenly he got an idea which resulted in his fitting the smaller stick in the hole of the bigger one. He then used the two together to draw the banana inward. The two sticks disintegrated but he fitted them together again. He then pulled in everything within reach as if he were trying out his discovery. The next day he took far less time to fit the two together. It is a peculiarity of insight that once the solution is learnt, it is not forgotten though its memory may become hazy with the passage of time.

The above experiments make it quite obvious that learning by insight has certain characteristics of its own. They are briefly as follows :

1. Insight is sudden.

2. Insight alters perception.

3. Old objects appear in new patterns and organization by virtue of insight.

4. Insight is relative to the intellectual level. The higher species of animals including human beings have more insight than the members of lower species.

5. In insight understanding is more useful than dexterity of hands.

6. In Woodworth's opinion, insight is sometimes hindsight and at others is foresight. To quote him "Foresight is seeing the way to the goal before taking it or perceiving the uselessness of a certain lead without buying it and hindsight is observing that a lead is good or bad after trying it. When the whole situation is clear and above-board,

there is a good chance for foresight, but when important characteristics of the situation have to be discovered by exploration and manipulation, hindsight is the best, we can expect.

7. Previous experience is of assistance in insight, though the excess of previous experience does not necessarily increase insight because organized perception too is an essential factor in learning.

8. Maturity also effects insight as evidenced by the smoother working of insight in older age than in adolescence.

9. If the pieces essential for the solution of the puzzle are present together when perceived, insight comes about earlier.

10. Some psychologists say that learning by insight is associative learning. Insight appears suddenly after the manipulation of thoughts or objects for a small though significant length of time.

11. The insight gained in particular circumstances is of assistance in other circumstances. A verbal formula is generally extracted by people learning by insight and this formula is capable of facile application to other circumstances.

The above mentioned characteristics of learning through insight apply both to human and animal learning. The solitary difference is the fact that a human being by virtue of his superior capacities of experiencing and understanding, observes relation between various objects quickly and sees the patterns concealed in them with alacrity. He is assisted in this by language. As a matter of fact, insight occurs only when the learner perceives the related link hidden in the activity. The learning curve is altered suddenly due to insight. Insight is impossible in an extremely unfamiliar problem because familiarity is very necessary for insight. A student of literature will have no insight in any scientific problem because he does not know even the a b c of science. When the subject of study becomes a part of life, insight becomes easier. History can be made alive by exhibitions, Geography by travelling, and Arithmetic by shop accounts. Familiarity is also important besides the theoretical study.

One example of human learning by insight will suffice. A student of Arithmetic tries hard to solve a difficult problem of Arithmetic. He tries many methods but fails to secure a solution. He gives up and lays it aside or goes to sleep. After sometime suddenly or when he is awakened the solution suggests itself and he notes it down in his note-book. When he is confronted with similar problems in the future, he will have no difficulty in solving them.

The insight method is superior to imitation or conditioned response because both the later methods take more time.

Trial and error emphasizes the acquisition of motor skill but in insight mental effort is stressed upon.

While insight depends upon perception, trial and error depends upon sensory motor co-ordination.

The person keeps an eye on the goal, in trial and error and all activity is goal directed but insight is in the unconscious mind which exerts the most while the conscious activities are either very few or aimless.

Every new problem has to be tackled from the very beginning if the trial and error method is used. On the other hand, both generalization and differentiation are present in insight, which adds to the possibilities of transfer of learning and the use of old insight in the solution of novel problems.

Students will be permanently helped by the use of the insight method of learning in place of the trial and error method in their study and other daily activities. They will also be able to conserve their energy. Suppose that a person has to arrange furniture in a room. An average person will determine the position of the table by using the trial and error method and shifting the table from place to place. An intelligent person will take up a position from where the whole room is visible, and imagine all the possible positions of the pieces of furniture in an imagined framework of the room and then place the respective pieces accordingly. But this does not mean that trial and error method is not meant for the intelligent. By no means is this so. In many novel situations progress is not possible without it. An intelligent person should use both these methods according to the needs of the situation.

Problem of Neuro-Physiology of Learning

In the study of learning process physiological psychologist aims to find out its physiological basis. What changes take place in the body or brain of the animal when after many trials in a puzzle box it learns to get out of the puzzle box? In other words, the aim is to find out the extent to which learning of the organism depends on his body and brain. In this connection, physiological psychologists are specially interested in conditioned response learning out of the various methods of learning. Pavlov did important experiments on the dogs and found out what changes took place in brain structures during conditioning. Similarly, experiments have been done with rats, cats and dogs on avoidance conditioning, instrumental learning and discriminative learning. Physiological psychologists have attempted to find out the role of brain, receptors and muscles in these three types of learning.

Methods of Research

Following main methods are used in physiological psychology to find out the physiological basis of learning :

(1) **Brain Lesions.** This is the oldest method for studying the functions of brain in Learning. In this method a particular area of the brain is

destroyed and its effect on learning is observed. In earlier days, various areas of the brain were surgically removed in the use of this method. But now-a-days deep lesions are made in sub-cortical areas and the information is obtained. Beside the cerebral cortex, these experiments have been done with thalamus, mid-brain, limbic system and spinal cord.

(2) **Experiments on Conditioning.** Most important experiments in connection with learning have been done on conditioning. Following three types of experiments fall in this area :

(i) *Classical Conditioning* : In classical conditioning experiment, typically, a signal is presented to the animal (dog or cat). This is followed by an electric shock to some region of the animal body. For this procedure to be called classical conditioning, shock must always follow the signal.

(ii) *Conditioned Emotional Response* : Conditioned fear or any other conditioned emotional response may be observed during conditioning. For example, the rat is placed in a skinner box and first given classical conditioning trials. A click is given and then follows the electric shock. After three minutes of this practice, one or two intense shocks are given. The emotional reaction which occurs to these shocks is well-established for a long period.

(iii) *Avoidance Conditioning* : Three different techniques are commonly used in this group : (a) Paw flexure, (b) Jumping response and (c) Shuttle response. In paw flexure technique, the animal learns to avoid the shock by raising its paw. This technique is also used to establish differential conditioning. In jumping response technique, the animal learns to avoid the shock by jumping. In the third technique of avoidance conditioning, the animal (rat, cat, dog or monkey) is placed in a box having two compartments. The compartments are separated by a hurdle. The animal gets the shock while crossing the hurdle. The animal learns to avoid the shock by shuttling over the hurdle.

Experiments on Brain

Many types of experiments have been done in connection with the role of brain structures in learning. Some are concerned with the removal of the total cerebral cortex, whereas in other experiments only a small part of this structure of the brain is removed. Some experiments have been done with the sensory areas and others are concerned with the frontal cortex. Following are some conclusions in this connection :

(1) **Complete Decortication.** Many experiments of this type have been done when the total cortex of the animal is removed. The decorticated animal has much difficulty in conditioning. But it has been observed that classical conditioning, avoidance conditioning and

differential conditioning can take place. These experiments have been specifically done on dog.

(2) **Partial Decortication.** Experiments have been done on cats and dogs with one side of the neo-cortex removed. Removing one side of the cortex causes a partial paralysis of organs on the opposite side in the body. Motor activities cannot take place. It has been found from these experiments that learning or retention of a conditioned response are not affected. Only the vigour of the response on the affected side is decreased.

(3) **Sensory Areas.** Experiments involving the lesions of different sensory areas of the cortex have been done. These experiments show several things. First, acquisition of a response is definitely impaired. Second, the animal may forget a response learned before the lesion. Third, simple avoidance responses may be retained after the operation while differential responses may be lost.

(4) **Experiments Involving Frontal Cortex.** In these experiments lesions are made in the frontal cortex and its effect upon learning is observed. In general, it can be said that frontal cortex is important in the retention of avoidance responses. But the effect in this connection depends on the degree and place of lesion and the particular technique used in learning. However, the results are not entirely clear from most of these studies.

Beside the above experiments, the role of the limbic system, thalamus, brain stem and spinal cord has been found in the learning of different animals. It has been observed that the region in the posterior thalamus has a special role in avoidance conditioning. No structure of the mid brain or hind brain seems to be important for conditioning employing shock. In fact, very few structures of the brain stem are essential for shock conditioning. In many studies, it has been observed that there is no loss in the retention of conditioned responses after lesions of the various structures of the brain. Some investigators have also raised the question whether the brain is really necessary for the learning of very simple responses. Perhaps conditioning can take place in the spinal cord also. But the results of the experiments on this question are very complex and contradictory. Therefore, at present, it is not possible to draw a final conclusion on the basis of these studies. Spinal cord has some definite contribution in conditioning. But what this role is, has not been settled yet.

Experiments on Discriminative Learning

Intensive experiments have been done in physiological psychology on discriminative learning. In these experiments the animal learns to discriminate between two or more stimuli, conditioning methods are many times used in such learning. An attempt is made in these experiments to find out the neural mechanisms of discriminative learning. The animal is trained to discriminate, between specific stimuli.

Then a test is made to see whether the animal remembers the discrimination learned after a particular part of the brain has been removed. This process though appears simple, has many difficulties in practice. First of all, we must distinguish between the sensory capacity and learning capacity of the animal. Secondly, the method of learning is very important. Besides this, some other influences on the animal are also important. For example, the influence of habit is one of these. Again, it is not always possible to find out as to which structure of the brain is essential in learning. Influence of the following four factors has become clear from the experiments on discrimination learning :

(1) Separate effects of brain lesions on sensory capacity and on learning capacity are observed.

(2) Influence of specific methods of learning is observed.

(3) Different effects of lesion on retention and relearning ability depending on time after the operation are seen.

(4) Effects of the injury of various specific brain structures are different.

Intensive experiments on different animals have been done in the field of discriminative learning with respect to various sensory capacities involved. In somaesthetic sense, experiments have been done on thermal discrimination, roughness discrimination and form discrimination. It has been inferred from these experiments that posterior parietal area of the cortex has a special role in somaesthetic discrimination learning. When this area is removed other parts of the brain may take over its function to a limited extent only.

In auditory discrimination, experiments have been done in connection with the intensity of sound, frequency of sound, tonal pattern and auditory localization in space. From all these experiments important facts have been found about auditory discrimination. Similar experiments have been done about visual sense. It has been attempted to find out as to which parts of the brain are responsible for the memory loss. In order to find out the function of different regions of the brain, each separate part has been partially or totally removed and its effect on learning and retention has been observed. Important facts have been found out from these experiments.

Study of Problem Solving Behaviour

One definition of learning is that it is a behaviour of solving problems. Various experiments have been done on this aspect of learning. Some experiments are about learning of mazes, simple or complex. Other experiments are done with problem box in which the animal gets some reward on learning a correct response. Beside these, experiments have been also done on delayed response learning. Experiments on mazes are the most extensive. Various types of mazes have been used by different psychologists in these experiments. In some experiments, mazes of different difficulties have been used. Greater ability to learn the maze is required as the difficulty of the maze is increased. Experiments on brain functions in maze learning have been done mainly on the rat. Various parts of the brain are removed and their effects on learning are observed. Most important example of the 'problem box' situation is the Skinner box. Lashley has used latches and bars in problem boxes in which the animal learns to open a latch or press the bar. On learning the correct response the animal gets food as a reward. Behaviours seen in these experiments have not been explained on the basis of same hypothesis by all psychologists. Some important questions are : "What does the animal learn?" Does his learning lie in the muscles or does he learn to make responses in the outer world? What is the contribution of senses or brain in the learning process? Definite conclusions have not been drawn about all these questions. The studies which have been described in chapter on localization of brain functions are also important in connection with the learning process.

Many experiments have also been done on the role of pre-frontal-lobe in memory functions, attentive functions and spatial factors etc., in the delayed-response learning.

It is clear from the above brief survey of different experiments, results and problems in the field of learning in physiological psychology that there is a great scope for further research in this area. It is right that definite conclusions cannot be drawn from the investigations done so far. The reason is that various structures of the brain do not work independently. On the other hand, the total brain works as a unit. Therefore, when a particular part of the brain is removed many of its functions are taken over by the other parts. But even then it cannot be denied that work done by physiological psychologists in this field is of great importance. It is expected that definite conclusions will be drawn from the experiments done in near future.

QUESTIONS FOR EXERCISE

1. "Learning is a function of what is learned, how is it learned and who learns it?" Elaborate.
2. Write short note on Trial and Error Learning.
3. Write short note on Learning through insight.
4. What is the problem of neuro-physiology of learning? Discuss various methods of research in this area.
5. What are methods of learning? Explain with experimental data.
6. What do you understand by stimulus generalisation and discrimination? How is discrimination explained scientifically?
7. What is discriminative learning? Discuss experiments on discriminative learning.

18
ATTENTION AND INTEREST

Attention is a selective process. Man lives in an environment. The stimuli from the environment are always affecting him. But these stimuli do not affect him equally. It is a common place observation that some stimuli affect us more than others. This shows that man selects out of environmental stimuli. This tendency of selection shows that there is a motivational process in him which is known as attention. This attention is affected by interest, attitudes and set. It is a selective process which includes motivation, set and selection. The cat will attend to the mouse, one can see a definite set in it. This set is both physical as well as mental. To take an example from human beings, if a student is not motivated, he will attend to the class lecture. Again, while a professor is delivering a lecture in the class, there are several other sounds being made in other rooms and the surroundings. The student who hears the lecture selects professor's voice out of the noise in the surroundings. While a student is attentively hearing the lecture, one can very well note his physical set which is also symbolic of his mental set. Receptor adjustment, bodily adjustment, postural adjustment, muscle attention and central nervous adjustments are typical of bodily attitude in attention. Thus, in brief, attention can be defined as a process which compels the individual to select some particular stimulus according to his interest and attitude out of the multiplicity of stimuli present in the environment.

CONDITIONS OF ATTENTION

As a selective act of the mind, attention depends upon several conditions. These conditions may be of two types — external or objective and internal or subjective. External or objective conditions are related with the environment. In the environment or surrounding of the individual there are several stimuli, but he does not attend to all of them at the same time, because some stimuli are stronger than others. The factors making these stimuli stronger than others, are known as external determinants of attention. Besides the external conditions the mental conditions, culture and heredity also influence attention. Due to these internal conditions some objects attract our attention more than others. These internal factors are internal determinants of attention. The methods of achieving attention are based upon these external and internal determinants of attention.

DETERMINANTS OF ATTENTION

The following are the most important external determinants of attention :

(1) **Nature of Stimulus.** Nature of stimulus means its type, *i.e.,* whether it is visual, gustatory, auditory, olfactory or tactual stimulus. It has been found by experiments that in comparison with other sensations, form, colour and sound attract more attention. Among the pictures, the pictures of human beings attract more attention than those of animals or objects. Among the pictures of human beings those of beautiful women attract more attention. Besides these, the coloured pictures attract more attention than black ones. All these factors are important in advertisement. In the auditory stimulus, the melodious voice attracts more attention than other voices.

(2) **Intensity of the Stimulus.** The intensity of the stimulus is a helpful condition in attention. In comparison with the weak stimuli the intense stimulus attracts more attention of the organism. High sound, excessive pressure and acute pain attract our attention. In the market, there is always some buzzing sound and yet the pedestrians hear the horn of the motor car, since the sound of the horn is louder than other sounds. But it is not always necessary that one should attend to the intensity of stimulus. Sometimes while walking on the road, calling of our name attracts so much attention that we fail to hear even the loud sound of the motor horn. As a matter of fact, the attraction of the attention does not depend on any single factor, but on several factors interconnected with one another. Hence, it can be said that other things being the same, the more intense stimulus will attract more attention.

(3) **Size of the Stimulus.** In the visual stimuli the size of the stimulus is also a determinant of attention. As a general rule the bigger size attracts more attention, but a small advertisement of a very wide background also attracts attention. Thus, the attraction of an object does not depend upon its size alone, but also on its background. To illustrate, a big black spot on black face will not attract so much attention as a very small black spot on a white face.

(4) **Location of the Stimulus.** The location of the stimulus also affects attention. In the visual stimuli, the most effective location is just in front of the eyes. The role of different pages in the newspapers or the magazine and the different places on the same page, is important in advertisement. It has been found by experiments that advertisements given on the front page or on the upper half of any page attract more attention.

(5) **Contrast of the Stimulus.** The contrast of the stimulus is also an important determinant of attention *i.e.,* the presence of a woman among men and that of a man among women definitely attracts more attention.

(6) Change of the Stimulus. Attention cannot be concentrated for a long time on some particular object. Hence, the change of the stimulus affects attention. Attention is sustained by change of the stimulus. The advertisers change their advertisements from time to time lest they may cease to be attractive.

(7) Isolation of the Stimulus. A man sitting alone in some corner of the park, hotel or club attracts more attention than others. A student sitting alone at the far corner of the class, is seen first. Thus, isolation is an important external determinant of attention. This fact is based upon the reason that the isolated individual is not mixed with other individuals and hence seen separately in his own background. By experiments in advertisement it has been found that only the fact of isolation attracts 30% more attention. In the British Journal of Educational Psychology of August 1951, D.B. Berlyne points out the following principles based upon latest experiments :

(a) In comparison with the un-changed stimulus the stimulus changed in the near past has more possibility of attracting attention.

(b) The effect of the change goes on diminishing with the passage of time.

(c) Whenever stimuli are changed together and in which one is left un-changed, the effect of change is not noticeable.

(d) If change goes on in the changed stimuli, the process of attention is permanent and strong.

The modes of change also influence the process of attention. If there is a change absolutely opposite to the present stimulus, it will definitely attract more attention. While studying one does not hear the sound of the clock or that of electric fan but if either of these suddenly stops, one cannot fail to attend to it. Man becomes used to regular changes and does not pay much attention to them. But if some irregular change or any sudden change occurs, it at once draws attention.

(8) Duration of the Stimulus. As a general rule, the stimulus having more duration, attracts more attention. Thus, duration of the stimulus is an important determinant of the attention. But sometimes the smallest flashing of a movement attracts more attention than the bigger stimuli, *e.g.*, a sudden flash of light for several seconds will attract more attention in a dark night than a continually burning lamp.

(9) Repetition of the Stimulus. Along with duration, repetition of stimulus is also an important determinant of attention. It is a common place observation that when the teacher has to attract the attention of students towards a particular phenomenon, he repeats it several times. But sometimes, man ceases to attend a phenomenon simply because it is repeated many times, *e.g.*, if a man says some thing about him, we take interest in it once or twice, but if we find that he always repeats the same thing, we cease to pay attention to it.

(10) **Movement in the Stimulus.** In comparison with the static, the moving stimuli attract more attention. The position of stimulus changes due to movements. An object lying in some corner of the room will not attract our attention, but even if there is some illusion of movement in it we cannot help attending to it. The influence of movement in stimulus is widely used by the shopkeepers and businessmen, who advertise through moving electric lights.

Internal Determinants of Attention

The conditions of attention as described so far are the external determinants of attention. These can also be called external laws of attention. The presence of these conditions in the environment is helpful for attention. Besides these external conditions, some internal conditions are also helpful in drawing attention. These conditions are related to motives. As a matter of fact, the influence of conditions depends on these internal conditions to a very great extent. The hungry man will attend to the form and stimuli of the food. A man with a full belly will not attend to food, however nice it might appear. In the advertisement those demonstrating the naked organs of the woman have the maximum power of attraction of attention. Those interested in cinema look to the advertisements of cinema at first sight. It is difficult to describe all the internal conditions helpful in attention. Hence, only the most important will be enumerated here :

(1) **Interest.** Innate and acquired interests draw the individual's attention to a particular object. Doctors, engineers, professors, all attend to the objects of their own interest. Even among the professors an object attracting the attention of a professor of geology need not attract the attention of a professor of philosophy as well. Thus, the innumerable differences in interests create innumerable determinants of attention in different men. The stimuli influencing innate tendencies attract more attention than those influencing acquired interest.

(2) **Basic Drives.** The basic drives or instincts of the individual are also important in drawing his attention. The animal attends to a particular stimulus when driven by the basic drives of hunger, thirst, sex, etc., *e.g.*, a normal man motivated by sex will naturally attend to individuals of opposite sex. We all know by experience that when hungry we may attend to even a distasteful object, but while our belly is full, we may not attend even to the most tasteful food. Among the instincts, the fear has got a definite influence upon attention. All men who fear snake will attend to all things resembling the snake. Like fear, curiosity also influences attention. We attend to even the smallest details of the object about which we have any curiosity.

Innate need also is very important in attention. The influence of sexual need in attention is very much exploited in the advertisements. Normally, the sexual need in human beings can be easily evoked. Hunger, thirst etc., are felt occasionally and the means to satisfy them are also readily available, but neither the sexual need is ever fully satisfied nor are the means of satisfying it available to all persons all the time. Hence, most of the advertisements draw attention by stimulating the sexual need in human beings.

(3) **Mental Set.** Mental set is one of the most important internal determinants of attention. Mental set means the tendency or attitude of the mind. A man will attend to these objects towards which his mind is set. In the days of examination, the mental set of students is generally towards the examination, and hence, even the smallest thing concerning the examination will attract their attention.

(4) **Aim.** Aim also influences attention. Every man has some immediate and some ultimate aims *e.g.*, the immediate aim of the student is to pass the examination while the ultimate aim may be to get a job to earn living or any thing else. The man whose aim is not to pass the examination will not be concerned with textbooks or notes etc., but one who has the aim to pass the examination will at once attend to them.

(5) **Meaning.** In comparison with meaningless things, meaningful things and talks attract more attention. A man will not attend to a thing which has no meaning for him. Men do not like to hear meaningless talk. If some persons are talking in Tamil, the Punjabi will not like to hear it since for him it has no meaning.

(6) **Habit.** Habit is also an important determinant of attention. If a man is habituated to rising early and winding his clock early in the morning, he must attend to the clock as soon as he gets up. It has been rightly pointed out that man learns as to which object he should attend to and to which he should not, and thus, develops habits of attending and not attending to things. Thus, habit has two aspects in relation to attention. On the one side man develops a habit of attending to necessary desirable things and on the other side he develops the habit of not attending to unnecessary and undesirable things. Both these kinds of habits help man in his daily routine.

(7) **Disposition and Temperament.** Both disposition and temperament are important internal determinants of attention, *e.g.*, a man having a religious disposition and rational temperament will attend to religious matters, while another person having a sexual disposition and passionate temperament will attend to matters concerning sex or crimes etc. William James has rightly pointed out that it is our tendency to take interest in particular things, a result of our innate disposition and mental development, that determines as to which among the crowd of sensations, should attract our attention.

(8) **Past Experience.** Past experience also affects attention. If we know it by our past experience that a particular person is sincere towards us, we shall pay attention to whatever he advises us. If we

know by experience that he is not sincere to us, we shall not attend even to his most serious advices.

(9) **Emotion.** Emotion is also an important determinant of attention. It is a matter of everyday experience that we attend even to the smallest fault of the person whom we hate while we do not attend even to the greatest blunder of a person whom we love. A mother seldom finds faults with her child. The lovers find the whole world singing and dancing and immersed in romance.

(10) **Social Motives.** Social motives are very important determinants of attention. In advertisements the human figures attract more attention than figures of animals and things. The reason is that man is guided by his social motives. The news about altruism, bravery and saving another's life by putting oneself in danger attracts our attention because we praise these qualities. Men attend to things concerning their duties because of social motives.

Besides the conditions described above, many other factors influence attention. Heredity, education and training have a wide influence on attention. The family, school, club, class and society of which an individual is a member, do have some influence on his attention. The physical condition, desire, purpose of the person concerned also affect his attention. Thus, all the factors affecting the personality of a man affect his attention as well. As a matter of fact, it is difficult to describe all direct and indirect determinants of attention. The description given, however, includes the most important of such factors.

KINDS OF ATTENTION

(1) **Voluntary Attention.** Voluntary attention (its name is indicative of its nature) is that attention which is willingly directed to an object. If, for example, a student attends to his studies of his own account and as a result of any external pressure, his attention will be called voluntary attention. An analysis reveals elements of desire and interest, aim and social adjustment in this voluntary attention. In the foregoing example, the student directs his attention because of particular aim like the passing of an examination, acquiring knowledge or one of a number of other goals. He takes an interest in studying. By passing the examination or acquiring knowledge he may be able to support a family or gain social standing and status. Like other activities, attention is just another form of adjustment. The difference between the voluntary and involuntary attention is that while the former is secured by the motivating elements in the individual, the motivating elements exist without in the latter case. Thus, when attention is suddenly attracted by a song, the attention is called involuntary.

(2) **Involuntary Attention.** As has been explained above, involuntary attention is not only directed by the individual's desire or motivation, it may even be against it. It hinders the process of goal seeking sometimes, not always. If, for example, your attention is attracted by a song while

you are studying, your studies will be hindered. Social adjustment is similarly obstructed by involuntary attention. The proper adjustment of a student can be the outcome only of an undisturbed attention to his studies. On account of the fact that one can pay attention to only one thing at a time, the student will not be able to attend to his studies if his attention continually wanders in other directions. Obviously, a person forgets his goal owing to involuntary attention and cannot effect his adjustment.

(3) **Habitual Attention.** Besides the two types of attention mentioned above, there is a third type, the habitual or non-voluntary attention. The difference between non-voluntary and involuntary attention is that the former type is the result of some habit or practice and the motivation is in the individual but the reason or attention in the latter type is in the object. Habitual attention is different from voluntary attention because habitual attention has no need for a desire as the latter does. But continued application of voluntary attention converts it to habitual attention. For example, a student pays voluntary attention to study in the beginning but it is gradually transformed into habitual attention towards reading or writing. Thus, the position of habitual attention is in between voluntary and involuntary types of attention.

Actually, the above distinctions made in attention are not very clear. The difference between voluntary and involuntary attention is often only just discernible. No attention can be said to belong to any one of the three types completely. A scholar has to exercise his desire in spite of his involuntary attention in reading. There is an unconscious desire to pay attention to an object which involuntarily draws your attention. In this way, the difference in the types of attention is small though it is of great importance from the psychological viewpoint.

The nature of attention permits of its concentration in only one direction at one time. Direction of attention to two or more objects means either their acceptance as one or such an oscillation of attention between all of them as gives the impression of simultaneous attention. But experiments have proved, beyond doubt, that a person can pay attention to only one object at a time.

DISTRACTION

Distraction means the dividing of attention or some interference in attention. For example, when one is studying, the sound of a song or noise breaks in upon attention. The object which causes the distraction is called the distractor. In fact, broken attention is not absence of attention because the distractor is associated with the activity, often, though not always, and it no longer interferes with the activity.

Distraction does not always Interfere

Thus, the notion that distraction invariably hinders work is misleading, it being seen, for example, that the labourer produces more when there is music. Some labourers, men and women, sing at work in view of this fact. Not a few people do their reading and writing while the radio is playing. Some people work better in a noisy environment than in a peaceful one. Experiments conducted by Morgan indicated that at first distraction caused a drop in the speed of typewriting but it latter became constant. Pursuing the work in the disturbed condition increased the speed than it again dropped when the distraction was removed. But distraction in some experiments by Weber caused harm. Though it cannot be definitely said that distraction increases the speed of the work, it is possible to say with some degree of confidence that a decrease in speed due to distraction is not inevitable. Actually, the effect of a distraction on some work depends in no small measure upon the capacity, interest, practice, skill and mental set of the worker. If the distraction is suitable the speed will be increased but if it is unsuitable the speed will drop.

Forms of Distraction

Roughly, distraction can be divided into two forms :

(1) Continuous Distraction. As the name suggests, it is the continuous distraction of attention. Some examples of it are the sound of radio or gramophone played continuously, the noise of the market place etc. Experiments have led to the conclusion that adjustment to continuous distraction takes place quickly.

(2) Discontinuous Distraction. This type is irregular, being interspersed with intervals e.g., the hearing of somebody's voice every now and then. It interferes with work because of an impossibility of adjustment.

Means of Removing Distraction

Some major means of removing distraction are :

(1) Being Active in Work. Work in distraction calls for more energy, so that one way of adjustment to it, or removing it, is to become more active in work.

(2) Disregard of Distraction. The presence of a distracting factor while a man works is no extraordinary condition, and so, the best way to remove this element is to disregard it. The distraction is effective only when attention is directed to it, so that in attention, even the most serious distraction will keep that activity from being interfered within any way.

(3) Making the Distraction a Part of the Work. Distraction is an obstacle only when it is distinct from the activity or against it since attention can be focused just on one object at one time. Therefore, another method of making a distraction ineffective is to make it a part of the work. Some people work better when listening to a song because they make it a part of their work. But this approach is very difficult because in this the interests, nature and capacities of the person are involved. It is very difficult to make an uninteresting and contradictory distraction a part of the work.

SPAN OF ATTENTION

Suppose that many kinds of things are placed on a table before you. The table is covered with a sheet of cloth. Now, I remove the cloth from the table for a few moments and then ask you to name the articles placed on the table. The span of your attention will be found out from your answer. In ancient times, many philosophers believed that only one thing at a time can enter human consciousness, which means that an individual can pay attention to only one stimulus at one time. But later it was proved through several experiments and experiences that attention can be paid to more than one stimulus at a time. Then the question arose as to how many stimuli an individual can pay attention to at one time. This will depend on the span of attention of an individual. Different psychologists have reached different conclusions about the span of attention through their experiments. According to A. Tucker, span of attention is limited to six articles. According to Charles Bonet, only six stimuli can be attended to at one time. Other psychologists have found in some individuals a span of attention from 11 to 12 articles. Through his experiments made with the help of pebbles, Hamilton saw that the span of attention of a subject was limited to six or seven pebbles. When the pebbles were placed in a group, the span of attention was found to be greater. Jevons was the first to say that the span of attention is different with different individuals and that in one and the same individual, the span of attention is different on different occasions. In this way, the span of attention is variable. The span of attention in children is less than that in adults. Apart from age, practice, physical condition, liking, mentality and the form of the object of attention also affect the span of attention. Their difference in different circumstances can create difference in the span of attention.

Experiments have been made with the help of different kinds of stimuli, in order to measure the span of attention. Most of these experiments have been in connection with visual span of attention. In an experiments, first of all some words or figures are written on some slides. Now, these slides are gradually presented before the subjects through an apparatus to measure span of attention. It is so arranged that a slide may be seen at the most for one-tenth of a second so that the subject may not be given a chance to move his eyes more than once. The subject has to tell what word or figure he has seen. This is the span of his attention. The subject is given many chances and their average is taken out. Cattle was the first psychologist to carry out an experiment to measure the span of attention in the year 1885-86.

It is clear from the aforesaid explanation that more than one stimulus are included in the span of attention. In connection with the question why it so happens, it has been explained that we see the different stimuli in the form of one group or pattern. It has been found out from the experiments made by Freeman that in a condition of simple groupism, the span of attention is greater.

DIVISION OF ATTENTION

It is a matter of common experience that an individual sometimes does two or three acts together. For example, people sing while they are taking a bath; women knit while they are gossiping and many people keep eating groundnuts while they are seeing a film, such two acts are possible at the same time because attention is divided between them. In this division, attention cannot be paid to both the acts in an active form. Ordinarily, if you pay attention to eating groundnuts, you will not be able to see the film. Seeing of a film is possible only when your acts of eating ground nuts is mechanical. It is also true in all those conditions in which any two acts are done together. Out of the two acts, if one is made mechanical, you need not pay attention to it and it goes on by itself. This depends on practice. Even two complicated acts are possible at one and the same time through practice. But, if the act is difficult, attention in such a condition is often diverted and not divided. It means that attention is very quickly diverted from one thing to the other, although we do not actually feel this diversion. Guilford, while giving an example of doing two acts by making them a single pattern, writes in his book that when a person has learnt to play on piano with both the hands separately, he can also play on piano with both the hands together.

Here a question arises as to what is the effect of division of attention on that act. Some psychologists maintain that the effect of the division of attention on the production of work is harmful, while others say that it is useful. In one experiment, Michell asked the subject to compare two weights and to count the number of ringing sounds upto six at one and the same time. At first, the act of counting was somewhat disturbed, but later, the act of comparison also, along with the act of counting, was good. Psychologists have concluded, from some other experiments of this kind, that by doing two acts together no hindrance is caused in the product, but it is, on the contrary, more convenient and there is an increase in production. It has been seen through the experiments that the acts of knocking, reading and adding, when done together at the same time, are more satisfactory than when done separately at different times. But evidences in favour of the division of attention are not available through all experiments. Paulham, by allotting a subject the act of reading one poem and of writing another, saw that some disturbance or the other was caused in doing both the acts together. Similar conclusions were drawn from the experiments made by Binet. Laurange saw through his experiment, made with the help of the apparatus measuring span of attention, that the division of attention reduces the span of attention. Spetch, on getting the act of counting done along with a free associative experimentation, saw that the division of attention had a bad effect on the form as well as on the result of work-product.

It is clear from the above explanation that all psychologists do not reach similar conclusion of experimentation about the effect of the division of attention on work-product. The truth is that the effect of the division of attention on work-product depends much on the ability, liking, practice and the form of actions of the subject. There are certain actions which can be easily performed together, and, on the other hand, there are certain actions which cannot be performed together. For example, to solve a difficult mathematical question and to understand some difficult portion of a poem is not possible at one and the same time. It is so, because no one pattern can be made of such uncommon actions. On the other hand, those actions a pattern of which can be formed, are done together better than they are done separately.

QUESTIONS FOR EXERCISE

1. What do you understand by attention? Give analysis of its conditions.
2. Write short note on Determinants of attention.
3. Distinguish between voluntary and involuntary attention. Can attention be divided between two distinct tasks at the same moment?
4. Write a short note on Distraction.
5. What is the meaning of span of attention? Describe an experiment on measuring span of attention.

19

MEMORY AND FORGETTING

The conscious level of the human mind is not the solitary level of mental activity. The impressions of various experiences become permanent at the subconscious stages and they come to the conscious level whenever they are needed or when there is that relevant context. The experiences are not obliterated from the mind with the passage of time, but rather, they remain in the mind permanently, in the memory and can be recalled with effort and recognised. But, it is common experience that people do not remember their experiences completely, and a major part is not remembered and it is forgotten. Thus, remembering and forgetting are subjects of daily experience. Memory is a general word which includes several mental activities like recall, recognition or retention. We see indications of memory all around us. A person or animal experiences ease in relearning an activity which he had learnt previously but had forgotten. This proves very obviously that the previous learning had not been wiped out completely but had left an impression on the mind or a chance in the nerves which indicated relearning. People do not completely forget the story of any movie they have seen but recount it with ease when they are requested to do so by a friend. If someone else takes on the tedious task of telling the story of the same film, they affirm it because they are reminded of it, and if they hear any song from the film played any where they are easily reminded of that too. Thus, there is retention, recall and recognition in the memory of a perceived experience, which makes it a complete activity.

Memory is a Physical Activity

Bentley and his followers said that experience or learning acquired by a person leave impressions or marks on the mind, which are memory traces. They are the basis of memory in the form of functional tendency, because retention ends when these traces are wiped off. These psychologists have established by giving proofs that retention is a psychological process.

Memory is a Psycho-physiological Activity

But Bartlett, Piron and Gibson and some other psychologists have attempted to show that memory is a mental activity independent of memory traces. They have proved by examples of stories, pictures, etc., that memory depends more on mental states like interests, motivation, biases etc., than on repetition of experience. This makes memory a mental activity. But just as every mental activity has a psychological base, so does memory has a psychological foundation. Briefly, memory is a psycho-physiological activity.

Memory is preceded by learning and therefore, memory has four processes in general. They are as follows :

1. Learning
2. Retention
3. Recall
4. Recognition.

Two of these four activities namely learning and retention, are essential to memory. Recall succeeds learning but there is no recognition. Sometimes, retention is followed by recognition without any recall. Besides learning and retention both recall and recognition are necessary for complete memory. Sometimes, it is recall which takes place first to be followed by recognition but equally often the order of the two activities is reversed.

(1) Learning. It will be quite in keeping with the context to give a brief description of each of these activities. As has been mentioned above, the first step of activity is learning. If the learning is good, memory will also be good. Thus, the methods which assist learning do the same for memory. Learning creates memory traces on the mind, on the basis of which recollection is effected.

(2) Retention. The second activity in memory is retention, which means making permanent the remains of experience. The remains of experiences are left on the mind in the form of memory traces where they are safe though they are acted upon by interest and other mental states. The proofs of retention are recollection, recognition and relearning. Though recollection is a proof of memory, its absence is not the proof of the absence of memory because a person often remembers something at a later date which had eluded him at the earlier occasion. Same is the case with recognition because while its presence indicates memory, its absence is no proof that there is no memory. If we come face to face with a long separated friend and find ourselves unable to identify him, we cannot take this to mean that all the experiences related to that person have been obliterated from the memory because the next moment we might be astonished when at last, we succeed in identifying him. The most convincing proof of retention is furnished by relearning in the absence of which retention cannot be accepted. If there is no progress in relearning it will be concluded that there was no retention. After experiencing anything the activity of its consolidation goes on for sometime. This is proved by the fact that a poem will linger in one's brain for some time after one has learnt it, even though there is no effort to recall it. Students preparing for some examination would have experienced this activity.

Levels of Retention

Retention, as has been mentioned above, is the making permanent of the remains of experiences. The different forms taken by these remains of experiences indicate that there are different levels of retention. Something remains on the fringe of consciousness and can be recalled into consciousness effortlessly. About some things we feel as if these had been experienced yesterday and can be recalled at will. The same cannot be said of others which we forget and can remember only when someone reminds us of them or when some new event takes place. In this way, efforts are to be made in order to remember things in the conscious, subconscious and unconscious level. The facts in the unconscious cannot be remembered and can be recovered only by word association, dream analysis and other methods.

(3) **Recall.** The third activity in memory is that of recall. It is the activity by which the remains of experiences made permanent, are brought back to the conscious level. A student studies for his examinations all the year round and a major part of his learning is present in a permanent and healthy state in his mind. While answering the question paper in the examination hall he recalls this learning existing in the memory and puts it down in black and white. Though this recollection cannot be identical to the original learning, its matter resembles the original and a major part of the learning can be remembered in the same form if suitable efforts are made. Actually, recall is something novel and not just a mere reproduction of the past experience or perception. In spite of the fact that it depends on retention, recollection is not fashioned entirely by it. It is not necessary that if retention is good, recollection will also be good.

Nature of Recall

Ebbinghaus experimented to see whether recollection is creative or reproductive, *i.e.*, whether the person concerned puts something alien with the recollection or does he make a faithful reproduction. Ebbinghaus taught some senseless stanzas to some people and asked them to recall these stanzas after different time intervals. From the results, he concluded that recollection is reproductive, a view with which Bartlett and his followers do not agree, and to prove their point he experimented with the recollection of a story. A student was made to read a story with care and was given to recall it fifteen minutes later. This reproduced story was given to another student to read and he, too, was asked to recall it. In this way, students were made to recall a story by this chain method and it was concluded that in the last reproduction, the conclusion and even names of the character had been changed.

(4) Recognition. The last step in memory is recognition. Sometimes recall comes after recognition as, for example, when we recognize an old friend the moment we set eyes on him and then we are reminded of many things about him. On other occasions, meanwhile, it is recall which precedes recognition. Suppose that I am travelling in a train and I am confronted with the embarrassing situation of someone asking me whether I had recognised him. I apologise doubtfully and confess my inability to recognise him. The person says : "When ten years ago we lived in Saket, Meerut, we were neighbours." And this statement starts a reaction, reminding me of my experiences of ten years ago. I then recognise the person, shake hands and start talking of this and that. This example shows that recognition sometimes follows recollection.

Recognition may either be definite or indefinite. A person recognises a friend immediately he sees him and is perfectly aware of everything about this person, this being an example of definite recognition. An example of indefinite recognition would be the inability of a person to remember the time, place and context in which he first heard the story which has just been related to him in spite of the fact that he recognises the story itself. The person knows when, where, how and by whom, in fact everything of the recognised subject.

In recognition, the recognised person or subject is separated from other subjects or people. When a person recognises a friend in a crowd, he distinguishes his friend from the rest. This differentiation has a lot of significance in recognition and the more exact it is, the better will be the recognition. And, recognition is impossible in the absence of differentiation. Recognition literally means cognising again, and, it is therefore, the cognition of some subject seen before. Thus, recognition comes after cognition.

To study the favourable conditions in memory, it is necessary to study the favourable conditions for learning, retention, recall and recognition.

FAVOURABLE CONDITIONS IN RETENTION

Many experiments have been carried out on this subject and many physiological and psychological conditions have proved useful in learning. Some of the main conditions which favour retention are :

(1) Nature of Material. The following specialities in the material to be retained help in its retention to a large extent :

(i) *Intensity* : The intensity of the stimulus assists in the retention of a subject. Weak or indistinct sensations do not stick in the mind for any length of time. Clear photographs can be remembered with ease.

(ii) *Distinctness* : Distinct sensations like strong light, extreme beauty or ugliness and such like can be retained for a long time. We forget an ordinary person easily but we remember one for a long time if he be out of the ordinary in any way.

(iii) *Recency* : Recent experiences are retained for a longer time and a diminution in their retention occurs with the passage of time.

(iv) *Meaning* : Meaningless sensations do not linger long in the mind while meaningful ones can be retained for long with little effort.

(2) Duration. A sensation which continues for a longer time, can be retained for a longer time in the mind. A sensation of a shorter duration will be, correspondingly, retained for a shorter duration.

(3) Amount of Material. If the subject being pursued is long, it will be retained for a longer time while a shorter subject will take less time before it is forgotten. The amount of material to be learnt has a favourable effect on its retention, there being two reasons for the phenomenon, (a) A man has to make less exertion in order to learn a shorter subject, while a longer subject demands more effort and therefore, the retention is more lasting. (b) In the longer subject, as compared to the shorter, the person finds the meaning and relates the various parts of the subject together, all this is the power of retention.

(4) Amount of Learning. The extent of retention is directly proportional to the amount of learning that is to say that retention will be more if the amount of learning is large. A subject studied more stays longer in the mind while one studied less will remain in the mind for a shorter period. Overlearning has a favourable effect on the retention.

But this does not mean that retention will go on increasing with the learning because after a certain limit disinterest, fatigue, and monotony may have a derogatory effect on retention. Therefore, the increasing and strengthening effects of overlearning confine themselves to a certain limit.

(5) Methods of Learning. The methods of learning, too, do not fail to impress their importance on the retention of a subject. Learning by the whole method instead of the part method, the spaced method instead of the unspaced method and the active method instead of the passive method result in better and longer retention.

(6) Speed of Learning. The faster the learning, the better the retention. This is the principle in accordance with which people learning faster seem to retain the subject learnt for longer periods as compared to the slower learners. For example, a child grasped mathematics later than his contemporaries, but when it came to language, making no pretensions he was far quicker at it. His retention of language was far more than that of mathematics. Actually, the speed of learning indicates the inclination of the boy towards a subject and interest he takes in it, and due to these he learns it faster and retains it longer.

(7) **Feeling.** Freud and other psychologists assert that we retain pleasant experiences for a longer time whereas we forget painful experience quickly. Even, if all psychologists do not accept this view of the psychoanalysts no one denies that pleasant experiences are remembered longer than painful ones. With the passage of time man becomes indifferent to all past experiences wiped out from the board of memory.

(8) **Attention.** While studying a subject, if greater attention is paid to the subject the retention will be better. On the contrary, the retention will be weakened by inattention.

(9) **Sleep.** Some time elapses, after study, before the subject is retained in the mind and if this time of strengthening and retention is used for sleep, the memory traces get a good opportunity to be etched upon the memory. Psychologists differ in regard to the cause of the effect which sleep has on retention.

(10) **Mental Review.** If some experience is incessantly contemplated upon its retention is better than one about which the mind does not trouble itself. Really speaking, by mental review a repetition of the subject is caused which strengthens retention.

(11) **Mental Set.** A person retains those things for a longer period which coincide with his mental inclinations. A religious person remembers idea relating to religion for a long time and a sensuous man remembers things of sexual interest.

(12) **Apperception.** Apperception means the assimilating of learned subject with the knowledge already present. The retention of a newly learned subject is greatly facilitated if it is assimilated with the present store of knowledge to start with. And on the other hand, a longer time is needed for retention if this assimilation is not effected.

(13) **Intention.** This, too, is not far behind in making its presence felt, on retention. If a subject is learned with the express intention of being retained, the aim will be fulfilled with extraordinary success. But if there is no such intention, the subject removes itself from the memory of the person after sometime. Learning gathered with a view to appearing in the examinations is remembered better and things picked up here and there, in the ordinary course, are easily forgotten unless the person has a special inclination towards them.

But it cannot be concluded from this that any learning carried out for retention will of necessity be retained. The only thing implied is that retention is better if there is intention to retain the subject than when there is no such intention.

(14) **Massive Experience.** The retention will be more if the experience is massive. If a person has ever loved, he never forgets it because it affects his whole personality and it is a fact that we remember that thing longer which affects us more. The meaning of the importance of

experience is also implied in the extent of experience. A person retains that experience longer which is of greater value to him than other experiences. When the value attached to the experience is lost, the experience, too, slips out of the mind.

FAVOURABLE CONDITIONS IN RECALL

Generally, the factors which favour retention also have a good effect on recollection. In other words, it means that recollection is better if the retention is good. But this is not always so. There are some factors which favour the recollection of experiences over and above the factors favourable to retention. The major ones are :

(1) **Suitable Mental and Physical Conditions.** Recall is comparatively easy when both the mind and the body are healthy and fresh. And, adverse and indifferent physical and mental conditions hinder recollection.

(2) **Perfection of Clues.** Recall is done with the help of clues which are stimulators of recall. To take an example, if we learn a poem, we cannot recall it without the help of the title, the first line or the clue to some part of it, and clues are necessary for the recall of anything in the mind. The completeness of the recall depends upon the completeness of these clues.

(3) **Mental Set.** The mental set of the individual, too affects recall. A religious minded person remembers religious subjects easily while a sensuous person will find it easy to remember things associated with sex.

(4) **Context.** Context too helps recall. When writing an essay, or talking, things pertinent to the context keep on suggesting themselves to the mind. The recollection due to context does not stop with only one thing, one leads to another and this reminds the person of a third thing thus forming a chain of linked thoughts and experience which often take a person so far afield that he forgets the context in which the conversation had originated.

(5) **Motives.** When a person is under the extreme influence of a motive, he has such clear recollection of related incidents that he sometimes has hallucinations.

(6) **Feeling.** Recollection is not immune to feelings of pleasure and pain. These feelings and experiences of pain and pleasure are recollected easily than indifferent feelings while pleasurable experiences are comparatively easily recollected.

(7) **Effort.** This has a very significant effect on recollection. Unless the extreme limit of effort has been passed, recollection generally increases with the effort. When this limit has been exceeded or passed over activities become fragmented and recollection becomes difficult. In reality, it is the wrong type of effort which hinders recollection and it can take a variety of forms like the effort made in the absence of the

clues. But if, on the other hand, the effort is made while the emotions are kept in check, and with confidence, keeping in view the clues, recollection will be affected favourably.

(8) Absence of Inhibition. Recollection is better in the absence of any inhibition, because inhibition obstructs recollection and it may be caused by the conflict of the simultaneous arising of two activities or by repression and again, by fear or other emotions. A student forgets everything in the examination because he is nervous. A doctor cannot remember the name of the patient in whose treatment he was completely unsuccessful. Sometimes a name cannot be recalled while useless names are constantly remembered. These three examples respectively illustrate the effects of emotion, repression and conflict on recollection. Their only solution is the elimination of the inhibition, if recollection is to be improved. These obstacles in recollection are called reproductive inhibitions. As a general rule, the conditions found favourable for retention and real are equally favourable to recognition, and in view of this fact, only two conditions will be mentioned here.

FAVOURABLE CONDITIONS IN RECOGNITION

(1) Mental Set. Recognition is helped by the mental set, in the manner in which other factors assist memory. Recognition is correct when the mental set is favourable and it is incorrect when the mental set is unfavourable. For example, we recognize the same voice if the element of expectancy is absent. But on the other hand, mental set may cause faulty recognition because you may take every knock at the door to be the one made by the person whom you are waiting for.

(2) Confidence. This, too, is an indispensable element in recognition. In its absence, even correct recognition becomes infested with doubt and a mistake is the outcome. In reality, only trial and error can regulate the amount of self-confidence, which one may have in a particular situation.

HOW TO MEMORISE

Many experiments were conducted in psychology with a view to effecting economy in memorizing. In these experiments, attempts were made, after experimenting with different methods of memorization, to find that method by which the maximum material may be memorised in the shortest possible time. The economy of the following methods has been brought to light :

(1) Recitation. The mental repetition of something is called recitation. Recitation makes the subject firmer than if it were read over and over again or repeated. Mental repetition is an active way of study. This saves time, at the same time assuming the longer retention of the subject.

(2) Spaced and Unspaced Methods. As the name suggests, the spaced method of memorizing is one in which there are time intervals in the memorization and the subject is connected to memory after various sittings. On the contrary, the memorization in the unspaced method is done at one sitting, without any intervals being introduced.

Many experiments were done in order to assess the economy affected by these two methods. In Ebbinghau's opinion, the spaced method is more economical in the memorisation of meaningless things. Belborn and Villian opined that the spaced method is better in the memorization of poetry and prose. Lashley considered the spaced method to be better while Cook approved of the unspaced method.

The economy in the use of either the spaced or the unspaced methods depends upon the abilities of the individual and the nature and extent of the material. A short poem of 8 to 10 lines should be memorised at one sitting. On the other hand, it is generally difficult to memorise a poem comprising 100 lines at one sitting because the possibilities of fatigue in attempting to learn so long a poem without rest are very great. Actually, the spaced method has many advantages over the unspaced method. Not only is the fatigue eliminated in the interval, but there is an opportunity to contemplate on the subject learnt. This helps to remove the monotony caused by long periods of study and it enables a person to keep his attention focused on learning. The interval also eliminates any wrong activities and prevents their repetition. There is no general rule as to the interval between two sitting and it depends on the individual and the subject taught. It can be said that the interval should be long enough to remove the fatigue of the last sitting and strengthen the memory traces.

(3) **Part and Whole Methods.** To study something by the part method is to divide it into parts before studying or memorizing it. On the other hand, a subject is read according to the whole method when it is read from start to finish, as a whole. The experiments carried out to measure the superiority of these methods over each other have not yielded consistent results. Sometimes, the part method showed better results while on the other occasions it was the whole-method, which excelled. Lotti Steffens concluded from his experiments on children and grown-ups who were required to study meaningless material, that the whole method saved 12 per cent of time as compared to the part method. Contrary to this Pechstein, in an experiment, instructed 6 persons to learn 32 times employing the whole method, at the same time instructing 6 others to do the same by using the part method. When the results were compared, the people using the part method in memorizing had taken less time than the other six. Pechstein concluded from this that the part method is more advantageous than the whole method.

Actually, the two methods part and whole are not contradictory. The application of one or the other method to the memorizing of certain subject is decided by its extent and nature and by the ability of the individual. The whole method is better than the part method when it comes to learning a short poem but the part method proves more advantageous if the poem is a long poem. In this case, it would be advisable to go through the whole poem to start with, in order to relate the different parts of the poem and to follow this up by learning it a small piece at a time. It is generally better to use the whole method if the subject be difficult because it is easier to understand its different parts individually. But, at the same time, it is essential to use the part method in making sense out of the difficult portion of the subject. Thus, time can be saved in using the whole method with a short subject and the part method in the perusal of a lengthy and difficult one, but in reality, the subject will have to act according to his personal capabilities besides the general law when he wants to decide on any particular method. If we tire easily by the whole method, the part method is unquestionably better for us.

(4) **Active and Passive Methods.** Memorising by utterance is the active method while mental repetition is the passive method. Many experiments have been carried out to measure the economy, which these methods may affect. Gates, Ebbinghaus and his followers concluded from their experiments that the active method is better than the passive method.

Actually, the active method is better than the passive in many respects.

1. The activity in memorising is increased.

2. The desire to learn and the effort are maintained while the relation between the various parts is established easily and naturally.

3. The subject is understood and the rhythmical grouping and localisation of the various parts of the material also takes place.

4. The method forms a sort of pattern of the subject in the mind of the learner and anything missing from this pattern can be recalled easily.

5. This method reduces mental distraction. But this does not mean that the passive method is always less useful than the active method. Actually, in learning anything new it is always advisable to memorise it mentally before memorising it by reading it aloud.

(5) **Rote and Intelligent Methods.** If a person is learning or memorising something without understanding it, he is said to be using the rote or unintelligent method. There is no apperception in this. On the other hand, by use of the intelligent method, it involves the understanding of the subject and apperception does come about.

The experiment to measure the economy of either of this subject reveals the consistent superiority of the intelligent over the unintelligent or mechanical method. The mechanical method does not form any association between the material and the thoughts in the mind and the matter is thus not strengthened, which results in its early elimination. On the other hand, the intelligent method lends firmness to the memory, which becomes more permanent.

(6) **Grouping and Rhythm.** Memorization is considerably facilitated by rhythm and grouping. It is easier to memorise poetry than prose but by the rhythm scheme. One couplet contains enough meaning to be spread over several pages, but the rhythm makes the memorization easier.

(7) **Association.** Association as a factor which keeps memorization is not less important than the other. Suppose that we have to remember that the first step in a solution of arithmetical problem is the bracket and the successive steps are of, division, multiplication, subtraction and addition and in order to facilitate it, an association between 'B' and bracket, O and of, D and division, I and into or multiplication, S and subtraction and, A and addition may be formed, keeping in mind that the letters represent the first letter of each word. These letters should now be put together to form the word BODISA; which, when remembered, will keep this law in mind. Other association in different subjects may be formed similarly.

Besides the method of memorization detailed above, all the favourable factors in retention should be used comprehensively. The desire to memorise affords considerable assistance in remembering, because of the case in concentration, which is absolutely essential. Rest and sleep also affect memorization and attention should be paid to them. The use of similar images, similar to the subject also helps memorization and retention.

FORGETTING

The difficulty, or inability of a subject in being remembered on coming to the consciousness in the mental activity, is due to forgetting. It contradicts remembering and it is the failure of retention. Sometime, almost too often, the thought is retained even though it is not recalled. Its inability to come to the conscious level can be attributed to a variety of reasons. Therefore, mere failure to recollect is not the same thing as forgetting. But lack of progress in learning is definitely forgetting. Briefly, failure of recollection is partial or temporary forgetting, the failure of retention is complete or permanent forgetting.

According to Ebbinghaus, forgetting is a passive mental process. The activity continues automatically with the passage of time and the mind does not interfere with it. The activity of forgetting proceeds with good speed for some four to six hours after the learning of meaningless pieces but by the time 5 to 7 days have passed, the enthusiasm dies out and the activity is very slow, so much so that the difference between the forgetting of the 10th and 21st days is almost impermeable.

Some psychologists have not accepted the opinion expressed by Ebbinghaus. They think that forgetting is an active-passive process implying that the mind too takes a hand, the other being the passage of time, in forgetting. Forgetting is effected in no small measure by the mental processes, which take place in the interval between remembering and forgetting. The least amount of forgetting takes place in sleep but if the person engages in some other activity, it is comparatively more. Forgetting is also speeded up by some injury to the brain, consumption of alcoholic liquids, feeling, emotion, mental tension etc. In this way, forgetting is both an active and passive process.

Causes of Forgetting

Many theories about causes of forgetting are current Ebbinghaus attributes forgetting to passage of time while Freud and Bartlett are more inclined to blame the activities, which take place in the interval of forgetting. Roughly speaking, most psychologists have given the following causes for forgetting :

(1) **Interpolated Activity.** As far as the behaviourists are concerned, it is the interpolated activity after learning which causes forgetting, the extent of forgetting depending upon the divergence of these activities from the material learnt.

(2) **Disuse.** The theory of disuse postulates that any learnt activity or accumulated knowledge will be gradually forgotten if it is not regularly practiced. Psychologists who do not agree with this view assert that forgetting is due not only to disuse but also to the activities after learning.

(3) **Retroactive Inhibition.** Some learning tends to contradict some previous learning, a tendency entitled retroactive inhibition, meaning the fatal effect of interpolated activity on learning. This theory was first proved by Muller and Pilzecker. Retroactive inhibition is specially affected by the following four things :

(a) *Similarly, between past learning and interpolated learning* : Experiments have proved that the retroactive inhibition will increase with similarity with the past learning and interpolated activities.

(b) *Difference in quantities of past learning and interpolated-learning* : Retroactive inhibition will be more if the quantities of past learning and interpolated learning are vastly different in favour of the latter. But if the latter is less, the hindrance will also be less.

(c) *Temporal relation of the Interpolated activities* : If the interpolated activities take place soon after the previous learning the hindrance will be accentuated. The most harmful interpolated activities are those, which take place either immediately after learning or just before recollection while the least harmful is the one taking place in the middle of the retention period.

(d) *Intelligence and age of the learner* : Retroactive inhibition is reduced with every increase in the age and intelligence of the learner.

The two-factor theory expounded by Melton and Lackun singles out two factors as having extraordinary effect on retroactive inhibition. The learning of a new thing causes the forgetting of the old by hindering its relearning and the other factor is the competition between the old and new memory traces.

(4) Repression. The psychoanalysis believe that the major cause of forgetting is repression, *i.e.*, the pushing of the experience or thoughts into the unconscious. Freud said that it is natural in human beings to repress sorrowful thoughts because of the pain of the cause if remembered. It was the theory of repression on which Freud founded his successful analysis of everyday forgetting in writing, speaking, recognizing and the forgetting of the mental patients but the description of forgetting, in things other than these, cannot accept repression as the sole cause.

(5) Factors Affecting Learning. All the factors which affect learning also affect forgetting because forgetting is the unlearning of a learnt subject. The major factors are :

(a) *Method of learning* : As a general rule it can be said that forgetting is less in the case of whole, spaced, active and insightful learning than in the case of part, unspaced, passive and unintelligent methods of learning.

(b) *Quantity of learning* : Within a limit, the absence of over learning may bring about forgetting, while the same effect may be produced by over learning outside the limit. Inside the limit, forgetting will be less if there is over learning.

(c) *Speed of learning* : Faster learning censures retention while slower learning is forgotten relatively quicker.

(d) *Instrument of learning* : Forgetting is more in the use of a small and less extensive instrument than in the use of bigger and more extensive instrument. Similarly, there is more forgetting in the case of sorrowful or meaningless instruments than in the case of happy or meaningful instrument.

(6) Deficiency of Thinking and Repetition. Mental thinking and repetition assist retention and recollection and in the same manner these factors also affect forgetting, *i.e.*, in the absence of these factors forgetting increases.

(7) Deficiency of the Mental Set. Mental set is another factor of assistance in the retention and recollection of a subject so that its greater concurrence will reduce forgetting.

(8) Brain Injury. Often when a person suffers a brain injury he forgets many incidents and experiences and the extent of the forgetting depends upon the seriousness of the injury.

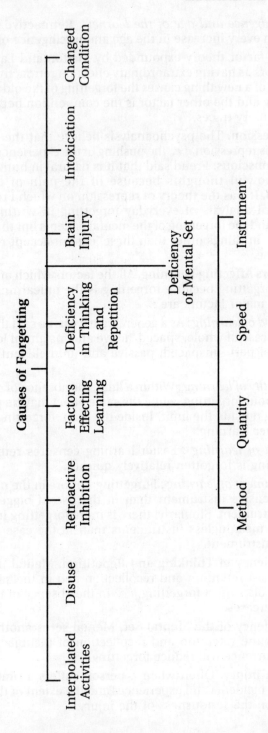

(9) Uses of Stimulants. Wine and other stimulants have a detrimental effect on the brain, because they weaken the memory traces. Thus, forgetting will be increased if such intoxicants are used.

(10) Altered Stimulus Condition. If there is an association between the stimulus and the situation of the stimulus, then forgetting is facilitated by any change in the situation or condition of the stimulus. People who stay abroad for long forget their correct dialect.

Besides, the causes mentioned above, the factors which influence retention and recollection may also cause forgetting. In brief, every factor which hinders memorization causes forgetting. The chart given on previous page makes clear the causes of forgetting.

QUESTIONS FOR EXERCISE

1. What is memory? Analyse the factors in memory and briefly indicate their nature.
2. Describe the condition favourable to memorization. What does good memory consist in? Name and illustrate some factors that help retention.
3. Write an essay on how to build up a good memory.
4. What are the causes of forgetting? Briefly, discuss the theory of retroactive inhibition.

20

ASSOCIATION

Ebbinghaus occupies an important place in the history of modern psychology in Germany. His influence on German psychological thought is confined to the later half of the nineteenth century. He was born in 1850 in a trader's family. He was educated at the Bonn University where he studied history and physiology. For his higher education he went to Halle and Berlin. In 1870, he joined the armed forces but three years later he resigned from his commission and returned to Bonn and secured the degree of doctor of philosophy. The subject of his thesis was 'nature of the unconscious'. This led to Ebbinghaus developing an interest in psychology in pursuit of which he studied Fechner's book on the subject. After that he independently took up research work in psychology because he had no acquaintance with the contemporary psychologists and he could not invade their sanctum. He visited England and France where he picked up considerable knowledge of psychology. In 1886, he was appointed to the post of Assistant Professor at the Berlin University but he subsequently joined Breslau and then finally Halle University. His most important work consists of his experiments on memory.

Ebbinghaus' initial experiment with memory were performed upon himself and for these experiments he invented what are called nonsense syllables. With the help of these syllables he found a solution to the problem of association. Associationists believe that association is the basis of every experience. In his examination of memory Ebbinghaus used the nonsense syllables to control the association and thereby gained control over those elements which could influence memory.

Ebbinghaus' experiment on memory can be described approximately. Thus, he wrote down the nonsense syllables on separate cards and then placed them in a specific order. After that he started examining them from one end. When all the cards had been seen he tried to employ his memory and write down the syllables in the order in which he had seen them. From this experiment Ebbinghaus concluded that if the number of nonsense syllables is seven then they can be memorised and reproduced correctly after one single viewing. No more than three seconds would be necessary for the purpose. In the same way if the number of nonsense syllables is 12 then they can be reproduced correctly after 17 seconds taking 82 seconds. From his experiments, he gained the following data :

Number of nonsense syllables	Number of recollection	Time in seconds	Average time secs. per word
7	1	3	.4
10	13	52	5.2
12	17	82	6.8
16	30	196	12.0
24	44	422	17.6
36	55	792	22.0

In this way Ebbinghaus proved from his experiments that repetition and time play an important role in memory. As the number of nonsense syllables increases the number of recollections and the time also increases, a fact which is apparent from the above table.

Ebbinghaus' experiments with memory in fact provided a wealth of detail. For example, examining the relation between learning and retention Ebbinghaus found out the number of recollections which would be necessary for a list of 16 nonsense syllables, which was learnt 24 hours previously, can be reproduced exactly. He found that the relearning of a thing learnt 24 hours previously can lead to an economy in time of about 10%. This method of memory testing evolved by Ebbinghaus is known by the name of saving method.

Through his experiments Ebbinghaus also learnt that it is possible to calculate the time that would be needed to forget something which had been learnt. Besides, what facility can be achieved if the thing learnt is relearnt or recollected at frequent intervals? What are the best methods of memorising for longest retention? He also proved that the study of memory can be given a scientific basis and the facts related to it examined.

Ebbinghaus published a detailed account of his research work in two volumes : *Theory of Colour Vision* and *Ground Work of Psychology*. The latter in particular achieved considerable fame and was for years treated as a standard treatise on the subject suitable for use as a text-book. The style of the author was lively and attractive which was one of the reasons for the popularity of his books. Ebbinghaus occupies a premier position in German psychology, and the facts derived from experiments with memory, constitute a completely original contribution to psychology. Besides, one of the most important aspects of his work is that he proved conclusively that such elusive mental activities as memory could be studied in the laboratory, literally under the microscope, a thing which had hitherto been considered well nigh impossible. And his work is an implicit assertion of the scientific nature of psychology, an eloquent testimonial.

KINDS OF ASSOCIATION

There are two kinds of associations — controlled association and uncontrolled association. Ordinarily, our association in different actions of our daily life is settled, and therefore, almost controlled. The pattern of how we shall solve problem, when it presents itself before us, is almost already settled. How little a time we took in doing so and how correctly the work was done is something important. The following two kinds of controlled associations have been accepted.

(1) **Partially Controlled Association.** The process of association, in this, is not completely controlled. The subject selects one of the many words. In an experiment of this kind, the experimenter instructs the subjects like this, "I shall speak out the name of some thing and you will speak out the name of anyone part of it." Now suppose he says 'school', so many things are included in school and the subject can name anyone of them.

(2) **Completely Controlled Association.** In this, as is clear from its name, the process of association is completely pre-settled and controlled. For example, night is the antonym for day, bad for good, white for black, big for small and high for low. Now, if anyone of these words is spoken before the subject, he will certainly give its antonym.

Experiments on Association

As has been already said, the subject's knowledge about language and words is tested from the result of controlled association. On the other hand, complexes are found out through an experiment of free association. Associative reaction time is studied through the experiments of association. In this connection, experiments are made, sometimes by speaking a word and sometimes by presenting it. In the same way, a subject expresses his response, sometimes by speaking, sometimes by writing and sometimes by naming it. Cattel, Woodworth and Wells have made many experiments about the test of reaction period through the name of an object. In this, a picture of familiar objects or colours was shown to the subject and he was asked to tell their names. It was seen from these experiments that more time was taken in expressing the names of the objects than what was taken in reading them, because more practice was needed in naming the objects than what was needed in reading them. Secondly, in naming an object, many names enter the mind together and time is taken in selecting the correct name from among them, while there is no need of selection in reading it. In studying association reaction time about reading, Cattel presented some words, letters and figures before the subject and asked him to make response by reading them loudly and hurriedly. It was found out from these experiments that the reaction time for bigger words and figures was greater than that for smaller words and figures. It was so because more time was taken in setting them.

Besides the above methods, the study of association reaction time is also made through controlled association method. In this, the subject has to speak out a word opposite or coordinating to the stimulating word. In testing completely controlled association, only one opposite word is spoken and the reaction time is therefore less. In testing partially controlled association, the subject has a chance to make a selection and the reaction time is therefore greater. But then, similar conclusions are not reached about all the subjects. In testing completely controlled association, the reaction period of the subjects, possessing a small vocabulary, is long, because sometimes they do not know even the opposites. Murphy, Young, Wreschner, Cason and other psychologists have studied the reaction through a free association method. It has been found out from the experiments made by Menzorath and Wells that reaction time can be reduced by the practice, because, through practice, the subject adjusts himself to the situation and therefore does not take much time in reacting. It has been found out from the experiments made by Anderson that the reaction time in case of adults is less than that in case of children.

Through his experiments, Wreschner has reached the conclusion that the reaction period in free association is less than that in the controlled association. In 1917, a psychologist, named Mag, concluded from his experiments that the reaction time in free association is greater than that in controlled association. Nevertheless, no definite conclusion in this connection could yet be established to decide whether a difference in the controlled and free reaction period to any stimulating word is unavoidable, caused or not. It has been found out from the experiments made by the psychologists, named Jhumb and Marbe, that the reaction period of a word is decreased by repeating it again and again. This fact has been verified through the experiments made by other scientists. According to Cason, a specified word, in the absence of repetition, does not remain united with the stimulating word and the reaction period is therefore increased. Thus, the reaction period is reduced by repetition.

Determinants of Associative Reaction Time.

Associative reaction period depends on various factors. Many experiments have been made about the effect of these factors. In a concrete form, the factors effecting the associative reaction period are given below :

(1) **Indirect Response.** Indirect response is that which the subject does not express but keeps it hidden in his brain and presents some other word instead to represent response. In this way, in case of indirect response, the associative reaction period is increased.

(2) **Interfering Response Words.** In order to associate some words, many words often present themselves before the subject and time is

taken in making a selection among them. So, in the presence of such interfering response words, association reaction period is increased.

(3) **Internal Distraction.** Sometimes, the attention of the subject is internally distracted by a stimulating word on the recollection of some happy or sad event. It is clear that it will cause some delay in making response and the association reaction time will increase.

(4) **Absence of Response Word.** Sometimes it so happens that, on presentation of some word, no other word or idea in the form of response enters the mind of the subject immediately, and a delay is therefore caused in making response and the association reaction period is increased.

(5) **Mental Condition.** The effect of mental condition on the associative reaction period is important. If the subject is mentally alert, he makes the response at once and the associative reaction period is less. On the other hand, if the subject is not mentally alert, the response is delayed and the associative reaction period is more. Besides the mental alertness, complexes, relation between stimulating and responding words and many other mental factors affect the associative reaction period.

FREE ASSOCIATION

Association is not fixed and controlled in free association. The results of free association, in a concrete form, have been used with two kinds of purposes.

(1) **Detective.** Free association method has been used in many countries to detect a crime. In this method, a list of atleast twenty stimulating words, which are related to the circumstances of the crime, is made. Now, besides these, some eighty such words are selected, which have no special relation with the circumstances of the crime. The list of these hundred words is presented before the accused and he is instructed to express the first word that enters his mind atonce after the stimulating word is spoken. Now, the stimulating words are spoken, one after the other gradually, and it is found out with the help of stop-watch as to how much time does the accused take in responding the various words. Along with this examination, the gestures of the accused in making response are also taken into account. Blood pressure is also sometimes noted. The first psychologist to detect crime through this method was a German psychologist, named Wertheimer. After that, many other psychologists have successfully used this method. The psychological principle at the root of this success is that, when such stimulating words, which are connected with the criminal incident, are presented before the accused, the accused tries to repress the response which presents itself in his mind and this increases his reaction period to those words. Now, if some accused takes more time in response to most of the twenty specified words given in the list,

there is sufficient ground to believe that he has committed the crime, or else he would not have behaved like that. Here it is necessary to note how much time more an accused has taken in making response to the words relating to the incident. This fact can be ascertained by comparing his reaction time with the reaction time of other accused persons. Now, if the accused person is only one, it will not be proper to consider him as guilty or guiltless only on the grounds of his reaction time, because it cannot be decided whether his reaction time in case of those specified words is more than the time normally taken or not. Therefore, a crime can be detected through free association test only when this test is given to more than one accused persons. It is clear that a great care is necessary in detecting a crime through this method.

(2) **Diagnostic.** It has already been said that the response words are closely related to the mental feelings and emotions of a person. Mental physicians, therefore, use this method in finding out internal complexes of the mental patients. First of all, the psychologists, named Jung and Riklin, used this method in diagnostic experiments. This method has special importance in diagnostic process, because the mental patients themselves do not know their own complexes and they cannot tell anything, if they are directly asked about them. In making response to stimulating words, a mental patient unknowingly expresses his mental responses to different objects. It is clear that, for diagnostic purpose, the list of stimulating words should be such as to include words relating to the important aspects of the patient's life. After a list of words relating to the patient's profession, his married life and family etc., is prepared, the patient is asked to sit in a separate room. Here, the experimenter presents before the patient all the words, one by one, and instructs him to express his response to every word immediately and without any hesitation. After once obtaining responses to all the words in this way, the list is again presented before the patient. The subject is instructed to make, from his memory, the same responses which he had made on the previous occasion. Such responses are often different and, in that case, the experimenter takes note of them. Many things, such as mistaking the stimulating word to be some other word, giving an irrelevant response, showing surprise, laughing, smiling, stammering, growing pale, inability to remember the individual response or the first response etc. are seen, in the responses made by the patient to the stimulating words, closely related to his mental condition. The words, to which such specified responses are given are taken to be connected with the mental complexes of the patient. Mental complexes have been found out in this way in many patients on the basis of a free association test. It is necessary in this experiment that the subject should give full cooperation to the experimenter and that there should be no obstruction of any kind in the association at the time of experiment. No correct conclusion can, otherwise, be reached,

from the results of the experiments. In brief, if a proper use is made of a free association test it is bound to prove helpful in diagnosing the complexes of the mental patients.

CONSTRAINED ASSOCIATION

It is a matter of common experience that different ideas get mixed together in the mind due to various reasons. This process is called association. There are two kinds of association — Free and Constrained. In a free association, there is no impediment of any kind in the process of association and it works quite freely. In constrained association, on the other hand, there are impediments in the process of association as its very name signifies. In this kind of experiment, the experimenter limits the association area of the subject. The subject can have the same association with the stimulating words as has been fixed by the experimenter.

There are two forms of constrained association — partial constraint and full constraint. In the partial constraint, as is clear from its name, the process of association is partially fixed. In this, the subject can select some reactions within a fixed limited area. On the other hand, in the condition of full constraint the reaction of the subject is fixed before hand.

The main kinds of partial constrained association are given below :

(1) Coordinates. In this, the names of the objects, similar to the given word, have to be told. For example, if the stimulating word is plant, the name of the plant has to be given, if it is an animal, the name of the animal has to be given and so on in case of other things, such as mango, jamboo, pigeon, crow, cow and a buffalo etc.

(2) Subordinate-Superordinate Relation. In this, there is a subordinate-superordinate relation between the given names and the words spoken through association. For example, the book is made of paper, and therefore, there is a subordinate-superordinate relation between them. Similar examples can be of house and bricks or the machine and its parts etc.

(3) Species-Genus. In this, when the name of some group is given, the name of its kind has to be spoken, and if the name of the kind is given, the name of the group is spoken, such as animal — monkey, fruit — apple etc. and Ram — man, rose — flower etc.

The kinds of complete constrained association are given below :

(1) Opposites. In this, the subject has to tell the antonym of a stimulating word, such as small-big, light-heavy, fair-black, fat-thin etc.

(2) Analogous. As is clear from its name, the subject has to present, in this, the words analogous to the stimulating words. For example, if the experimenter says "coal : black", it has to be seen in this that a word, which has the same relation with stimulating word, as black colour has with coal, should be given in the form of reaction, just as 'black' will be spoken after 'coal' and white after 'milk'. In this, the experimenter first speaks two words and then presents the third stimulating word and the subject in reaction presents the fourth word which has the same relation with the third word which the second word has with the first.

Some of its examples are given below :

Japan : Japanese. India : (Indian)

Moon : Night. Sun : (Day)

Three : Four. Five : (Six)

The above examples can also be given about species-genus, figure sequence etc. For example, a problem can be presented like this — If Mohan is fatter than Sohan and Rama is fatter than Mohan, who is the fattest of the three? Or, Sita was the wife of Rama and Laxman was Rama's brother, how was Sita related to Laxman? etc.

First of all, Galton, in the 19th century, conducted experiments about association. The first experiments about constrained association were conducted in the laboratory of Wundt in Germany. Experiments by Cattel are regarded as authentic even now. After that, Brayant and Kent threw light on the problem of constrained association.

Experiment

Date......Day......Time.......Place.......Environment.......Name of the subject...... Age of the subject...... Mental condition of the subject....... .

Problem — Study of the subject's reaction to the stimulating words in partial and fully constrained condition.

Instruments and Apparatus — (Five) lists of stimulating words, shop watch, wooden screen, paper, pen and pencil.

Method of Experiment

To conduct this experiment, the experimenter should first prepare five lists of stimulating words. Each list will contain twenty words. The first two or three words of these, will be for practice, so that the subject may know from them as to what he has to do. Out of these five lists, there shall be two lists of partial constraint, two of complete constraint and one list of free association. One list out of the two lists of partial constraint will include the association words of coordinates and the other will contain the association words of species-genus. Out of the two lists of completely constrained association, one list will contain the words of opposite association and the other will contain the words of analogous association. Along with these five lists, proforma to note the reaction word and time will also be prepared.

Before starting the experiment, the experimenter will wind and examine the stop-watch. He will then ask the subject to sit in an arm-chair before him and will place the wooden screen between himself and the subject in such a way that all the instruments and apparatus such as stop-watch, paper, pencil, lists etc., will remain behind the screen and the experimenter will be able to see the subject plainly.

Instructions. Now the experimenter instructs the subject about the association. Before beginning each list, instructions, suited to the same, are given. For example, separate instructions, to be gradually given for different five lists, mentioned above, are noted on next page.

(1) Partially Constrained Association List

(a) *Co-ordinator* : "Now some words will be spoken before you, one by one. At once after hearing one word, you have to speak out hurriedly the word that enters your mind in a way of reaction, such as pen-inkpot, paper-pencil etc."

(b) *Species-genus* : "Now some words will be spoken before you, one by one. As soon you hear a word, you have to tell the genus, if it is species, and you have to tell the species, if it is genus, such as men — Mohan, fruit — apple, Sita — girl, cow — animal etc."

(2) Completely Constrained Association

(a) *Opposites* : "Now some words will be spoken before you, one by one. You have to speak its opposite word in way of reaction, such as black-white, small-big, fat-thin etc."

(b) *Analogous* : "Now some problems will be presented before you, one by one. The first two words of each problem will have special relation. You have to make out that relation. Now the third word will be spoken and in reaction to it, you have to speak such analogous word which should have the same relation with the third word which the second has with the first word, such as black crow, white swan, three-four and six-eight etc."

In the above examples, black is the colour of the crow. Whose colour is white? The word 'swan' will be spoken in answer to this question. Similarly, three is half of six. Whose half the four will be? Eight will be spoken in answer to it. In both the examples, the relation which exists between the first two words, is also seen between the third and the fourth.

(3) Free Association

"Now, some words will be spoken before you, one by one. On hearing each word, the word which strikes your mind in the beginning in the form of reaction should at once be spoken by you hurriedly without the least attempt to hide it."

Process of Experiment. When the arrangement of the experiment is complete, all the five association lists are presented, one after the other. Before starting the first list, suitable instruction is given to the subject and it is ascertained that he has understood the instruction.

Now, as soon as a word from the list is spoken, the stop-watch is made to work, and when the subject's reaction to it is received, the watch is stopped. The reaction word and the reaction time is noted against the stimulating word in the proforma attached to the list. The first two words for practice and the next 20 words for actual experiment are given in the list. When the whole list is finished, an introspective report is taken from the subject about his association reactions. In this report, the subject describes his experiences about the nature of the difficulty that he came across in some association and about the problem, emotion and his own individual feelings. The mental process of the subject is known from this. Thus, introspective report is also added to the proforma. The subject is allowed some rest after presentation of a list. If the experimenter and the subject are fellow-students, they often change places between them. In this way, the reactions of association about all the five lists, one by one, are obtained. The experiment being long, there is generally a possibility of the subject getting tired. This experiment, is therefore, completed in two sittings in two days. On the first day, three lists are presented and, on the next day, the remaining two lists are presented. All the aforesaid five lists should be presented in such sequence that every list should have a greater quantity of constraint than its previous list. There is no constraint in the list of free association and, it is therefore, presented first. After this the list of partial constraint and, last of all, the lists of complete constraint are taken for experiment. Among the lists of partial constraint, the lists of coordinate associations are taken first and the list of species-genus associations are presented next. In the list of complete constraint, the lists of opposite association are presented next.

Precautions. Attention is paid to the following precautions in conducting this experiment :

1. In every list, there should be at least two words for practice and then twenty words for experiment.

2. After the completion of each list, the subject should be allowed some rest before starting the next list, and the experimenter and the subject, if they are fellow students, should change places between them.

3. As soon as each list is finished, the subject should be asked to submit introspective report and an attempt should be made to understand his mental process through it.

4. Before presenting each list, instructions should be given in clear words and with examples. It should be ascertained from the subject that he has followed the instructions quite well.

5. The environment at the time of making experiments should always be very peaceful or else there is a possibility of an obstruction creeping in the association process of the subject.

Results. In this experiment, quantitative and qualitative results are drawn on the basis of received data in the following way :

(a) Quantitative Results

1. *To find out the average reaction period of every list separately* : For this the figures in the column of the reaction period of each proforma are added and divided by the number of words in that proforma. For example, if the total of seconds in the column of reaction period is 50 and the number of words is 20, then 50 is divided by 20 and the average reaction period will be 2.5 seconds.

2. The average reaction period of the partial and completely constrained association is taken out separately and compared with the reaction period of free association.

3. The average reaction period of every subject is compared with the average reaction period of other persons of the group.

(b) Qualitative Results

To find out the qualitative result of the data, the following things are noted in their reactions of partial and complete associations :

1. The occasions when the subject has given wrong reactions.

2. The occasions when the subject has not reacted at all.

3. The reaction period which is too long.

The causes of the above three things are examined on the basis of the introspective report. Any other thing which is found out from this report, besides the above things, should also be noted.

Explanation. Attention is paid to the following things in explaining the data :

1. Why and in what condition was the average reaction period long? The average reaction period in free association is generally the shortest, it is longer in partially constrained association and it is longest in completely constrained association. If the result in case of some subject is different from this, the cause of it should be examined.

2. Individual differences also have their effect on the average reaction period. In the given experiment, the effect is shown by comparing the subject with other individuals of the group.

3. It should be shown from the explanation of the qualitative results of a subject that the greater is the knowledge of words of an individual, the shorter will be his reaction period, because he does not take much time in selecting the words. On the other hand, the smaller is the vocabulary of an individual, the longer will be his reaction period and greater will be the number of his failures.

4. The mental actions such as perception, memory and thinking etc. also affect the reaction of association. If these mental actions are

of a high standard, the very form of association undergoes a change. But it needs a long time to examine the effects of all these factors, and therefore, they are not to be examined in the present experiment.

5. Mind also has an important effect on association. The mental range of the subject in the present experiment can be examined and its effect on association can be shown.

6. If the mental condition of an individual has affected association, it should also be shown clearly.

Conclusion. The following conclusions about the reaction of constrained association, are reached through the present experiment :

1. Along with increase in constraint and resultant limitation of the field of selection, the reaction period goes on increasing. The reaction period, therefore, is the shortest in free association, a little longer in partially constrained association and it is the longest in completely constrained association.

2. Difficulties are more or less, seen in various kinds of association. For example, in the process of association, the difficulty in free association is the least, it is greater in a partial constraint and it is the greatest in complete constraint association. Even in partially constrained association, the difficulty in co-ordination is less than that in other kinds. In completely constrained association, the difficulty in opposites is less than that in analogous. Along with an increase in difficulties, the reaction period also goes on increasing.

3. Mind, vocabulary and individual differences also affect the constrained association.

4. Due to the effect of the process of constrained association on the process of thinking, the laws of thinking, formulated by spearman, can be proved on the basis of this experiment.

Practical Advantages

1. Experience and its association have an important effect on our daily thinking.

2. The mind, thinking, emotions and complexes of an individual can be found out from this experiment.

3. This experiment throws light on the form of reaction period and also on the factors affecting it.

QUESTIONS FOR EXERCISE

1. Discuss the main contribution of Ebbinghaus to the growth of experimental psychology.
2. Discuss various rules of association. What is the distinction between primary and secondary laws? Explain with examples.
3. Write short note on Constrained Association.

4. What causes influence association? What type of stimuli are used in experiment on constrained association?

5. What is controlled association? Describe an appropriate experiment to study controlled association.

6. Write short note on Free Association.

21

IMAGERY

In studying imagery, psychologists have approved the following methods :

(1) Learning Method. It is a matter of common experience that imageries are helpful in learning. Different kinds of imageries work in different kinds of learning. Imageries of the words spoken before us are often presented in our brains on hearing them. The kinds of imageries, which are strong in an individual, help him in learning the same kinds of words easily and quickly. In the method of learning, some such fixed words, as are related to various imageries, are presented before the subject. The kind of imagery, which help the subject in learning the word, related to it, easily and quickly, has to be discovered. The kinds of imageries, which are numerous among them, are discovered from this. But there is one difficulty here. It is true that, if the word which presents a particular kind of imageries in a particular subject, is discovered, the abundance of imageries can be found out from the ease with which the words are learnt. But the word and the kind of imageries it presents in the brain of a particular subject cannot be known definitely. This method, therefore, cannot be said to be satisfactory.

(2) Distraction Method. In this method, the subject is engaged in some work and then a distraction is related in his work through various kinds of stimuli. Now, the subject is believed to have, in abundance, the same kind of imageries as the kind of distraction which creates a great obstruction in his work. There is one difficulty here. It is this that, generally, some particular kinds of distractions affect all the subjects more in comparison with other kinds of distractions. For example, the works done with the help of the eyes are more affected by a distraction of the ears, and similarly, works done with the help of the ears are more affected by a distraction of the eyes. Thus, distraction depends on the kind of work also. The imageries, therefore, cannot correctly be studied through the distraction method.

(3) Association Method. In this, the subject is instructed to write, for five to seven minutes, the names of some objects related to every kind of imagery. The imagery of the subject is found out from the names of the objects he writes. The subject is believed to possess, in abundance, the kinds of imageries similar to the words which are numerous. The chief defect in this method is that, to interpret, from the utterance or retention of a certain word, that an imagery related to it is also present in the brain of the subject, would be wrong. For example, when he says 'flute', it is not necessary that an imagery of the flute is also there in his brain, sometimes it so happens that the retention of some object, event or expedience is possible without considering its qualities. In such a condition, to accept the presence of an imagery, similar to a word, would not be proper.

(4) **Method of Writing Analysis.** In this method, as is clear from its name, the mental imageries of a subject are discovered from the analysis of his writing. This method is based on the common experience that the mental imagery of the topic, object or scenery, that an individual describes, is present in his brain at the time of writing it. Therefore, the imageries related to the objects, about which he writes more can be believed to be in abundance in his brain. But this fact is not applicable to all the individuals. Some such examples are available, wherein the writer could describe some words related to some special kind of imageries, even in the absolute absence of those imageries. Had it not been so, how some poets, blind from their birth, could give so beautiful descriptions of various topics? It is, therefore, baseless to imagine the presence of some special kinds of imageries in an individual on seeing his writing.

(5) **Picture Description Method.** In this method, a particular picture is shown to the subject for some time and then he is asked to write a detailed description of the same. After the writing is finished, many questions about the picture are put to the subject, and the answers are taken down. It is believed that the subject in order to describe the picture, needs verbal and visual imageries. Therefore, the better is the description of the picture, the better will be the imageries of the subject. Fernold, Muller, Binet and many other psychologists made use of the letter squares in the picture description method. Picture description method will not be considered satisfactory through psychological point of view, because to imagine the mental imageries of the describer from his description of the picture is not reasonable.

(6) **Questionnaire Method.** In this method, some questions about the various forms of imageries are put to the subject, in answer to which he gives a description of his imageries. He tells through introspection, whether the imagery is clear or dim. An average is taken by evaluating the description of this manifestation. Now, the greater is the average evaluation of an imagery, the stronger will the imageries of that kind in the subject be regarded. Correct conclusions to a great extent, can be drawn about the imageries by using the questionnaire method properly. But, some precautions should be taken in this connection. For example, the number of questions relating to every imagery should be equal. Secondly, the questions should be distinct and simple. The questions should be about such imageries that there

may not be any difficulty in experimenting upon them. The questions should be direct and small. In spite of all these precautions, the conclusions drawn through this method can be sometimes wrong, because an individual difference is found about the imageries.

It is clear from the above description of the various methods studying imagery that the questionnaire method is considered to be the best among them.

METHODS OF STUDYING IMAGINATION

Psychologists have made use of the following main methods to carry out experimental study of imagination :

(1) **Ink Blot Test.** First of all, Binet and Henry made use of this test to examine the fertility of imagination. After that, Whipple made use of 20 ink blot cards. The following two methods are employed in testing the fertility of imagination through ink blot tests.

(a) The subject is allowed to see any one of the ink blots. He goes on noting down the imaginations which arise in his mind on seeing a blot. All the ink blot cards are presented, one after the other. The fertility of subject's imagination is found out with the help of the time taken in presentation of the cards and the imagination that arose on seeing them.

(b) All the ink blot cards are placed, upside down, before the subject. Now, he is instructed to pick them up, one by one, and to express the imaginations, which enter his mind, one by one. The time taken in this act is noted. When all the cards are deal with, attention is paid to the time taken in one imagination. The fertility of the subject's imagination is found out all the more distinctly through this method, because the greater is the fertility of imagination in an individual, the greater will be the number of objects imagined. On the other hand, the less is the power of imagination in an individual, the less will be the number of objects seen in ink blots.

(2) **Word Building Method.** The constructive aspect of imagination is found out through this method of studying imagination. In this, the subject is asked to make as many words as possible, of six letters each, within five minutes, with the condition that no letter should be used more than once in one word. The constructive imagination of the subject is found out from the number of words successfully built in this way, within five minutes.

(3) **Completion Testing Method.** There is yet another method, known as completion testing method, to study the constructivity of imagination. Ebbinghaus used it, first of all. In this, the subject is given a form in which there are many places left out blank. The subject is instructed to fill up these blanks. The constructive aspect of his imagination is found out from this. The difficulty in this is that it is the mind which is used here more than the imagination. Correct conclusions,

therefore, cannot be drawn through this method. Some psychologists ask the subject to write a story with the help of some words. This method of testing the constructive ability has been proved to be more useful than the method of Ebbinghaus.

(4) **Binet Method.** The psychologist, Alfred Binet has presented another method similar to the method of Ebbinghaus to test imagination. In this, the subject is given the first portions of a sentence and he is asked to complete the sentence. This throws light on the various aspects of a parson's imagination. Constructivity in imagination is found out from a sentence made beautifully.

(5) **Maskelyne Method.** The psychologist, Maskelyne, has also presented a method of testing the constructive ability of imagination. In this, the subject was instructed to make as many sentences as he could with the help of some words within five minutes. These words included nouns and verbs. An estimate of the constructive ability of the subject's imagination could be had from the sentences he made. A great defect in this method is that, in doing this act, mind is employed more than imagination.

Fertility of imagination and constructive ability is found out through the aforesaid methods of studying imagination. In fact, imagination is needed in constructive acts of any kind, and therefore, the greater is the number of constructive acts that a person does, the greater is the imaginative power which that person is supposed to possess. In the same way, the most important among the kinds of imageries included in the imagination of a particular individual can be found out through the kind of constructive acts and the mediums like poetry and painting etc. Experiments are still being made in this connection to explore better methods of studying imageries and imagination in future.

QUESTION FOR EXERCISE
1. Describe different methods of studying imagery.

22

THINKING

What is Thinking?

Thinking, which is complex mental activity, cannot be easily separated from learning, memorising, imagining etc. As Warren puts it, "Thinking is an activity concerning idea. It is symbolic in character, initiated by a problem or task which the individual is facing, involving some trial and errors but under the directing influence of that problem and ultimately leading to a conclusion or solution of the problem." Thus, the activity of thinking originates from some problem, and is the response of the individual to his problem. The solution of the problem takes place internally and not in the form of external activities. Thinking starts with a problem and concludes with its solution. This activity of thinking continues till either the solution is found or till the person becomes fatigued by the effort. There cannot be any thinking in the absence of some problem. Problems in human life come in an incessant stream and they have to be solved by thinking. No general rule can be laid down as to the circumstances which create problems. The reactions of the same individual to different situations and of different individuals to the same situations are not identical or even similar. One situation may appear problematic to one person while a number of other persons may find nothing of the nature of a problem in it. The problems of different persons like philosophers, scientists and religious minded persons are dissimilar. The problems of a logician appear meaningless to the uninitiated but the logician is immersed day and night, in a search for their solutions. Some problems are theoretical while others are practical. The problems of study in B.A. are practical but the problems of the logician are theoretical. The solution of practical problems assists day to day life while the solutions of theoretical problems lead to the satisfaction of curiosity.

FORMS OF THINKING

Thinking, the mental solution of problems, makes use of the symbols of objects instead of the objects. Thinking attempts the solution of problems by employing the trial and error method. There is a kind of flow in the activity of thinking, one problem leading to the thinking of another by reminding the person of that other problem. Thus, many things come to the thinker's mind when he is thinking. The instruments of thinking — images, imagination, signs, indications, and such-like are also internal. Thinking continues to be an internal activity unless and until it takes the form of verbal thinking.

The aim of purposeful thinking may be discovery, but it may equally well be invention. When there is a problem, either a solution to it is found or, instead, some new idea is found. The inventions make use of both analysis and synthesis. There is foresight in thinking because the remotest possibilities of the future are thought of in advance. Hind sight is also an element of thinking because it makes use of material collected from past experiences. Thinking is done with the help of abstract signs of real objects, which adds to thinking the element of abstraction. The major form of thinking is reasoning, which works on the basis of trial and error. It economises time and energy because of mental research instead of motor exploration.

INSTRUMENTS OF THINKING

Thinking calls for the assistance of percepts, images, concepts, signs and formulae, of which it makes abundant use. These are the essential instruments of thinking.

(1) **Perceptions.** Percepts are important factors in thinking, affording material to it. They also stimulate thinking. Suppose we have seen our friend doing something. This perception will set us thinking in order to discover ways and means of preventing our friend from this bad act. Many other percepts will assist in this thinking. We will, with the help of memory, try to recall the perceptions of the past behaviour of our friend in order to see the causes which may have set him on this wrong path of life in the hope of discovering ways and means which may be expected to cure him.

(2) **Image.** Image, too, is a kind of symbol which includes the faint recollection of perceptions. Past experiences of an individual move around in his mind in the form of images. Images may be recalled through a conscious effort but they also flash on the mind involuntarily. Many experiments have indicated that images are not quite as essential to thinking as they were previously considered to be. The use of images in thinking depends in no small measure upon the method of thinking which the individual employs. Some people use other symbols in their thinking, instead of images. It is not essential that a singer must have auditory images in order to be good. Thinking in philosophy and political science makes better use of words than images. Similarly, subjects like arithmetic make very infrequent use of images. Sometimes, a person experiences difficulty in making the other person comprehend his thoughts just because they differ in their ways of thinking.

(3) **Concept.** Concepts are the abstract forms of past experiences. Humanity is the quality of the human species, found equally in all human beings. A concept is a general idea and, as the example makes clear, it is founded upon perception. The concept of humanity cannot

be formed without the perception of human beings, because humanity is the common element in the perception of human beings. An abstraction of humanity from human beings is necessary in order to proceed from perception to concept. Concept, formed with the help of abstraction, is mental. Concepts extend the limits of thinking to include both the past and the future. Reasoning cannot be done without concepts, which are both abstract and general. These are the indispensible elements of thinking. Classification of objects is done on the basis of concepts. While it differentiates between different classes of objects and creatures, it also shows the similarity between individuals of the same class. Conceptual thinking takes less time because it facilitates the thinking of innumerable things by a few concepts. Thus, one concept is the symbol of many objects. But all concepts are not equally extensive. For example, creature is more comprehensive than human beings which in its turn, is more comprehensive than Indians. Indians are included in human beings who are included in creatures.

(4) **Symbols and Signs.** Concepts are made use of in thinking mainly with the help of symbols, which are the representatives of general thoughts. Whenever our thoughts turn to human beings, the human figure, which occupies our mind is a general figure, not that of any specific person. The image of a dog is a symbol of dogs in general. One or its numeral equivalents are symbols of unity while two or 2 symbolises dualism. The sound of a whistle may be the symbol of a policeman or a watchman. The noise of the fire engine is the symbol of fire. Thus, the use of symbols in thinking saves time and energy.

Symbols and signs are intimately related. Symbols change to signs. In daily behaviour symbols are used extensively in the form of signs. The whistle of the watchman is a sign of his presence, and the green flag is a sign of the departure of the train. Arithmetic makes extensive use of signs *e.g.* + indicates addition, — subtraction, × multiplication. Similarly a^2 means $a \times a$. The use of symbols as signs simplifies thinking even further. There is some difficulty in establishing the symbol of the concept and the sign for the symbols in the beginning but once this difficulty is overcome the activity of thinking proceeds at a greater speed. Once we get used to them, we make use of these symbols without any conscious thought about their meaning or representation. The learning of a language presents an initial difficulty in the recognition of letters, but their subsequent use in understanding the meanings and in thinking is greatly facilitated. Though the understanding of signs in algebra takes some time, problems can easily be solved afterwards. The facility in the use of language in thinking is due to the use of symbols. The letters are symbols in language, but in other languages, pictures serve the same purpose. Some languages replace symbols by signs.

(5) **Formulae.** Besides the symbols and signs, the use of formulae also results in the economy of time and energy. One small formula

contains a world of meaning. Comprehensive use of formulae is made in arithmetic and science. In Geometry, for example, the formula r^2 represents the relation between the radius and the circle. The compound 'water' is represented by H_2O, which means that two atoms of hydrogen and one of oxygen combine to form water.

Thus, thinking makes very extensive use of percepts, images, concepts, symbols and formulae. Among them, concepts, symbols and formulae indicate the importance of language in thinking.

CONCEPT FORMATION

Thus, the element active in the development of concepts from the age of three to twelve is Animism. And it is not the only active element, being assisted in its work of developing concepts by anthropomorphism though the development of concepts of directly perceived objects takes place according to realism and mechanism. Milk, rice etc., are at the start, considered living but with the passage of time these concepts too, become mechanised. Originally, the concepts in the mind of the child take the form of the impressions of objects and creatures which he receives, but later on these egocentric concepts are replaced by mechanistic concepts, these latter concepts help the individual to react to the environmental objects. They also help him to behave in society.

Activities in Concept Formation

Several mental activities take part in the formation of concepts, some of the important ones being :

(1) **Perception.** The formation of concepts or conception, starts with perception. The concept of human beings cannot be conceived if human beings are not perceived or if only one human being is observed. The observation of many human beings is essential to this concept formation. Thus, comprehensive perception is the first step towards the formation of concepts.

(2) **Analysis.** Analysis of the qualities of the concepts is the second step towards concept formation. It is not possible to identify a man as a human being and as distinct from other living creatures unless his characteristics are analysed. Thus, the analysis of human beings is essential to the concept of human beings.

(3) **Comparison.** It is the third step towards concept formation. In the previous example, comparison of the analysed traits of various persons is also necessary. This comparison supplies us with the knowledge of the similarity or identity and dissimilarity or diversity of human beings. Analysis of qualities alone is not enough to form concepts. The comparison of the qualities is also essential.

(4) **Synthesis.** The next step, after analysis, is the synthesis of similar qualities for concept formation. This synthesis of similar traits is arrived at with the help of abstraction, rather than the addition of qualities. Dissimilar qualities are disregarded in synthesis. Discrimination

is needed for the separation of similar and dissimilar qualities, after which the generalisation of the similar ones is effected though this would leave the process of synthesis incomplete unless assimilation were also effected. Some psychologists separate these activities from synthesis.

(5) **Naming.** Naming is the final step in concept formation and as every concept has a name, naming of every concept is essential. Consequently, after synthesis, each concept gets a name. For example, the name 'human will' is given to it after the peculiarities of human beings have been synthesised and then the concept of human will be ready.

Now concepts originate in the mind with the increase and extension of knowledge, but the individual does not make any conscious effort towards their formation which goes on automatically. If someone asks us for our idea of a human being, the answer may not suggest itself all of a sudden. All we would possibly say is that a human being is one who has humanity. The definition of humanity would be more difficult. But, we make frequent use of the word 'human' in our daily lives and find no difficulty in it. In reality, the above steps in the development of concepts have been discovered by analysis.

STUDIES BY WURZBURG SCHOOL

Wurzburg movement is among the famous movements of the twentieth century in modern psychology. It was the forerunner of gestalt psychology started by Wertheimer in 1912. This movement was started by Brenteno. Brenteno created a psychology in which more importance was given to action than to experience. Brenteno differentiated between the core of experience and the process of experience. Instead of differentiating between experience and the action of recognising it Brenteno differentiated between the structural and functional forms of experience. For example, difference between red colour and its sensations can be seen. According to Brenteno the subject matter of psychology is the action of experiencing red and not red colour. In this way, psychology studies that action which occurs in the mind at the time when an experience of red colour takes place. This experience is dynamic where as red colour is a passive matter. According to Brenteno the core of the mind points out towards an object outside the mind.

Mach. The second psychologist to make important contribution to the Wurzburg Movement was Mach. He was a structuralist. According to Mach, there is no difference between the subject matter of physics and psychology. But in psychology attention has to be given to certain sensations which are not in the physical things but exist in the relationships between them. If we see three different spots and react towards each of them something in addition to these blots arises in our experience. This is their spatial relation and just as we feel the dots differently, similarly we also feel this spatial relation. In fact, this spatial relation can be seen by introspection in the same way as any other fact. In order to examine this, arrange the same spots at that place but in a different pattern and then see that we have different spatial sensations. In this way, Mach found the traditional categories of sensory experience to be insufficient. His form of thinking was structuralist.

Von Ehrenfels. After Mach, Von Ehrenfels presented important psychological principles in Germany. He was the founder of the famous school 'Gestalt qualitat'. The meaning of this word is 'The quality conferred by a pattern'. It is clear that according to this school in every perception some qualities are seen which are in addition to the sensations gained from the various scenes. These qualities are the qualities of the form, the structure or the pattern of the object perceived. This principle is different from Wundt's theory of 'Creative Synthesis'. In creative process synthesis of elements has been accepted. On the other hand, according to Von Ehrenfels in every perception the form of the object is a distinct quality. For example, in any sweet music the sound of different musical instruments which have created the music cannot be recognised. This is because all these sounds combine to form such a pattern the sound of which is different from the various individual sounds of the instruments. Here, it must be noted that as yet nothing has been proved in the Wurzburg school by the experimental method.

Kulpe. The work was done by Kulpe for the first time. He was the chairman of an experimental laboratory in Wurzburg. He found out some elements by experimental analysis. For example, he analysed the factors responsible for self-determinant actions. Kulpe's work started in the early stages of the 20th century. His laboratory at Wurzburg became centre for research where experiments were performed on many such problems which were neglected by the school of Wundt.

Marbe. In this first comes the study of Marbe. In this, the subject was kept in a situation in which he had to arrive at a decision and provide also a respect on the actions taking place between excitement and decision on the basis of introspection. The problem of decision was, for example, to distinguish the heavier of any two things. This judgment could be done in the form of words or any external action which the person performing the experiment could give in this study towards the mental processes which occur before the decision.

Watt and Messer. After the study of Marbe, Watt and Messer found out a method by experimenting upon association by which the thought processes between the utterance of a word and reaction towards it could be found. It was found by these experiments that many elements were found by introspection which cannot be included in the description of sensory experience. These experiences were quite similar to the stream of consciousness described by James. In other words, experience seems like a flow and like a collection of disintegrated parts. These can also be called conscious tendencies. These are nuclear and indefinite and these cannot be changed into simple sensations, images and feelings. These experiences are quite similar to Stout's imageless thoughts. The conscious feelings of doubt and determination, acceptance and refusal are included. Watt pointed towards actions which influence the action of decision and thought though they are not present in the conscious mind.

Ach. In addition to the above problems, Ach analysed the process by which a man reaches decision. He saw that before any decision, conscious feelings are accompanied by inclinations which although beyond consciousness, influence the thought process and thus the decision. By this analysis, Ach classified the men into "decisive kinds" on the basis of introspection. Ach's research supports the views of Kulpe. By this Watt's study is also verified. Ach has called these elements, which are important in the process of decision, the decisive tendencies. These elements have a close relation with meaning. Ach said that consciousness of meaning is completely managed and directed by the unconscious tools. If there is any meaning of an object in consciousness, then the reason for it is those ideas which have been excited in the unconscious. In this way, meaning does not depend on conscious elements. It depends on the excitation of the associated ideas. Ach also attracted attention towards consciousness.

Karl Buhler. In 1907, a new era started in the Wurzburg school due to the findings of Buhler. At this period in America, Woodworth was doing research work on the process of thought. In France, Binet was independently experimenting on the process of thought. In his experiments on thought process Woodworth stressed the reality of thoughts and feelings of relationship. According to Woodworth the definition of feeling cannot be given in structural words. In the process of thought Woodworth stressed, like Ach, two different forms of meaningful consciousness. Buhler conducted research by the method used by Woodworth and with a similar purpose. Buhler particularly paid attention to reality of sensational thought processes. Till then, no attention had been paid to this in the Wurzburg School. In the experiments of Buhler a long interval of 5 to 20 seconds was given between problems and their solutions. This increased the possibility of error in introspection. Hence, Wundt challenged its experimental validity. In this way, a clear opposition occurred between Wundt and the Wurzburg school. Buhler proved the existence of such elements in feeling which were not sensational. Before this, psychologists had seen relations only in the form of relations, but Buhler accepted them to be new structural elements, elements of thought. In this way, he proved the relation between conscious elements of introspection. In the process of thought it is an important part of the content.

Wundt's Criticism

As has been mentioned earlier the Wurzburg school had to become the prey of Wundt's criticism. On the other side in America, Titchener did not accept the experimental conclusions of the Wurzburg school and ignored them. Wundt was greatly respected in Germany. He had long experience of experimenting with the introspection method. Hence, his criticisms had great effect on the experimenters of the Wurzburg school and they tried to safeguard their theories. According to Wundt, the Wurzburg research related to the tendencies which determine thought current. Wundt praised their work in this sphere. But on the other side, he criticized the Wurzburg School for presenting many such experiments and ideas which could never become a part of organised psychology.

Titchener's Criticism

Titchener of America, who was a structural psychologist, only accepted sensation, images and feelings as elements of consciousness. He refused to accept the concept of imageless thought. He defined the experimental elements of Buhler and conscious tendencies of Watt in terms of structuralism. According to Titchener, the so-called conscious tendencies are a complex organization of sensations originating in the sense organs. To accept them as extrasensory was due to the wrong use of the introspection method. As far as the question of meaning goes according to Titchener, they came under the sphere of logic and not under that of psychology. Therefore, the Wurzburg research related to meaning cannot be included in psychology.

Search for Experimental Proofs

By the lectures and experiments of Titchener, the difference between him and the Wurzburg School became clear. The experimenters of Wurzburg School concluded from the objections of Titchener that they had given sufficient experimental proof of their conclusions. Therefore, they engaged themselves in collecting sufficient experimental proof for the given mental conditions. They experimented to safeguard their fundamental theories. One of this kind of effort was T.V. Moore's experiment regarding the relation of meaning and image. Moore concluded from this experiment that meaning and image were two different psychological elements. Hence, contrary to Titchener's principle Moore accepted a fourth independent element other than sensation, image and meaning. To prove the presence of meaning Moore performed some experiments. He gave a list of some words to 9 persons to read and hear. He gave instruction in compiling this list that as soon as the meaning of the word becomes clear, at once the subject was to lift up his hand from a telegraph key. In the second experiment he gave instruction that as soon as an image appeared in reaction to a word the subject was to lift his hand from the telegraph key. It was seen in these experiments that except for one person, meaning invariably appeared earlier than image, in the case of all eight subjects. Whereas, it takes half a second for the appearance of a meaning it takes, on an average, twice the time for the appearance of an image. By this experiment Moore criticized Titchener's contention that there were only three elements in consciousness — sensation, image and feeling.

Importance of Wurzburg School

In the history of experimental psychology Wurzburg school has its own importance. The main facts related to it are :

(1) **Importance of Tendencies and Feelings.** In the Wurzburg school research work was done on the concepts of feelings and tendencies. This affected all the aspects of psychology.

(2) **Research Related to Thinking.** After Buhler's experiments, a flow of research work resulted in the sphere of thought. Tremendous research literature was compiled on the process of thought. Experimental studies were conducted on problems related to structure of concepts, thoughts, signs and symbols, mathematics, logic, aesthetics and ethics and also regarding research of unknown relations in the process of thought. Some of these studies were traditional in Wurzburg whereas others started from different traditions.

(3) **The Emergence of Experimental Psychology in Thought.** Whatever may be the allegation by the opponents on the experiment related to thought in the Wurzburg School, Kulpe's research work and study of thought outside the Wurzburg school combined to create solid experimental psychology of thought. Mostly, evolutionary study has been done in the psychology of thought. In other words, it was endeavoured to find in what circumstances different kinds of thought start in the life of men. In this way, in the psychology of thought, questions relating to thought are concerned with problems of development and learning. In this way, gradually in the psychology of thought, the problems did not retain the same form which they had for the experimenters of the Wurzburg School. Still we cannot refuse to accept the truth that the experiments of the Wurzburg school laid the foundation of the experimental psychology of thought.

(4) **The Background of Gestalt Psychology.** As has been indicated earlier the Wurzburg school presented the background for Gestalt psychology. In this respect Mach's analysis of sensations is of great importance. Mach said that in changing that organisation of elements there occurs a change in the qualities of perception. Therefore, he has accepted spatial sensations which are distinct from the sensations of the elements of perception. It is clear that these experiments prove that the element of organisation presents some new facts in perception. In 1890, Von Ehrenfels wrote in an article that there is something more than the order of different sounds in music. A note in different music does different functions. In this way, different music can be created from similar sounds. Hence, Von Ehrenfels concluded that, other than the main elements, the organised forms have their own qualities. This

he termed as Gestalt Qualitate, or quality of organisation. From these theories of Ehrenfels the main basis of Gestalt school is formed.

Still all studies of the Wurzburg school have a permanent place in the history of psychology. Regarding determination and thought the conclusions of Wurzburg school were not accepted in that form later on. Woodworth and Titchener did not accept the imageless thought and neither could the experimenters of the Wurzburg school prove it definitely. The problems which Kulpe had presented for discussion, now come under the psychology of learning.

THEORIES OF THINKING

(1) **Central Theory.** The ancient theory about the definition of thinking is called the central theory. In this, as is clear from its name, the definition of thinking is done through the processes of the central brain and it is accepted that, at the time of thinking, there are actions only in the brain and there are no other physiological actions. No experimental evidence to prove the central theory could be given.

(2) **Motor or Peripheral Theory.** This theory was presented by the behaviourist psychologist, Watson. As is clear from its name, more importance, in this, is attached to various physiological actions in place of the brain actions. In thinking, Watson laid special stress on the actions of the larynx and regarded language and thinking as inseparable. Other behaviourists accept the presence of some other physiological actions also besides the actions of the larynx in thinking. This second opinion is considered to be important specially, although the experiments, which were made to prove it could not furnish a common conclusion. An absence of sufficiently minute instruments is said to be the cause of difference in results of the experiments. It was found out from some experiments that there is an implicit movement in the tongue at the time of thinking, although this has not been proved fully. It was found out by noting down the movements of teeth and tongue at the time of thinking that these movements in thinking are not necessary. Here, some of the psychologists maintain that, whenever the actions of these organs are not seen, its cause is not the absence of actions but the absence of minute instruments to show them. In 1932, to prove Jakson's motor theory of thinking, experiment was done on twenty subjects to know whether there was some action in neuro-muscular system at the time of thinking or not. It was concluded from the results of experiments that there was surely some action in the neuro-muscular system at the time of thinking, although it was difficult to ascertain it through an external inspection. In 1935, through his experiments on dumb and normal subjects, Max proved that there is no neuro action current in a dreamless sleep condition, while this action increases at the time of a dream. According to motor theory, the same kind of action is seen in the fingers of the deaf and the dumb at the time of thinking as is seen in the larynx of ordinary persons. It

is clear from the various experiments that an action does take place in the nerves of many parts of the body at the time of thinking, but it does not prove that this action is compulsory for all kinds of thinking. Therefore, all kinds of thinking cannot be denied through motor theory. If the central theory of thinking has not been proved through experiments, it could not, at the same time, be disproved. In the present condition, therefore, it cannot be said with any certainty as to how thinking of various kind is performed. None of the present theories is capable of defining all kinds of thinking.

TRIAL AND ERROR IN THINKING

Solution of a problem is sought in thinking. In most of the cases, trial and error method is used in the process of this solution. Although Kohler and many other psychologists have tried to make use of insight instead of trial and error in solving problems, yet most of the psychologists do not deny the use of trial and error in solving them. Even in experiments made by Kohler, Chimpanzees tried trial and error many times before reaching insight. In explaining this, Woodworth showed that, due to the presence of a gap in circumstances, solution of a problem is not seen immediately, and therefore help from trial and error is taken. The solution of this gap is the real insight. The truth is that even the gestalt psychologists have given some importance or the other to trial and error in solving problems. As Woodworth has pointed out, trial and error does not mean doing an action aimlessly or without thinking. If it is accepted, most of the objections raised by gestalt psychologists can be removed. In making experiment on children, Wertheimer saw that in solving geometrical problems, help from trial and error was also taken along with that from insight. But Wertheimer accepts no importance of trial and error in creative thinking. Other psychologists do not agree with him in this. The truth is that even great psychologists have taken help from trial and error to reach their difficult theories.

Gestalt psychologists do not accept the importance of past feelings in the solution of present problems. On the other hand, great stress has been laid on past experience in trial and error theory. In one experiment, Durkin divided a problem into many parts and asked various subjects to solve it separately. After that, he presented the whole problem. It was observed that the subjects solved the whole problem easily. On the other hand, the subjects, before whom the whole problem was presented at one and the same time, felt great difficulty in solving it. This experiment proved the importance of past experience in solving a problem. But it does not prove that the importance of insight in solving a problem is less in any way. In fact, it is from trial and error that we reach insight gradually. Therefore, the importance of trial and error in solving a problem cannot be denied.

THINKING AND LANGUAGE

Among all animals only man can think. One of its main reasons is that he is given the power of language. Behaviourist psychologists have gone so far as to regard thinking as an implicit speech. Although this theory has not yet been proved yet no psychologist denies the importance of language in thinking. Not only Watson, but even Binet, before him, regarded thinking as sub vocal speech. Mueller differentiates between thinking without a language and thinking with a language. To prove the behaviourist theory of thinking, Clark, Thomson and other psychologists made experiments with the help of such instruments in which the movements of the larynx in the process of thinking could be seen. In the result of all these experiments, the movements of the larynx in the process of thinking could not be seen on all occasions. Even then, many behaviourists maintain that the absence of still more minute instruments is the cause of it and that the movement of the larynx in the process of thinking is not lacking.

It has been seen from common experience that all kinds of thinking cannot be explained through behaviourist theory. Sometimes, it so happens that an individual speaks something and thinks something else. In such a condition, the relation of thinking with language cannot be regarded as compulsory. After studying some patients of aphasia, Held saw that although they could not express their ideas through language, because of brain injury, yet the process of thinking still existed in them. Held has given an example of an English officer who showed the process of thinking even when he suffered from aphasia. This experiment proves that the process of thinking should not be regarded as a result of the action of the larynx but its cause. It is clear from the above explanation that thinking and language are closely related, although both of them cannot be said to be similar.

IMAGELESS THINKING

According to introspectionist psychologists, the existence of image is necessary in thinking. Thinking in the absence of image is impossible. In experiments made by Wundt and Titchener, the subjects, in expressing their experience at the time of considering problems, said that different kinds of images presented themselves during thinking. It was also observed that there was often no use of images in thinking. In this way, introspectionists established the importance of image in thinking, but later, psychologists of the Wurzburg class advocated imageless thinking through their experiments. Wundt of Germany, Binet of France and Woodworth of America made experiments in this connection, but the most important experiments in this connection were made by the psychologists of the Wurzburg school, named Kulpe, Marbe, Mueller, Messar and Buhler.

According to Wurzburg school, thinking is an integrated process which cannot be divided into different parts as sensations and images etc. In 1901, the psychologists of the Wurzburg school, in their experiments, found thinking to be imageless on the basis of the subject's introspection. Kulpe was the first psychologist to make experiments in this direction. After Kulpe, Marbe, in an experiment, instructed the subjects to compare two weights. It was not found from the information given by the subjects as to how they could discriminate between heavy and light. Marbe, with the help of G.E. Mueller and other psychologists, proved that images and sensations had no hand in discriminating between light and heavy. Some conscious tendencies like doubt, trust and hesitation etc., were surely there in the subjects. Marbe gave importance to these tendencies in place of sensation, image and feeling etc., to be at the root of thinking. Through his experiments, Titchener tried to show that many kinds of images were present in conscious tendency itself. Contradicting this statement, Titchener, the psychologist of Wurzburg school of society, named Messer and Buhler, refused to acknowledge the presence of image and sensation in conscious tendency. The psychologist, Alfred Binet also advocated imageless thinking by experimenting on his own daughters.

Here, it is necessary to pay attention to the fact that the psychologists of the Wurzburg class do not deny the presence of images of all kinds of thinking. They only do not regard image to be unavoidable for thinking. It has been shown through experiments that there are symbols in thinking and images rise from these symbols. Imageless thinking has been proved to be impossible through the experiments of Woodworth, Comstock, Crossland, Gleason and other psychologists who proved the importance of image in thinking on the basis of experiments. Hollingworth, Bonsfield and Berry also drew conclusions of a similar kind from their experiments. By giving some mathematical questions, Bonsfield and Berry wanted to know the kinds of images and their range of action in the thinking process of the subjects. The subjects said that the visual images of the figures were helpful in solving the questions. These images were settled, stable and clear. Ideatic images, lasting for a long time, were seen in subjects at the time of thinking and no change was seen in their form and kind. On the basis of this conclusion, Bonsfield and Berry showed the importance of memory images in thinking, and proved that images were helpful in thinking. Among the experiments made separately by Okabe, Clarke, Pyle and Jacobson in Cornell laboratory of Titchener to know the importance of image in thinking, they gave no proof of imageless thinking. On the basis of his experiment, Clarke showed that the idea of imageless thinking was, in fact, based on impediments created by a difference in the meaning and subjects matter of thinking. Contradicting the conclusions reached through experiments made in Cornell laboratory, Ogden said that the images in thinking were seen by the subjects because they were instructed to tell the presence of those images.

It is clear, from the above explanation of the various experiments made in connection with the importance of image in thinking, that, while sometimes there is an image in thinking, the thinking is sometimes imageless. The first kind of thinking can be called concrete and the second kind of thinking can be called abstract.

SET IN THINKING

The psychologists of the Wurzburg school have accepted the importance of a determining set in thinking along with a conscious tendency. A determining set means that a solution to a problem is imagined to a special extent limit which helps the process of thinking to flow in a special direction. In the absence of this determining set, an individual cannot have a sure solution to a problem present before him, although it cannot be concluded from this that a solution through a determining set is compulsory, because this set can also have a wrong direction. It is necessary that a determining set is in a correct direction, because then alone it can help in solving a problem. As has been said before, the psychologists of the Wurzburg school advocate their opinion on the basis of various experiments.

By giving hypnotic suggestions to the subjects, Ach showed, through his experiments, connected with thinking, that, not only conscious but even unconscious determining set affects thinking. It is because of this determining set that thinking becomes controlled and full of aim.

In every psychological experiment, there are three kinds of instructions. Besides the instructions given by the experimenter, the subject has self-instruction also and some other instructions he has to follow due to the situation of the experiment. Because of a particular situation, the past experience of the subject also effects instruction. Determining sets are therefore created by controlling instructions and past feelings in the subjects. Maier showed, through his experiments, that there is a recombination of past experiences in thinking and a new relation among various things is seen through the same. Maier made the following experiments in this connection.

(1) The aim of this experiment is to find out the extent of the importance of past experiences in thinking. The subjects were made to sit in a room with a low ceiling where there was a big table, two long poles with about seven and a half feet each in length, two poles with more than three feet each in length, a big table clamp, two small clamps, wire of an electric bell, pieces of zinc tubes and some other things. All these things were not needed in the process of thinking. The subject was then instructed thus, "The problem before you is to make two pendulums, one of which will lie on this point and the other on that point. Both the pendulums should be made in such a way that small pieces may be kept connected to both of them through which signs may be made on both the points." To solve this problem, knowledge of pendulum and the skill of joining two small poles into a big one

through wedging was necessary along the knowledge of the wedging principle. The subjects were divided into five different groups. The first group was given neither any instruction nor the partial or full solution of the problem. Only the problem was placed before it. The second group was given a partial solution of the problem but the subjects were told that the presentation was made merely to acquaint them with the material. The third group was given the problem as well as the practical solution and was also told to simplify the solution of the problem by joining the present material correctly. The fourth group was asked to solve the problem. The fifth group was given the problem, asked to solve it and was also informed that the joining of the material was helpful in finding the solution. Besides this a determining set, through proper presentation, was also created in the subjects of this group. In this way, only the subjects of the fifth group alone were given all the instructions completely. Eight, out of twenty-two subjects of this group solved the problem. Other subjects failed because of their making inadequate determining set. Only one subject, out of sixty two subjects of the first four groups, could solve the problem. In this way, Maier concluded from this experiment that the importance of determining set in thinking was clear.

(2) Two ropes were hung from the ceiling of a room at such a distance that it was not possible to catch hold of both of them at one and the same time. There could be many ways to catch hold of both the ropes, but Maier was to test only one way in which the subject was to stand with one rope in his hand, was to tie a heavy object at the end of the other rope and was to swing the other rope so hard that it reached near the first rope to be caught easily. The subject was given ten minutes to solve the problem. Many unnecessary articles were present in the room. When the subject failed, two hints were given to him and the rope was made to swing hard once more. The other subject was given a weight and was told that it could help in solving the problem. It was seen in the result of the experiment that thirty-nine per cent subjects solved the problem without any hint. After a hint was given, other thirty-eight per cent subjects solved the problem. From this, Maier concluded that a solution of a problem was easy after receiving sure hints.

(3) The subjects connected with this experiment were such as could not solve the problem due to a change in behaviour. In the experiment, the subjects were divided into two groups. The first group was told for twenty minutes the various actions of solution to the problem. The second group was not told anything. It was told that if the problem was not solved, the behaviour should be changed and another alternative should atonce be used. Three kinds of problems were placed before the subjects. In one problem, the instruction was given to put out a lighted lamp placed at a distance through small tubes and clamps. In the second problem, the rope problem, described

before, was presented. In the third problem, instruction was given to unite the planks with the help of clamps and then to make a peg to hang a hat on. The rope problem was successfully solved by about five per cent subjects belonging to both the groups. In this way, in solving this problem, there was no difference in both the groups, although it was certainly seen that the subjects of the controlled group, as compared to those of the experimental group, took some more time in solving the problem. The problem of putting out the lamp was solved by about twenty-five per cent subjects of both the groups. Even among these, the subjects of the controlled group, in comparison to the subjects of the experimental groups, took a long time more. In the third problem, while sixty-eight per cent subjects of the experimental group were successful, only forty-seven per cent subjects of the controlled group could succeed. From this, the importance of the determining set in solving a problem becomes clear.

From all the three experiments of Maier, given above, the importance of the determining set in solving a problem becomes clear.

As has been said before, when the determining set is wrong, it makes the solution of a problem still more difficult, instead of helping it, in the same way a favourable determining set helps in changing a difficult problem into an easy one. A psychologist named Luchins concluded from his experiments that the subjects, after solving many difficult problems, could not solve a very simple problem, because at the time of solving difficult problems, a determining set favourable to them was formed in the subjects and this same determining set proved an impediment in solving a simple problem. It is thus clear that a favourable determining set is very necessary for solving problems.

QUESTIONS FOR EXERCISE

1. What is thinking? Analyse the process of thinking in solving a problem with the help of a suitable example.
2. Write short note on Concept formation.
3. Deal briefly with the studies on thought processes by the Wurzburg school.
4. Write short note on theories of thinking.
5. Write short note on importance of trial and error in thinking.

23

INTELLIGENCE AND INTELLIGENCE TESTS

Definition of Intelligence

The word intelligence forms part of our ordinary stock of words which we use everyday. In the field of psychology too, the word intelligence finds a fairly comprehensive use, but it has been defined in a number of ways by the scientists. Some of these definitions are given below :

(1) Intelligence is the Ability of Adjusting in a New Situation. According to Wells, "Intelligence is the property of recombining our behaviour pattern so as to act better in a novel situation." In William Sterns' opinion, "Intelligence is the ability to adjust oneself to a new situation."

These definitions are faulty in the following respects :

(a) They fail to clarify the full scope of intelligence.

(b) Intelligence and adjustibility are not the same. Intelligence is innate but adjustibility is mostly learnt.

(2) Intelligence is the Ability to Avail of Past Experience. Both Ebbinghaus and Thorndike define intelligence as the ability to make profitable use of past experience. In other words, intelligence is the ability of learning.

The definition has the following defects :

(a) Learning and intelligence are not identical because learning depends on many things besides the latter.

(b) This definition does not describe the full scope of intelligence.

(3) Intelligence is the Ability of Abstract Thinking. According to Garret, one may define inelligence as including "the abilities demanded in the solution of problems which require the comprehension and use of symbols." In Terman's opinion "Intelligence is the ability to think abstractly."

This definition suffers from the following defects :

(a) Abstract thinking is not intelligence, it is only a part of intelligence.

(b) This definition fails to describe the complete scope of intelligence.

(4) **Intelligence is the Conglomeration of Many Powers.** In Wechsler's opinion, "Intelligence is the aggregate or global capacity of an individual to act purposefully, to think rationally and to deal effectively with his environment." Computing the different powers of intelligence, Husband has said : "An intelligent person uses past experience effectively, is able to concentrate and keep his attention focused for longer periods of time, adjusts himself to a new and unaccustomed situation rapidly, with less confusion and with fewer false moves, shows variability and versatility of response, is able to see distinct relationships, can carry on abstract thinking, has a greater capacity of inhibition or delay and is capable of exercising self-criticism."

Actually, Husband has given a very good description of an intelligent person but intelligence cannot be accepted to be the sum total of all these qualities. The psychologists, however, differ in their assessment of intelligence as a power or a collection of many powers. A description of the different theories concerning the nature of intelligence will help us to understand the various interpretations of the form of intelligence.

THEORIES OF INTELLIGENCE

The following are the main theories concerning the nature of intelligence.

(1) **Monarchic Theory.** This theory holds that intelligence is one power or energy which effects all the activities of the individual. According to Victoria Hazlitt, intelligence is a general ability which determines the various specific abilities. This theory has been proved to be fallacious. Prominent people show a less than average ability in many activities. For example, Darwin had a very bad handwriting.

(2) **Oligarchic Theory.** This theory postulates that intelligence is an aggregate of mutually independent powers. Binet believed this theory. Experiments disproved this theory by showing that mental powers are interdependent.

(3) **Multifactor or Anarchic Theory.** Thorndike is the most prominent among those who believe this theory. This theory holds that intelligence is the mean of undetermined independent rudimentary elements. But Spearman has criticised this theory.

(4) **Two Factor Theory.** This theory was conceived by Spearman who holds that intelligence has two parts : (1) General Intelligence or G, and (2) Specific Intelligence or S. General intelligence effects every activity but the effects of the specific intelligence are confined to specific activities. General intelligence is found in lesser or greater degree in every one. Specific intelligence is of various types, the several types being independent of each other. They differ from individual to individual. This intelligence of a person depends on his general intelligence.

Staffens and Brown have upheld Spearman's theory on an experimental foundation. But Pears asserts that adequate experimental data, in its favour, is not available and consequently even Spearman's theory cannot be said to be universally acceptable.

In reality enough experiments are still needed to formulate an all-embracing definition of intelligence. In this connection, a 'universally acceptable theory has yet to be worked out.

TYPES OF INTELLIGENCE TESTS

Intelligence tests are classified according to the activities prescribed in them :

1. Verbal Tests.
2. Non-Verbal Tests.

As the name itself suggests, Verbal tests make use of language while the non-verbal tests include such activities which do not necessitate the use of language. Both these types are suitable for individual as well as group tests. Consequently, verbal and non-verbal tests are capable of further sub-division into two classes — individual and group. Thus, finally there are four types of intelligence tests :

1. Verbal Individual Intelligence Tests.
2. Non-verbal Individual Intelligence Tests.
3. Verbal Group Intelligence Tests.
4. Non-verbal Group Intelligence Tests.

Verbal Individual Intelligence Tests

The very name verbal individual intelligence tests, suggests that these are intelligence tests given to individuals, or in other words they are meant to test the intelligence of the individual. Language finds adequate use in them. Binet Simon tests and the various revisions are all included in this classification.

Hindi Version of the Terman-Merrill Scale

The Central Bureau of Psychology of Uttar Pradesh has made a Hindi Version of the Terman Merrill Scale. This revision includes a variety of material, from solid objects to difficult questions. The activities in the beginning are simple like constructing a bridge or a tower of blocks or fitting in irregular wooden block in their proper place supplied for them. At the same time, at the end of the tests there are difficult questions which need considerable thinking. This test is divided into numerous age groups. The higher age groups use language to a considerable extent and its use gradually declines with the age group. For example, the two years group include the following activities :

1. The form panel with three holes.
2. Recognition of objects by name.
3. Recognising the organs of the body.
4. Making a tower of blocks.
5. Naming an object from its picture.
6. Word order.

The various types of activities in the "superior adult third" are as follows :

1. Vocabulary.
2. Sense of direction.
3. Paper cutting.
4. Logical reasoning.
5. Repeating nine digits.

Non-verbal Individual Intelligence Tests

It is quite apparent from the above example that in verbal tests, the child's knowledge of language is more in demand, and therefore, the use of these tests is limited to students or literate persons. But these verbal tests cannot be used in the case of illiterate individuals as these tests involve an extensive use of language which fails as a medium to measure the individual differences between the illiterates. Consequently, illiterate individuals are tested with the help of Non-verbal individual intelligence tests. The name itself indicates the nature of these tests. These tests involve the least possible use of the linguistic ability and are similarly almost unaffected by knowledge derived from books. One example of these non-verbal tests is the performance intelligence tests.

Performance Intelligence Tests

It would be in keeping with the context of our discussion to understand in detail the performance intelligence test as an example of the non-verbal individual intelligence tests. According to Munn, "The word performance is usually applied to tests which require a minimum use of understanding and language." Thus, these tests make use of items requiring responses and not language and these tests can be applied to children, illiterates, feebleminded individuals as well as to foreigners.

Pintner-Patterson Performance Scale

One example of the performance intelligence tests is the Pintner-Patterson Performance Scale. It was evolved by Pintner and Patterson in 1917. In this scale there are 15 types of tests, of which 7 are form boards, 6 picture completion, memory span and the rest are picture puzzles and imitations etc.

Porteus Maze Tests

Another example of the performance intelligence tests is the Porteus Maze tests. In it, paper and pencil mazes are used. For his tests, Porteus created mazes for children from 3 to 14 years.

QUESTIONS FOR EXERCISE

1. What is the nature of intelligence? How is it measured?
2. What do you understand by intelligence?
3. Write short note on Types of Intelligence Tests.

24
PERSONALITY

Ordinarily, personality is taken as the external appearance of the individual. In philosophy the meaning of personality has been interpreted in the sense of the internal self. But in psychology neither is the personality the external appearance nor is it the internal self, but it includes both and much more. The word personality has been derived from the Latin word persona. The word persona was used for the cover, utilised by the actors to change their appearance, but in the roman times it was taken as the particular character itself. This second meaning has been taken in the modern word personality. Thus, personality is not a fixed state but a dynamic totality which is continuously changing due to interaction with the environment. Personality is known by the conduct, behaviour, activities, movements and everything else concerning the individual. It is the way of responding to the environment. The way in which an individual adjusts with the external environment is personality. In the words of Munn, "Personality may be defined as the most characteristic integration of an individual's structure, modes of behaviour, interests, attitudes, capacities, abilities and aptitudes." Behaviour requires integration. This integration of various traits is found differently in different persons. As a general rule every healthy individual has some sort of integration. The peculiar forms of integration in a particular individual are his personality traits. Thus, personality is the most characteristic integration of an individual. It is personality which marks distinction in one man and another. In the words of Gordon Allport, "Personality is the dynamic organisation within the individual of those psycho-physical systems that determine his unique adjustment to his environment." The personality is the organisation of the internal and external activities. It includes the external appearance, qualities, aptitudes and capacities etc. It is the result of the interaction of the individual with the environment. It is not a collection of the traits, but a particular organisation of them. It is the total quality of the individual's behaviour. Individual affects other individuals through his personality. Thus, personality is manifested in his various activities. In short, personality is the total quality of the behaviour, attitudes, interests, capacities, aptitudes, and behaviour patterns, which are manifested in his relation with the environment.

For some time there was discussion among the psychologists about the relation of heredity and environment in the development of personality. In this discussion arguments were given from both sides and much matter was gathered on the basis of observation and experimentation. It was found by this data that the development of personality depends upon both the heredity and the environment. Hence, modern psychology includes both heredity and environment in the factors influencing personality.

According to Gordon Allport only the relatively stable aspects of behaviour should be recognised as personality traits. In his book, "*Personality : a psychological interpretation,*" Allport writes, "From the evidence now in hand, four important conclusions may be drawn :

(1) Personality, defined as the distinctive mode of adjustment adopted by each individual in his efforts to live, is not formed at birth, but it may be said to have begun at birth.

(2) The earliest distinctive adjustment in respect to which infants can be said to differ, are in the intensity and frequency of their spontaneous activity (mobility) and in their emotional expression (temperament). Both these factors are primarily products of inheritance.

(3) Probably not before the fourth month is there sufficient learning and maturation to form distinctive habits of adjustment or rudimentry traits. But by the second half of the first year, adoptive response to the physical environment and to behaviour so marks distinctiveness.

(4) Distinctive qualities noted early in life tend to persist.

The child seems pre-disposed to learn certain modes of adjustment and reject others. Even before these adoptive forms are clearly defined an observer can often, by the method of 'prophecy' predict later traits. Irrespective of the method used in the study of the consistency of early development, the evidence is positive, virtually in every case." Thus, heredity influences the biological features of personality. As a matter of fact, the heredity does not determine personality completely, nor is it ineffective in it.

FACTORS AFFECTING PERSONALITY

The factors affecting personality can be divided into two classes : (1) Biological and (2) Social. The biological factors affecting the development of personality are of three types : (i) Ductless Glands, (ii) Physique and (iii) Nervous System.

Endocrine Glands

Ductless glands send their secretions directly to the blood without ducts. Their secretions are called hormones. These hormones are responsible for many changes in the personality. Different glands secrete one or more type of hormones. A description of the effect of some of the ductless glands will show the extent to which personality is influenced by them.

(1) **Pancreas.** Pancreas send insulin to the blood. The amount of sugar in the blood depends upon the amount of insulin in it. When the deficiency of insulin *i.e.*, sugar, is in the body the mental powers are weakened and the personality of the individual seems less balanced. His mood is changed, temperament becomes irritated and fear increases.

(2) **Thyroid Gland.** Thyroid gland has a very important function in the development of physical structures as well as mental development. If it is absent since the very birth the intellect of the child does not improve. Cretins, imbeciles etc., are the result of the absence of thyroid glands. Its destruction causes a disease known as myxoedema. This disease creates laziness in man. The activities of the mind as well as those of muscles are slackened. The memory becomes weak, man is not easily concentrated and thinking becomes difficult. In the period of development the excess of the activity of thyroid results in rapid physical growth, specially the development of height. An excessive activity of this gland results in rapid physical growth, specially the development of height. A deficient activity of this gland results in tension, irritation, worry and instability in man's personality. Thus, with the increase or deficiency in the activity of thyroid glands, the activity of the body as well as of the mind also increases and decreases. But this does not mean that the increase and decrease of the activity in the body is always due to the effect of thyroid gland. Occasionally, it might be due to other causes as well, but thyroid gland does play an important part in them.

(3) **Adrenal Gland.** Adrenal gland secretes adrenaline. Adrenaline has an important influence upon personality. Its excess creates the sexual traits in men or women. Its excess in women is responsible for the absence of the rounded contours and feminine voice. It organises the organic capacities in the time of emergency. The excess of adrenaline causes rapid heart-beat, high blood pressure and the postponement of the activity of the intestines. The individual having less adrenaline feels relaxation in the muscles, more sweat and the pupils of the eye are extended. An entire absence of adrenaline results in the disease known as addison's disease. In this disease one feels weakness and lethary in the body, power of resisting disease is lessened, the interest in sex activity disappears and metabolism becomes low. The skin becomes black, the power of resisting heat and cold is lessened and behaviour becomes irritable.

(4) **Gonads.** The secretion of the gonads *i.e.*, sex glands, is an important factor influencing personality. Gonads separate sex hormones. Sex hormones are very much helpful in the increase of sex interest. In adolescence there is a special increment in the hormones. Hence, changes are observed in the individuals according to their sex. In man one finds the manifestation of masculine characteristics such as beard, moustaches, high pitch in voice etc., while in the female there is development of mammary glands and other womanly traits. The

processes concerning pregnancy *e.g.* mensus, pregnancy, the bearing of the child and maternal behaviour is very much influenced by the sex hormones.

(5) **Pituitary Gland.** The hormones secreted by the pituitary gland control other glands. The hormones secreted by the front part of the pituitary gland increase the activity of other glands as well. The hormones created by the back part of the pituitary gland control the blood pressure and the metabolism of water in the physical activities. These hormones also affect physical growth. In the time of physical growth the bones and muscles of the individual grow speedily due to the activity of this gland. In its excess, the height can go even upto 7 to 9 feet. But because after excessive activity this gland becomes very much inactive, these very tall persons die at an early age. If the activity of the pituitary gland is very much deficient in the period of development, individual remains a midget, though his intellect is normal and the physical structure is not un-attractive. If the activity of this gland is normal during the development period and becomes excessive afterwards, the hands, feet, nose and lower jaw etc., become broad. This state is known as acromegaly.

The effect of the hormones is influenced by the heredity as well as by the environmental factors. But still the excess or deficiency in their activity create some changes quite apparent in the personality of the individual. It is not necessary that the excess of the secretion of any one of the particular gland should always show some special influence in the body *e.g.,* the excess of sex tendency should not always be supposed as due to the excess of the secretion of the sex gland, since different glands also interact upon each other due to which the activity of some is increased while that of others is decreased. The sex behaviour, for example, is very much influenced by social norms, customs, circumstances, habits and many other things. Hence, in spite of the deficiency of the sex hormones, the individual may appear to be very much interested in sex activities. On the other hand, in spite of excess of the sex hormones, the individual may not appear to be interested in sexual activities.

Physique

Another important biological factor affecting personality is physical structure. It is seen in daily life that often the fat men are easy going and social, while the thin persons are self-controlled, irritated and un-social. Thus, the physical structure has some relation with the temperament. But even the instances contrary to this rule are also existing. As a matter of fact, the relation of physical structure and the temperament has not been definitely established. More experiments are required in this direction. The experiments conducted so far have been mostly on college students. Before one arrives at some definite conclusion, experiments must be conducted on adult persons as well.

But even after that, the problem of the basis of correlation remains un-answered. Simply by correlation the temperament cannot be taken as a result of physical structure. It should also be remembered in this context that the physical structure makes a difference in other's behaviour towards different individuals and is modified, to some extent, according to their physical structure. This difference in our behaviour makes a change in their personality. Hence, a particular difference should not be supposed due to physical structure alone but also due to other's behaviour towards the particular person, though the former may be more important.

Body Chemistry

Another important biological factor affecting personality is body chemistry. In ancient times, the differences of temperament were supposed to be due to difference of chemical elements in different men. Thus, the nervous personality was taken as the result of excess of nervous fluid. It was supposed that the sanguine persons have an excess of blood, the choleric persons an excess of bile, phlegmatic persons an excess of phlegam and the melancholic persons, an excess of spleen. This principle is not accepted in modern psychology, but still no psychologist denies the relation of personality with the proportion of chemical elements in the body. These chemical elements are of two types. Some reach the body from outside while some are created in the body itself. Thus, the drugs have sufficient effect on personality. The behaviour of the drunkard is an example of such effect. Different types of intoxicating drugs have a clear influence upon the personality of the individual. The deficiency of different vitamins also causes some change in the personality. With the increase or decrease of the quantity of sugar in the body, the physical and mental state of the man is very much changed. In convalescence one finds a difference in the individual's personality. Difference is also noticed after long illness.

Besides the above mentioned biological factors many other factors influence personality, *e.g.*, sex, intelligence, intellect and nervous system etc. The difference in the sex of male and female creates an essential difference in their personality, though it has been established that much of this difference is caused by social and cultural environment. Galton and Goddard believe that intellect is absolutely hereditary. The modern psychologists do not agree with this hereditary view though the influence of heredity is not denied. The environment affects intellect, but the development of intellect is ultimately limited. The influence of special talents, as that of music, mathematics etc., on human personality is very well-known. Like the intellect, the talents are also generally hereditary. According to Kempf, the author of *The Autonomic Function and Personality*, the nervous system is one of the important determinants of personality.

Social Factors Influencing Personality

The environments of different individuals are very much different from one another and so also their effects, but the influence of environment on personality can roughly be divided into that of home, school and society. All these three play an important part in the development of personality.

INFLUENCE OF HOME ON PERSONALITY

The environment of the home has a wide influence on the development of personality. This influence, as a general rule, is according to the pattern found in particular culture. In the family the relation of child with the parents is the most intimate. The cultural development of the child is very much influenced by the behaviour of the parents, *e.g.,* a child brought up in Indian family will be very much different in his behaviour than another brought up in Western culture. But even in the same culture much difference can be observed in the parent-child relationship in different families, *e.g.,* generally, the child has a respectable place in Indian family, but all Indian parents do not sufficiently love and sympathise with the child. In such circumstances much repression is observed in child's behaviour. He becomes an introvert and often enjoys in his dreams, day dreams and imaginations things which are denied to him by his parents. The influence of the presence of the parental love is again not the same in the case of all children. A child may become aggressive while another may become submissive in the same circumstances. On the other hand, if the parents show excessive affection towards the child, the child may become an extremist and excessively dependent upon the parents. A child excessively ignored shows different types of conflicts in his personality. Children brought in the psychological clinics for the cure of defects of personality showed that an important cause of their defects was the behaviour of their parents towards them. According to Sigmund Freud, the tendency to depend upon the parents in the childhood is manifested in the tendency to depend upon the leader in the adult age. If the child is allowed freedom in the matter concerning his belongings food, clothes, books etc., he will develop a habit of free will, if all these are divided by his parents he will not get an opportunity to utilize his judgment and so become over-dependent and submissive.

Parents are more powerful and efficient than the child. Hence, they are the ideals before him. The child wants to become like his parents. Thus, he establishes his identification with either of the parents and tries to follow his manners, ways and behaviour. The child also fulfils his frustrated desires through his identification. It has been observed that the little boy wears the big shirt of the father and walks proudly like him with a stick in his hand. This identification with the parents in the childhood is later converted into the identification of the individual with the leader. By the identification with the leader the individual is happy in the leader's achievements and sorry in his failures.

In the absence of affection and sympathy, the child often turns criminal. While discussing the causes of criminal tendencies, Healy and Bronner have emphasized three factors, the effort to get rid of the painful circumstances, the tendency to revenge for the misbehaviour of the father, the efforts to satisfy the frustrating desires. Often the child has the curiosity as to wherefrom the younger brother or sister has come. The answer to this question by the parents has an important effect on his personality. The child has a natural curiosity towards the sex tendency. Often the parents try to suppress his curiosity towards sex or they just rebuke when he asks such questions. But the child is not silenced by this. He tries to enquire from the servants or friends in the house. But this leads to guilt conscience. The reactions in the parents about the everyday matters in the family also affect the personality of the child. The relations of the mother and father among themselves also affect the personality of the child. In short, even behaviour of mother or father and the circumstances in family affect the personality of the child more or less.

It has been observed that the behaviour of the eldest and the youngest, the elder or the younger is not the same in the family. Similarly, it has been found that the parents' behaviour towards them is not also the same. This has led the psychologist Alfred Adler, to emphasize the importance of birth order in the development of personality. The birth order of the child fixes the status in the family which decides his roles which affect his personality. The youngest child is treated with affection by everyone, hence he becomes over-dependent. The eldest child becomes self-sufficient and tyrant, because being the only child for sometime he does not share his rights and things with others. The birth of another child in the family has an important influence on the first child, since it takes away his monopoly in affection and sometimes he is neglected altogether. Hence, he feels jealous with the younger child and tries to regain his rights. On the other hand, the new child is anxious to make his place in his family. The above description of the child's problems based upon the conception of birth order has been conclusively proved. The researchers have found similar conflicts in different birth orders. Adler has truly said that the individual develops his style of life from the pattern of his early life in the family, but there are no grounds to suppose that this style of life remains un-changed in future. It cannot be denied that the environment in the childhood is one of the most important factors determining personality, but it is difficult to believe with Freud and Adler that the personality of an individual is completely determined in childhood.

QUESTIONS FOR EXERCISE

1. What is meant by personality? What are the factors, which determine it?

2. Discuss fully the biological determinants of personality.

3. Bring out the contribution of social factors to the development of personality.

4. Explain the role of family and school situations in the development of personality.

5. What do you understand by measurement of personality? Describe in brief the important methods of personality assessment?

25
WORK AND FATIGUE

What is Work

Work can be defined as an action performed with the object of achieving some particular objective. Hence, work is an action with a particular aim which is fulfilled by the action. Human beings do various kinds of work to earn their livelihood. Apart from the earning of livelihood actions may have some other objectives such as study, earning, prestige, etc. Here, it may be objected that play also has an objective and for that reason it would be difficult to distinguish play from work. But two things must be kept in mind. In the first place the player does get some satisfaction of his physical and psychological needs, but he does not start by considering this satisfaction as his goal. In the second place, it is not possible to draw a dividing line between play and work. The same activity may be a game for one individual and work for another, depending upon the attitude. For example, just as the player devotes his entire attention to playing the game without being overtly conscious of the results, the determined worker may perform some activity with complete concentration and be oblivious to the actual results. On the other hand, every player does think in terms of winning and losing, irrespective of how much sporting spirit he has. Hence, while the definition of work given above shows its relative difference from play, it does not indicate that there is a complete difference between the two. As far as the pleasurable and interesting aspect of play is concerned, the same can be and is many times true of work also. The secret of the success of many great people lies in the fact that they found as great pleasure in doing work as they did in play.

Kinds of Work

Work is broadly divided into two categories — muscular work and mental work. Before going on to a detailed description of these two kinds it is necessary to remember that the two are so intimately connected with each other that the distinction between the two is merely verbal and a matter of practical expediency. Muscular work requires physical energy. On the other hand, mental work requires the expenditure of nervous energy but there is no physical work which does not require some mental participation just as much as there is no mental work which does not consume some physical energy. Hence, both kinds of work are mutually dependent, not mutually exclusive.

MUSCULAR WORK

Every human being performs a multitude of muscular actions everyday in his life. Muscular work, depending upon the difficulty involved, results in more or less fatigue, sooner or later and one then arrives at a stage when one stops work due to fatigue. This limit differs from individual to individual and from work to work.

Measurement of Fatigue in Muscular Work

The fatigue which is consequent upon all muscular work is measured by the ergograph, an instrument which measures the contraction of the muscles. Although many kinds of ergographs are in use, the most commonly used are Mosso's and Kraeplin's ergographs. In using the ergograph the right or the left arm of the subject is tied in such a way that he can move only the middle finger. Before starting the experiment the instrument for measuring rhythm is fixed at 60°. Then the subject pulls the thread fixed to the ergograph at the first beat of the metronome and relaxes it at the second beat. The contraction and expansion of the muscles in the middle finger are recorded on a sheet of smoked paper through a niddle. Since, this work of pulling and relaxing the string is continued over a long period and since the string is loaded with some weight the subject's finger becomes fatigued until a stage is reached when the finger cannot pull the thread at all. As fatigue increases, the height of the marking on the smoked paper begins to fall and at the time of total fatigue the markings take the form of a straight-line. In this manner the ergograph helps in the study of the effects of fatigue on muscular work.

Effect of Rest on Muscular Fatigue

Muscular work leads to the exhaustion of the muscles and if the muscles are allowed to rest at this time, the fatigue is reduced. It may even be completely eliminated. Many experiments have been conducted to observe the effect of rest on muscular fatigue. Many important facts about the length and the frequency of the rest period have thus been discovered. For example, in one experiment the subject was given a six kilogram weight to lift. Lifting of the weight caused muscular contraction and putting it down led to relaxation of the muscles. The subject was given a ten second rest after every lifting. As a result the subject continued to lift the weight at ten second intervals for an indefinite period. After sometime, in a second experiment, the rest interval was reduced from ten seconds to only two seconds and it was found that within one minute the subject became so tired that he could not lift the weight at all. Besides, he had to rest for two hours to get rid of the fatigue accumulated in that one minute of work. It is, therefore, evident from this that it is not only the rest given which is effective in removing fatigue. The rest interval must be given with the right frequency and it must be in proportion to the time spent in work.

Influence of Mental Factors on Muscular Work

The extent of fatigue and time in which it occurs also depend to a great extent upon mental factors. It has been seen that if the individual takes interest in his work he can produce more work for a long time and still not complain of fatigue. Generally, mental fatigue has an adverse effect on muscular activity, although there are many exceptions to this. Sometimes individuals are seen performing mental work with great skill and application despite mental fatigue. Yet, mental factors do undoubtedly influence muscular work.

Other Factors in Muscular Work

In addition to the above mentioned factors, many other factors also effectively influence muscular work. For example, it has been observed that women get tired more quickly than men in doing muscular work. Lombard's studies had a very favourable influence upon the introduction of rest as well as practice, food and alcoholic drinks. Harley's studies showed that tobacco has a detrimental effect on muscular work.

Study of Muscular Work by the Hand Dynamometer

All the above examples of muscular study were made by the ergograph. But it is also measured and studied by the use of hand dynamometer. In this instrument the subject fits his finger into the dynamometer and pulls it with his entire strength and then relaxes it. The meter is fixed at 60°. An interval of four seconds is allowed between two successive acts of pulling the handle. The subject performs this function for one minute and in every case the force exerted by the subject is measured in terms of kilograms. If the subject does not take rest but performs the action continuously he tries rapidly and a diminution in his energy is soon apparent. But if he takes rest at regular intervals then he can continue to do this work for a much longer time since he does not become fatigued so quickly.

Value of the Study of Muscular Work

As has been pointed out earlier, the study of muscular work is valuable from the psychological point of view. It is a matter of common experience that output can be increased if muscular fatigue can be prevented. Therefore, many measures are adopted to reduce muscular fatigue in most factories and offices. Generally, the workers are allowed to have one or two rest intervals during the working hours, and the period of rest varies from half an hour to one hour. Arrangements are also made for refreshments. Efforts are also made to make the work interesting. In some organisations music is played to the workers while they are working. Then, normally only men are employed to do muscular work while children and women are allowed to do only light muscular work because they become tired much quicker. Studies are still being conducted to discover ways and means of reducing fatigue. In addition to this bonuses are offered to improve the motivation of the workers. It need hardly be pointed out that the worker's efficiency and skill can be vastly improved by these studies of muscular work.

MENTAL WORK

What is Mental Work?

Mental work involves the use of mental energy. All individuals are not endowed with the same amount of mental energy, and therefore all people cannot be expected to perform the same kind of mental work. One common example of mental work is the work of study. In this kind of work, too, some functions are difficult and hard while others are simple and easy. It is, for example, easier to take notes than to write a book. Hence, individuals with varying amounts of mental energy are required to perform these simple and complex tasks. Individual differences in respect of mental energy are seen just as they are present in the case of muscular energy. Besides this, some individuals have exceptional mental capacity for certain specific kind of tasks but negligible capacity for other tasks. For example, a good teacher is not always a good writer while a good writer may or may not be a good teacher.

Study of Mental Work

Among the many methods adopted in the study of mental work, the more commonly used are :

(1) **Letter Elimination Method.** As is evident from the name itself, in this method the subject has to eliminate certain words from the list provided. He is made to sit comfortably and then given a list and a pencil with which to eliminate letters. This work can be done for any fixed period, from half an hour to one hour. The subject is informed of the completion of the work a minute or two before it actually ends. At the end of the test the subject's personal examination is also recorded. Now the letters cancelled by him, the letters left untouched and the letters cancelled incorrectly are counted and an evaluation of his work is made. From this one can evaluate the mental efficiency of the subject.

(2) **By Addition or Subtraction.** In this, the subject is required to do some addition and subtraction and his work and its quality is evaluated on the basis of the right and wrong answers produced by him.

WORK CURVE

Work curve, as is evident from the term itself, is that line upon a graph which indicates the work done by an individual. Work curves can be prepared both for mental work and muscular work. The work curve of an individual's performance possesses the following three features :

(1) Initial Spurt. Whenever an individual begins to do some work, he sits down to it fresh and for that reason his production progresses rapidly in the initial stages of the work. Hence, the work curve progresses quickly in the beginning.

(2) Plateau. This initial spurt or rapidity is not maintained for a long time because the individual invariably begins to get exhausted as he continues to work. For this reason his progress begins to fall and then stops increasing.

(3) Final Spurt Near the End. Whenever the individual learns that his work is coming to an end he puts in a special effort near the end. This also leads to a rise in the work curve although this spurt lasts for only a short time. In this stage the individual works enthusiastically although he is exhausted.

The above sketch of the nature of the work curve does indicate the extent and variety of factors that influence production. But it does not suggest that the work curve declines due to fatigue. Fatigue is delayed if the worker has practice in his work. On the other hand, fatigue also has a detrimental effect on the habits formed by practice. Sometimes the worker produces as much in a fatigued condition as otherwise but in that case the quality of the work is definitely inferior to his normal production. All these factors are known as the factors which influence production of work.

FACTORS INFLUENCING PRODUCTION

The factors influencing production have been discovered after many experiments. Some of these factors help production and increase it while other hinder and retard it. Basically, these factors can be divided into the personal and environmental categories. Personal factors are again of two kinds — the mental and the physical.

(a) Personal Factors. These are the factors which are inherent in the worker himself. Every kind of work is the consequence of the worker's mental and physical application and it needs the use of mental and physical energy. For that reason the personal factors influencing production are psychological as well as physical.

(1) Psychological Factors. This category includes all those factors which are part of the worker's psychology and have some influence upon the work produced by him. The main ones are the following :

(i) *Motivation* : Motivation is the most important factor in production because it increases when motivation increases and falls when motivation is reduced to a lower level. Although motivation alone is not enough to increase production when the individual is completely exhausted it does influence production under more normal circumstances. It is of even greater importance when the work is difficult and complex. The truth of the matter is that motivation will have great influence upon production when the work is more difficult.

(ii) *Incitement* : Many experiments have established that production can be increased by incitement. It is difficult to be skilled in one's work if this is lacking. Its influence is not very apparent in work which is done continuously but it can be seen in all work which is done at intervals. The fact has been established by the experiments of Robinson and Haren. For this reason the workers are given incitement in different professions so that they may produce more.

(iii) *Interest* : It is a commonly accepted fact that production increases if there is interest and decreases if there is not. Interest helps to delay fatigue and also to reduce it. Many experiments have shown that interest is the cause of application and dedication to a task and this increases production.

(iv) *Reward and Punishment* : The consequences of an individual's work influence his production. If the result is reward he tends to return to his work with even greater enthusiasm. The reward may be material, as in the case of money, or verbal, as in the case of praise etc. Different individuals react differently to various kinds of rewards but it has some effect, more or less. But the more effective reward is one which is neither too easily available nor impossible to attain. It also should not be so cheap as to have no real value and neither should it be so valuable that the worker may show greed for it. The effect of reward and punishment can be seen clearly in the case of students. It has very great importance for games.

(v) *Coordination* : In any industry the production achieved by a worker depends upon his coordination with the work. It has been seen in the experiments of Kraeplin that in the absence of coordination there is much greater distraction of attention. When their coordination improves the loss of attention is considerably less with the result that they can concentrate on their work and produce more.

(vi) *Establishing rapport between the workers* : If many workers are to work simultaneously to complete some work then rapport must be established between them. Besides, production is better also when the relations between the workers are friendly and cordial. On the other hand, absence of such relations leads to loss of production in terms of quantity as well as quality.

(vii) *Blocking* : The effect of blocking on production can be seen in the experiments conducted by Bills. According to him no person can perform some mental work continuously. In certain cases the frequency of blocking is as high as four or five times within one minute. Sometimes, the period of blocking itself may last for one minute. In the duration of blocking the worker's mental condition is more or less stunned. Although it is impossible to say why blocking occurs at all, it cannot be denied that it does occur and that the frequency and the actual length of blocking varies from one person to another and even from one kind of task to another in case of the same person.

(2) **Physiological Factors.** The physiological factors which influence production are those which depend upon the bodily condition of the worker. The main factors are :

(i) *Health and capacity of physical organs* : Different bodily organs such as hands, feet, eyes, etc., are employed during different kinds of task. If these organs are defective or weak then production is very adversely affected. On the other hand, more production can be done if these physical organs are healthy and strong. Hence, the total quantity of work done by a worker depends upon the condition of his bodily organs.

(ii) *Fasting* : Fasting also influences production. The experiments conducted by Glaze indicate that fasting for more than one day has a distinct influence upon production although fasting for a day or less may have no apparent effect. Glaze experimented upon three subjects and observed that the production went down in each case due to fasting. Later on the skill was regained when the fasting was stopped.

(iii) *Sleep* : Sleep has an important influence upon production because lack of adequate sleep leads to a fall in the quantity and quality of production. Adequate sleep has a beneficial effect on production.

(iv) *Drug addiction* : Almost all experiments in this connection have proved that drug addiction is bad. Hollingworth has substantiated this view after conducting an experiment on six subjects.

(v) *Use of tobacco* : The experiments conducted upon the effect of tobacco chewing on production have not yielded uniform results. In the case of middle-aged people addicted to smoking, it was found that tobacco has a beneficial effect. On the other hand, if tobacco is taken by people not accustomed to it, their production registers a sudden and sharp fall because tobacco renders their mental and physical condition abnormal.

(b) Environmental Factors

The environmental factors influencing production include all those circumstances and conditions which alter production in any way. The more important ones are the following :

(1) **Light.** In every kind of industry some degree of light is necessary. But if the intensity of the light is more or less than required then production suffers. The quality of light, in addition to its quantity, also affect production. The best light is the natural light of the sun. It not only helps vision but also has a good effect on the health but in its absence white light is believed to be the best substitute. In addition to the quantity and quality the distribution of the light available is another effective factor. The light should be so distributed over the working area that it should light up and illuminate the machines and other instruments being used by the workers. But it should not fall

directly upon the eyes of any worker because this may dazzle him and lead to accidents. If the light is adequate it will avoid straining the eyes and in this manner contribute to the skill of the worker.

(2) **Ventilation.** If many people work together on the same premises it becomes necessary to make provisions for the flow of clean air into place and of stale air out of the place. Besides, in many kinds of work many harmful gases are generated in the process of production. It is essential that such gases must be ejected as rapidly as possible. All kinds of experiments have indicated that proper ventilation has a positive effect on production and the absence of such arrangements leads to the ill health of the workers and a subsequent fall in production.

(3) **Temperature.** In many offices and factories it becomes necessary to control the room temperature in the premises in order to maintain the efficiency of the staff because excessive heat or excessive cold have an adverse effect on production. The proper temperature can be determined only by the nature of the work, the local climate, the location of the factory and also by the average health of the workers. But it can be said definitely that it is necessary to maintain proper temperature for good production. For this reason many laboratories are air-conditioned now a days.

(4) **Noise.** Some experiments conducted upon the effect that noise has upon production indicated definitely that when it rises above a certain pitch it is definitely harmful. The pitch of noise that can be tolerated depends upon the habits of the worker, his skill and the nature of the work. Many experiments have been conducted in this connection and many means devised to reduce the volume of noise in factories. Many modern laboratories are sound-proofed to external noise so that the workers within are not disturbed.

In this account of the factors influencing production, only the more prominent personal and environmental factors have been taken into account. In actual fact, it is not possible to list the total number of factors. Besides, psychologists attached to different industries continue to study these factors and make experiments. They help in revealing many new facts.

(5) **Rest Pauses.** It has been found that adequately timed rest pauses of proper duration have a positive influence upon production. It is possible to determine by experiment the length and frequency of the rest pauses which will be adequate for a particular individual. Vernon and Bedford conducted an experiment on 17 young girls in which the girls were given a rest of ten minutes after every hour of work. A twenty per cent increase in production was observed. In another experiment in which seven girls were involved a thirteen per cent increase in production was noticed when they were allowed to rest after every hour. In an experiment by Ermaski it was seen that when a five minutes interval was introduced after every hour of work and a

fifteen minute interval after every hour and quarter of work, twenty-five per cent improvement in production was noted. Graff conducted some experiment and concluded that production is increased if a rest of two minutes is given after forty minutes of mental work and a rest of five minutes after eighty minutes of mental work. On the basis of experiments it was found that a rest pause of 6 to 10 minutes after every two hours of work proves useful and beneficial in the case of middle aged workers. Some other experiments have shown that if the rest pause is more or less than a particular limit then it will hinder production instead of helping it. If the rest pause is too long it is harmful because the worker's enthusiasm cools down and it amounts to beginning a fresh. Besides, it also leads to boredom and disgust. In an experiment by Amberg a rest pause of 5 minutes was found useful while a rest pause of 15 minutes proved definitely detrimental. In the same way different lengths and varying frequencies of rest pauses can be determined for different persons. The basic fact is that the rest pause should be long enough to eliminate fatigue and make the worker fresh but it should not be so long that it may induce boredom, lethargy and disinterest. It is only natural that different rest intervals will be required for individuals with varying personal interests, capabilities, abilities, etc. Hence, it is the worker who himself can tell how much rest he requires and after what interval of time. The basic principle governing the timing of the rest pause is that it should be introduced after the period of maximum production because soon after this production begins to fall. If rest is provided at this time, this inevitable fall in production can be eliminated.

(6) **Group Situation.** Psychologists have conducted many experiments to find out whether production improves while working in a group or if it is better when the individual is working alone. Modi induced a group of youngsters to do muscular work on the hand dynamometer first individually and then in pairs, and came to the conclusion that production was two per cent more in the group situation than while it was done alone. In his experiments college students Whitmore saw that production was twenty-six per cent more when work was performed in a group situation. The main reason for this increase in production in the group situation is that a definite competitive spirit comes into play while working together. As a result the individual worker is induced to bring into work his entire energies. But this kind of increase in production is mainly quantitative because in terms of quality the work generally deteriorates. The reason for this phenomenon is that the worker is constantly interested in the total work done by others and in trying to do better than them he fails to consider the quality of his own work. Although, generally the more skilful individuals retain their skill while working collectively, some individuals are found to perform better while working alone. This fact depends on the one side upon the individual nature and working habits of the person, and

on other side upon the nature of work. For example, mental work in which quality counts, the creation of art or literature, is better done alone because in a group situation there is too much distraction of attention. But this fact cannot be said to be true of all writers and artists, because much depends upon the working habits of each individual. On the other hand mechanical, physical and work in which quantity alone is important, are normally better performed collectively.

FATIGUE

What is Fatigue?

Fatigue may be defined as a reduction in the capacity of the mind or the body, and a condition in which a person cannot work or he works less. A tired animal lies inactive. In Hepner's words "Fatigue is the reduced capacity of our organism to work properly, that capacity is accompanied with some feeling also which is known as feeling of fatigue." A person naturally experiences a feeling of fatigue after working for a number of hours. The time for which a person can work, at a certain occasion, is another matter but every person feels tired after having worked to his full capacity, because by this his capacity to work is reduced. Decrease in capacity to work accompanies an increase in fatigue. Speaking briefly, fatigue is the reduction of capacity.

Kinds of Fatigue

Fatigue is of many kinds just as capacity takes a variety of forms. It is generally believed to be of four kinds :

1. Subjective or Mental.
2. Objective or Physical.
3. Nervous Fatigue.
4. Boredom.

(1) Mental Fatigue. Mental work, or any kind of strain on the mind reduces the capacity of the mind for work and causes mental fatigue. Thus, in mental fatigue, the mind tires or the capacity of its minute fibres for work is diminished.

(2) Physical Fatigue. This type of fatigue results in the reduction in the capacity of the muscles of the body and a feeling of fatigue. In this way, physical fatigue is brought about by physical exertion. Even though the body feels tired due to mental exertion which should normally result in mental fatigue, yet on account of the close relation of the two, it also produces physical fatigue. Thus, mental fatigue is unavoidable and it leads to physical fatigue.

(3) Nervous Fatigue. The subconscious mind of man is extremely active and since in the process of its work it consumes energy in due course of time it naturally produces a feeling of fatigue and depression. Nervous fatigue can also result if the subconscious is extremely tired due to mental conflict.

(4) Boredom. Boredom and fatigue are not identical. Fatigue is the result of the use of energy but boredom is the feeling of tiredness due to an incomplete or improper expulsion of energy. If you go to a friend and he is busy in some work you become bored. Similarly, you get bored if a person persists in talking about the same thing day after day. Boredom results in restlessness, a state induced by our inability to find proper use for our capacity for work as is the case with the young lady who gets bored with her unemotional lover because she does not get a chance to express her feelings.

Means of Removing Fatigue

Many experiments have been carried out in psychology to discover ways and means of getting rid of fatigue, and these experiments have evolved the following ways :

(1) Sleep. Sleep is by far the best means of banishing fatigue because in sleep both the fibres in the mind and the fibres in the body are at rest while waste matter is expelled from the body. The capacity of the mind and the energy thus gained replaces fatigue.

(2) Relaxation. Sitting or lying in a relaxed position also eliminates fatigue because both the body and mind are at rest in a comfortable posture and the mental as well as physical capacity is thus restored.

(3) Balance of Work and Rest. As we have mentioned earlier, too much work, over work and no work at all, cause fatigue. Thus, for the elimination of fatigue, work and rest are equally necessary. It is best to alternate rest and work in a manner that should bring about a proper balance.

(4) Change in Work. Due to the fact that different types of work cause strain on different parts of the body, more work is possible if the type of work is altered every now and then. Same type of mental exertion continued for a long time also induces boredom because our other capabilities do not get a chance of expression. Thus, change in work is necessary to avoid and eliminate physical and mental fatigue.

(5) Recreation. Recreation creates an opportunity for the unexpressed capabilities to express themselves, at the same time it reduces mental and bodily tension. Thus, it is a useful means of avoiding fatigue.

(6) Change in Emotions. Another factor which introduces fatigue is an unrelenting application to work and a consistent, hard and laborious way of life. Thus, a change of emotions once in a while will also reduce fatigue.

These factors which eliminate fatigue generally apply to everyone but a person may pick and choose according to his own interests. There may be other factors especially suited to persons with particular tastes, inclinations and interests.

QUESTIONS FOR EXERCISE

1. What is work? Explain muscular work and mental work.
2. Write short note on factors influencing production.
3. What do you understand by fatigue? State and describe the various kinds of fatigue.
4. Write short note on Mental Fatigue.